STEPHEN A. GEPPI PRESENTS

THE OVERSTREET COMIC BOOK PRICE GUIDE TO
LOST UNIVERSES

BY ROBERT M. OVERSTREET,
J.C. VAUGHN & SCOTT BRADEN

PAUL CASTIGLIA + MARK F. DAVIS + JOSH DECK + GREG HOLLAND
CHARLES S. NOVINSKIE + RIK OFFENBERGER + ADAM POST
JEFF KEVIN + AMANDA SHERIFF + JASON VERSAGGI + CARRIE WOOD
CONTRIBUTING WRITERS

MARK HUESMAN + AMANDA SHERIFF
EDITORS

YOLANDA RAMIREZ
PRICING EDITOR

MARK HUESMAN + DAWN GUZZO
LAYOUT & DESIGN

CHARLES S. NOVINSKIE + JASON C. ODOM
PROOFING & EDITORIAL ASSISTANCE

SPECIAL THANKS TO

JAMES BELLA + BIG APPLE CON + MIKE CARBONARO + HOWARD CHAYKIN + BRADY DARVIN
DAVE & ADAM'S CARD WORLD + BRENDAN DENEEN + DIAMOND COMIC DISTRIBUTORS + DIAMOND INTERNATIONAL GALLERIES
GARY DOLGOFF COMICS + SKIP FARRELL + JOSH GEPPI + G-MAN COMICS + JASON GOODMAN + GARY GUZZO
HAKE'S AUCTIONS + HERITAGE AUCTIONS + HEROES AREN'T HARD TO FIND + DAVID HILLMAN + ART HOLCOMB
JIM HOLLISTER + WILLIAM HUGHES VINTAGE COLLECTABLES + JAYJAY JACKSON + JOSEPH A. JAMES
GEORGES JEANTY + J.G. JONES + NICK KATRADIS + DAVID LAPHAM + TOM MASON + DAN MOLER
MYCOMICSHOP.COM + TIM PERKINS + ED POLGARDY + KEVIN POLING + SANDY PLUNKETT
THE ESTATE OF PAUL RYAN + JIM SALICRUP + CONAN SAUNDERS + LEE SEITZ + JIM SHOOTER
J. CLARK SMITH + NEIL VOKES + PAULINE WEISS + MARK WHEATLEY + DEAN ZACHARY + DWIGHT JON ZIMMERMAN

GEMSTONE PUBLISHING • HUNT VALLEY, MARYLAND
WWW.GEMSTONEPUB.COM

THE OVERSTREET COMIC BOOK PRICE GUIDE TO LOST UNIVERSES.
Copyright © 2022 by Gemstone Publishing, Inc. All rights reserved.
Printed in Canada. No part of this book may be used or reproduced in
any manner whatsoever without written permission except in the case of
brief quotations embodied in critical articles and reviews.
For information, write to: Gemstone Publishing, 10150 York Rd., Suite 300,
Hunt Valley, MD 21030
or email feedback@gemstonepub.com

All rights reserved. **THE OVERSTREET COMIC BOOK PRICE GUIDE TO
LOST UNIVERSES** is an original publication of Gemstone Publishing, Inc.
This edition has never before appeared in book form.

Mighty Crusaders cover by Jerry Ordway. Mighty Crusaders ©2022
Archie Comic Publications. Ironjaw cover by Lee Weeks. Ironjaw ©2022
Nemesis, Ltd. Star Brand cover by Alex Saviuk, Tom Palmer & Mort Todd.
Star Brand ©2022 MARVEL. Dark Dominion cover by J.G. Jones. ©2022
Successors to Enlightened Entertainment, LLC.

Overstreet® is a Registered Trademark of Gemstone Publishing, Inc.

Mighty Crusaders Hardcover Edition ISBN: 978-1-60360-286-0
Mighty Crusaders Soft Cover Edition ISBN: 978-1-60360-285-3

Ironjaw Hardcover Edition ISBN: 978-1-60360-591-5
Ironjaw Soft Cover Edition ISBN: 978-1-60360-592-2

Star Brand Hardcover Edition ISBN: 978-1-60360-594-6
Star Brand Soft Cover Edition ISBN: 978-1-60360-593-9

Dark Dominion S&N Hardcover Edition ISBN: 978-1-60360-287-7
Dark Dominion Deluxe S&N Hardcover Ed. ISBN: 978-1-60360-288-4

Printed in Canada

First Edition: February 2022

GEMSTONE PUBLISHING

STEVE GEPPI
PRESIDENT

J.C. VAUGHN
VICE-PRESIDENT
OF PUBLISHING

ROBERT M. OVERSTREET
PUBLISHER

MARK HUESMAN
CREATIVE DIRECTOR

AMANDA SHERIFF
ASSOCIATE EDITOR

YOLANDA RAMIREZ
PRICING EDITOR

MIKE WILBUR
WAREHOUSE OPERATIONS

TOM GAREY
KATHY WEAVER
BRETT CANBY
ANGELA PHILLIPS-MILLS
ACCOUNTING SERVICES

WWW.GEMSTONEPUB.COM

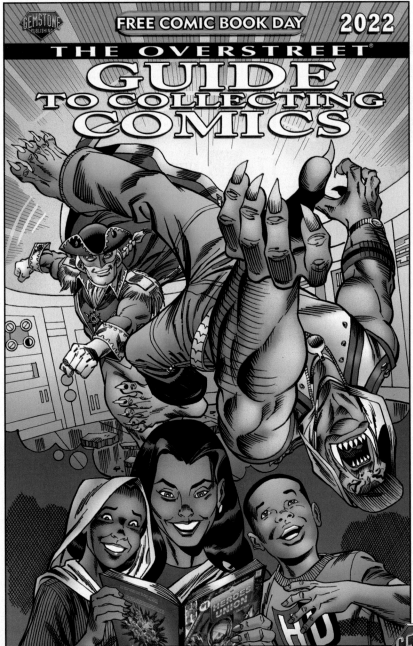

TABLE OF CONTENTS

PUBLISHER'S NOTE

These are, as the saying goes, interesting times.

We've seen staggering new record prices established, only to have them fall at the next major auction. We've seen a handful of new comics over the $1 Million or more mark in just the past few months alone. It certainly seems as if we're in a time when no record is truly safe.

Just a few years ago, we could have called some of the prices realized "insane," whereas now we just sit back and see what comes next. *The Overstreet Comic Book Price Guide* has never been in the business of predicting where the market will go.

I've been asked to do that many times, and it's just never been our thing.

We reflect the market. We don't dictate to it, speculate on it, or direct it. That doesn't, though, mean that we don't see things from which we can draw some conclusions.

First, there are some truly different economic dynamics going on right now. While many individuals and businesses have been severely impacted by COVID-19 and its fallout, others have done okay or even prospered in this situation. In some cases, people who haven't been able to travel have taken the money they would have spent going to a convention (airfare, hotel, food) and instead targeted a big-ticket item that they'd always wanted.

Second, none of us know how long these conditions will last.

Third, when things are expensive enough that they move out of our price range, market forces suggest that we will look for something less expensive.

That brings us to this book, *The Overstreet Comic Book Price Guide To Lost Universes.* While we have indeed seen an amazing number of record prices in recent times, there are still many, many accessible, affordable comic books to be had on the back issue market. And many of them are gateways to incredible storytelling and offer new universes to discover.

For years, many collectors have referred to "dead universes," but it's comics, and in comics we're always ripe for a comeback. Hence the term "Lost Universes." As we've seen with Milestone, Valiant, MLJ/Archie, and even characters from Marvel's New Universe, given a chance, characters, stories, and worlds that once faded have returned in powerful ways.

Think about what's packed in this book: Atlas-Seaboard, Comics' Greatest World from Dark Horse, Continuity, CrossGen, DEFIANT, Future Comics, the Kirbyverse from Topps, the Mighty Crusaders, original Milestone, New Universe from Marvel, Tower's *T.H.U.N.D.E.R. Agents*, Triumphant, the Ultraverse from Malibu, and original Valiant populate this new volume. Every comic that is priced is also pictured.

We've also included a tremendous amount of behind-the-scenes information, copious amounts of original art, and no small amount of thought in this book. Many, though certainly not all, of the comics listed herein are *very* affordable. We suspect – but don't know – that as our fellow enthusiasts help us discover the true scarcity of some of these issues, that may change in years to come.

This is your invitation to discover worlds you might have missed or even dismissed previously, and this is a call to remember that in comics there are always new worlds to discover, and that some of them are just as addictive as those you already collect.

Bob

Robert M. Overstreet
Author & Publisher

San Diego, 1994. It was my first trip to Comic-Con International: San Diego. I had only recently broken in as a freelancer for Overstreet Publications, among others, and I was standing there talking to *the* Bob Overstreet.

He *seemed* like a normal human being, but this was *the guy*. This was the creator of *The Overstreet Comic Book Price Guide*, the monumentally influential book that I'd first seen at Eide's Entertainment in Pittsburgh in 1976. This was the guy who had added definition to our hobby, backed it up with thoroughness and longevity, and delivered time and time again. And I was talking to him like it was a normal thing.

In the here-and-now, after his incredible work on 51 annual editions of the *Guide*, you probably don't need me to pitch you on his resumé.

At the time, though, it was a total geek out moment, and I managed to survive it somehow without looking like an idiot (or at least not a complete one). I was already churning, working hard to turn my freelance gigs into an actual job, but I was a bit dazed by the moment. I definitely did not suspect that by the time San Diego rolled around the next year, both Bob and I would have been working for Steve Geppi's Gemstone Publishing for months.

But we were. I joined the staff as Associate Editor, and I could just walk down the hall and ask Bob Overstreet questions about comics history. It seemed a bit unreal, even after I'd been doing it a while.

One of my co-workers then was Scott Braden. We'd been hired to work on the company's magazine, *Overstreet's FAN*, but the stature, power, and long-term impact of the *Guide* was the reason we even had the opportunity.

We had some tastes that overlapped and others that didn't, which made for great conversations, but both Scott and I saw *The Overstreet Comic Book Price Guide* and strongly believed that it and what is now *The Overstreet Guide To Grading Comics* should not be the only Overstreet books about our favorite subject, comic books.

The Overstreet Comic Book Price Guide To Lost Universes springs from those early discussions and many others we've had over the years. It adds a *Photo-Journal* aspect to the trusted elements of the *Guide*, and we are confident you are going to love the results as much as we loved creating and working on this book.

Special thanks to Editor/designer Mark Huesman, who handled the heavy lifting on all the listings, Editor Amanda Sheriff, who organized our corrections, designer Dawn Guzzo, who took care of all the feature articles, Pricing Editor Yolanda Ramirez, who worked with Bob on the pricing updates, our proofers, Charles S. Novinskie and Jason C. Odom, who turned the pages around so quickly, and to Conan Saunders for the last minute save.

Our sincere thanks to everyone who contributed to this one, and particularly to you for picking it up. We look forward to your reactions!

J.C. Vaughn
Author & Vice-President of Publishing

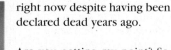

"Lost Universes."

Let's explore that phrase's nigh-magical meaning, shall we? The term makes one consider these wonderful planes of fast-paced fiction which you will discover (or at least, rediscover) within the pages of this book are truly lost to us, never to be found again.

But are they really?

When readers and comic book fans can reintroduce themselves to these celestial worlds upon worlds via back issue bins at comic shops and conventions around the planet, are they really ever lost? When they can be tracked down from online retailers, can we say they're not coming back?

When it comes to comics and the notion that dead and gone truly means dead and gone for good, there are a trio of answers to the question: *Nada*, *negative*, and *no*.

Of course, you, dear reader, can fill in the blank however you see fit.

For the sake of argument, though, these comic book universes – most of which are not being published currently – do come back time to time.

Tower Comics' *T.H.U.N.DE.R. Agents* is a great example of this, since the heroes of this mighty mythos have been published by a number of companies over the years. Perhaps more distinctly, the Mighty Crusaders have been appearing, disappearing, and reappearing for literally decades from the same publisher!

Then, there are the original Valiant and original Milestone universes, four-color fiefdoms that just refuse to die. Multiple incarnations in both cases, and in both cases they're also being published

right now despite having been declared dead years ago.

Are you getting my point? So, instead of referring to these Lost Universes as dead and gone – for that would be sheer folly – consider them as future reading and an expansion of a comic book curriculum that millions of fans can enjoy this day and, well, the next.

If you're not collecting them, you should be.

Get out there!

Scott Braden
Author

P.S. For many of us, comics are as much about the relationships we forge as they are about the Lost Universes we discover. We owe a deep debt of gratitude to all of the creative professionals, retailers, historians, and our fellow fans, all of whom have shared so much with us and helped make this book a reality. And if you happen to enjoy this edition, please support the businesses that advertised in it. Their support also made this book – and we hope a second one – possible.

Scott Braden, a former Gemstone Publishing staffer, is an Overstreet Advisor and regular contributor to our publications, including our Scoop *email newsletter. As a journalist he has covered everything from comics to elections. He's also the creator of the comic book* Kent Menace.

Values for items listed and pictured in this book are based on author's experience, consultations with a network of advisors including collectors specializing in various categories, and actual prices realized for specific items sold through private sales and auctions. The values offered in this book are approximations influenced by many factors including condition, rarity and demand, and they should serve only as guidelines, presenting an average range of what one might expect to pay for the items.

In the marketplace, knowledge and opinions held by both sellers and buyers determine prices asked and prices paid. This is not a price list of items for sale or items wanted by the author or publisher. The author and the publisher shall not be held responsible for losses that may occur in the purchase, sale or other transaction of property because of information contained herein. Efforts have been made to present accurate information, but the possibility of error exists.

Unlike the main edition of *The Overstreet Comic Book Price Guide*, this book only includes three pricing columns, representing the grades 2.0 (Good or GD), 6.0 (Fine or FN), and 9.2 (Near Mint-minus or NM-). You will see the three prices listed under the images of the comics, as in the top example.

However, some of the comics listed in this volume have yet to accrue significant value below grade 9.2 (Near Mint-minus or NM-). For such issues, we have only listed the single 9.2 price, as in the lower example.

It may seem odd advice to get from a price guide, but whatever price the market assesses to your comics, remember that in the end you determine what they are worth *to you*. Collect what you love and it's difficult to overpay!

Readers who believe that they have discovered an error are invited to mail corrective information to the author, Robert M. Overstreet, at Gemstone Publishing, 10150 York Rd., Suite 300, Hunt Valley, MD 21030. Verified corrections will be incorporated into future editions.

SHIELD-WIZARD COMICS #1
SUMMER 1940
$450 $1350 $10,000

STATIC #8
JANUARY 1994
$4

G-MAN COMICS

World's Finest Micro Publisher

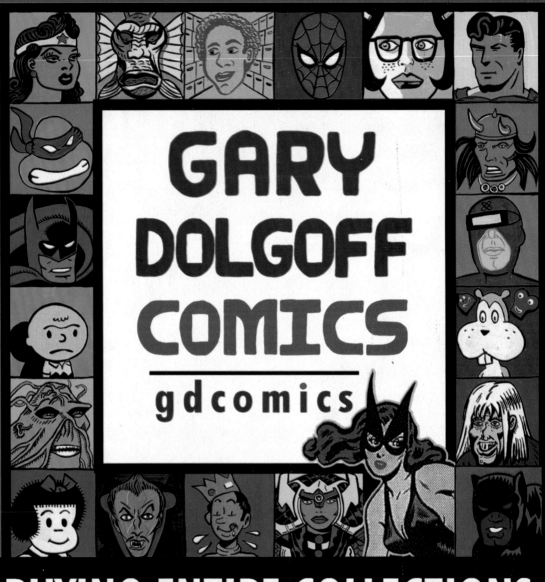

Publisher Martin Goodman had sold Magazine Management (and its Marvel subsidiary) to Perfect Film & Chemical in 1968. A provision of the sale was that Martin's son Charles ("Chip") would run the editorial. For various reasons – notably conflict between Chip and Stan Lee and the evolution of Perfect to the larger, conflict-averse Cadence Industries – Chip was let go. Outraged, Martin established Seaboard Periodicals in 1974 with Chip in charge. Like Magazine Management, Seaboard would publish a variety of magazines including detective, confessional, film, cheesecake, puzzle, and pulp titles…anchored by comics. The name Atlas, of course, was a nod to Martin's old Marvel imprint.

I was a 22-year-old fan who answered an ad in the *New York Times* and was hired. With Martin in a corner office, my weekly meetings or calls with Stan (who offered advice), and palpable fear at my former home DC, I anticipated success. I articulated a "vision" to all the artists and writers: the glittering Silver Age plopped in a world inspired by the dirty, crime-ridden, bankrupt New York of the early 1970s. My assistant Ric Meyers and I confidently and ambitiously plotted two universes full of characters. The Atlas universe was laid out in a diagram showing how everything interrelated. After hours, Ric and I conceived a second, never-published line. That imprint was to be called Timeless, honoring Martin's Timely imprint. Atlas had 90-plus characters, Timeless 50-plus – the latter including a few that Martin rejected for the initial Atlas launch, like The Headless Horsewoman and Hellflower (a concept by my dear friend and Parsons student, the late Dick Siegel). The link between the imprints was to have been the villain Haydes.

My datebooks are jammed full of co-plotting with writers, reviewing thumbnails and designs with artists, checking finished art, arguing with the Comics Code Authority and, increasingly, meeting with Martin who was displeased with the direction of the comics. Before we had any sales reports he was insisting, more and more – and then demanding – that the titles look more like Marvel comics.

The challenges were plentiful but so were the rewards, in particular working with writer John Albano, a good friend from DC; can-do-anything artist Ernie Colon, who I had met at Skywald (and who continued to work with me until his death); the inspired and inspiring artist Sal Amendola; writer Archie Goodwin and artist Pat Boyette, both of whom I knew from Warren; crusty Leo Summers, an *Analog* and DC artist whom I sought out; artist Walt Simonson, whose unpublished Kaiju saga was a gem; and the great Jeff Jones, another Skywald alumnus.

Then and now, the keyword for Atlas was "promise." The creative personnel believed there was potential in every comic. The first two issues of most titles had strengths and disappointments. But on the whole, I believed – and still do – we were on to something new and worthwhile.

Unfortunately, our deadlines were murderous and few of us got to do our best work. After two issues, when Martin issued the Make Mine Marvel mandate – instructing characters to be revamped and frankly bowdlerized – the plans for our universe, for Timeless, for *everything* faltered badly.

I quit in frustration. At the time, I would not have believed we would still be talking about Atlas. That said, someone asked me recently what I would say to Martin if he were still with us. I was surprised at my answer: "Thanks for giving me the opportunity to craft something we're talking about 45 years later."

- Jeff Rovin

The former editor of Atlas, Jeff Rovin wrote Zero-G *with William Shatner, the* EarthEnd Saga *with Gillian Anderson, continues to write the* Tom Clancy's Op-Center *novels, westerns, and work on IP litigation for Hollywood and NY law firms.*

FIRST PUBLICATION:
Grim Ghost #1, *Ironjaw* #1, *Phoenix* #1, *Weird Tales of the Macabre* #1 (All January 1975)

LAST PUBLICATION:
The Phoenix #4 (October 1975)

REVIVAL(S):
Ardden Entertainment published three six-issue series and an incomplete mini-series beginning with *Grim Ghost* #0 (October 2010), *Phoenix* #0 (October 2010), *Wulf* #1 (March 2011), and *Atlas Unified* #0 (November 2011). Atlas Originals has released four prose offerings, *Targitt* (June 2020), *Bog Beast* (July 2020), *Wrecage* (September 2020), and *Thrilling Adventure Stories* (November 2020).

Splash page from *Ironjaw #2* by Pablo Marcos.
Image courtesy of Nick Katradis.

BARBARIANS #1
JUNE 1975
$3 $9 $28

BLAZING BATTLE TALES #1
JULY 1975
$3 $9 $30

THE BRUTE #1
FEBRUARY 1975
$3 $9 $35

THE BRUTE #2
APRIL 1975
$2 $6 $18

THE BRUTE #3
JULY 1975
$2 $6 $22

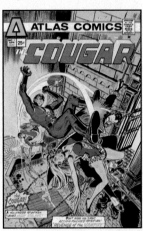

THE COUGAR #1
APRIL 1975
$2 $6 $20

THE COUGAR #2
JULY 1975
$2 $6 $20

DEMON-HUNTER #1
SEPTEMBER 1975
$3 $9 $25

THE DESTRUCTOR #1
FEBRUARY 1975
$3 $9 $26

THE DESTRUCTOR #2
APRIL 1975
$2 $6 $16

THE DESTRUCTOR #3
JUNE 1975
$2 $6 $16

THE DESTRUCTOR #4
AUGUST 1975
$2 $6 $16

FRIGHT #1
AUGUST 1975
$3 $9 $30

THE GRIM GHOST #1
JANUARY 1975
$2 $6 $22

THE GRIM GHOST #2
MARCH 1975
$2 $6 $22

THE GRIM GHOST #3
JULY 1975
$2 $6 $22

HANDS OF THE DRAGON #1
JUNE 1975
$3 $9 $24

IRONJAW #1
JANUARY 1975
$3 $9 $28

IRONJAW #2
MARCH 1975
$3 $9 $28

IRONJAW #3
MAY 1975
$2 $6 $16

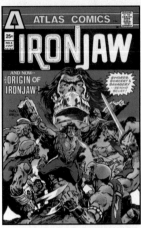

IRONJAW #4
JULY 1975
$2 $6 $16

MORLOCK 2001 #1
FEBRUARY 1975
$2 $6 $20

MORLOCK 2001 #2
APRIL 1975
$2 $6 $20

MORLOCK 2001 #3
JULY 1975
$3 $9 $28

PHOENIX #1
JANUARY 1975
$2 $6 $22

PHOENIX #2
MARCH 1975
$2 $6 $16

PHOENIX #3
JUNE 1975
$2 $6 $16

PHOENIX #4
OCTOBER 1975
$2 $6 $16

PLANET OF VAMPIRES #1
FEBRUARY 1975
$3 $9 $35

PLANET OF VAMPIRES #2
APRIL 1975
$2 $6 $24

PLANET OF VAMPIRES #3
JULY 1975
$2 $6 $22

POLICE ACTION #1
FEBRUARY 1975
$2 $6 $18

POLICE ACTION #2
APRIL 1975
$2 $6 $18

POLICE ACTION #3
JUNE 1975
$2 $6 $18

SAVAGE COMBAT TALES #1
FEBRUARY 1975
$2 $6 $20

SAVAGE COMBAT TALES #2
APRIL 1975
$2 $6 $22

SAVAGE COMBAT TALES #3
JULY 1975
$2 $6 $20

THE SCORPION #1
FEBRUARY 1975
$3 $9 $28

THE SCORPION #2
MAY 1975
$3 $9 $28

THE SCORPION #3
JULY 1975
$2 $6 $20

TALES OF EVIL #1
FEBRUARY 1975
$2 $6 $22

TALES OF EVIL #2
APRIL 1975
$2 $6 $22

TALES OF EVIL #3
JULY 1975
$2 $6 $22

TARGITT #1
MARCH 1975
$2 $6 $18

TARGITT #2
JUNE 1975
$2 $6 $18

TARGITT #3
JULY 1975
$2 $6 $18

TIGERMAN #1
APRIL 1975
$2 $6 $20

TIGERMAN #2
JUNE 1975
$2 $6 $20

TIGERMAN #3
SEPTEMBER 1975
$2 $6 $20

VICKI #1
FEBRUARY 1975
$5 $15 $85

VICKI #2
APRIL 1975
$5 $15 $85

VICKI #3
JUNE 1975
$5 $15 $90

VICKI #4
AUGUST 1975
$5 $15 $90

WEIRD SUSPENSE #1
FEBRUARY 1975
$2 $6 $20

WEIRD SUSPENSE #2
APRIL 1975
$2 $6 $20

WEIRD SUSPENSE #3
JUNE 1975
$2 $6 $20

WESTERN ACTION #1
FEBRUARY 1975
$2 $6 $20

WULF THE BARBARIAN #1
FEBRUARY 1975
$3 $9 $24

WULF THE BARBARIAN #2
APRIL 1975
$3 $9 $24

WULF THE BARBARIAN #3
JULY 1975
$2 $6 $18

WULF THE BARBARIAN #4
SEPTEMBER 1975
$2 $6 $18

DEVILINA #1
JANUARY 1975
$5 $15 $75

DEVILINA #2
MAY 1975
$5 $15 $80

GOTHIC ROMANCES #1
DECEMBER 1974
$31 $93 $800

MOVIE MONSTERS #1
DECEMBER 1974
$4 $12 $65

MOVIE MONSTERS #2
FEBRUARY 1975
$4 $12 $650

MOVIE MONSTERS #3
APRIL 1975
$4 $12 $60

MOVIE MONSTERS #4
AUGUST 1975
$4 $12 $60

THRILLING ADVENTURE STORIES #1
FEBRUARY 1975
$3 $9 $45

THRILLING ADVENTURE STORIES #2
AUGUST 1975
$4 $12 $55

WEIRD TALES OF THE MACABRE #1
JANUARY 1975
$5 $15 $80

WEIRD TALES OF THE MACABRE #2
MARCH 1975
$5 $15 $85

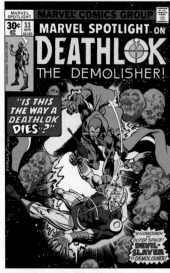

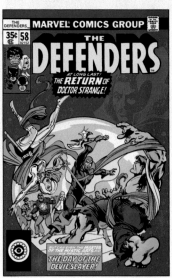

The Atlas-Seaboard character with perhaps the oddest existence (or most existences) was Demon-Hunter. In his Atlas origin story (and only issue), Gideon Cross had renounced the demon cult which had granted him incredible powers and now stood opposed to them. Their goal was "Xenogenisis," the rebirth of a demon race on earth. David Anthony Kraft (*Comics Interview*) wrote it and Rich Buckler plotted and illustrated it.

Meanwhile, over at Marvel, Buckler's "Deathlok The Demolisher" series in *Astonishing Tales* had been canceled mid-story. The story was to be more or less wrapped up in *Marvel Spotlight* #33 (1977), although it would also carry into *Marvel Two-in-One* #27 before fading into the great land of permanently dangling storylines. Again, with Kraft writing and Buckler illustrating, Deathlok returned ostensibly for the wrap-up story. Only it was easily as much the origin story for Devil-Slayer.

Devil-Slayer was Eric Simon Payne. He had renounced the demon cult which had granted him incredible powers and now stood opposed to them. Their goal, and stop me if you've heard this before, was "Xenogenisis," the rebirth of a demon race on earth. His costume was blue with an orange cape where Demon-Hunter's was red with a blue cape, but otherwise it's the same guy.

Devil-Slayer went on to pop up in Kraft's *The Defenders* #58-60 (1978) for a three-part story entitled, not surprisingly, "Xenogenisis."

He wasn't done there. Well, Devil-Slayer was, as was Eric Simon Payne, but Gideon Cross wasn't. Cross came back as Bloodwing, in the Buckler-published *Galaxia Magazine* (1981). This one didn't get as far as mentioning Xenogenisis, but there was mention of a demonic "Crimson Brotherhood." The character looked the same as his Marvel incarnation on the color cover (interiors were black and white), but the feel was a little more rough and tumble.

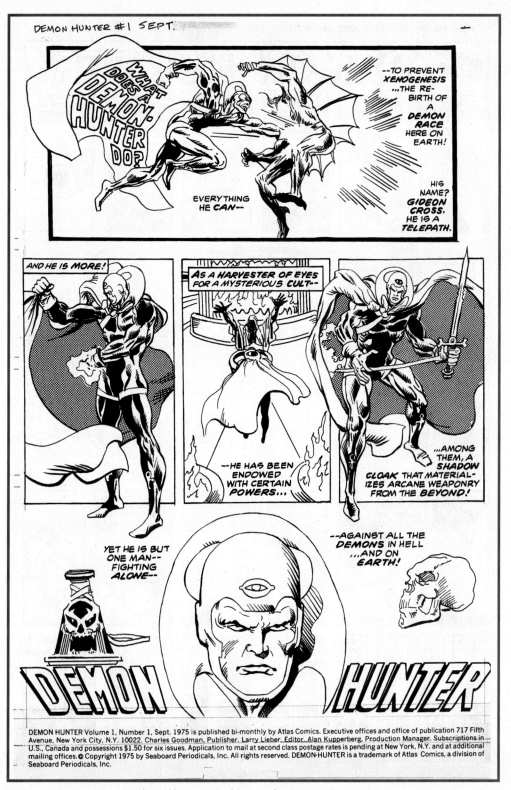

Rich Buckler's original Page 1 for *Demon-Hunter #1*.
Image courtesy of Nick Katradis.

Rich Buckler's original Page 2 for *Demon-Hunter #1*.
Image courtesy of Nick Katradis.

An unpublished Bloodwing page by Rich Buckler and Sam de la Rosa intended for *Galaxia Magazine #2*.
Image courtesy of Heritage Auctions.

ATLAS 2.0 (Ardden)

Ardden Entertainment, the publishers of what's become known as "Atlas 2.0," started out in comics with licensed properties, specifically Flash Gordon. From there, they acquired the rights to do a "modern" Casper/Wendy/Hot Stuff comic, and they were considering other options

"I was racking my brain, trying to think of other properties that I loved as a kid, and remembered Atlas. At some point when I was in high school and obsessively collecting comics, I had found nearly the entire Atlas run in a dollar bin," said former Ardden publisher Brendan Deneen.

"I loved the characters and the history of the company, even as a teenager. I did some online sleuthing and eventually found my way to Jason Goodman [the grandson of Timely, Marvel, and Atlas founder Martin Goodman]. I sent him an out-of-the-blue email. I must have said something that Jason liked because he responded, and we started talking on the phone a couple times a week about potential ways forward. I believe that Jason liked that I worked in both publishing and the film industry. We hit it off almost immediately," he said.

Soon, Ardden launched the Atlas line, with *Phoenix* (written by Deneen and *Earth-X* scribe Jim Krueger) *The Grim Ghost* (written by Tony Isabella and screenwriter Stephen Susco) and *Wulf* (written by *30 Days of Night* creator Steve Niles).

"I always knew that I wanted to do the three we chose. They seemed like the most obvious, though we also heavily flirted with *Planet of Vampires* and *Destructor*," he said.

Deneen said he knew from the outset that he wanted to write *Phoenix*, but he called the choice of writers for *The Grim Ghost* "a little

FIRST PUBLICATION:
The Grim Ghost #0 and *Phoenix* #0 (October 2010)

LAST PUBLICATION:
Wulf #6 (September 2012)

REVIVAL(S):
Atlas Originals has issued four prose projects, *Targitt* (June 2020), *Bog Beast* (July 2020), *Wrecage* (September 2020), and *Thrilling Adventure Stories* (November 2020).

more complex," and said the situation led to Ardden's Editor-in-Chief, J.M. DeMatteis, departing. "…luckily J.M. and I are still friends," he said.

"Writing *Phoenix* was definitely the high point for me because I love that character, and I think it was the best of the three reboots (but I'm biased). I also loved the early days, when Jason and I were batting creative ideas back and forth. It's always fun to play with characters that existed before you were born, and to try to come up with new ways to approach them while also being respectful to their histories," he said.

In addition to the departure of DeMatteis, the company had some serious difficulties with some of the creators and ran into deadline problems. The Atlas line ended in the middle of the *Atlas Unified*, a mini-series that was bringing all of the Atlas characters together distinctly in the same universe for the first time.

"I think it just came down to sales. I honestly believe the delays in the first three titles doomed us. I'm a collector of comics myself and delays between issues are interest killers. Like I said, I wish we had been able to complete *Atlas Unified* because it was a brilliant storyline that would have gone in some very cool directions," he said.

Since Atlas 2.0, Deneen has written three novels, including an original Morbius story for Marvel/ Titan, a four-book picture book series for Marvel starting with *Night Night, Groot*, and has a middle grade Green Arrow graphic novel coming out from DC in 2022 entitled *Stranded*. In 2015, he launched Scout, a successful new comics start-up, where he is CEO, and he continues to work in publishing and the film and television industries.

Dean Zachary's original cover for the New York Comic Con exclusive limited edition of *Atlas Unified* #0 featuring Wulf, Phoenix, Grim Ghost, and Lomax (left to right). Image courtesy of Dean Zachary.

ATLAS RETAILER SAMPLER
2010
$3

ATLAS UNIFIED #0
MULTIVERSE GIVEAWAY
OCTOBER 2011
$3

ATLAS UNIFIED #0
NEW YORK COMIC CON EDITION
OCTOBER 2011
$3

ATLAS UNIFIED #0
NYCC EDITION • SALGADO SKETCH COVER
OCTOBER 2011
$3

ATLAS UNIFIED #0
NYCC EDITION • ZACHARY SKETCH COVER
OCTOBER 2011
$3

ATLAS UNIFIED #0
RETAILER PREVIEW EDITION
OCTOBER 2011
$3

ATLAS UNIFIED #1
WULF COVER
NOVEMBER 2011
$3

ATLAS UNIFIED #1
GRIM GHOST COVER
NOVEMBER 2011
$3

ATLAS UNIFIED #1
PHOENIX & LOMAX COVER
NOVEMBER 2011
$3

ATLAS UNIFIED #1
FOLD-OUT COVER
NOVEMBER 2011
$3

ATLAS UNIFIED #2
FEBRUARY 2012
$3

THE GRIM GHOST #0
OCTOBER 2010
$3

THE GRIM GHOST #0
LIMITED B&W COVER EDITION
OCTOBER 2010
$3

THE GRIM GHOST #0
NEW YORK COMIC CON EDITION
OCTOBER 2010
$3

THE GRIM GHOST #1
MARCH 2011
$3

THE GRIM GHOST #1
SKETCH COVER
MARCH 2011
$3

THE GRIM GHOST #1
KAPOW! COMIC CON VARIANT
MARCH 2011
$3

THE GRIM GHOST #2
MAY 2011
$3

THE GRIM GHOST #2
ONLINE EXCLUSIVE EDITION
MAY 2011
$3

THE GRIM GHOST #3
JULY 2011
$3

THE GRIM GHOST #4
AUGUST 2011
$3

THE GRIM GHOST #5
SEPTEMBER 2011
$3

THE GRIM GHOST #6
NOVEMBER 2011
$3

PHOENIX #0
NEW YORK COMIC CON EDITION
OCTOBER 2010
$3

PHOENIX #0
LIMITED B&W COVER EDITION
OCTOBER 2010
$3

PHOENIX #1
MARCH 2011
$3

PHOENIX #1
B&W SKETCH COVER
MARCH 2011
$3

PHOENIX #1
KAPOW! COMIC CON VARIANT
MARCH 2011
$3

PHOENIX #2
MAY 2011
$3

PHOENIX #2
ONLINE EXCLUSIVE EDITION
MAY 2011
$3

PHOENIX #3
JULY 2011
$3

PHOENIX #4
SEPTEMBER 2011
$3

PHOENIX #5
FEBRUARY 2012
$3

PHOENIX #6
AUGUST 2012
$3

WULF #1
MARCH 2011
$3

WULF #1
B&W VARIANT COVER
MARCH 2011
$3

WULF #1
KAPOW! COMIC CON VARIANT
MARCH 2011
$3

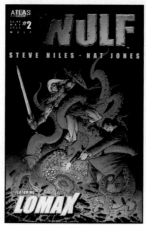

WULF #2
MAY 2011
$3

WULF #2
ONLINE EXCLUSIVE EDITION
MAY 2011
$3

WULF #3
SEPTEMBER 2011
$3

WULF #3
IRONJAW VARIANT COVER
SEPTEMBER 2011
$3

WULF #4
OCTOBER 2011
$3

WULF #5
FEBRUARY 2012
$3

WULF #6
SEPTEMBER 2012
$3

PHOENIX #1 ORIGINAL PRINTING

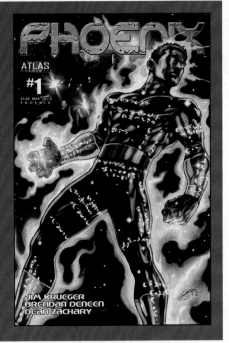

The interiors of the original, unreleased printing of *Phoenix* #1 were printed very dark. Most of the dark blue colors, particularly in Phoenix's costume, ran toward purple-black in this printing, where as in the released "first" printing the were slightly lighter than Navy blue. These pages can also be readily compared to those reproduced in the *Atlas Retailer Sampler*, which was printed at approximately the same time as the original printing. At the instruction of Atlas owner Jason Goodman, this overwhelming bulk of this printing was pulped (destroyed). However, some copies, which had already been delivered to the Atlas offices, are known to exit.

THE "ATLAS AT LAST!" EXHIBIT

On Friday, March 11, 2011, "Atlas At Last," a visual tour through the 73 color comic books and black & white magazines produced by Seaboard Periodicals, opened at Geppi's Entertainment Museum in Baltimore.

In attendance for the event were Guest Curator Mike Wilbur, from Diamond International Galleries, the late Phil Zolli, whose AtlasArchives.com site had focused attention on the line since 2003, Guest Curator J.C. Vaughn, who spearheaded the development of the exhibit, and Gemstone Publishing's Creative Director, Mark Huesman, who edited the exhibit's companion publication, a special *Comic Book Marketplace* #1.

Wilbur's and Zolli's respective collections made up the backbone of the exhibit, which included the rare *Gothic Romances* magazine (which features text and accompanying spot illustrations) and almost never seen *My Secret*, a confessions-type magazine, of which even some diehard Atlas fans are unaware.

In addition to the publications, the exhibit included an extensive survey of original comic book art with than a dozen covers, two color guides, and character sketches. Also included were two unpublished covers, *Planet of Vampires* #4 by Pablo Marcos and an undesignated *Phoenix* piece by Sal Amendola.

John Santangelo, Sr. and Ed Levy launched T.W.O. Charles Company, named after the co-founders' sons, both of whom were named Charles, in 1940. The company became Charlton Publications in 1945, and it included the Charlton Comics imprint, which continued until 1986. During its long run, Charlton successfully embraced different genres including war, Western, horror, crime, science fiction, and romance comics, as well as superheroes.

With magazines, puzzle books, and other publications in its line-up, the company's first comic book was *Yellowjacket Comics* #1 (September 1944), just months before the company adopted the Charlton name.

Charlton's superhero characters were not in a coherent universe, but they certainly got close in the Silver Age. Perhaps the initial spark came when Captain Atom was introduced in *Space Adventures* #33 (March 1960) by Joe Gill and Steve Ditko. Whether that was the case or not, the notion would take a few years to gestate.

Introducing... THAT DARLING OF DARKNESS, NIGHTSHADE, WHO TEAMS UP WITH OUR ATOMIC FIREBALL TO COMBAT "OPERATION GOLDEN GHOST," AN INGENIOUS, EVIL PLOT TO UNDERMINE THE SECURITY OF OUR NATION... AND THE WORLD!!!

Ted Kord, a new version of Blue Beetle, the Fox Comics character (Dan Garrett) that first appeared in *Mystery Men Comics* #1 (August 1939, published by Fox, acquired by Charlton in the '50s), was created by Gil and artists Bill Fraccio and Tony Tallarico for *Blue Beetle* #1 (June 1964). The Question, another character from Ditko, was launched as a back-up feature in that same issue.

In 1965, editor Dick Giordano introduced Charlton's "Action Heroes" line. While still not a universe in the continuity sense, there was definitely something of a sensibility building in their superhero comics.

Son of Vulcan, created by writer Pat Masulli and Fraccio debuted in *Mysteries of Unexplored Worlds* #46 (May 1965). Beginning with *Strange Suspense Stories* #75 (June 1965), Charlton reprinted the earlier Gill/Ditko Captain Atom stories. The series was retitled *Captain Atom* with #78 and Ditko returned to illustrate new adventures of the character. Judomaster was introduced by Gill and artist Frank McLaughlin in *Special War Series* #4 (November 1965). Peacemaker first appeared in *Fightin' 5* #40 (November 1966) by Gill and artist Pat Boyette.

Writer-artist Pete Morisi introduced the title character in *Peter Cannon ... Thunderbolt* #1 (January 1966), which then took over the numbering of *Son of Vulcan* for #51-60 (March/April 1966 – November 1967). While the practice of changing titles and continuing numbering was not unusual in prior decades, Charlton made something of an art of it.

Captain Atom #82 (September 1966), which introduced Nightshade, saw the only true team-up for the "Action Heroes" line. Between the comic's covers, the government paired Captain Atom and Nightshade, and history – or at least a footnote – was made.

Captain Atom, Blue Beetle, the Question and Nightshade did eventually come together as the Sentinels of Justice, a superhero team featured in *Americomics Special* #1 (August 1983) after Charlton stopped publishing and before the characters' trademarks were acquired by DC Comics, by then Giordano's employer, in 1985.

At DC, the original concept for Alan Moore and Dave Gibbons was to use the Charlton characters for the story that became *Watchmen*, but instead the altered versions familiar to readers were created. Instead, the Charlton superheroes were introduced on Earth-4 in *Crisis on Infinite Earths* and became part of DC's post-Crisis continuity. Captain Atom, Blue Beetle, and The Question would go on to experience multiple runs at DC.

COMICS' GREATEST WORLD

Comics' Greatest World was reportedly conceived in 1990, well before the onslaught of comic book universes that would hit the marketplace just a few years later. Spearheaded by Dark Horse Comics President and Publisher Mike Richardson, Creative Director Randy Stradley, Managing Editor Barbara Kesel, Editorial Coordinator Jerry Prosser, and Editor/designer Chris Warner, it took time to develop before finally seeing the light of day in 1993.

Dark Horse, of course, was no stranger to the comic book business. In July 1986 it had entered the fray with the anthology title *Dark Horse Presents* (with lead features such as Paul Chadwick's *Concrete* and Warner's *Black Cross*) and *Boris The Bear*. The line expanded rapidly to include *Hellboy*, *The American*, *The Mask*, *Trekker*, and *Sin City*, as well as licensed properties such as *Aliens*, *Predator*, and *Star Wars*, among others. The combination franchise *Aliens vs. Predator* got its start in comics from the company.

> **FIRST PUBLICATION:**
> *Dark Horse Comics #8 (March 1993)*
>
> **LAST PUBLICATION:**
> *Ghost #36 (April 1998)*
>
> **REVIVAL(S):**
> *Ghost* - Volume 2
> (September 1998 - August 2000)

In *Dark Horse Comics* #8-10, the anthology title featured the prelude story "Who is X?" (later reprinted in *X: One Shot to the Head*) before the Comics' Greatest World series rolled out with 16 weekly issues. The releases were organized into groups of four, each of which was focused on a specific region: Arcadia, Golden City, Steel Harbor, and Cinnibar Flats (location of The Vortex), in a somewhat alternate version of the United States.

The through-line story focused on the Searchers from an alien group called the Reavor Swarm, who had come to Earth to track down "the Heretic," whose experiments on 1930s and '40s humankind generated the metahuman activity that was then springing up across the world.

The initial 16 weekly issues, which together introduced all of the critical characters in the universe, included *Arcadia* Week 1: X, Week 2: Pit Bulls, Week 3: Ghost, and Week 4: Monster; *Golden City* Week 1: Rebel, Week 2: Mecha, Week 3: Titan, and Week 4: Catalyst: Agents of Change; *Steel Harbor* Week 1: Barb Wire, Week 2: The Machine, Week 3: Wolf Gang, and Week 4: Motorhead; and *Vortex* Week 1: Division 13, Week 2: Hero Zero, Week 3: King Tiger, and Week 4: Out of the Vortex.

Prosser provided the scripts for the *Arcadia* titles, Kesel wrote the *Golden City* issues, Warner scripted the *Steel Harbor* comics, and Stradley authored the four for *The Vortex*. Notable cover artists included Frank Miller, Dave Dorman, Jerry Ordway, George Peréz, and Geoff Darrow, among others.

Whatever its origins, *Comics' Greatest World* was released into a retail terrain that was changing into something far different than the one in which it was originally conceived. The speculator boom of the early '90s was in the process of giving way to a glut, which made for challenging times for a number of publishers.

Ghost (36 regular issues in its first run) and *X* (25 regular issues and a few specials) proved to be the most durable of the characters. *Barb Wire* got a feature film. *Will To Power* and *Out of the Vortex* each lasted 12 issues. *Catalyst: Agents of Change* stuck around for seven. *Agents of Law* and *Motorhead* totaled six issues each. *Division 13* and *The Machine* each ran four.

By the time *Ghost* #1, *Motorhead* #1, and *Agents of Law* #1 were released, the name Comics' Greatest World had given way to "Dark Horse Heroes." It wouldn't last long either.

Given the bleak outlook for their superhero world, and the fact that the company had many other comics that were selling just fine, it's probably not surprising that in the end this experiment just ran its own course. That said, there are still some very intriguing stories and characters in this universe, as its fans know.

Jerry Ordway's preliminary illustration for the cover to Dark Horse's
Will to Power #7 (Comics' Greatest World) featuring Titan, Grace,
and Rebel. Image courtesy of Heritage Auctions.

DARK HORSE COMICS #8
MARCH 1993
$1 $3 $8

DARK HORSE COMICS #9
APRIL 1993
$5

DARK HORSE COMICS #10
MAY 1993
$5

DARK HORSE COMICS #19
MARCH 1994
$4

DARK HORSE COMICS #20
APRIL 1994
$4

DARK HORSE COMICS #21
MAY 1994
$4

DARK HORSE COMICS #22
JUNE 1994
$4

DARK HORSE COMICS #23
JULY 1994
$4

DARK HORSE COMICS #24
AUGUST 1994
$4

**COMICS' GREATEST WORLD:
SOURCEBOOK**
MARCH 1993
$5

**COMICS' GREATEST WORLD:
X**
JUNE 1993
$3

**COMICS' GREATEST WORLD:
X**
B&W PRESS PROOF ED. • JUNE 1993
$1 $4 $10

**COMICS' GREATEST WORLD:
X**
DIAMOND LIMITED ED. • JUNE 1993
$5

**COMICS' GREATEST WORLD:
X**
DIAMOND FOIL ED. • JUNE 1993
$1 $3 $8

**COMICS' GREATEST WORLD:
X**
HEROES WORLD FOIL ED. • JUNE 1993
$1 $3 $8

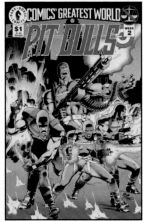

**COMICS' GREATEST WORLD:
PIT BULLS**
JUNE 1993
$3

**COMICS' GREATEST WORLD:
GHOST**
JUNE 1993
$4

**COMICS' GREATEST WORLD:
MONSTER**
JULY 1993
$3

**COMICS' GREATEST WORLD:
REBEL**
JULY 1993
$3

**COMICS' GREATEST WORLD:
REBEL**
SPECIAL LIMITED ED. • JULY 1993
$4

**COMICS' GREATEST WORLD:
REBEL**
HEROES WORLD FOIL ED. • JULY 1993
$6

**COMICS' GREATEST WORLD:
MECHA**
JULY 1993
$3

**COMICS' GREATEST WORLD:
TITAN**
JULY 1993
$3

**COMICS' GREATEST WORLD:
CATALYST: AGENTS OF CHANGE**
AUGUST 1993
$3

**COMICS' GREATEST WORLD:
BARB WIRE**
AUGUST 1993
$4

**COMICS' GREATEST WORLD:
BARB WIRE**
SPECIAL LIMITED ED. • AUGUST 1993
$5

**COMICS' GREATEST WORLD:
BARB WIRE**
HEROES WORLD FOIL ED. • AUGUST 1993
$1 $3 $8

**COMICS' GREATEST WORLD:
THE MACHINE**
AUGUST 1993
$3

**COMICS' GREATEST WORLD:
WOLF GANG**
AUGUST 1993
$3

**COMICS' GREATEST WORLD:
MOTORHEAD**
AUGUST 1993
$3

**COMICS' GREATEST WORLD:
DIVISION 13**
SEPTEMBER 1993
$3

**COMICS' GREATEST WORLD:
DIVISION 13**
SPECIAL LIMITED ED. • SEPTEMBER 1993
$5

**COMICS' GREATEST WORLD:
DIVISION 13**
HEROES WORLD FOIL ED. • SEPTEMBER 1993
$6

**COMICS' GREATEST WORLD:
HERO ZERO**
SEPTEMBER 1993
$3

**COMICS' GREATEST WORLD:
KING TIGER**
SEPTEMBER 1993
$3

**COMICS' GREATEST WORLD:
OUT OF THE VORTEX**
SEPTEMBER 1993
$3

AGENTS OF LAW #1
MARCH 1995
$3

AGENTS OF LAW #2
APRIL 1995
$3

AGENTS OF LAW #3
MAY 1995
$3

AGENTS OF LAW #4
JUNE 1995
$3

AGENTS OF LAW #5
JULY 1995
$3

AGENTS OF LAW #6
SEPTEMBER 1995
$3

BARB WIRE #1
APRIL 1994
$4

BARB WIRE #2
MAY 1994
$4

BARB WIRE #3
JUNE 1994
$4

BARB WIRE #4
AUGUST 1994
$4

BARB WIRE #5
SEPTEMBER 1994
$4

BARB WIRE #6
OCTOBER 1994
$4

BARB WIRE #7
NOVEMBER 1994
$4

BARB WIRE #8
JANUARY 1995
$4

BARB WIRE #9
FEBRUARY 1995
$4

**BARB WIRE:
ACE OF SPADES #1**
MAY 1996
$4

**BARB WIRE:
ACE OF SPADES #2**
JUNE 1996
$4

**BARB WIRE:
ACE OF SPADES #3**
JULY 1996
$4

**BARB WIRE:
ACE OF SPADES #4**
SEPTEMBER 1996
$4

**CATALYST:
AGENTS OF CHANGE #1**
FEBRUARY 1994
$3

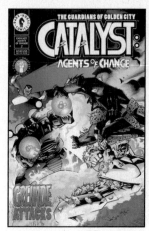

**CATALYST:
AGENTS OF CHANGE #2**
MARCH 1994
$3

**CATALYST:
AGENTS OF CHANGE #3**
APRIL 1994
$3

**CATALYST:
AGENTS OF CHANGE #4**
MAY 1994
$3

**CATALYST:
AGENTS OF CHANGE #5**
JUNE 1994
$3

**CATALYST:
AGENTS OF CHANGE #6**
AUGUST 1994
$3

**CATALYST:
AGENTS OF CHANGE #7**
SEPTEMBER 1994
$3

DIVISION 13 #1
SEPTEMBER 1994
$4

DIVISION 13 #2
OCTOBER 1994
$4

DIVISION 13 #3
DECEMBER 1994
$4

DIVISION 13 #4
JANUARY 1995
$4

GHOST #1
APRIL 1995
$1 **$4** **$10**

GHOST #2
MAY 1995
$5

GHOST #3
JUNE 1995
$5

GHOST #4
JULY 1995
$4

GHOST #5
AUGUST 1995
$4

GHOST #6
SEPTEMBER 1995
$4

GHOST #7
OCTOBER 1995
$4

GHOST #8
NOVEMBER 1995
$4

GHOST #9
DECEMBER 1995
$4

GHOST #10
JANUARY 1996
$4

GHOST #11
FEBRUARY 1996
$4

GHOST #12
MARCH 1996
$4

GHOST #13
APRIL 1996
$4

GHOST #14
MAY 1996
$4

GHOST #15
JUNE 1996
$4

GHOST #16
JULY 1996
$4

GHOST #17
AUGUST 1996
$4

GHOST #18
SEPTEMBER 1996
$4

GHOST #19
NOVEMBER 1996
$4

GHOST #20
DECEMBER 1996
$4

GHOST #21
JANUARY 1997
$4

GHOST #22
FEBRUARY 1997
$4

GHOST #23
MARCH 1997
$4

GHOST #24
APRIL 1997
$4

GHOST #25
MAY 1997
$5

GHOST #26
JUNE 1997
$4

GHOST #27
JULY 1997
$4

GHOST #28
AUGUST 1997
$4

GHOST #29
SEPTEMBER 1997
$4

GHOST #30
OCTOBER 1997
$4

GHOST #31
NOVEMBER 1997
$4

GHOST #32
DECEMBER 1997
$4

GHOST #33
JANUARY 1998
$4

GHOST #34
FEBRUARY 1998
$4

GHOST #35
MARCH 1998
$4

GHOST #36
APRIL 1998
$4

GHOST SPECIAL #1
JULY 1994
$1 **$3** **$7**

GHOST SPECIAL #2
JUNE 1998
$5

GHOST SPECIAL #3
DECEMBER 1998
$4

GODZILLA VS. HERO ZERO #1
JULY 1995
$5

HERO ZERO #0
SEPTEMBER 1994
$3

**KING TIGER &
MOTORHEAD #1**
AUGUST 1996
$3

**KING TIGER &
MOTORHEAD #2**
SEPTEMBER 1996
$3

THE MACHINE #1
NOVEMBER 1994
$3

THE MACHINE #2
DECEMBER 1994
$3

THE MACHINE #3
JANUARY 1995
$3

THE MACHINE #4
FEBRUARY 1995
$3

THE MASK WORLD TOUR #1
DECEMBER 1995
$4

THE MASK WORLD TOUR #2
JANUARY 1996
$4

THE MASK WORLD TOUR #3
FEBRUARY 1996
$4

THE MASK WORLD TOUR #4
MARCH 1996
$4

MECHA SPECIAL #1
MAY 1995
$3

MOTORHEAD #1
AUGUST 1995
$3

MOTORHEAD #2
SEPTEMBER 1995
$3

MOTORHEAD #3
OCTOBER 1995
$3

MOTORHEAD #4
NOVEMBERT 1995
$3

MOTORHEAD #5
DECEMBER 1995
$3

MOTORHEAD #6
JANUARY 1996
$3

MOTORHEAD SPECIAL #1
MARCH 1994
$4

OUT OF THE VORTEX #1
OCTOBER 1993
$3

OUT OF THE VORTEX #1
SPECIAL LIMITED EDITION
OCTOBER 1993
$4

OUT OF THE VORTEX #2
NOVEMBER 1993
$3

OUT OF THE VORTEX #3
DECEMBER 1993
$3

OUT OF THE VORTEX #4
JANUARY 1994
$3

OUT OF THE VORTEX #5
FEBRUARY 1994
$3

OUT OF THE VORTEX #6
MARCH 1994
$3

OUT OF THE VORTEX #7
APRIL 1994
$3

OUT OF THE VORTEX #8
MAY 1994
$3

OUT OF THE VORTEX #9
JUNE 1994
$3

OUT OF THE VORTEX #10
JULY 1994
$3

OUT OF THE VORTEX #11
SEPTEMBER 1994
$3

OUT OF THE VORTEX #12
OCTOBER 1994
$3

TITAN SPECIAL #1
JUNE 1994
$4

WILL TO POWER #1
JUNE 1994
$3

WILL TO POWER #2
JUNE 1994
$3

WILL TO POWER #3
JUNE 1994
$3

WILL TO POWER #4
JULY 1994
$3

WILL TO POWER #5
JULY 1994
$3

WILL TO POWER #6
JULY 1994
$3

WILL TO POWER #7
JULY 1994
$3

WILL TO POWER #8
AUGUST 1994
$3

WILL TO POWER #9
AUGUST 1994
$3

WILL TO POWER #10
AUGUST 1994
$3

WILL TO POWER #11
AUGUST 1994
$3

WILL TO POWER #12
AUGUST 1994
$3

COMICS' GREATEST WORLD:
X #1
FEBRUARY 1994
$3

X #2
TITLE CHANGES TO X WITH #2
MARCH 1994
$3

X #3
APRIL 1994
$3

X #4
MAY 1994
$3

X #5
JUNE 1994
$3

X #6
AUGUST 1994
$3

X #7
SEPTEMBER 1994
$3

X #8
OCTOBER 1994
$3

X #9
NOVEMBER 1994
$3

X #10
DECEMBER 1994
$3

X #11
FEBRUARY 1995
$3

X #12
MARCH 1995
$3

X #13
APRIL 1995
$3

X #14
MAY 1995
$3

X #15
JUNE 1995
$3

X #16
JULY 1995
$3

X #17
AUGUST 1995
$3

X #18
SEPTEMBER 1995
$3

X #18
NEWSSTAND EDITION
SEPTEMBER 1995
$3

X #19
OCTOBER 1995
$3

X #20
NOVEMBER 1995
$3

X #21
DECEMBER 1995
$3

X #22
JANUARY 1996
$3

X #23
FEBRUARY 1996
$3

X #24
MARCH 1996
$3

X #25
APRIL 1996
$3

**X / HERO ILLUSTRATED
SPECIAL #1**
JUNE 1994
$3

**X / HERO ILLUSTRATED
SPECIAL #2**
JUNE 1994
$3

**X: ONE SHOT TO THE
HEAD #1**
AUGUST 1994
$3

CONTINUITY COMICS

What is known as the Continuity Comics Universe began in 1979 with the *New Heroes Portfolio*. It was the introduction of the Continuity Comics' universe. They weren't Continuity Comics at the time, and they made a pit stop at Pacific Comics, where the original *Ms. Mystic* #1 garnered huge sales, before eventually launching their own comic line.

The Continuity Comics heroes consisted of Armor, Bucky O'Hare, Crazyman, Cyberrad, Hybrids (Mite, Hyperion, Shealth, Gymcrack, Cyclone, Spanng, and Horror), Megalith, Ms. Mystic, Samuree, Shaman, Toyboy, and Valeria She-Bat.

Was this a launching pad for a new comics universe for Adams?

"No, it was just a thing called the *New Heroes Portfolio*. I created these characters and did them. What happened was that Sal Quartuccio said, 'If you were going to create new characters, what would they be?' I said, 'I don't know.' He said, 'How about creating a portfolio of new characters? You can get them out there; you can protect your copyright,'" Adams said.

"So, once a month I did a new character and they did a portfolio. There were these characters that I sort of created off the top of my head and did them in the *New Heroes Portfolio*, never with the thought in mind of necessarily taking them any further. Things evolve, the process moves forward and the things that you did suddenly become something else. I tend to create things with lives of their own. I don't start off saying this is simply this. I create what it's all about. Even when I did those portfolio pieces, I wrote [little histories], where they came from, what [they're] all about. I can't just draw a picture. It has to have a history. So essentially that's what happened," he said.

These new heroes were the core of the 1984 launch of Continuity Comics, which was basically a side project for Continuity Studios. As a result,

FIRST PUBLICATION:
New Heroes Portfolio (1979)

LAST PUBLICATION:
Megalith #7 (January 1994)

REVIVAL(S):
"Blood" in *Dark Horse Presents* #1 (April 2011).

the comics had an extremely erratic shipping schedule.

"From Continuity's point of view, it was not a moneymaker. We did the comic books when we could. We weren't really publishers. We got into it walking backwards and we turned out our comic books when we could get them done," Adams said.

The "Deathwatch 2000" event and the "Rise of Magic" storyline that followed were the first universe feel for the characters that were included. In the short term, it paid off for Continuity Comics.

"To be an independent publisher but still be in the mainstream was very, very difficult. It was the kind of thing you wouldn't do. But what happened was Image came in afterward and basically took our model and used it for very, very successful publishing. So, if I look back at it, I don't think I could have done it a different way, because I don't think I could have blasted out there and been immediately successful. I had to sort of make the tramping grounds, then everyone else could come along and do it. I was right. Big deal. Now why don't we do *Deathwatch 2000* and really kick out with a series that is a moneymaker and is successful on a commercial basis? And it was, we sold 10 times as many comics, 10 times per title than any other comic we did before that. We were selling like 15,000 copies, we went to 150,000 copies," he said.

The industry, though, was going through a substantial upheaval. Continuity Comics ceased publishing in January 1994. Acclaim Comics would release six issues of *Knighthawk*, and two issues each of *Samuree* and *Valeria The She-Bat* in 1995, but that would be it for Continuity Comics until Adams unveiled "Blood" in the pages of *Dark Horse Presents* #1 (April 2011).

– Rik Offenberger

The cover image from Neal Adams' New Heroes Portfolio (1979).
The portfolio was a springboard for a number of Continuity Comics characters.
Image courtesy of Rik Offenberger.

ARMOR #1
APRIL 1993
$3

ARMOR #1
BAGGED VERSION
APRIL 1993
$3

ARMOR #2
MAY 1993
$3

ARMOR #3
AUGUST 1993
$3

ARMOR #3
BAGGED WITH CARD
APRIL 1993
$3

ARMOR #4
OCTOBER 1993
$3

ARMOR #5
NOVEMBER 1993
$3

ARMOR #6
NOVEMBER 1993
$3

CYBERRAD #1
APRIL 1993
$4

CYBERRAD #2
JULY 1993
$4

EARTH 4 #1
APRIL 1993
$4

EARTH 4 #2
MAY 1993
$4

EARTH 4 #3
AUGUST 1993
$4

**HYBRIDS
DEATHWATCH 2000 #0**
APRIL 1993
$4

**HYBRIDS
DEATHWATCH 2000 #0**
RED FOIL VARIANT • APRIL 1993
$4

**HYBRIDS
DEATHWATCH 2000 #1**
APRIL 1993
$4

**HYBRIDS
DEATHWATCH 2000 #2**
JUNE 1993
$4

**HYBRIDS
DEATHWATCH 2000 #3**
AUGUST 1993
$4

**HYBRIDS
DEATHWATCH 2000 #3**
BAGGED WITH CARD • AUGUST 1993
$4

HYBRIDS #1
JANUARY 1994
$4

MEGALITH #0
APRIL 1993
$3

MEGALITH #1
APRIL 1993
$3

MEGALITH #2
JUNE 1993
$3

MEGALITH #3
AUGUST 1993
$3

MEGALITH #3
BAGGED WITH CARD
AUGUST 1993
$3

MEGALITH #4
OCTOBERL 1993
$3

MEGALITH #5
DECEMBER 1993
$3

MEGALITH #6
DECEMBER 1993
$3

MEGALITH #7
JANUARY 1994
$3

MS. MYSTIC #1
MAY 1993
$3

MS. MYSTIC #2
JUNE 1993
$3

MS. MYSTIC #2
BAGGED WITH CARD
JUNE 1993
$3

MS. MYSTIC #3
AUGUST 1993
$3

MS. MYSTIC VOL. 2 #1
OCTOBER 1993
$3

MS. MYSTIC VOL. 2 #2
NOVEMBER 1993
$3

MS. MYSTIC VOL. 2 #3
DECEMBER 1993
$3

Ms. Mystic Vol. 2 #4
January 1994
$3

Samuree Vol. 2 #1
May 1993
$4

Samuree Vol. 2 #2
July 1993
$4

Samuree Vol. 2 #3
December 1993
$4

Samuree Vol. 2 #4
January 1994
$4

Shaman #0
Janaury 1994
$3

Valeria The She-Bat #1
May 1993
$1 $4 $10

Valeria The She-Bat #1
May 1993
$1 $4 $10

Valeria The She-Bat #5
November 1993
$5

CROSSGEN COMICS

CrossGenesis #1, a preview issue for the universe and its concepts, launched the CrossGen universe in January 2000. Founder Mark Alessi and Gina M. Villa wrote the story bible of the "Sigilverse," as the complex set of series and characters spread across many different genres was alternately known. All of the company's universe titles were distinctly not superhero comics, something Alessi told *The Overstreet Comic Book Price Guide* at the time that he wanted to avoid. Magic, science fiction, horror, swordplay, espionage, high seas piracy, and many others, though, were fair game.

The Sigil marks, frequently seen branded onto characters, were a common thread for the characters in the universe. While the CrossGen titles were clearly a universe from the ground up, it was the mystery of the Sigils and the powers frequently associated with them that held the concept together rather than a significant number of crossovers.

Unlike most publishers, for which editorial staff works with teams of independent freelancers, the creators employed by the company were all salaried employees and worked together at CrossGen's headquarters in Oldsmar, Florida. Over the company's history, creators on the company's roster included Chuck Dixon, Butch Guice, Drew Geraci, Steve Epting, Jeff Johnson, Barbara Kesel, Ben Lai, Greg Land, Ron Marz, Brandon Peterson, Bart Sears, Andy Smith, Dexter Vines, and Mark Waid, among others. This policy would be relaxed somewhat later in deals with creators including George Pérez and J.M. DeMatteis.

The company's initial offerings included *CrossGen Chronicles* #1 (June 2000) and *Sigil* #1, *Mystic* #1, *Meridian* #1, and *Scion* #1 (all July 2000). They ranged from space opera and magic to Arthurian-style adventures. The latter four would prove to be some of the company's longest-running titles. *The First* #1 (November 2000) rounded out the launches for that calendar year.

The company continued to expand their line-up. *Crux* #1 (May 2001), *Sojourn* #0 (July 2001), *Ruse* #1 (November 2001), and *Negation* #0 (December 2001) followed the first year's releases. *The Path* #1 (April 2002), *Way of the Rat* #1 (June 2002), *Route 666* #1 (July 2002), *Brath* #0 (February 2003), *Chimera* #1 (March 2003), *Mark of Charon* (April 2003), *Solus* (April 2003), and *El Cazador* #1 (October 2003) continued the expansion.

CrossGen Comics, Inc. rebranded as CrossGen Entertainment, Inc. (CGE) in 2003 and added a number of subsidiary companies, including the Code 6 imprint, which was to publish non-universe titles co-owned by the company and their respective creators.

In June 2004, the company declared bankruptcy and stopped publishing, leaving many stories incomplete, including *Negation War*, the company's first true crossover title. On November 15, 2004, The Walt Disney Company purchased CrossGen's assets, largely so they could acquire J.M. DeMatteis and artist Mike Ploog's non-universe series, *Abadazad*, which they published as three prose novels that include art segments beginning in 2006.

Checker Books published trade paperback editions of some of the CrossGen material, but they included no new material and did not reprint all of the previously published issues.

Disney eventually handed the CrossGen properties to their better-known comic book company, Marvel. *Ruse* #1, with original writer Mark Waid, and *Sigil* #1, with a very different take on the title, debuted as four-issue mini-series in March 2011. *Mystic* #1, also a distinctly different version of the story, was also released as the first of a four-issue mini-series in November 2011. Further CrossGen revivals at Marvel were announced, but they never came to fruition.

> **FIRST PUBLICATION:**
> *CrossGenesis* #1 (January 2000)
>
> **LAST PUBLICATION:**
> *Brath* #14, *El Cazador* #6, *Kiss Kiss Bang Bang* #5, *Negation War* #2, *Route 666* #24 and *Way of the Rat* #24 (all June 2004)
>
> **REVIVAL(S):**
> *Ruse* #1 and *Sigil* #1 (March 2011), *Mystic* #1 (August 2011) at Marvel Comics.

Greg Land and Drew Geraci's original cover art for *Sojourn* #14 featuring Arwyn and Rahm. Image courtesy of Heritage Auctions.

ARCHARD'S AGENTS #1
JANUARY 2003
$3

ARCHARD'S AGENTS: THE CASE OF THE PUZZLED PUGILIST
NOVEMBER 2003
$3

ARCHARD'S AGENTS VOL. 3 - DEADLY DARE
APRIL 2004
$3

BRATH PREQUEL
FEBRUARY 2003
$3

BRATH #1
MARCH 2003
$3

BRATH #2
APRIL 2003
$3

BRATH #3
MAY 2003
$3

BRATH #4
JUNE 2003
$3

BRATH #5
JULY 2003
$3

BRATH #6
AUGUST 2003
$3

BRATH #7
SEPTEMBER 2003
$3

BRATH #8
NOVEMBER 2003
$3

BRATH #9
DECEMBER 2003
$3

BRATH #10
JANUARY 2004
$3

BRATH #11
FEBRUARY 2004
$3

BRATH #12
MARCH 2004
$3

BRATH #13
MAY 2004
$3

BRATH #14
JUNE 2004
$3

CHIMERA #1
MARCH 2003
$3

CHIMERA #2
APRIL 2003
$3

CHIMERA #3
MAY 2003
$3

CHIMERA #4
JULY 2003
$3

CROSSGEN CHRONICLES #1
JUNE 2000
$4

CROSSGEN CHRONICLES #1
CUSTOMER REVIEW EDITION
JUNE 2000
$4

CROSSGEN CHRONICLES #2
MARCH 2001
$4

CROSSGEN CHRONICLES #3
JUNE 2001
$4

CROSSGEN CHRONICLES #4
SEPTEMBER 2001
$4

CrossGen Chronicles #5
DECEMBER 2001
$4

CrossGen Chronicles #6
MARCH 2002
$4

CrossGen Chronicles #7
MAY 2002
$4

CrossGen Chronicles #8
JULY 2002
$4

CrossGenesis #1
JANUARY 2000
$3

CrossGen Primer
JANUARY 2000
$3

CrossGen Sampler
FEBRUARY 2000
$3

Crux #1
MAY 2001
$3

Crux #2
JUNE 2001
$3

CRUX #3
JULY 2001
$3

CRUX #4
AUGUST 2001
$3

CRUX #5
SEPTEMBER 2001
$3

CRUX #6
OCTOBER 2001
$3

CRUX #7
NOVEMBER 2001
$3

CRUX #8
DECEMBER 2001
$3

CRUX #9
JANUARY 2002
$3

CRUX #10
FEBRUARY 2002
$3

CRUX #11
MARCH 2002
$3

CRUX #12
APRIL 2002
$3

CRUX #13
MAY 2002
$3

CRUX #14
JUNE 2002
$3

CRUX #15
JULY 2002
$3

CRUX #16
AUGUST 2002
$3

CRUX #17
SEPTEMBER 2002
$3

CRUX #18
OCTOBER 2002
$3

CRUX #19
NOVEMBER 2002
$3

CRUX #20
DECEMBER 2002
$3

CRUX #21
JANUARY 2003
$3

CRUX #22
FEBRUARY 2003
$3

CRUX #23
MARCH 2003
$3

CRUX #24
APRIL 2003
$3

CRUX #25
MAY 2003
$3

CRUX #26
JUNE 2003
$3

CRUX #27
JULY 2003
$3

CRUX #28
AUGUST 2003
$3

CRUX #29
NOVEMBER 2003
$3

CRUX #30
NOVEMBER 2003
$3

CRUX #31
DECEMBER 2003
$3

CRUX #32
DECEMBER 2003
$3

CRUX #33
FEBRUARY 2004
$3

EL CAZADOR #1
OCTOBER 2003
$5

EL CAZADOR #2
NOVEMBER 2003
$3

EL CAZADOR #3
DECEMBER 2003
$3

EL CAZADOR #4
JANUARY 2004
$3

EL CAZADOR #5
MARCH 2004
$3

EL CAZADOR #6
JUNE 2004
$3

EL CAZADOR: THE BLOODY BALLAD OF BLACKJACK TOM #1
APRIL 2004
$3

THE FIRST PREVIEW
NOVEMBER 2000
$x $x $x

THE FIRST #1
NOVEMBER 2000
$4

THE FIRST #2
JANUARY 2001
$4

THE FIRST #3
FEBRUARY 2001
$4

THE FIRST #4
MARCH 2001
$4

THE FIRST #5
APRIL 2001
$4

THE FIRST #6
MAY 2001
$4

THE FIRST #7
JUNE 2001
$4

THE FIRST #8
JULY 2001
$4

THE FIRST #9
AUGUST 2001
$4

THE FIRST #10
SEPTEMBER 2001
$4

THE FIRST #11
OCTOBER 2001
$3

THE FIRST #12
NOVEMBER 2001
$3

THE FIRST #13
DECEMBER 2001
$3

THE FIRST #14
JANUARY 2002
$3

THE FIRST #15
FEBRUARY 2002
$3

THE FIRST #16
MARCH 2002
$3

THE FIRST #17
APRIL 2002
$3

THE FIRST #18
MAY 2002
$3

THE FIRST #19
JUNE 2002
$3

THE FIRST #20
JULY 2002
$3

THE FIRST #21
AUGUST 2002
$3

THE FIRST #22
SEPTEMBER 2002
$3

THE FIRST #23
OCTOBER 2002
$3

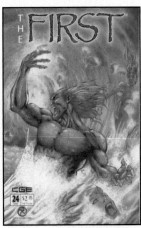

THE FIRST #24
NOVEMBER 2002
$3

THE FIRST #25
DECEMBER 2002
$3

THE FIRST #26
JANUARY 2003
$3

THE FIRST #27
FEBRUARY 2003
$3

THE FIRST #28
MARCH 2003
$3

THE FIRST #29
APRIL 2003
$3

THE FIRST #30
MAY 2003
$3

THE FIRST #31
JUNE 2003
$3

THE FIRST #32
JULY 2003
$3

THE FIRST #33
AUGUST 2003
$3

THE FIRST #34
SEPTEMBER 2003
$3

THE FIRST #35
NOVEMBER 2003
$3

THE FIRST #36
NOVEMBER 2003
$3

THE FIRST #37
DECEMBER 2003
$3

KISS KISS BANG BANG #1
FEBRUARY 2004
$3

KISS KISS BANG BANG #2
MARCH 2004
$3

KISS KISS BANG BANG #3
APRIL 2004
$3

KISS KISS BANG BANG #4
MAY 2004
$3

KISS KISS BANG BANG #5
JUNE 2004
$3

MARK OF CHARON #1
APRIL 2003
$3

MARK OF CHARON #2
MAY 2003
$3

MARK OF CHARON #3
JUNE 2003
$3

MARK OF CHARON #4
JULY 2003
$3

MARK OF CHARON #5
AUGUST 2003
$3

MERIDIAN #1
JULY 2000
$3

MERIDIAN #1
CUSTOMER REVIEW EDITION
JULY 2000
$3

MERIDIAN #2
AUGUST 2000
$3

MERIDIAN #3
SEPTEMBER 2000
$3

MERIDIAN #4
OCTOBER 2000
$3

MERIDIAN #5
NOVEMBER 2000
$3

MERIDIAN #6
DECEMBER 2000
$3

MERIDIAN #7
JANUARY 2001
$3

MERIDIAN #8
FEBRUARY 2001
$3

MERIDIAN #9
MARCH 2001
$3

MERIDIAN #10
APRIL 2001
$3

MERIDIAN #11
MAY 2001
$3

MERIDIAN #12
JUNE 2001
$3

MERIDIAN #13
JULY 2001
$3

MERIDIAN #14
AUGUST 2001
$3

MERIDIAN #15
SEPTEMBER 2001
$3

MERIDIAN #16
OCTOBER 2001
$3

MERIDIAN #17
NOVEMBER 2001
$3

MERIDIAN #18
DECEMBER 2001
$3

MERIDIAN #19
JANUARY 2002
$3

MERIDIAN #20
FEBRUARY 2002
$3

MERIDIAN #21
MARCH 2002
$3

MERIDIAN #22
APRIL 2002
$3

MERIDIAN #23
MAY 2002
$3

MERIDIAN #24
JUNE 2002
$3

MERIDIAN #25
JULY 2002
$3

MERIDIAN #26
AUGUST 2002
$3

MERIDIAN #27
SEPTEMBER 2002
$3

MERIDIAN #28
OCTOBER 2002
$3

MERIDIAN #29
NOVEMBER 2002
$3

MERIDIAN #30
DECEMBER 2002
$3

MERIDIAN #31
JANUARY 2003
$3

MERIDIAN #32
FEBRUARY 2003
$3

MERIDIAN #33
MARCH 2003
$3

MERIDIAN #34
APRIL 2003
$3

MERIDIAN #35
MAY 2003
$3

MERIDIAN #36
JUNE 2003
$3

MERIDIAN #37
JULY 2003
$3

MERIDIAN #38
AUGUST 2003
$3

MERIDIAN #39
NOVEMBER 2003
$3

MERIDIAN #40
DECEMBER 2003
$3

MERIDIAN #41
JANUARY 2004
$3

MERIDIAN #42
JANUARY 2004
$3

MERIDIAN #43
MARCH 2004
$3

MERIDIAN #44
APRIL 2004
$3

MYSTIC #1
JULY 2000
$3

MYSTIC #2
AUGUST 2000
$3

MYSTIC #3
SEPTEMBER 2000
$3

MYSTIC #4
OCTOBER 2000
$3

MYSTIC #5
NOVEMBER 2000
$3

MYSTIC #6
DECEMBER 2000
$3

MYSTIC #7
JANUARY 2001
$3

MYSTIC #8
FEBRUARY 2001
$3

MYSTIC #9
MARCH 2001
$3

MYSTIC #10
APRIL 2001
$3

MYSTIC #11
MAY 2001
$3

MYSTIC #12
JUNE 2001
$3

MYSTIC #13
JULY 2001
$3

MYSTIC #14
AUGUST 2001
$3

MYSTIC #15
SEPTEMBER 2001
$3

MYSTIC #16
OCTOBER 2001
$3

MYSTIC #17
NOVEMBER 2001
$3

MYSTIC #18
DECEMBER 2001
$3

MYSTIC #19
JANUARY 2002
$3

MYSTIC #20
FEBRUARY 2002
$3

MYSTIC #21
MARCH 2002
$3

MYSTIC #22
APRIL 2002
$3

MYSTIC #23
MAY 2002
$3

MYSTIC #24
JUNE 2002
$3

MYSTIC #25
JULY 2002
$3

MYSTIC #26
AUGUST 2002
$3

MYSTIC #27
SEPTEMBER 2002
$3

MYSTIC #28
OCTOBER 2002
$3

MYSTIC #29
NOVEMBER 2002
$3

MYSTIC #30
DECEMBER 2002
$3

MYSTIC #31
JANUARY 2003
$3

MYSTIC #32
FEBRUARY 2003
$3

MYSTIC #33
MARCH 2003
$3

MYSTIC #34
APRIL 2003
$3

MYSTIC #35
MAY 2003
$3

MYSTIC #36
JUNE 2003
$3

MYSTIC #37
JULY 2003
$3

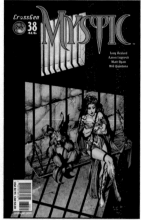

MYSTIC #38
AUGUST 2003
$3

MYSTIC #39
SEPTEMBER 2003
$3

MYSTIC #40
NOVEMBER 2003
$3

MYSTIC #41
NOVEMBER 2003
$3

MYSTIC #42
DECEMBER 2003
$3

MYSTIC #43
JANUARY 2004
$3

NEGATION PREQUEL
DECEMBER 2001
$3

NEGATION #1
JANUARY 2002
$3

NEGATION #2
FEBRUARY 2002
$3

NEGATION #3
MARCH 2002
$3

NEGATION #4
APRIL 2002
$3

NEGATION #5
MAY 2002
$3

NEGATION #6
JUNE 2002
$3

NEGATION #7
JULY 2002
$3

NEGATION #8
AUGUST 2002
$3

NEGATION #9
SEPTEMBER 2002
$3

NEGATION #10
OCTOBER 2002
$3

NEGATION #11
NOVEMBER 2002
$3

NEGATION #12
DECEMBER 2002
$3

NEGATION #13
JANUARY 2003
$3

NEGATION #14
FEBRUARY 2003
$3

NEGATION #15
MARCH 2003
$3

NEGATION #16
APRIL 2003
$3

NEGATION #17
MAY 2003
$3

NEGATION #18
JUNE 2003
$3

NEGATION #19
JULY 2003
$3

NEGATION #20
AUGUST 2003
$3

NEGATION #21
SEPTEMBER 2003
$3

NEGATION #22
NOVEMBER 2003
$3

NEGATION #23
NOVEMBER 2003
$3

NEGATION #24
DECEMBER 2003
$3

NEGATION #25
JANUARY 2004
$3

NEGATION #26
FEBRUARY 2004
$3

NEGATION #27
MARCH 2004
$3

NEGATION LAWBRINGER #1
NOVEMBER 2002
$3

NEGATION WAR #1
APRIL 2004
$3

NEGATION WAR #2
JUNE 2004
$3

THE PATH PREQUEL
MARCH 2002
$3

THE PATH #1
APRIL 2002
$3

THE PATH #2
MAY 2002
$3

THE PATH #3
JUNE 2002
$3

THE PATH #4
JULY 2002
$3

THE PATH #5
AUGUST 2002
$3

THE PATH #6
SEPTEMBER 2002
$3

THE PATH #7
OCTOBER 2002
$3

THE PATH #8
NOVEMBER 2002
$3

THE PATH #9
DECEMBER 2002
$3

THE PATH #10
JANUARY 2003
$3

THE PATH #11
FEBRUARY 2003
$3

THE PATH #12
MARCH 2003
$3

THE PATH #13
APRIL 2003
$3

THE PATH #14
MAY 2003
$3

THE PATH #15
JUNE 2003
$3

THE PATH #16
JULY 2003
$3

THE PATH #17
AUGUST 2003
$3

THE PATH #18
SEPTEMBER 2003
$3

THE PATH #19
NOVEMBER 2003
$3

THE PATH #20
DECEMBER 2003
$3

THE PATH #21
JANUARY 2004
$3

THE PATH #22
MARCH 2004
$3

THE PATH #23
APRIL 2004
$3

ROUTE 666 #1
JULY 2002
$3

ROUTE 666 #2
AUGUST 2002
$3

ROUTE 666 #3
SEPTEMBER 2002
$3

ROUTE 666 #4
OCTOBER 2002
$3

ROUTE 666 #5
NOVEMBER 2002
$3

ROUTE 666 #6
DECEMBER 2002
$3

ROUTE 666 #7
JANUARY 2003
$3

ROUTE 666 #8
FEBRUARY 2003
$3

ROUTE 666 #9
MARCH 2003
$3

ROUTE 666 #10
APRIL 2003
$3

ROUTE 666 #11
MAY 2003
$3

ROUTE 666 #12
JUNE 2003
$3

ROUTE 666 #13
JULY 2003
$3

ROUTE 666 #14
AUGUST 2003
$3

ROUTE 666 #15
SEPTEMBER 2003
$3

ROUTE 666 #16
NOVEMBER 2003
$3

ROUTE 666 #17
DECEMBER 2003
$3

ROUTE 666 #18
DECEMBER 2003
$3

ROUTE 666 #19
FEBRUARY 2004
$3

ROUTE 666 #20
MARCH 2004
$3

ROUTE 666 #21
APRIL 2004
$3

ROUTE 666 #22
JUNE 2004
$3

RUSE #1
NOVEMBER 2001
$5

RUSE #2
DECEMBER 2001
$3

RUSE #3
JANUARY 2002
$3

RUSE #4
FEBRUARY 2002
$3

RUSE #5
MARCH 2002
$3

RUSE #6
APRIL 2002
$3

RUSE #7
MAY 2002
$3

RUSE #8
JUNE 2002
$3

RUSE #9
JULY 2002
$3

RUSE #10
AUGUST 2002
$3

RUSE #11
SEPTEMBER 2002
$3

RUSE #12
OCTOBER 2002
$3

RUSE #13
NOVEMBER 2002
$3

RUSE #14
DECEMBER 2002
$3

RUSE #15
JANUARY 2003
$3

RUSE #16
FEBRUARY 2003
$3

RUSE #17
MARCH 2003
$3

RUSE #18
APRIL 2003
$3

RUSE #19
MAY 2003
$3

RUSE #20
JUNE 2003
$3

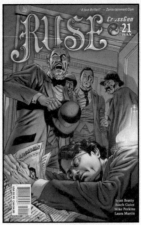

RUSE #21
JULY 2003
$3

RUSE #22
AUGUST 2003
$3

RUSE #23
SEPTEMBER 2003
$3

RUSE #24
NOVEMBER 2003
$3

RUSE #25
DECEMBER 2003
$3

RUSE #26
JANUARY 2004
$3

**SAURIANS: UNNATURAL
SELECTION #1**
FEBRUARY 2002
$3

**SAURIANS: UNNATURAL
SELECTION #2**
MARCH 2002
$3

SCION #1
JULY 2000
$3

SCION #1
CUSTOMER REVIEW COPY
JULY 2000
$3

SCION #2
AUGUST 2000
$3

SCION #3
SEPTEMBER 2000
$3

SCION #4
OCTOBER 2000
$3

SCION #5
NOVEMBER 2000
$3

SCION #6
DECEMBER 2000
$3

SCION #7
JANUARY 2001
$3

SCION #8
FEBRUARY 2001
$3

SCION #9
MARCH 2001
$3

SCION #10
APRIL 2001
$3

SCION #11
MAY 2001
$3

SCION #12
JUNE 2001
$3

SCION #13
JULY 2001
$3

SCION #14
AUGUST 2001
$3

SCION #15
SEPTEMBER 2001
$3

SCION #16
OCTOBER 2001
$3

SCION #17
NOVEMBER 2001
$3

SCION #18
DECEMBER 2001
$3

SCION #19
JANUARY 2002
$3

SCION #20
FEBRUARY 2002
$3

SCION #21
MARCH 2002
$3

SCION #22
APRIL 2002
$3

SCION #23
MAY 2002
$3

SCION #24
JUNE 2002
$3

SCION #25
JULY 2002
$3

SCION #26
AUGUST 2002
$3

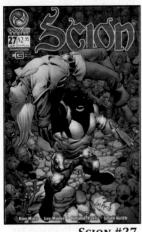

SCION #27
SEPTEMBER 2002
$3

SCION #28
OCTOBER 2002
$3

SCION #29
NOVEMBER 2002
$3

SCION #30
DECEMBER 2002
$3

SCION #31
JANUARY 2003
$3

SCION #32
FEBRUARY 2003
$3

SCION #33
MARCH 2003
$3

SCION #34
APRIL 2003
$3

SCION #35
MAY 2003
$3

SCION #36
JUNE 2003
$3

SCION #37
JULY 2003
$3

SCION #38
AUGUST 2003
$3

SCION #39
SEPTEMBER 2003
$3

SCION #40
NOVEMBER 2003
$3

SCION #41
DECEMBER 2003
$3

SCION #42
FEBRUARY 2004
$3

SCION #43
APRIL 2004
$3

SIGIL #1
JULY 2000
$3

SIGIL #1
CUSTOMER REVIEW COPY
JULY 2000
$3

SIGIL #2
AUGUST 2000
$3

SIGIL #3
SEPTEMBER 2000
$3

SIGIL #4
OCTOBER 2000
$3

SIGIL #5
NOVEMBER 2000
$3

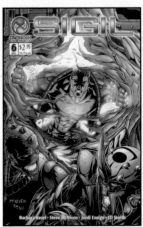

SIGIL #6
DECEMBER 2000
$3

SIGIL #7
JANUARY 2001
$3

SIGIL #8
FEBRUARY 2001
$3

SIGIL #9
MARCH 2001
$3

SIGIL #10
APRIL 2001
$3

SIGIL #11
MAY 2001
$3

SIGIL #12
JUNE 2001
$3

SIGIL #13
JULY 2001
$3

SIGIL #14
AUGUST 2001
$3

SIGIL #15
SEPTEMBER 2001
$3

SIGIL #16
OCTOBER 2001
$3

SIGIL #17
NOVEMBER 2001
$3

SIGIL #18
DECEMBER 2001
$3

SIGIL #19
JANUARY 2002
$3

SIGIL #20
FEBRUARY 2002
$3

SIGIL #21
MARCH 2002
$3

SIGIL #22
APRIL 2002
$3

SIGIL #23
MAY 2002
$3

SIGIL #24
JUNE 2002
$3

SIGIL #25
JULY 2002
$3

SIGIL #26
AUGUST 2002
$3

SIGIL #27
SEPTEMBER 2002
$3

SIGIL #28
OCTOBER 2002
$3

SIGIL #29
NOVEMBER 2002
$3

SIGIL #30
DECEMBER 2002
$3

SIGIL #31
JANUARY 2003
$3

SIGIL #32
FEBRUARY 2003
$3

SIGIL #33
MARCH 2003
$3

SIGIL #34
APRIL 2003
$3

SIGIL #35
MAY 2003
$3

SIGIL #36
JUNE 2003
$3

SIGIL #37
JULY 2003
$3

SIGIL #38
AUGUST 2003
$3

SIGIL #39
SEPTEMBER 2003
$3

SIGIL #40
NOVEMBER 2003
$3

SIGIL #41
NOVEMBER 2003
$3

SIGIL #42
DECEMBER 2003
$3

SILKEN GHOST #1
JUNE 2003
$3

SILKEN GHOST #2
JULY 2003
$3

SILKEN GHOST #3
AUGUST 2003
$3

SILKEN GHOST #4
SEPTEMBER 2003
$3

SILKEN GHOST #5
OCTOBER 2003
$3

SOJOURN PREQUEL
JULY 2001
$3

SOJOURN #1
AUGUST 2001
$6

SOJOURN #2
SEPTEMBER 2001
$5

SOJOURN #3
OCTOBER 2001
$5

SOJOURN #4
NOVEMBER 2001
$3

SOJOURN #5
DECEMBER 2001
$3

SOJOURN #6
JANUARY 2002
$3

SOJOURN #7
FEBRUARY 2002
$3

SOJOURN #8
MARCH 2002
$3

SOJOURN #9
APRIL 2002
$3

SOJOURN #10
MAY 2002
$3

SOJOURN #11
JUNE 2002
$3

SOJOURN #12
JULY 2002
$3

SOJOURN #13
AUGUST 2002
$3

SOJOURN #14
SEPTEMBER 2002
$3

SOJOURN #15
OCTOBER 2002
$3

SOJOURN #16
NOVEMBER 2002
$3

SOJOURN #17
DECEMBER 2002
$3

SOJOURN #18
JANUARY 2003
$3

SOJOURN #19
FEBRUARY 2003
$3

SOJOURN #20
MARCH 2003
$3

SOJOURN #21
APRIL 2003
$3

SOJOURN #22
MAY 2003
$3

SOJOURN #23
JUNE 2003
$3

SOJOURN #24
JULY 2003
$3

SOJOURN #25
AUGUST 2003
$3

SOJOURN #26
SEPTEMBER 2003
$3

SOJOURN #27
OCTOBER 2003
$3

SOJOURN #28
NOVEMBER 2003
$3

SOJOURN #29
DECEMBER 2003
$3

SOJOURN #30
JANUARY 2004
$3

SOJOURN #31
FEBRUARY 2004
$3

SOJOURN #32
MARCH 2004
$3

SOJOURN #33
APRIL 2004
$3

SOJOURN #34
MAY 2004
$3

SOLUS #1
APRIL 2003
$3

SOLUS #2
MAY 2003
$3

SOLUS #3
JUNE 2003
$3

SOLUS #4
JULY 2003
$3

SOLUS #5
AUGUST 2003
$3

SOLUS #6
SEPTEMBER 2003
$3

SOLUS #7
NOVEMBER 2003
$3

SOLUS #8
DECEMBER 2003
$3

WAY OF THE RAT #1
JUNE 2002
$3

WAY OF THE RAT #2
JULY 2002
$3

WAY OF THE RAT #3
AUGUST 2002
$3

WAY OF THE RAT #4
SEPTEMBER 2002
$3

WAY OF THE RAT #5
OCTOBER 2002
$3

WAY OF THE RAT #6
NOVEMBER 2002
$3

WAY OF THE RAT #7
DECEMBER 2002
$3

WAY OF THE RAT #8
JANUARY 2003
$3

WAY OF THE RAT #9
FEBRUARY 2003
$3

WAY OF THE RAT #10
MARCH 2003
$3

WAY OF THE RAT #11
APRIL 2003
$3

WAY OF THE RAT #12
MAY 2003
$3

WAY OF THE RAT #13
JUNE 2003
$3

WAY OF THE RAT #14
JULY 2003
$3

WAY OF THE RAT #15
AUGUST 2003
$3

WAY OF THE RAT #16
SEPTEMBER 2003
$3

WAY OF THE RAT #17
OCTOBER 2003
$3

WAY OF THE RAT #18
NOVEMBER 2003
$3

WAY OF THE RAT #19
DECEMBER 2003
$3

WAY OF THE RAT #20
JANUARY 2004
$3

WAY OF THE RAT #21
FEBRUARY 2004
$3

WAY OF THE RAT #22
APRIL 2004
$3

WAY OF THE RAT #23
MAY 2004
$3

WAY OF THE RAT #24
JUNE 2004
$3

WAY OF THE RAT
FREE COMIC BOOK DAY SPECIAL
JUNE 2003
$3

DEFIANT

DEFIANT (stylized in all caps) was founded by Jim Shooter with an investment from The River Group following his departure from Valiant and a period during which he was contractually unable to work for other publishers. Once that period had passed and when the company was funded, his first hires were Valiant veterans Winston Fowlkes (CFO), Debbie Fix (administrator/editor), JayJay Jackson (writer/editor/colorist), and David Lapham (artist).

They were joined by J. Clark Smith (Vice-President of Marketing and Development), who years earlier had been part of Shooter's team in a bid to acquire Marvel. Artist/editor Joe James, who Shooter and Jackson had met while consulting for Milestone Media, was another early addition to the company's roster.

"The creative spirit was amazing. And it's all top-down. But just being around a room of artists and writers was fantastic, and they were literally all over the place. And everyone got along with each other, too," Smith said. "While Jim had already plotted the first four issues prior to founding DEFIANT, there was a lot of development work done in my New York apartment on that title before we moved to our offices on Madison Avenue."

Future superstar artists J.G. Jones, Charlie Adlard, and Adam Pollina signed on, as did established creators such as Len Wein, Dave Cockrum, Chris Claremont, Steve Ditko, and Alan Weiss, among others.

The company announced that the first issue of their first title, *Plasm*, would be released in the form of trading cards and an album from The River Group. It was written by Shooter, penciled by Lapham, inked by Mike Witherby, colored by Jackson and a team of colorists, lettered by Kenny Lopez, and edited by Deborah Purcell.

The stage for most of the story was The Org of Plasm, a living planet that conquered other worlds to sustain itself and its abilities to genetically grow (rather than make) ships and create troops. Most of The Org's citizens subscribed to the theory that to be "mulched" – devoured by the Org – was to live on in the great cycle of life. A few rebels, though, believed that each individual life is sacred, something almost completely alien to the majority. It was into this world that a small group of previously normal humans from Earth were catapulted.

Marvel alleged – wrongly, as the courts decided – that *Plasm* had appropriated their Marvel UK property *Plasmer*. DEFIANT changed its name to *Warriors of Plasm* and continued. Marvel filed suit.

In the meantime, the company launched *Dark Dominion* (which also debuted with a Zero issue card set and album) and *The Good Guys*, followed by *Charlemagne*, *Dogs of War*, *Prudence & Caution*, and *War Dancer*, as well as the *Warriors of Plasm: Home For the Holidays* graphic novel.

The stories were all building toward a big event called *Schism*, which would be a universe-altering, four-issue mini-series and run through all of the company's titles. The court case against Marvel had been decided in DEFIANT's favor, though all was not good.

"Judge (and future Attorney General of the U.S.) Michael B. Mukasey ruled emphatically in our favor. He also warned Marvel's lawyers, quote, 'If you ever use my court as a business weapon again, you will sincerely regret it,'" Shooter said.

The damage was done, though. "Winning" cost DEFIANT $300,000 and delayed a multi-million-dollar deal with Mattel long enough that the deal was cancelled. DEFIANT was out of business.

Of the *Schism* crossover event, only *Warriors of Plasm* #13 and *Dogs of War* #5 made it to the stands.

"I didn't know it was coming until I walked in one day and everyone was either very quiet or was crying," colorist David Hillman said of the day the company shut down. "I looked around and asked, 'Who died?'"

FIRST PUBLICATION:
Plasm #0 (July 1993)

LAST PUBLICATIONS:
Warriors of Plasm #13,
Dogs of War #5 (August 1994)

REVIVAL(S):
None to date.

David Lapham's unpublished *Warriors of Plasm* #14 Page 14, part of the Schism crossover event. Image courtesy of David Lapham.

The Birth of the Defiant Universe #1
May 1993
$5 $15 $75

Charlemagne #0
February 1994
$3

Charlemagne #1
March 1994
$4

Charlemagne #2
April 1994
$3

Charlemagne #3
May 1994
$3

Charlemagne #4
June 1994
$4

Charlemagne #5
July 1994
$3

Dark Dominion #1
October 1993
$3

Dark Dominion #2
November 1993
$3

DARK DOMINION #3
DECEMBER 1993
$3

DARK DOMINION #4
JANUARY 1994
$3

DARK DOMINION #5
FEBRUARY 1994
$3

DARK DOMINION #6
MARCH 1994
$3

DARK DOMINION #7
APRIL 1994
$3

DARK DOMINION #8
MAY 1994
v$3

DARK DOMINION #9
JUNE 1994
$3

DARK DOMINION #10
JULY 1994
$3

DOGS OF WAR #1
APRIL 1994
$4

DOGS OF WAR #2
MAY 1994
$4

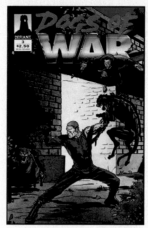

DOGS OF WAR #3
JUNE 1994
$4

DOGS OF WAR #4
JULY 1994
$4

DOGS OF WAR #5
AUGUST 1994
$4

THE GOOD GUYS #1
NOVEMBER 1993
$4

THE GOOD GUYS #2
DECEMBER 1993
$3

THE GOOD GUYS #3
JANUARY 1994
$3

THE GOOD GUYS #4
FEBRUARY 1994
$4

THE GOOD GUYS #5
MARCH 1994
$3

THE GOOD GUYS #6
APRIL 1994
$3

THE GOOD GUYS #7
MAY 1994
$3

THE GOOD GUYS #8
JUNE 1994
$3

THE GOOD GUYS #9
JULY 1994
$3

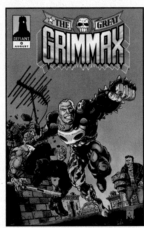

THE GREAT GRIMMAX #1
AUGUST 1994
$4

THE ORIGIN OF THE
DEFIANT UNIVERSE #1
FEBRUARY 1994
$5

PLASM #0
JUNE 1993
$3 $9 $25

PRUDENCE & CAUTION #1
MAY 1994
$4

PRUDENCE & CAUTION #1
SPANISH EDITION
MAY 1994
$4

PRUDENCE & CAUTION #2
JUNE 1994
$3

PRUDENCE & CAUTION #2
SPANISH EDITION
JUNE 1994
$3

SPLATTERBALL
JUNE 1993
FIRST EDITION **$100**
SECOND EDITION **$15**

WAR DANCER #1
FEBRUARY 1994
$3

WAR DANCER #2
MARCH 1994
$3

WAR DANCER #3
APRIL 1994
$3

WAR DANCER #4
MAY 1994
$4

WAR DANCER #5
JUNE 1994
$3

WAR DANCER #6
JULY 1994
$3

WARRIORS OF PLASM #1
AUGUST 1993
$4

WARRIORS OF PLASM #2
SEPTEMBER 1993
$4

WARRIORS OF PLASM #3
OCTOBER 1993
$4

WARRIORS OF PLASM #4
NOVEMBER 1993
$4

WARRIORS OF PLASM #5
DECEMBER 1993
$3

WARRIORS OF PLASM #6
JANUARY 1994
$3

WARRIORS OF PLASM #7
FEBRUARY 1994
$3

WARRIORS OF PLASM #8
MARCH 1994
$4

WARRIORS OF PLASM #9
APRIL 1994
$4

WARRIORS OF PLASM #10
MAY 1994
$3

WARRIORS OF PLASM #11
JUNE 1994
$3

WARRIORS OF PLASM #12
JULY 1994
$3

WARRIORS OF PLASM #13
AUGUST 1994
$3

**WARRIORS OF PLASM
(HOME FOR THE HOLIDAYS)**
NOVEMBER 1993
$6

**WARRIORS OF PLASM
THE COLLECTED EDITION**
FEBRUARY 1994
$14

DEFIANT RARITIES & MULTIPLE PRINTINGS

Although DEFIANT did not exist during the current, variant-crazed modern era, some of their products did have multiple iterations. In addition to the various formats in which *Plasm* #0 appeared (see Page 145), the binder for the *Plasm* #0 card set saw different versions, as did the *Splatterbowl* comic book insert paired with those binders (there is one version of *Splatterbowl* that has no edition stamp, for instance). Additionally, *The Good Guys* #2 saw a misprint – Jim Shooter's editorial page did not have its traditional DEFIANT blue background color – so there is a second printing that did have the blue background. There are reportedly a handful of unnumbered copies of the otherwise signed & numbered *Birth Of The DEFIANT Universe* comics as well.

In addition to being available in the form of the card set and binder, the *Plasm* #0 story was available as a comic book bound into *PREVIEWS* Volume 3 #6 (June 1993) from Diamond Comic Distributors. Image courtesy of Jim Hollister.

Among the iterations of DEFIANT's *Plasm* #0 were the bound-in version (see above) and a single-staple version, now highly prized by collectors. The issue was also reprinted in the *Warriors of Plasm* trade paperback. Image courtesy of Jim Hollister.

A *Plasm* promotional card not available elsewhere was included in the polybag with *Overstreet's Comic Book Monthly* #4 (August 1993), which featured Jim Shooter on the cover with his creation. Image courtesy of Jim Hollister.

In comic book terms, Year One of the DEFIANT Universe was one giant *Schism* #0. Within the pages of the company's offerings, readers had learned that the universe ran on one rule: The dreams of men beget their reality.

The company's slogan was "Beyond the Imaginary Limits," and that's precisely where the ill-fated *Schism* mini-series/crossover event was designed to take readers. Its creators had been setting the stage for it from the company's earliest releases onward.

Spanning four, 48-page issues, *Schism* was plotted by Jim Shooter, JayJay Jackson, Len Wein, Alan Weiss, David Lapham, Joe James, and Ed Polgardy. It would feature art by David Lapham, and finished art by Dave Taylor, Dick Giordano, and J.G. Jones.

The story was to take the threads that were already starting to come together in and between the various titles and play them out on a cosmic scale. The events would have been portrayed in DEFIANT's regular summer releases as well.

Set in exotic locales such as the mythical Avalon, majestic Thailand, otherworldly Plasm, and even Manhattan's eerie "Dark Dominion," *Schism* found Charlemagne, Glimmer, the Good Guys, the Great Grimmax, Prudence, the War Dancer, and all five Warriors of Plasm – as well as other supporting cast – on many fronts in 1994.

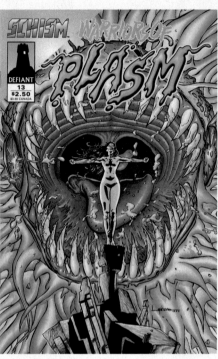

Warriors of Plasm #13, one of the last two comics DEFIANT published, was the only critical part of Schism to see print.

The Background

The first humans imagined a faraway place where the fantastic inventions of their dreams dwelt; a home of myths and long-lost legends called the Dreamtime. For untold millennia, the Dreamtime flourished as a heaven of human-kind's greatest inspirations, noblest ideas, and finest ideals – all made flesh. Due to the cataclysmic "Great Schism," the Dreamtime separated from "real space," and through the combination of magic and weird menace, became an aberrant life form itself.

Craving man's imaginative input, the Dreamtime horrifically rein-vented itself into the insatiable, all-consuming, world-beast known as the Org of Plasm – left to search dimensions for ripe, living planets in a desperate attempt to sate its ravenous hunger. Meanwhile, humanity continued to dream, creating a twisted new landscape of the Id just outside of human perception. This hellish dreamscape – warped by modern man's fears and frailties – came to be known as the "Substratum."

Now, with the boundaries set, Lorca and the ever-voracious Org of Plasm discover the Earth. Then, New York native and future guru Michael Alexander learns of the "Dark Dominion" that is the Substratum and its evil inhabitants, Chasm and Mule. And, a group of children (and one girl's father, who just happens to be a comic book retailer) have their wishes granted while attending a comic book convention. Meanwhile, the "Mayan god of rock 'n' roll" and Nietzsche's "Cosmic Dancer" – as DEFIANT described Arhq Tsolmec, the War Dancer, in *Birth of the DEFIANT Universe* – comes apocalyptically to end the Earth (the source for all dreams and wishes fulfilled), while his earthly challenger Charlemagne stands ready to defend the world at all costs. At the same time, denizens of Plasm and its human

David Lapham's unpublished *Warriors of Plasm* #14 Page 8, a major *Schism* tie-in.
Image courtesy of David Lapham.

manipulations travel throughout *Dogs of War*, *Prudence & Caution*, and the *Hero Illustrated* giveaway *The Great Grimmax* #0.

The Plot

The saga of *Schism* begins by bringing readers up-to-date with Sally Throckmorton, War Dancer's protégé, who is now a successful model. With people buzzing around her (including boyfriend/Bo hunk, Fabiano and her agent) Sally finds herself choosing whether to take a movie deal or a TV script. Suddenly, the quantum traveler Styx appears before her, transports her into the Substratum (Glimmer's "Dark Dominion") and takes her to mythical Avalon, the ancient home of the heroes.

Meanwhile, the ultimate fight between superman, Charlemagne, and man-god, War Dancer begins in Angor Wat. Igo, a spy from Avalon, has come across the epic battle and watches as Charlemagne falls before the Dancer. Igo leaves to report back to Avalon's leader, Thrakahl.

The only other comic published with the *Schism* crossover iconography (the corner box) was *Dogs of War #5* by Art Holcomb and Georges Jeanty.

The story then returns to Sally, who is touring Avalon and taken to a large library full of exotic maps, globes, and books. Sally is then introduced to Glimmer himself, Michael Alexander. He presents a beautiful, ornate book chronicling the origin of the DEFIANT Universe, as well as the origin of the Dancer. He opens the book and within its pages are pictures of "Atlantis" (yes, kids, Plasm was once the legendary Atlantis – pretty cool, huh?) and the contest between the Dancer and Thrakahl for the lovely Zahnree Ph'la's hand. Then, Sally is shown images of the original "Dance of Two" experiment between the Dancer and Zahnree, as well as its interruption by four evil magicians, the appearance of Feathered Serpent (the destructive force of Plasm), and Thralkahl's involvement in the debacle.

Sally then witnesses the sad conclusion of the failed experiment: Zahnree swallowed by the serpent; the Dancer flung into space; and Thrakhal set adrift on a lonely sea in the real world. Then Glimmer pulls out a map of the planes of existence, explaining

that the experiment created a barrier around a section of the quantum field that grew to become the Org of Plasm. He turns to an ornate globe and tells the story of how Lorca discovered Earth and pierced the barrier between Dreamtime and reality. As a result, denizens of Earth – including Sally and DEFIANT'S heroes and villains – found their wishes granted, and, in many cases, gained superpowers.

Sally is simultaneously hearing Glimmer's tale and being measured for an outfit by a servant girl. A mysterious man instructs Sally to prepare herself to act in Zahnree's stead, and perform the "Dance of Two" with Thrakahl, in order to complete the original magic spell and heal the Great Schism. Sally, bewildered, turns to Glimmer, who assures her this is indeed happening.

Thrakahl is on the other side of Avalon planning in his war room. Igo appears and informs the leader that the battle between the War Dancer and Charlemagne is going poorly for the latter. Hearing this, Thrakahl orders that they prepare Sally for the "Dance of Two." Sally dons Zahnree-type finery, while Thrakahl wears some magnificent garb. And, even though Sally is presented with great fanfare, the leader of Avalon turns her away – declaring that she is not the one.

Back on Earth, Nudge from *Warriors of Plasm* arrives at Zahnree's ancestral home, the Temple of Nimh, with a bottle holding the essence of the War Dancer's true love and his partner in the "Dance of Two."

When Nudge opens the bottle, suddenly, there is a flashback to the evolution of the Org of Plasm since the Schism. It appears that Zahnree is communicating to Nudge everything that has happened to her since the failed "Dance of Two." The two spirits then merge in a spectacular effect that lights up the temple.

In the meantime, on Plasm, Lorca and the remaining Warriors of Plasm are fighting the *Dark Dominion* thug-turned-dark god, Chasm. All the while, the Org

J.G. Jones original art for the unpublished *Dark Dominion* #11 Page 22, a *Schism* tie-in issue.
Art from Scott Braden's collection.

is going wild now that Zahnree's influence over the Feathered Serpent is gone and it is free and unbridled. It appears that Chasm has become so much more powerful since his early days in the Substratum that he now brushes the heroes away in a single stroke. In the process, though, he damages the Org and it strikes out at him. According to the *Schism* plot, readers – and Chasm himself – "have a clear demonstration of his power" when he successfully fights off the ravenous world's attacks.

Readers are then transported back to Thailand where the War Dancer and Charlemagne are still battling. The mighty Charlemagne, through sheer determination, finally defeats the Dancer. The Dancer then tells the Earth's champion that he can't destroy the world – Charlemagne must, in his stead. Although Charlamagne sees evidence of what the Dancer is saying all around him, with people becoming "unworthy gods," he still refuses to end the world, even though he now understands the stakes involved.

This previously unpublished Dark Dominion cover by J.G. Jones serves as the cover for the limited, signed edition of *The Overstreet Comic Book Price Guide To Lost Universes*.

The issue ends with Igo travelling back to Thailand to bring Charlemagne and the Dancer to Avalon. Styx brings Nudge and Sally (looking like Zahnree) to Avalon, as well. As they converge on Avalon, so does the dark god, Chasm!

The next pulse-pounding chapters of *Schism* begin with the evil Chasm attacking all of DEFIANT'S heroes! Even Avalon's leader, Thralkahl, gets thrashed by the dark god, just as Chasm turns his attention to a surprised Nudge and kidnaps her off the face of the heroic realm . . . forcibly taking her to the hell-on-earth called Pandemonium!

It's in Pandemonium where Nudge is nearly slashed to death by the claws of Demonica (a monstrous nightmare, and the right hand of Chasm), as Michael, who came to save Nudge, gets his heart ripped out of his chest by Chasm. This traumatic episode shows Michael that he can live on in his quantum state unharmed, though he may never be capable of becoming real again. He quickly grabs the dying

Nudge, transforms her into the quantum state, and transports both of them back to Avalon.

Michael and Nudge, in their quantum states, cross the span of the earth in an effort to reach Avalon. Then, finally reaching the mythical city of heroes, the quantum pair see firsthand the combined powers of the villains striking the mystical realm at all angles. Also, the Feathered Serpent, now without the calming element of Zahnree's spirit to guide him, strikes out at Avalon, too – only to be countered by Charlemagne in a brilliant display of power.

Meanwhile, War Dancer and Sally are performing the "Dance of Two," trying to end the Schism that has set chaos upon the worlds. And "Dance of Two," means they're having sex. They dance and dance, until finally, they find climax. Unfortunately, as seen within the last pages of *Warriors of Plasm* #13, the "Dance of Two" finds all the heroes transported to a grassy field on Earth – leaving the villains both time and resources to plan, and ultimately conquer, the realms of Plasm, our world, and beyond.

After *Schism*, the real fun would begin in the DEFIANT Universe. That's when the overarching storyline's true conflict would manifest itself, transforming the comic book universe's heroes into the potential saviors of many worlds. Mule would end up controlling Plasm, Nudge was going to become the brain of Plasm, and Chasm was going to end up ruling the Earth. The only people who would know about it would be DEFIANT'S heroes, who would be reduced to being resistance fighters.

The last page of *Schism* #4 featured the Dancer and Sally in a warm embrace underneath the sun and sky, looking forward to tomorrow. Maybe one of our tomorrows will see the release of the project and bring their happy ending to light.

Editor's note: *To read more about DEFIANT, check out our special section, The DEFIANT Ones, beginning on Page 568.*

Unpublished *Schism* #3 Page 23 by J.G. Jones.
Art from Scott Braden's collection.

After serving four years in the United States Army and making it through Desert Storm, Jim Hollister came home to Phoenix, Arizona. Always a fan of Ghost Rider and Superman comic books as a kid, "The Death of Superman" rekindled his interest in the medium. Then in the Summer 1993 his close friend, Marcelino Lopez, introduced him to DEFIANT.

Hollister started with one box of *Plasm* cards, in which he found a 1-in-every-1,080-packs Level 3 card. He was hooked. It's been a long ride since then, one filled with persistence and dogged determination.

In a small but very active core group of DEFIANT collectors, no one has stepped up to challenge or even question Hollister's supremacy in collecting the comic books, promotional items, and other materials from the short-lived publisher. Even after more than two decades collecting the material, though, occasionally he is still able to pick up something he doesn't already have.

That happened recently when he acquired a card and another item he's been after almost since he started.

"It was one card and one DEFIANT logo pin that I recently found. I've been scouring the Internet and connections I made through the comic book industry over many years, as searched for all the Level Three *Plasm* cards," he said.

"Up until recently, I had found seven of the eight cards. I was missing number four: The Great Grimmax. I actually found it misspelled on eBay for $2,500. I then contacted the seller, and we negotiated on a final price. I just received it about

one month ago as we're speaking, completing my Level Three Set for *Plasm*," he said.

"The DEFIANT logo pin I also recently acquired had a solid blue background with the DEFIANT castle icon. The common pins have a blue fade-to-white background," he said.

Collector Jim Hollister in one of his vintage DEFIANT T-shirts. Image courtesy of Jim Hollister.

If his attention to detail on a simple thing like a promotional pin gives you the idea that he's serious about collecting DEFIANT, that seems like a fair observation. When he says he was hooked from the start, that also seems accurate.

"I really thought the concept of having collector cards arranged in numerical order to make a comic book was so unique that it grabbed me instantly. No one else had done it before," he said. "I also really like all the promo stuff that DEFIANT put out. It was way above and beyond other companies. That made it very intriguing for me, because it was like a treasure hunt to find them all. You know how the saying goes: It's not the kill; it's the thrill of the chase."

Dealing with some dealers and other collectors isn't always the easiest. "Pretty much everybody that I've talked to has no idea what DEFIANT is unless they're a Jim Shooter fan," he said.

That has been changing of late thanks to the active DEFIANT Fans Facebook group. "I've seen a level of activity that I've never seen since this comic book company started in 1993. And more recently, I've actually seen the values starting to come up," he said.

He's been a collector in a general sense since he

was nine years old, he said, and now has almost 29 years under his belt as a DEFIANT collector.

He said his favorite piece wasn't necessarily the hardest to get. It's the *Plasm* #0 book, which is available in a number of formats ranging from the single-staple edition, to the version that was bound into the *PREVIEWS* catalog, to the card set and binder.

"It's a love story. Call me a hopeless romantic, but I like it," he said.

"I really love the marketing. There are so many things that they put out to promote their business. I really like the promo stuff a lot. So, you get more than just the comic book or the story; you get all the memorabilia that comes with it, and I really like that," he said.

In addition to the comics, trading cards, and binders, among the rarities he's assembled are promo cards, posters, buttons, uncut card sheets, T-shirts, watches, baseball caps, box cutters, mechanical pencils, and card tins, as well as the Triumphant comics from the "non-crossover crossover."

"I also collect Majestic Entertainment titles since they have a very similar platform to DEFIANT. I also collect 1968 *Hot Wheels* cars. That was the first year they came out, plus the year I was born. I [also] collect music and movies. Plus, I have quite the collection of scale model muscle cars from the 1960s and early '70s," he said.

"The motivation for me is the thrill of the chase. It's the challenge. I'm the type of person that it's either all or nothing. Unfortunately, I have never had the opportunity to meet Jim Shooter himself. It would certainly be a highlight of my life and showing him my collection would be such an honor. For that matter, I haven't met any of the creators. I'm betting they don't know I exist," he laughed, "but I would love the opportunity to meet any of them."

Despite his status among his fellow collectors, the hunt isn't over for him yet.

"I'm still missing the Heroes World 10-card Promo Set signed by Jim Shooter. Only 100 sets were autographed. Then there is the *Dark Dominion* t-shirt. Also, I really would like to own a copy of the *Birth of the DEFIANT Universe* unsigned, and unnumbered. From what I understand, only about eight exist. I'm also looking for the 'How to Create Comics' seminar packet," Hollister said.

In his first box of *Plasm* cards, in 1993, Jim Hollister found a 1-in-every-1,080-packs Level 3 card. It took him more than 25 years to track down this one, Level 3 Card #4, to complete the set.
Image courtesy of Jim Hollister.

One of Hollister's favorite promotional items is this two-piece Schism promo card with art by David Lapham and Bob Wiacek.
Image courtesy of Jim Hollister.

(From top, left to right): A CGC-certified 9.8 copy of *Birth of the DEFIANT Universe*, the Spanish language editions of *Prudence & Caution #1 & 2*, *Birth of the DEFIANT Universe* and Gary M. Carter's *Comic Book Marketplace* editorial identifying it as the most expensive comic ever produced to that date, Triumphant Comics issues featuring the "non-crossover crossover," a DEFIANT ballcap, the first edition of the *DEFIANT Newsletter*, *Mule vs. Chasm* card tins, and *Splatterball* insert with no edition stamp. Images courtesy of Jim Hollister.

(From top, left): A sealed case of *Plasm* #0 trading card tins, an open *Plasm* #0 trading card tin, a sealed case of 10 boxes of *Plasm* #0 trading cards, packs of *Plasm* #0 trading cards from the tins (including one signed by Jim Shooter), *Dark Dominion* promo card signed by Alan Weiss & Len Wein, *The Good Guys* promo card, sealed boxes of *Splatterbowl I* trading cards, and *Splatterbowl I* trading card tins. Images courtesy of Jim Hollister.

With the publication of Don McGregor's creator-owned, Paul Gulacy-illustrated graphic novel, *Sabre: Slow Fade of an Endangered Species*, Eclipse Enterprises was founded by brothers Jan and Dean Mullaney in 1977. It was the first to be sold to the direct market, or specifically comic book specialty shops.

The company, which was eventually known as Eclipse Comics, was a home to creator-ownership and a number of high-profile projects, including *Sabre* (a continuing series after the graphic novel), *Aztec Ace*, *Miracleman*, *DNAgents*, *Crossfire*, *Scout*, *Airboy*, *Ms. Tree*, *Winterworld*, and *Zot*, among others. With titles such as *Area 88*, and *Mai, the Psychic Girl*, Eclipse was also a pioneer in English-translated Japanese manga.

The line-up was entertaining, sometimes challenging, and always diverse. What it wasn't, though, was a universe. Naturally, in 1988 the company launched an event that would bring their disparate slate together in one project. Wait, what?

With covers by Bill Sienkiewicz, *Total Eclipse* was a five-issue, Prestige format mini-series designed to celebrate Eclipse's first decade. Marv Wolfman, who had just completed DC's *Crisis On Infinite Earths*, made the main story of *Total Eclipse* his next comic book event.

Kicking things off, *Total Eclipse* #1 ("Zzed") featured the origin of the Airboy villain Zzed as he goes up against Sgt. Strike and Airboy, as well as the New Wave and Misery in the lead story with pencils by Bo Hampton, inks by Will Blyberg. There's also the "The Prowler," written by Tim Truman with pencils by Brent Anderson and inks by Mike Dringenberg.

In *Total Eclipse* #2 ("Nightmares"), the Prowler, Miracleman, Liberty Project, Heap, and Aztec Ace join the action with pencils by Bo Hampton and Mark Johnson (assist) and inks by Will Blyberg, Rick Bryant, Tom Yeates, Sam de la Rosa, and Romeo Tanghal. The back-up story in the second issue featured Aztex Ace in "Anacromesh in the Meld" with script by Doug Moench, pencils by Tim Sale, and inks by Mark Pacella.

For *Total Eclipse* #3 ("Heroes and Villains"), Wolfman and company really widened the roster with Black Terror, Mr. Monster, and the denizens of Beanworld joining the conflict. Bo Hampton continued to handle the pencils, assisted by Jim Ritchie, B.C. Boyer, Trina Robbins, Terry Beatty, Mark Pacella, and Larry Marder, while Rick Bryant handled the inks. The back-up feature, "Home Again to Aanugal," was written by Steve Gerber and illustrated by Cynthia Martin.

Zzed becomes Doctor Eclipse in *Total Eclipse* #4, which saw the unlikely team-up of Miracleman, Aztec Ace, Sgt. Strike, Prowler, Airboy, Valkyrie, Skywolf, New Wave, Liberty Project, Beanish, Destroyer Duck, Black Terror, Nine Crocodile, Amelia Earhart, and Fred Noonan, among others. It was illustrated by Bo Hampton, Jim Ritchie, Larry Marder, Will Blyberg, Rick Bryant, Tom Yeates, Sam de la Rosa, Romeo Tanghal and Mark Buckingham. The back-up story spotlighted Miracleman in "Screaming" by Gaiman and Buckingham.

Bo Hampton, Rick Bryant, Larry Marder and Stan Woch illustrated the main story's conclusion in *Total Eclipse* #5 ("Finale!"). Doctor Eclipse, Miracleman, Aztec Ace, Airboy, Valkyrie, Skywolf, New Wave, The Heap, and even the Adolescent Radioactive Black Belt Hamsters, among others, made it into the mix. The back-up for this final issue was Chuck Dixon and Woch's Air Fighters story "Tumblin' Dice."

Each of the issues in the series included a text feature by Eclipse publisher Dean Mullaney reflecting on the company's 10-year (to that point) journey. There was also a tie-in comic, *Total Eclipse: The Seraphim Object* #1, which took place between the events of *Total Eclipse* #2 and #3. It was written by Kurt Busiek and illustrated by James Fry.

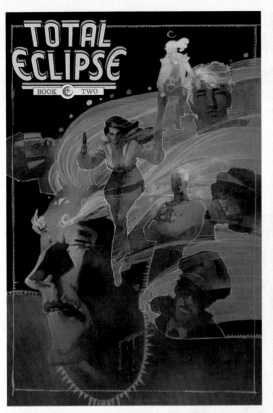

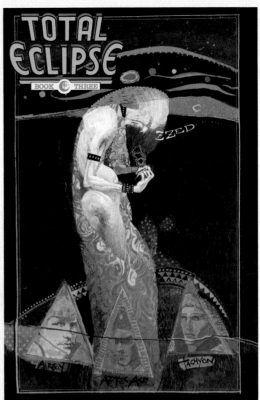

First Comics' CROSSROADS

First Comics, initially based in Evanston, Illinois and then eventually headquartered in Chicago, was co-founded by Ken F. Levin and Mike Gold in 1983. The company quickly set itself up as a home to a variety of creator-owned properties that had only their quality in common. Howard Chaykin's *American Flagg!*, a revival of Charlton's *E-Man*, Mike Grell's *Jon Sable, Freelance*, the continuation of Grell's *Starslayer* (originally at Pacific Comics), and the science fantasy series *Warp* led their early offerings.

The addition of *Grimjack* and *Mars*, the acquisition of *Nexus*, *Badger* and *Whisper* from Capital Comics, and Jim Starlin's *Dreadstar* moving over from Marvel's Epic imprint, among other titles, gave First an impressive roster.

While Nexus and Badger clearly inhabited the same universe, the rest of the company's line-up just as clearly did not. It was *Grimjack* that could have made any discussion of a crossover between their diverse titles possible. Grimjack is the nom de guerre of John Gaunt, a mercenary, veteran of many conflicts, double-crosses, and betrayals, and present owner of Munden's Bar in the pan-dimensional city of Cynosure. With access to a frequently changing array of other universes, the Cynosure itself provided the means to do crossovers without violating the continuity of the respective series.

Despite its obvious appeal, though, the city wasn't used as a story device for all of First's only epic crossover, *Crossroads*. A five-issue, prestige format mini-series that brought together many of First's characters – though not exclusively the headliners – *Crossroads* stood out on the stands thanks to its format and an impressive set of covers by artist and *Nexus* co-creator Steve Rude.

Crossroads #1 ("Dance To The End Of Love," July 1988) teamed Whisper and Jon Sable. It was

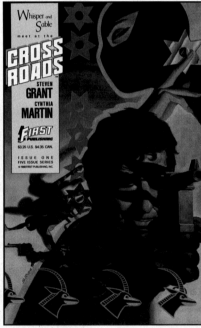

written by *Whisper* creator/writer Steven Grant and illustrated by Cynthia Martin. *Crossroads* #2 ("Payback, August 1988) featured Sable and Badger. The creative team for that issue was writer Mike Baron, creator of Badger, and artists Angel Medina and Rod Whigham. Both of the first two issues had a contemporary setting, so it more or less made sense that the characters could have interacted.

For *Crossroads* #3 ("Moon At Stonehenge, September 1988), which starred Badger and *American Flagg's* Luther Ironheart in a story by writer Roger Salick and *E-Man* co-creator and artist Joe Staton, the meeting of Badger and near-future Luther Ironhart required magic from *Badger* supporting character Ham the Weather Wizard.

Cynosure's pan-dimensional qualities at least come into play in *Crossroads* #4 ("Head Games, October 1988), putting the spotlight on Grimjack and *Nexus* supporting character Judah Maccabee in a tale by Salick and artist Shawn McManus. It sets the stage for the final issue, and in that way really only #4 and #5 are the only truly related stories in the mini-series. Events in *Grimjack*, *Dreadstar*, and *Nexus* also proceed the conclusion, though readers need not have read all of them to comprehend the story.

Nexus co-creator Baron returned to write *Crossroads* #5 ("Vicious Circle, November 1988), which brought together Grimjack, Dreadstar, and Nexus with art by Luke McDonnell. Since Nexus is plagued with dreams of mass murderers that continue until he eliminates the guilty, it actually makes a lot of sense that he would dream of Vanth Dreadstar when their universes overlap. Grimjack is more or less caught in the middle of the adventure, and there's a good bit of action (although there was little if any impact on the characters' regular series from events in the mini-series).

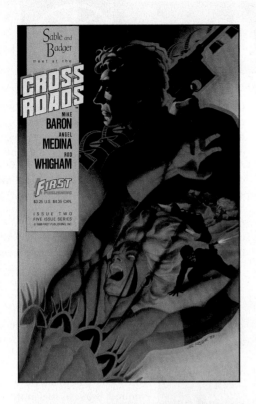

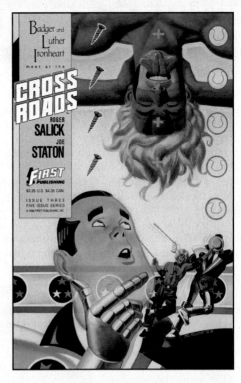

Former Valiant co-founder, editor, and inker Bob Layton, veteran writer David Michelinie, who had collaborated with Layton on an acclaimed run on *Iron Man* among other projects, and artist and former DC Comics Vice-President Dick Giordano founded Future Comics and brought in a roster of creators including Bob McLeod, Ron Lim, Mike Leeke, Bob Hall, and Brett Breeding, among them.

Layton and Michelinie had created Deathmask in the 1980s, but after a few false starts, nothing had happened with it. They revived their character concept for Future Comics.

"The Shadow could 'cloud men's minds,' but that was as far as his preternatural abilities went. Our guy used truly fantastic unearthly powers. And while The Punisher had no problem blowing people away with various firearms, he didn't turn bad guys' knives into steel snakes to run them through or create mini-tornadoes that sandblasted their skin off. And though Batman had evolved into a scary creature of the night type, he was still bound by his own code of ethics. Deathmask had no such restrictions," Michelinie said.

"Actually, we had planned to have the Deathmask be the thing that linked all of the original characters in the FCU. The liquid metal that formed the Metallix armour and the technology that enabled McKinsey Flint to inhabit the Edison Wilde android in *Freemind* were all to be linked to the source of the Deathmask power," he said.

"Although the character that became Deathmask was the concept that triggered Future Comics, it was decided that *Freemind* would be our first – and flagship – title. Bob had suggested a character who was a genius but was confined to a wheelchair, similar to Stephen Hawking. Except

that this character could transfer his consciousness into the body of an android which gave him superpowers. I liked the idea but wanted to add a twist that would give the character more dimension as well as make him different from other superheroes. The genius's initial goal was simple: he merely wanted to escape his useless body, to be able to walk around and do things his handicap prevented him from doing. But the transfer process unexpectedly freed up that part of the mind that most humans can't access – hence the project name, 'Freemind' – and gave the android incredible powers. Which turned our hero, McKinsey Flint, from one of the most helpless people on the planet to one of the most powerful, creating problems and responsibilities he hadn't foreseen. When all he really wanted was to be normal," Michelinie said

"Co-plotter Bob Layton had come up with the name 'Metallix' when we were collaborating on an *Iron Man* project (*The End*) at Marvel. Then, when we were developing characters for Future, he suggested an armored character whose armor was liquid metal that could alter on the spot. As a fan of the old *Challengers of the Unknown* at DC, I suggested the twist of making it a team book, since 'Metallix' kind of sounded plural anyway. The liquid armor could then be passed between the individual team members when their specialized skills – pilot, marksman, underwater expert, etc. – were called for," he said.

Deathmask #3, *Freemind* #7, *Metallix* #6, all cover-date June 2003, were Future Comics' last publications during their initial run. The company's fourth title, *Peacekeeper*, only appeared in ads and in a teaser appearance in the Free Comic Book Day edition of *Metallix* #1, until the printed version finally appeared in 2018.

FIRST PUBLICATION:
Freemind #0 (August 2002)

LAST PUBLICATION:
Deathmask #3, *Freemind* #7, *Metallix* #6 (All June 2003)

REVIVAL(S):
Colony (Non-universe Graphic Novel) published through IDW Publishing (2012); *Deathmask* #4-5, *Freemind* #8, *Metallix* #7, and *Peacekeeper* #1 Made available to order in 2018. Company is periodically active on Facebook.

An unpublished Pat Broderick/Bob Layton image from *Freemind #9*.
Image courtesy of Skip Farrell/Future Comics.

DEATHMASK #1
APRIL 2003
$3

DEATHMASK #1
VARIANT COVER
APRIL 2003
$5

DEATHMASK #2
MAY 2003
$3

DEATHMASK #3
JUNE 2003
$3

DEATHMASK #4
NOVEMBER 2018
$5

DEATHMASK #5
NOVEMBER 2018
$5

FREEMIND #0
AUGUST 2002
$3

FREEMIND #0
VARIANT COVER
AUGUST 2002
$3

FREEMIND #0
DYNAMIC FORCES VARIANT COVER
AUGUST 2002
$3

FREEMIND #1
NOVEMBER 2002
$3.50

FREEMIND #1
VARIANT COVER
NOVEMBER 2002
$3.50

FREEMIND #2
DECEMBER 2002
$3.50

FREEMIND #3
JANUARY 2003
$3.50

FREEMIND #4
FEBRUARY 2003
$3.50

FREEMIND #5
APRIL 2003
$3.50

FREEMIND #6
MAY 2003
$3.50

FREEMIND #7
JUNE 2003
$3.50

FREEMIND #8
NOVEMBER 2018
$5

FREEMIND TPB
APRIL 2003
$15

METALLIX #0
JUNE 2003
$3.50

METALLIX #1
DECEMBER 2003
$3.50

METALLIX #1
VARIANT COVER
DECEMBER 2003
$3.50

METALLIX #1
FREE COMIC BOOK DAY EDITION
APRIL 2003
$3

METALLIX #2
JANUARY 2003
$3.50

METALLIX #3
FEBRUARY 2003
$3.50

METALLIX #4
MARCH 2003
$3.50

METALLIX #5
MAY 2003
$3.50

METALLIX #6
JUNE 2003
$3.50

METALLIX #7
NOVEMBER 2018
$5

PEACEKEEPER #1
NOVEMBER 2018
$5

THE ORIGIN OF DEATHMASK

"Back in the 1980s, when independent publishing was in its infancy, Bob and I were contacted by a gentleman in Michigan with a request to write and draw a graphic novel which this fellow would then publish. Bob had had an idea about a Native American shaman who used real magic to fight crime, a character he called 'Seneca Blackstone.' So we fleshed out the character, changed his name to 'Seneca St. Synn,' and came up with a plot for a graphic novel we called *Sorcerer*," writer and Future Comics co-founder David Michelinie said.

"The story was penciled and scripted, but then delays and complications arose and we ended up parting ways with the original publisher. Years later, we offered the project to Marvel, who accepted it but wanted us to add another 10 pages or so to reach their minimum length for a graphic novel," he said.

"Once again, plotting, pencils and script were done but, for whatever reasons, the book was never published. So, after many more years Bob suggested we publish the story ourselves as a one-shot or two-part comic, selling it over the Internet. I agreed. But then Bob went to Orlando Megacon and got so much enthusiastic response from fans that he came home having decided that we would publish four monthly comics instead! And thus, with the addition of Dick Giordano to the administrative team, Future Comics was born," he said.

"By then, Marvel had introduced their own character called 'The Sorcerer,' and another indie project had come along called (I believe) *Saint Sinner*, so our guy underwent more changes and saw print as Jacob Nakai, 'Deathmask,'" he said.

Unpublished *Deathmask* #7 cover in progress.
Image courtesy of Skip Farrell/Future Comics.

KIRBYVERSE (Topps)

From 1993 to 1994, Topps Comics' Kirbyverse was a line of titles and a comic book universe based on previously unpublished character designs and story concepts by comics grandmaster Jack Kirby. Of course, by this time, Kirby's place in comics history had been secured by his prodigious output and well-documented imagination over five decades in the industry, but the team at Topps thought there was life in some of his previously unpublished concepts.

Talent enlisted to bring the King's latter-day myths to life included writers Roy Thomas, Kurt Busiek, Gerry Conway, Gary Friedrich, Tony Isabella, and artists Dick Ayers, Steve Ditko, Keith Giffen, Don Heck, John Severin, Walter Simonson, and Kirby himself, among others.

The Kirbyverse began with the giveaway comic *Jack Kirby's Secret City Saga* #0, written by Thomas and illustrated by Simonson. The story then continued in a trilogy of character-centric one-shots, *Captain Glory*, *Bombast*, and *Nightglider*, all of which featured covers by Kirby and interior art by Steve Ditko, Dick Ayers and John Severin, and Don Heck, respectively.

The *Secret City Saga*, developed and written by Thomas, involved a race of humankind called "the Ninth Men," The enlightened and technologically advanced Ninth Men ruled over the world in fabulous cities like Gazra.

The heroes of the tale and a handful of others survived a cycle of doom that happens every 150 centuries. The same devastation had felled the eight prior races of humankind. The remaining Ninth Men had to defeat the villainous General Ortiz and Dr. Roag, save then-President Bill Clinton (*Secret City Saga* #3 came bagged with a sax-playing Clinton trading card), and at the same time stop the cyclical apocalypse from destroying modern man, by their standards the "Tenth Men."

Secret City Saga #1-4 featured interior art by Ditko,

who seemed very well suited to the material.

The additional Kirbyverse series included *Satan's Six*, *Jack Kirby's TeenAgents*, *Jack Kirby's Silver Star*, and *Victory* (Captain Victory), the last two of which had previously appeared in Kirby's creator-owned series at Pacific Comics. *Satan's Six* had a follow-on series, *Satan's Six: Hellspawn*.

Published in June of 1994, *Victory* was written by Busiek, illustrated by Keith Giffen and Jimmy Palmiotti, this series was to have everyone in it – from *Secret City Saga*'s Ninth Men (all in redesigned costumes courtesy of Giffen), to the TeenAgents, to a never-revealed new Kirby hero that might have launched into a new series of his/her own. It instead became the comic book line's swansong and the genesis of Kirbyverse's role as a "Lost Universe."

Given Topps' main business, it's not surprising that each of the one-shots came polybagged with three "Kirbychrome" chromium cards that combined to form a small set.

In his editorial in *Victory* #1, then-Assistant Editor Charles Novinskie called Kirby "a drawing/thinking machine." He wrote, "Few people can imagine the scope of [Kirby's] genius without seeing the number of characters he has created that have yet to see the light of day."

"I was lucky enough to interview Jack for *PREVIEWS* in advance of the launch of these Topps Comics titles – and he was a real sweetheart," said Diamond Comic Distributors *PREVIEWS* catalog editor Marty Grosser. "His wife, Roz, was on the line listening in, and helping out when needed. Jack was 76 years old at the time, so he was not a young man obviously, but he was still enthusiastic about the line and the people he was working with to bring his personal creations to life."

The Kirbyverse characters were revisited in Dynamite's *Kirby Genesis* series.

FIRST PUBLICATION:
Jack Kirby's Secret City Saga #0 (April 1993)

LAST PUBLICATION:
Victory #1 (June 1994)

REVIVAL(S):
Kirby Genesis #0-8 (2011-2012) and its related series (2011-2013) *Kirby: Genesis - Captain Victory* #1-6, *Kirby: Genesis - Dragonsbane* #1-4, and *Kirby: Genesis - Silver Star* #1-6 from Dynamite.

The Neil Vokes/Terry Austin cover for *Jack Kirby's TeenAgents* #1.
Image courtesy of Neil Vokes.

BOMBAST #1
1993
$4

CAPTAIN GLORY #1
APRIL 1993
$4

JACK KIRBY'S SECRET CITY SAGA #0
APRIL 1993
$4

JACK KIRBY'S SECRET CITY SAGA #0
GOLD VARIANT COVER
APRIL 1993
$10

JACK KIRBY'S SECRET CITY SAGA #0
SILVER VARIANT COVER
APRIL 1993
$10

JACK KIRBY'S SECRET CITY SAGA #0
RED VARIANT COVER
APRIL 1993
$10

JACK KIRBY'S SECRET CITY SAGA #1
MAY 1993
$4

JACK KIRBY'S SECRET CITY SAGA #2
JUNE 1993
$4

JACK KIRBY'S SECRET CITY SAGA #3
JULY 1993
$4

JACK KIRBY'S SECRET CITY SAGA #4
AUGUST 1993
$4

JACK KIRBY'S SILVER STAR #1
OCTOBER 1993
$4

JACK KIRBY'S TEENAGENTS #1
AUGUST 1993
$4

JACK KIRBY'S TEENAGENTS #2
SEPTEMBER 1993
$4

JACK KIRBY'S TEENAGENTS #3
OCTOBER 1993
$4

JACK KIRBY'S TEENAGENTS #4
NOVEMBER 1993
$4

NIGHT GLIDER #1
APRIL 1993
$4

SATAN'S SIX #1
APRIL 1993
$4

SATAN'S SIX #2
MAY 1993
$4

SATAN'S SIX #3
JUNE 1993
$4

SATAN'S SIX #4
JULY 1993
$2 $6 $12

SATAN'S SIX: HELLSPAWN #1
JUNE 1993
$3

SATAN'S SIX: HELLSPAWN #2
JUNE 1993
$3

SATAN'S SIX: HELLSPAWN #3
JULY 1993
$3

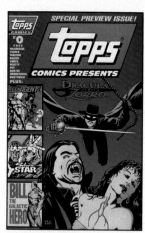

TOPPS COMICS PRESENTS #0
1993
$3

TOPPS COMICS PREVIEW #0
SPRING 1994
$3

VICTORY #1
JUNE 1994
$3

VICTORY #1
ROB LIEFELD VARIANT COVER
JUNE 1994
$3

The final page of the six-page of "Command Decision," the B&W TeenAgents Prologue featured in the 1993 preview comic *Topps Comics Presents #0*. It later appeared in color in *Satan's Six #4*.

Inside The Kirbyverse

During the height of the comic boom in the early 1990s, trading card giant The Topps Company expanded into the world of comics. Former Marvel editor Jim Salicrup joined the company as Editor-in-Chief and teamed with publisher Ira Friedman in 1992. Dwight Jon Zimmerman, following a stint at Marvel, also signed on.

Following the successful launch of Bram Stoker's Dracula, Topps Comics plunged into the world of superheroes with the Kirbyverse, a slate of characters conceived and designed by Jack Kirby and executed by a roster of Silver Age greats and newer creators.

Overstreet: Following Topps' wildly successful launch of *Bram Stoker's Dracula*, Topps shifted gears and turned to a superhero universe starring characters created by the legendary Jack Kirby. How did that deal come about?

Jim Salicrup (JS): When Topps Comics was first announced, we were bombarded with all sorts of projects to consider as comics. At some point we were offered a Jack Kirby project, that although we did sign on to do it, we never followed through on it, instead creating the Kirbyverse directly with Jack Kirby. The best part of the negotiations was visiting Jack Kirby and his wife Roz at their home in California. Then-Topps Chairman Arthur Shurin, Topps Comics publisher Ira Friedman, and I had brought the Kirbys bagels from New York City as a special treat.

Overstreet: How long did negotiations take? How was Kirby compensated?

JS: Negotiations didn't take that long. The

Topps Comics Editor-in-chief Jim Salicrup (top) and Editor Dwight Jon Zimmerman (above) at Topps in 1994. Photos courtesy of Charles S. Novinskie.

Kirbyverse was treated very much like a licensed property—Jack owned it, and Topps Comics licensed it. Like with many licenses, a fee is paid up front, then royalties are paid based on sales. The initial comics were released toward the end of the comics boom, so sales were strong. Not only did Jack do well, but so did contributors such as Steve Ditko, Don Heck, Dick Ayers, John Severin, and others, getting great royalties for their contributions.

Overstreet: Whose idea was it to draw in Silver Age creators to work on the series?

Dwight Jon Zimmerman (DJZ): I don't recall specifics, but I do remember being excited about the idea, even though I knew having Kirby draw the stories was not in the cards. I grew up reading Marvel Comics in the 1960s, so the opportunity to be working with some of the creators whose stories I enjoyed back then was something I looked forward to.

JS: My idea. When I was kid, my dream was to work at Marvel Comics; this was back in the 60s. I started at Marvel back in '72 and the company had changed dramatically. It simply wasn't the 60s Mighty Marvel Bullpen, and it became less so with every passing year. So, in order to finally work at the Marvel of the '60s I had dreamed about, I had to rebuild it back in the '90s. I was able to get almost everyone I wanted. Unfortunately, Stan Lee couldn't contribute as he was still exclusive to Marvel at that point.

Overstreet: The original series started with *Jack Kirby's Secret City Saga* developed and written by Roy Thomas. How much of that series was created by Roy, and how much was inspired by Kirby?

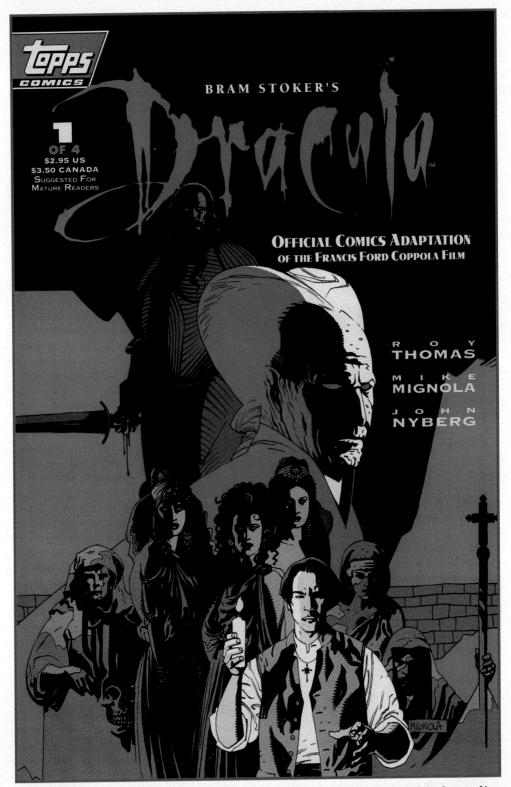

Topps scored a hit with the Roy Thomas/Mike Mignola/John Nyberg adaption of the feature film *Bram Stoker's Dracula*. The Kirbyverse titles were their first entry into the superhero market.

DJZ: Jim can correct me on this, but as I recall, Kirby supplied the character designs and the high concepts and that Roy, Kurt Busiek, and Tony Isabella fleshed them out.

JS: There was a several page, single-spaced typed outline by Jack Kirby that provided the background and set-up for the characters which Roy was fairly faithful to. I'd say it was 80-90% Kirby. Moving past that initial issue, the stories were mostly Roy's.

Overstreet: *Secret City Saga* #0 was a giveaway comic ahead of the release of issue #1. What was the response like from readers?

DJZ: As I recall it was well-received initially. Topps Comics was the new kids on the block, as it were, with the resources of The Topps Company, the #1 sports trading card company in the nation, so the spotlight was on us.

JS: Great! Of the initial offerings, this comic may've been the best. If only Walter Simonson could've drawn the entire series…

Former Topps Editor Dwight Jon Zimmerman in a recent photo. Photo courtesy of Dwight John Zimmerman.

Overstreet: Like all Topps books at the time, (except #0), issues were polybagged and contained a series of three original trading cards, which made sense because, after all, this was Topps. In hindsight, do you think the cards and polybags helped or hindered sales?

DJZ: Well, given that we were a division of The Topps Company, it was a natural for us to include trading cards with the comics. Unfortunately, the bagged-with-trading-cards concept proved to hurt, rather than help, sales and the Kirbyverse suffered as a result.

JS: Depends on who you ask. People who enjoy trading cards were happy, while fans who saw it as a gimmick probably weren't pleased.

Overstreet: *Secret City Saga* #0 by Roy Thomas and Walter Simonson set the tone for the series and introduced a number of key players such as the Ninth Men, leading up to the release of a number of one-shot publications, including Bombast,

Nightglider, Captain Glory, and Satan's Six. Did you have a favorite title/character?

JS: Each series has tremendous potential, and it would've been interesting to see these series develop the way early Marvel titles evolved over the years. How can I resist a Kirby character actually named Bombast? Satan's Six was like The Demon meets The Dingbats of Danger Street—total Kirby craziness. Who knows? Maybe I'll get another shot at editing them some day?

Overstreet: The talent involved on the Kirbyverse was like a *Who's Who* of comic royalty. What was it like working with someone like Steve Ditko? Steve was a pretty private guy; how did the artwork make it to the offices?

DJZ: To answer your second question first: that was FedEx. A piece of trivia: At the time Topps was based in Brooklyn, and it was FedEx's second-biggest account in the borough after the U.S. Coast Guard. As for your first question, my most vivid memory was sitting in my small office and having the artwork of Steve Ditko, Dick Ayers, John Severin, and Don Heck in three stacks on my desk. As I'm going through the pages, I'm thinking of that kid back in North Dakota during the 1960s buying comics created by these people. Now I'm working with them. To say that it was a thrill only begins to describe the experience. Insofar as day-to-day contact, that was all by telephone.

JS: As you know, Topps was originally headquartered in Brooklyn, and then we moved along with the rest of The Topps Company to new offices in Manhattan. Those artists who lived nearby could bring their art to the offices, the rest was through FedEx.

I had worked with all the artists previously at Marvel, so it wasn't anything new. Steve Ditko was always a delight to work with and was only private in the sense that he didn't want to grant interviews or be photographed. In person, he was easy to get along with once you got to know him.

Jack Kirby and Steve Ditko's original Page 13 for *Satan's Six* #1.
Image courtesy of Heritage Auctions.

One great memory from that period is that I had asked Batton Lash, the creator of *Wolff and Byrd, Counselors of the Macabre* to do a back-up strip for *Satan's Six*, featuring his characters. Batton drew the strip in the style of his favorite artist, Steve Ditko, thinking Ditko often did the back-up strips in those Atlas monster mags, where Kirby did the lead feature. When I got the penciled pages in from Bat, I couldn't resist asking Ditko to ink it. Ditko agreed and did an amazing job—showing in his inks how to do what Batton was aiming for in his pencils. Batton loved it! He said if he knew Ditko was going to ink it he would've frozen-up and never would've been able to pencil it. Ditko appreciated Batton's tribute to him and insisted that all the originals be given to Batton, forsaking the pages that would've been returned to him.

At one point there was a convention in Los Angeles, and they wanted to celebrate Topps Comics. I'll never forget they had a panel with Jack Kirby, Don Heck, Ray Bradbury, me, and others on it. Before the panel, Jack Kirby had asked Don Heck, "So, did Ditko ever find himself a woman?"

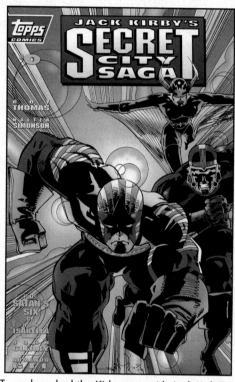

Topps launched the Kirbyverse with *Jack Kirby's Secret City Saga* #0 by writer Roy Thomas and artist Walter Simonson.

Overstreet: Maybe a few thoughts on what each of these creators brought to the Kirbyverse:
Bombast: Dick Ayers, John Severin?
DJZ: This was an opportunity to see exactly what each brought to the table with their art. It was a fascinating education in art collaboration.
JS: I always loved this art team, even if Severin himself wasn't so thrilled about it. Dick had a better layout sense, and could design more exciting pages, while Severin was an incredible artist who would fix all the weaknesses in Dick's drawing. These characters were a Kirby blend of super-heroes and soldiers (like Captain America, Fighting America, OMAC, etc.) and Dick and John had plenty of experience at Marvel together doing *Sgt. Fury and His Howling Commandos* and *The Incredible Hulk*.

Overstreet: *Captain Glory*: Steve Ditko?
DJZ: Ditko's storytelling was unsurpassed. He was such a master that he made it look easy.
JS: Ditko was great with faceless characters or characters with full-face masks. Of the three characters, because of his relative seriousness, I thought Ditko would work best on *Captain Glory*.

Overstreet: *Silver Star*: James Fry, Terry Austin, Kurt Busiek?
DJZ: This was a great fast-paced, action-packed adventure that sadly never took off.
JS: Despite the character's name, this was a character with which we moved away from the Silver Age approach and tried a somewhat more (at the time) modern, pre-Image-style approach.

Overstreet: *TeenAgents*: Neil Vokes, Kurt Busiek?
DJZ: I loved what Kurt and Neil did on *TeenAgents*. Just like what Stan and Jack did with The Fantastic Four, Kurt and Neil took the concept of a superhero team and reinvented it. And I thought their work on the villain Lord Ghast and his Valley Girl daughter was brilliant.
JS: Kurt had a great understanding of what made teen-age superhero groups work, and I wanted to tap into that with this title.

Overstreet: *Satan's Six*: Tony Isabella, John Cleary?
DJZ: Here's where I made my one contribution to the Kirbyverse. We were in a meeting to discuss art teams for the titles. Earlier I had gone through some unsolicited art samples, and those of John Cleary's caught my eye. His work was reminiscent of Todd McFarlane's. I told Jim about John, showed him the samples, Jim liked what he saw, and John got the job.
JS: This title probably was closest to the

Don Heck's original Page 2 for *Nightglider* #1.
Image courtesy of Heritage Auctions.

Image-style at the time, thanks to John Cleary's art style. Tony Isabella probably consulted with Kirby on his scripts more than other writers working on these titles, which was greatly appreciated.

Overstreet: *Victory*: Keith Giffen, Rob Liefeld?

DJZ: I remember being blown away by Keith's story.

JS: Who would've guessed that Keith Giffen would abandon his Kirbyesque style when actually drawing Kirby characters? Liefeld did a cover, which was an attempt to get the Image fans to pay attention.

Overstreet: What was it like to be playing in Kirby's universe?

JS: Well, I'd certainly had experience working on Lee/Kirby and Simon/Kirby characters at Marvel. Everything from *The Fantastic Four* (with John Byrne) to *Captain America*. With the *Secret City* heroes, it was an attempt to recreate the feel of the early Marvel comics, mostly for the sake of fun and nostalgia. Sometime after working on these titles, I had a talk with Alan Moore about the Kirbyverse, and he said he was trying for a similar type of thing in his Image comics series *1963*.

Neil Vokes illustrated this Kirbyverse promotional art. Image courtesy of Neil Vokes.

He suggested that maybe what we both should've done was have him write the Kirbyverse while keeping the Silver Age artists. I regret we weren't able to do that.

DJZ: Truth to tell, I was just on the editorial sidelines cheering the creators on. The writers and artists were the ones playing in it.

Overstreet: Given that the comic industry had fallen on tough times, sadly, the Kirbyverse was truncated before it could really build momentum. What plans were there for the future of the Kirbyverse, and how much material was produced that never saw the light of day?

DJZ: I remember a second *Silver Star* story. Jim Fry's art on it was jaw-dropping and Kurt's script was wonderful. Unfortunately, by that time poor sales caused the line to be canceled. Jim can tell you more.

JS: *Victory* was to be the next ongoing title, but at a time when creators could finally create and own their own characters at Image and elsewhere, it was difficult to attract the top talent needed to really be competitive in the super-hero market. A few more issues were produced (not by Giffen) but we ultimately decided they weren't what we wanted to come back with at that time.

Overstreet: Any closing thoughts on the Kirbyverse or time spent at Topps in general?

DJZ: For me, signing on with Topps Comics was the opportunity of a lifetime. We worked with some of the best creators in the industry and produced some great comics. We were still profitable when Topps decided to shut down the division. It was a strategically smart move given what happened industry-wide following Marvel's bankruptcy filing.

JS: After working 20 years at Marvel, I really wasn't looking to do more superheroes somewhere else, but the opportunity to work with those legendary creators, and manage to help get them the kind of royalties they never got before in their careers was something I'm very proud to have done. At a San Diego Comic-Con dinner with the Kirbys' and friends, Jack kept thanking me for the Topps Comics deal. Finally, I had to tell Jack to stop thanking me. That everyone working at that point in comics, including me, are the ones who should be thanking him—the true King of Comics.

– Charles S. Novinskie

Hero Initiative disbursement secretary/board member and frequent Overstreet contributor Charles S. Novinskie served as sales and promotions manager for Topps Comics and fondly remembers his time spent there and the many friendships developed over the years. He also emphatically enjoyed the Kirbyverse books and wishes there were more.

Don Heck's original Page 3 for *Nightglider* #1.
Image courtesy of Heritage Auctions.

MIGHTY CRUSADERS
(MLJ/ARCHIE)

The MLJ/Archie superheroes, known colloquially as the Mighty Crusaders, didn't actually team up under that name until 1965, despite the fact that the characters had been the company's earliest creations.

Blue Ribbon Comics #2 (December 1939) witnessed the debut of MLJ's first superhero, Bob Phantom. The Shield, which would become the company's top selling superhero, and which was also the country's first patriotic superhero, first appeared in Pep Comics #1 (January 1940). That same issue included the first story of The Comet. They would be joined by others. Shield-Wizard Comics #1 (June 1940) launched the Shield's second title, and The Black Hood arrived in Top-Notch Comics #9 (October 1940).

The end of the original run of the MLJ superheroes came about as superhero sales for all of the publishers sharply declined after World War II, particularly in comparison to the company's steady success with their non-superhero character, Archie Andrews, for whom the company was eventually renamed. The last comic of their original era was Pep Comics #65 (January 1948).

After the Silver Age at DC began, but before it reached the company that would become Marvel Comics, Archie revived the heroes, eventually placing them under the Mighty Comics imprint. After the heroes teamed up to help Fly Man (later simply The Fly), they were spun off into their own series. While the Mighty Crusaders title was short-lived, the name stuck.

The 1980s and the rise of comic book specialty shops saw another of the periodic resurgences of these characters under the Red Circle Comics imprint (later Archie Adventure Series). For a brief period during this time, The Mighty Crusaders and Archie's superhero line attracted top name super-

hero comics creators and they produced some of the most popular offerings in the characters' long histories.

The 1990s saw DC Comics license the MLJ/Archie superheroes for a new line called Impact Comics. The Comet and The Legend of the Shield in July 1991, followed by The Fly #1 and Jaguar #1 the following month. In September they added The Web, followed in December by The Black Hood and in May 1992 with The Crusaders. In addition to specials and annuals, DC offered three issues of Who's Who that showcased the Impact versions of all the MLJ heroes. In February 1993, The Crucible mini-series was launched, but Archie Comics decided that they didn't like the direction the Impact line was taking, and the project was canceled. The Crucible ended up becoming the wrap-up for this iteration of the heroes.

After another foray at DC that would have seen the characters integrated into the main DC Universe, the characters were returned to Archie. It would be 2012 before another effort saw the light of day. When the villain Brain Emperor returned from exile, it set in motion the children of the original Mighty Crusaders called upon to stop him as the New Crusaders.

After the animation style New Crusaders, the company launched the Dark Circle Comics imprint. While two mini-series featuring The Fox were light-hearted, three mini-series starring The Black Hood were distinctly aimed at a serious crime fiction audience.

Most recently a four-issue series of character specific one-shots was announced with Rob Liefeld (Youngblood) set to provide the story and art. However, after just one issue, The Mighty Crusaders: The Shield #1 (August 2021), Liefeld withdrew from the project.

FIRST PUBLICATION:
Blue Ribbon Comics #2
(December 1939)

LAST PUBLICATION:
Pep Comics #65 (January 1948)

REVIVAL(S):
Multiple revivals from the late 1950s to the present under the Mighty Comics, Red Circle Comics, Archie Adventure Series, Impact Comics (DC), and Dark Circle Comics imprints.

Rick Burchett's original art for *The Black Hood* #7 Page 15 (1992)
from the Impact Comics imprint, which featured the MLJ/Archie
heroes at DC Comics. Image courtesy of Heritage Auctions.

BLACK HOOD COMICS #9
WINTER 1943
$161 $483 $2500

BLACK HOOD COMICS #10
SPRING 1944
$103 $309 $1600

BLACK HOOD COMICS #11
SUMMER 1944
$77 $231 $1200

BLACK HOOD COMICS #12
FALL 1944
$69 $207 $1075

BLACK HOOD COMICS #13
WINTER 1945
$69 $207 $1075

BLACK HOOD COMICS #14
SPRING 1945
$123 $369 $1900

BLACK HOOD COMICS #15
SUMMER 1945
$69 $207 $1075

BLACK HOOD COMICS #16
FALL 1945
$69 $207 $1075

BLACK HOOD COMICS #17
WINTER 1946
$69 $207 $1075

BLACK HOOD COMICS #18
SPRING 1946
$69 $207 $1075

BLACK HOOD COMICS #19
SUMMER 1946
$87 $261 $1350

BLUE RIBBON COMICS #1
NOVEMBER 1939
$290 $870 $4500

BLUE RIBBON COMICS #2
DECEMBER 1939
$148 $444 $2300

BLUE RIBBON COMICS #3
JANUARY 1940
$100 $300 $1550

BLUE RIBBON COMICS #4
JUNE 1940
$110 $330 $1700

BLUE RIBBON COMICS #5
JULY 1940
$87 $261 $1350

BLUE RIBBON COMICS #6
SEPTEMBER 1940
$87 $261 $1350

BLUE RIBBON COMICS #7
NOVEMBER 1940
$87 $261 $1350

BLUE RIBBON COMICS #8
JANUARY 1941
$87 $261 $1350

BLUE RIBBON COMICS #9
FEBRUARY 1941
$356 $1068 $6400

BLUE RIBBON COMICS #10
MARCH 1941
$161 $483 $2500

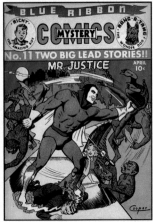

BLUE RIBBON COMICS #11
APRIL 1941
$161 $483 $2500

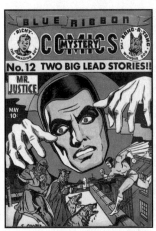

BLUE RIBBON COMICS #12
MAY 1941
$161 $483 $2500

BLUE RIBBON COMICS #13
JUNE 1941
$161 $483 $2500

BLUE RIBBON COMICS #14
JULY 1941
$129 $387 $2000

BLUE RIBBON COMICS #15
AUGUST 1941
$129 $387 $2000

BLUE RIBBON COMICS #16
SEPTEMBER 1941
$194 $582 $3000

BLUE RIBBON COMICS #17
OCTOBER 1941
$129 $387 $2000

BLUE RIBBON COMICS #18
NOVEMBER 1941
$129 $387 $2000

BLUE RIBBON COMICS #19
DECEMBER 1941
$116 $348 $1800

BLUE RIBBON COMICS #20
JANUARY 1942
$116 $348 $1800

BLUE RIBBON COMICS #21
FEBRUARY 1942
$300 $900 $5000

BLUE RIBBON COMICS #22
MARCH 1942
$116 $348 $1800

SPECIAL COMICS #1
TITLE CHANGES TO HANGMAN COMICS
WINTER 1942
$420 $1260 $7400

HANGMAN COMICS #2
SPRING 1942
$400 $1200 $7000

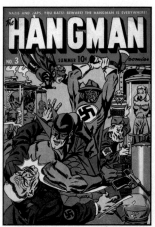

HANGMAN COMICS #3
SUMMER 1942
$541 $1623 $10,000

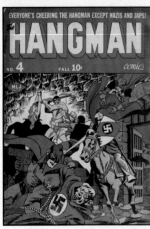

HANGMAN COMICS #4
FALL 1942
$432 $1296 $8000

HANGMAN COMICS #5
WINTER 1942-43
$290 $870 $4500

HANGMAN COMICS #6
SPRING 1943
$271 $813 $4200

HANGMAN COMICS #7
SUMMER 1943
$252 $756 $3900

HANGMAN COMICS #8
FALL 1943
$252 $756 $3900

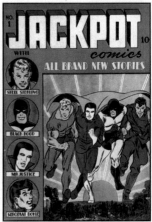

JACKPOT COMICS #1
SPRING 1941
$400 $1200 $7000

JACKPOT COMICS #2
SUMMER 1941
$174 $522 $2700

JACKPOT COMICS #3
FALL 1941
$168 $504 $2600

JACKPOT COMICS #4
WINTER 1941
$3900 $11,700 $36,000

JACKPOT COMICS #5
SPRING 1942
$757 $2271 $14,000

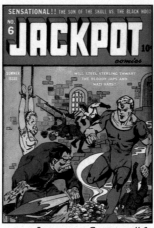

JACKPOT COMICS #6
SUMMER 1942
$300 $900 $5000

JACKPOT COMICS #7
FALL 1942
$300 $900 $5000

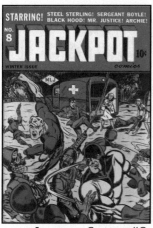

JACKPOT COMICS #8
WINTER 1942
$271 $813 $4200

JACKPOT COMICS #9
SPRING 1943
$271 $813 $4200

PEP COMICS #1
JANUARY 1940
$1050 $3150 $21,000

PEP COMICS #2
FEBRUARY 1940
$347 $1041 $5900

PEP COMICS #3
APRIL 1940
$272 $816 $4300

PEP COMICS #4
MAY 1940
$271 $813 $4200

PEP COMICS #5
JUNE 1940
$258 $774 $4000

PEP COMICS #6
JULY 1940
$206 $618 $3200

PEP COMICS #7
AUGUST 1940
$258 $774 $4000

PEP COMICS #8
SEPTEMBER 1940
$343 $1029 $6000

PEP COMICS #9
NOVEMBER 1940
$206 $618 $3200

PEP COMICS #10
DECEMBER 1940
$206 $618 $3200

PEP COMICS #11
JANUARY 1941
$226 $678 $3500

PEP COMICS #12
FEBRUARY 1941
$239 $717 $3700

PEP COMICS #13
MARCH 1941
$206 $618 $3200

PEP COMICS #14
APRIL 1941
$206 $618 $3200

PEP COMICS #15
MAY 1941
$206 $618 $3200

PEP COMICS #16
JUNE 1941
$423 $1269 $7500

PEP COMICS #17
JULY 1941
$865 $2595 $162,000

PEP COMICS #18
AUGUST 1941
$200 $600 $3100

PEP COMICS #19
SEPTEMBER 1941
$200 $600 $3100

PEP COMICS #20
OCTOBER 1941
$1000 $3000 $20,000

PEP COMICS #21
NOVEMBER 1941
$200 $600 $3100

PEP COMICS #22
1ST APP. ARCHIE, BETTY & JUGHEAD
DECEMBER 1941
$32,700 $98,100 $425,000

PEP COMICS #23
JANUARY 1942
$2900 $8700 $32,000

PEP COMICS #24
FEBRUARY 1942
$865 $2595 $16,000

PEP COMICS #25
MARCH 1942
$541 $1623 $10,000

PEP COMICS #26
APRIL 1942
$1500 $4500 $30,000

PEP COMICS #27
MAY 1942
$541 $1623 $10,000

PEP COMICS #28
JUNE 1942
$459 $1377 $8500

PEP COMICS #29
JULY 1942
$400 $1200 $7000

PEP COMICS #30
AUGUST 1942
$400 $1200 $7000

PEP COMICS #31
SEPTEMBER 1942
$459 $1277 $8500

PEP COMICS #32
OCTOBER 1942
$354 $1062 $6200

PEP COMICS #33
NOVEMBER 1942
$300 $900 $6000

PEP COMICS #34
DECEMBER 1942
$2600 $7800 $34,000

PEP COMICS #35
JANUARY 1943
$341 $1023 $5800

PEP COMICS #36
FEBRUARY 1942
$1950 $5850 $32,000

PEP COMICS #37
MARCH 1943
$300 $900 $6000

PEP COMICS #38
APRIL 1943
$290 $870 $4500

PEP COMICS #39
MAY 1943
$284 $852 $4400

PEP COMICS #40
JULY 1943
$290 $810 $4500

PEP COMICS #41
AUGUST 1943
$334 $1002 $5900

PEP COMICS #42
SEPTEMBER 1943
$219 $657 $3400

PEP COMICS #43
OCTOBER 1943
$219 $657 $3400

PEP COMICS #44
DECEMBER 1943
$219 $657 $3400

PEP COMICS #45
JANUARY 1944
$219 $657 $3400

PEP COMICS #46
FEBRUARY 1944
$187 $561 $2900

PEP COMICS #47
MARCH 1944
$187 $561 $2900

PEP COMICS #48
MAY 1944
$245 $735 $3800

PEP COMICS #49
JUNE 1944
$187 $561 $2900

PEP COMICS #50
SEPTEMBER 1944
$187 $561 $2900

PEP COMICS #51
DECEMBER 1944
$94 $282 $1450

PEP COMICS #52
MARCH 1945
$94 $282 $1450

PEP COMICS #53
JUNE 1945
$94 $282 $1450

PEP COMICS #54
SEPTEMBER 1945
$94 $282 $1450

PEP COMICS #55
DECEMBER 1945
$94 $282 $1450

PEP COMICS #56
MARCH 1946
$94 $282 $1450

PEP COMICS #57
JUNE 1946
$94 $282 $1450

PEP COMICS #58
SEPTEMBER 1946
$94 $282 $1450

PEP COMICS #59
DECEMBER 1946
$94 $282 $1450

PEP COMICS #60
MARCH 1947
$94 $282 $1450

PEP COMICS #61
MAY 1947
$74 $222 $1150

PEP COMICS #62
JULY 1947
$74 $222 $1150

PEP COMICS #63
SEPTEMBER 1947
$74 $222 $1150

PEP COMICS #64
NOVEMBER 1947
$74 $222 $1150

PEP COMICS #65
JANUARY 1948
$$74 $222 $1150

SHIELD-WIZARD COMICS #1
SUMMER 1940
$450 $1350 $10,000

SHIELD-WIZARD COMICS #2
WINTER 1940
$290 $870 $4500

SHIELD-WIZARD COMICS #3
SPRING 1941
$206 $618 $3200

SHIELD-WIZARD COMICS #4
SUMMER 1941
$206 $618 $3200

SHIELD-WIZARD COMICS #5
FALL 1941
$181 $543 $2800

SHIELD-WIZARD COMICS #6
WINTER 1941-42
$168 $504 $2600

SHIELD-WIZARD COMICS #7
SUMMER 1942
$168 $504 $2600

SHIELD-WIZARD COMICS #8
FALL 1942
$300 $900 $5000

SHIELD-WIZARD COMICS #9
WINTER 1942-43
$206 $618 $3200

SHIELD-WIZARD COMICS #10
SPRING 1943
$258 $774 $4000

SHIELD-WIZARD COMICS #11
SUMMER 1943
$142 $426 $2200

SHIELD-WIZARD COMICS #12
FALL 1943
$300 $900 $5000

SHIELD-WIZARD COMICS #13
SPRING 1944
$258 $774 $4000

TOP-NOTCH COMICS #1
DECEMBER 1939
$541 $1623 $10,000

TOP-NOTCH COMICS #2
JANUARY 1940
$290 $870 $4500

TOP-NOTCH COMICS #3
FEBRUARY 1940
$200 $600 $3100

TOP-NOTCH COMICS #4
APRIL 1940
$181 $543 $2800

TOP-NOTCH COMICS #5
MAY 1940
$219 $657 $3400

TOP-NOTCH COMICS #6
JUNE 1940
$142 $426 $2200

TOP-NOTCH COMICS #7
AUGUST 1940
$168 $504 $2600

TOP-NOTCH COMICS #8
SEPTEMBER 1940
$174 $522 $2700

TOP-NOTCH COMICS #9
OCTOBER 1940
$676 $2028 $12,500

TOP-NOTCH COMICS #10
DECEMBER 1940
$245 $735 $3800

TOP-NOTCH COMICS #11
JANUARY 1941
$168 $504 $2600

TOP-NOTCH COMICS #12
FEBRUARY 1941
$139 $417 $2150

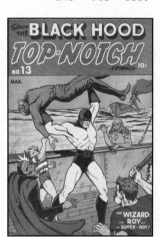

TOP-NOTCH COMICS #13
MARCH 1941
$139 $417 $2150

TOP-NOTCH COMICS #14
APRIL 1941
$139 $417 $2150

TOP-NOTCH COMICS #15
MAY 1941
$139 $417 $2150

TOP-NOTCH COMICS #16
JUNE 1941
$126 $378 $1950

TOP-NOTCH COMICS #17
JULY 1941
$126 $378 $1950

TOP-NOTCH COMICS #18
AUGUST 1941
$126 $378 $1950

TOP-NOTCH COMICS #19
SEPTEMBER 1941
$148 $444 $2300

TOP-NOTCH COMICS #20
OCTOBER 1941
$126 $378 $1950

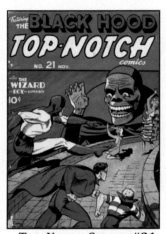

TOP-NOTCH COMICS #21
NOVEMBER 1941
$97 $291 $1500

TOP-NOTCH COMICS #22
DECEMBER 1941
$97 $291 $1500

TOP-NOTCH COMICS #23
JANUARY 1942
$97 $291 $1500

TOP-NOTCH COMICS #24
FEBRUARY 1942
$97 $291 $1500

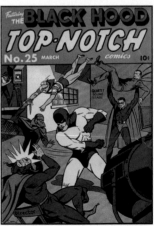

TOP-NOTCH COMICS #25
MARCH 1942
$97 $291 $1500

TOP-NOTCH COMICS #26
APRIL 1942
$97　$291　$1500

TOP-NOTCH COMICS #27
MAY 1942
$97　$291　$1500

**TOP-NOTCH
LAUGH COMICS #28**
JULY 1942
$97　$291　$1500

**TOP-NOTCH
LAUGH COMICS #29**
SEPTEMBER 1942
$97　$291　$1500

**TOP-NOTCH
LAUGH COMICS #30**
NOVEMBER 1942
$97　$291　$1500

**TOP-NOTCH
LAUGH COMICS #31**
DECEMBER 1942
$52　$156　$775

**TOP-NOTCH
LAUGH COMICS #32**
JANUARY 1943
$52　$156　$775

**TOP-NOTCH
LAUGH COMICS #33**
FEBRUARY 1943
$52　$156　$775

**TOP-NOTCH
LAUGH COMICS #34**
MARCH 1943
$52　$156　$775

**TOP-NOTCH
LAUGH COMICS #35**
APRIL 1943
$52　$156　$775

**TOP-NOTCH
LAUGH COMICS #36**
MAY 1943
$52　$156　$775

**TOP-NOTCH
LAUGH COMICS #37**
JULY 1943
$52　$156　$775

**TOP-NOTCH
LAUGH COMICS #38**
AUGUST 1943
$52　$156　$775

**TOP-NOTCH
LAUGH COMICS #39**
SEPTEMBER 1943
$52　$156　$775

**TOP-NOTCH
LAUGH COMICS #40**
OCTOBER 1943
$52　$156　$775

**TOP-NOTCH
LAUGH COMICS #41**
NOVEMBER 1943
$52　$156　$775

**TOP-NOTCH
LAUGH COMICS #42**
DECEMBER 1943
$52　$156　$775

**TOP-NOTCH
LAUGH COMICS #43**
FEBRUARY 1944
$52　$156　$775

**TOP-NOTCH
LAUGH COMICS #44**
APRIL 1944
$52 $156 $775

ZIP COMICS #1
FEBRUARY 1940
$465 $1395 $8600

ZIP COMICS #2
MARCH 1940
$275 $825 $4300

ZIP COMICS #3
APRIL 1940
$300 $900 $5000

ZIP COMICS #4
MAY 1940
$213 $639 $3300

ZIP COMICS #5
JUNE 1940
$213 $639 $3300

ZIP COMICS #6
JULY 1940
$200 $600 $3100

ZIP COMICS #7
AUGUST 1940
$200 $600 $3100

ZIP COMICS #8
SEPTEMBER 1940
$200 $600 $3100

ZIP COMICS #9
NOVEMBER 1940
$300 $900 $5000

ZIP COMICS #10
JANUARY 1941
$290 $870 $4500

ZIP COMICS #11
FEBRUARY 1941
$174 $522 $2700

ZIP COMICS #12
MARCH 1941
$206 $618 $3200

ZIP COMICS #13
APRIL 1941
$245 $735 $3800

ZIP COMICS #14
MAY 1941
$206 $618 $3200

ZIP COMICS #15
JUNE 1941
$232 $696 $3600

ZIP COMICS #16
JULY 1941
$252 $756 $3900

ZIP COMICS #17
AUGUST 1941
$432 $1296 $8000

ZIP COMICS #18
SEPTEMBER 1941
$541 $1623 $10,000

ZIP COMICS #19
OCTOBER 1941
$258 $774 $4000

ZIP COMICS #20
NOVEMBER 1941
$371 $1113 $6500

ZIP COMICS #21
DECEMBER 1941
$219 $657 $3400

ZIP COMICS #22
JANUARY 1942
$541 $1623 $10,000

ZIP COMICS #23
FEBRUARY 1942
$161 $483 $2500

ZIP COMICS #24
MARCH 1942
$145 $435 $2250

ZIP COMICS #25
APRIL 1942
$145 $435 $2250

ZIP COMICS #26
MAY 1942
$300 $900 $4800

ZIP COMICS #27
JULY 1942
$300 $900 $5000

ZIP COMICS #28
AUGUST 1942
$300 $900 $5000

ZIP COMICS #29
SEPTEMBER 1942
$271 $813 $4200

ZIP COMICS #30
OCTOBER 1942
$258 $774 $4000

ZIP COMICS #31
NOVEMBER 1942
$206 $618 $3200

ZIP COMICS #32
DECEMBER 1942
$343 $1029 $6000

ZIP COMICS #33
JANUARY 1943
$541 $1623 $10,000

ZIP COMICS #34
FEBRUARY 1943
$290 $870 $4500

ZIP COMICS #35
MARCH 1943
$206 $618 $3200

ZIP COMICS #36
APRIL 1943
$97 **$291** **$1500**

ZIP COMICS #37
MAY 1943
$97 **$291** **$1500**

ZIP COMICS #38
JULY 1943
$97 **$291** **$1500**

ZIP COMICS #39
AUGUST 1943
$74 **$222** **$1150**

ZIP COMICS #40
OCTOBER 1943
$61 **$183** **$950**

ZIP COMICS #41
NOVEMBER 1943
$61 **$183** **$950**

ZIP COMICS #42
DECEMBER 1943
$61 **$183** **$950**

ZIP COMICS #43
JANUARY 1944
$61 **$183** **$950**

ZIP COMICS #44
FEBRUARY 1944
$71 **$213** **$1100**

ZIP COMICS #45
APRIL 1944
$71 $213 $1100

ZIP COMICS #46
MAY 1944
$71 $213 $1100

ZIP COMICS #47
SUMMER 1944
$76 $228 $1175

SECOND UNIVERSE

JUNE 1959
—
OCTOBER 1967

ADVENTURES OF THE FLY #1
AUGUST 1959
$54 $162 $1500

ADVENTURES OF THE FLY #2
SEPTEMBER 1959
$29 $87 $725

ADVENTURES OF THE FLY #3
NOVEMBER 1959
$26 $78 $625

ADVENTURES OF THE FLY #4
JANUARY 1960
$36 $108 $900

ADVENTURES OF THE FLY #5
MARCH 1960
$12 $36 $260

ADVENTURES OF THE FLY #6
MAY 1960
$12 $36 $260

ADVENTURES OF THE FLY #7
JULY 1960
$17 $51 $400

ADVENTURES OF THE FLY #8
SEPTEMBER 1960
$17 $51 $400

ADVENTURES OF THE FLY #9
NOVEMBER 1960
$13 $39 $300

ADVENTURES OF THE FLY #10
JANUARY 1961
$12 $36 $260

ADVENTURES OF THE FLY #11
MARCH 1961
$8 $24 $145

ADVENTURES OF THE FLY #12
MAY 1961
$8 $24 $145

ADVENTURES OF THE FLY #13
JULY 1961
$8 $24 $145

ADVENTURES OF THE FLY #14
SEPTEMBER 1961
$9 $27 $165

ADVENTURES OF THE FLY #15
OCTOBER 1961
$8 $24 $145

ADVENTURES OF THE FLY #16
NOVEMBER 1961
$8 $24 $145

ADVENTURES OF THE FLY #17
JANUARY 1962
$8 $24 $145

ADVENTURES OF THE FLY #18
MARCH 1962
$8 $24 $145

ADVENTURES OF THE FLY #19
MAY 1962
$8 $24 $145

ADVENTURES OF THE FLY #20
JULY 1962
$8 $24 $145

ADVENTURES OF THE FLY #21
SEPTEMBER 1962
$6 $18 $110

ADVENTURES OF THE FLY #22
OCTOBER 1962
$6 $18 $110

ADVENTURES OF THE FLY #23
NOVEMBER 1962
$6 $18 $110

ADVENTURES OF THE FLY #24
FEBRUARY 1963
$6 $18 $110

ADVENTURES OF THE FLY #25
APRIL 1963
$6 $18 $110

ADVENTURES OF THE FLY #26
JULY 1963
$6 $18 $110

ADVENTURES OF THE FLY #27
SEPTEMBER 1963
$6 $18 $110

ADVENTURES OF THE FLY #28
OCTOBER 1963
$6 $18 $110

ADVENTURES OF THE FLY #29
JANUARY 1964
$6 $18 $110

ADVENTURES OF THE FLY #30
OCTOBER 1964
$6 $18 $110

ADVENTURES OF THE FLY #31
SERIES CONTINUES AS FLY MAN #32
MAY 1965
$6 $18 $115

**ADVENTURES OF
THE JAGUAR #1**
SEPTEMBER 1961
$23 $69 $550

**ADVENTURES OF
THE JAGUAR #2**
OCTOBER 1961
$11 $33 $240

**ADVENTURES OF
THE JAGUAR #3**
NOVEMBER 1961
$11 $33 $240

**ADVENTURES OF
THE JAGUAR #4**
JANUARY 1962
$8 $24 $160

**ADVENTURES OF
THE JAGUAR #5**
MARCH 1962
$8 $24 $160

**ADVENTURES OF
THE JAGUAR #6**
MAY 1962
$8 $24 $160

**ADVENTURES OF
THE JAGUAR #7**
JULY 1962
$7 $21 $125

**ADVENTURES OF
THE JAGUAR #8**
SEPTEMBER 1962
$7 $21 $125

**ADVENTURES OF
THE JAGUAR #9**
OCTOBER 1962
$7 $21 $125

**ADVENTURES OF
THE JAGUAR #10**
NOVEMBER 1962
$7 $21 $125

ADVENTURES OF THE JAGUAR #11
JANUARY 1963
$6 $18 $105

ADVENTURES OF THE JAGUAR #12
MAY 1963
$6 $18 $105

ADVENTURES OF THE JAGUAR #13
AUGUST 1963
$6 $18 $105

ADVENTURES OF THE JAGUAR #14
OCTOBER 1963
$6 $18 $105

ADVENTURES OF THE JAGUAR #15
NOVEMBER 1963
$6 $18 $105

THE DOUBLE LIFE OF PRIVATE STRONG #1
JUNE 1959
$34 $102 $850

THE DOUBLE LIFE OF PRIVATE STRONG #2
AUGUST 1959
$18 $54 $435

FLY MAN #32
NUMBERING CONTINUES FROM
ADVS. OF THE FLY #31 • JULY 1965
$5 $15 $85

FLY MAN #33
SEPTEMBER 1965
$5 $15 $85

FLY MAN #34
NOVEMBER 1965
$4 $12 $60

FLY MAN #35
JANUARY 1966
$4 $12 $60

FLY MAN #36
MARCH 1966
$4 $12 $60

FLY MAN #37
MAY 1966
$4 $12 $60

FLY MAN #38
JULY 1966
$4 $12 $60

FLY MAN #39
TITLE CONTINUES AS MIGHTY COMICS
SEPTEMBER 1966
$4 $12 $60

MIGHTY COMICS #40
FORMERLY TITLED FLY MAN
NOVEMBER 1966
$5 $15 $70

MIGHTY COMICS #41
DECEMBER 1966
$4 $12 $65

MIGHTY COMICS #42
JANUARY 1967
$4 $12 $65

MIGHTY COMICS #43
FEBRUARY 1967
$4 $12 $65

MIGHTY COMICS #44
MARCH 1967
$4 $12 $65

MIGHTY COMICS #45
APRIL 1967
$4 $12 $65

MIGHTY COMICS #46
MAY 1967
$4 $12 $65

MIGHTY COMICS #47
JUNE 1967
$4 $12 $65

MIGHTY COMICS #48
JULY 1967
$4 $12 $65

MIGHTY COMICS #49
AUGUST 1967
$4 $12 $65

MIGHTY COMICS #50
OCTOBER 1967
$4 $12 $65

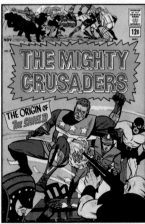

MIGHTY CRUSADERS #1
NOVEMBER 1965
$7 $21 $135

MIGHTY CRUSADERS #2
JANUARY 1966
$4 $12 $65

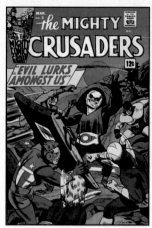

MIGHTY CRUSADERS #3
MARCH 1966
$4 $12 $60

MIGHTY CRUSADERS #4
APRIL 1966
$5 $15 $70

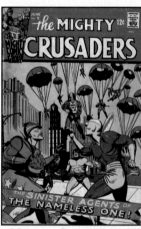

MIGHTY CRUSADERS #5
JUNE 1966
$4 $12 $60

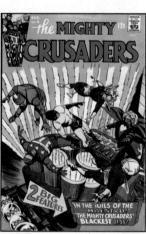

MIGHTY CRUSADERS #6
AUGUST 1966
$4 $12 $60

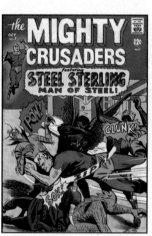

MIGHTY CRUSADERS #7
OCTOBER 1966
$4 $12 $60

THE SHADOW #1
AUGUST 1964
$9 $27 $175

THE SHADOW #2
SEPTEMBER 1964
$5 $15 $85

THE SHADOW #3
NOVEMBER 1964
$5 $15 $85

THE SHADOW #4
JANUARY 1965
$5 $15 $85

THE SHADOW #5
MARCH 1965
$5 $15 $85

THE SHADOW #6
MAY 1965
$5 $15 $85

THE SHADOW #7
JULY 1965
$5 $15 $85

THE SHADOW #8
SEPTEMBER 1965
$5 $15 $85

THIRD UNIVERSE

MARCH 1983
—
SEPTEMBER 1985

THE BLACK HOOD #1
JUNE 1983
$1 $3 $8

THE BLACK HOOD #2
AUGUST 1983
$4

THE BLACK HOOD #3
OCTOBER 1983
$4

BLUE RIBBON COMICS #1
NOVEMBER 1983
$1 $3 $10

BLUE RIBBON COMICS #2
NOVEMBER 1983
$6

BLUE RIBBON COMICS #3
DECEMBER 1983
$6

BLUE RIBBON COMICS #4
JANUARY 1984
$6

BLUE RIBBON COMICS #5
FEBRUARY 1984
$6

BLUE RIBBON COMICS #6
MARCH 1984
$6

BLUE RIBBON COMICS #7
APRIL 1984
$6

BLUE RIBBON COMICS #8
MAY 1984
$1 $3 $7

BLUE RIBBON COMICS #9
JUNE 1984
$6

BLUE RIBBON COMICS #10
JULY 1984
$6

BLUE RIBBON COMICS #11
AUGUST 1984
$6

BLUE RIBBON COMICS #12
SEPTEMBER 1984
$1 $3 $8

BLUE RIBBON COMICS #13
OCTOBER 1984
$6

BLUE RIBBON COMICS #14
DECEMBER 1984
$6

THE COMET #1
OCTOBER 1983
$6

THE COMET #2
DECEMBER 1983
$5

THE FLY #1
MAY 1983
$6

THE FLY #2
JULY 1983
$6

THE FLY #3
OCTOBER 1983
$5

THE FLY #4
DECEMBER 1983
$5

THE FLY #5
FEBRUARY 1984
$5

THE FLY #6
APRIL 1984
$6

THE FLY #7
JUNE 1984
$6

THE FLY #8
AUGUST 1984
$6

THE FLY #9
OCTOBER 1984
$6

MIGHTY CRUSADERS #1
MARCH 1983
$1 $3 $7

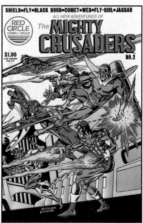

MIGHTY CRUSADERS #2
MAY 1983
$5

MIGHTY CRUSADERS #3
JULY 1983
$5

MIGHTY CRUSADERS #4
NOVEMBER 1983
$5

MIGHTY CRUSADERS #5
JANUARY 1984
$5

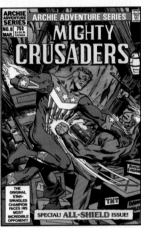

MIGHTY CRUSADERS #6
MARCH 1984
$5

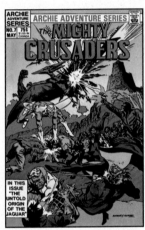

MIGHTY CRUSADERS #7
MAY 1984
$5

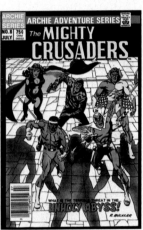

MIGHTY CRUSADERS #8
JULY 1984
$5

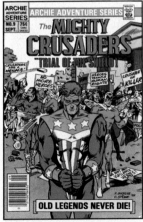

MIGHTY CRUSADERS #9
SEPTEMBER 1984
$5

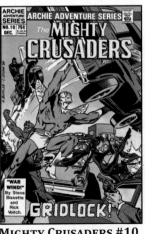

MIGHTY CRUSADERS #10
DECEMBER 1984
$5

MIGHTY CRUSADERS #11
MARCH 1985
$6

MIGHTY CRUSADERS #12
JUNE 1985
$6

MIGHTY CRUSADERS #13
SEPTEMBER 1985
$6

THE ORIGINAL SHIELD #1
APRIL 1984
$5

THE ORIGINAL SHIELD #2
JUNE 1984
$5

THE ORIGINAL SHIELD #3
AUGUST 1984
$5

THE ORIGINAL SHIELD #4
OCTOBER 1984
$5

THE SHIELD #1
JUNE 1983
$5

THE SHIELD #2
AUGUST 1983
$5

SHIELD - STEEL STERLING #3
DECEMBER 1983
$5

STEEL STERLING #4
JANUARY 1984
$5

STEEL STERLING #5
MARCH 1984
$5

STEEL STERLING #6
MAY 1984
$5

STEEL STERLING #7
JULY 1984
$5

FOURTH UNIVERSE

JULY 1991
–
JULY 1993

BLACK HOOD #1
DECEMBER 1991
$4

BLACK HOOD #2
JANUARY 1992
$3

BLACK HOOD #3
FEBRUARY 1992
$3

BLACK HOOD #4
MARCH 1992
$3

BLACK HOOD #5
MAY 1992
$3

BLACK HOOD #6
JUNE 1992
$3

BLACK HOOD #7
JULY 1992
$3

BLACK HOOD #8
AUGUST 1992
$3

BLACK HOOD #9
SEPTEMBER 1992
$3

BLACK HOOD #10
OCTOBER 1992
$3

BLACK HOOD #11
NOVEMBER 1992
$3

BLACK HOOD #12
DECEMBER 1992
$3

BLACK HOOD ANNUAL #1
JUNE 1992
$4

THE COMET #1
JULY 1991
$4

THE COMET #2
AUGUST 1991
$3

THE COMET #3
SEPTEMBER 1991
$3

THE COMET #4
OCTOBER 1991
$3

THE COMET #5
NOVEMBER 1991
$3

THE COMET #6
DECEMBER 1991
$3

THE COMET #7
JANUARY 1992
$3

THE COMET #8
FEBRUARY 1992
$3

THE COMET #9
MARCH 1992
$3

THE COMET #10
APRIL 1992
$3

THE COMET #11
MAY 1992
$3

THE COMET #12
JUNE 1992
$3

THE COMET #13
JULY 1992
$3

THE COMET #14
AUGUST 1992
$3

THE COMET #15
SEPTEMBER 1992
$3

THE COMET #16
OCTOBER 1992
$3

THE COMET #17
NOVEMBER 1992
$3

THE COMET #18
DECEMBER 1992
$3

THE COMET ANNUAL #1
1992
$4

CRUCIBLE #1
FEBRUARY 1993
$3

CRUCIBLE #2
MARCH 1993
$3

CRUCIBLE #3
APRIL 1993
$3

CRUCIBLE #4
MAY 1993
$3

CRUCIBLE #5
JUNE 1993
$3

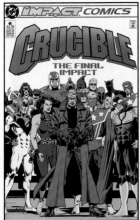

CRUCIBLE #6
JULY 1993
$3

THE CRUSADERS #1
MAY 1992
$4

THE CRUSADERS #2
JUNE 1992
$4

THE CRUSADERS #3
JULY 1992
$4

THE CRUSADERS #4
AUGUST 1992
$4

THE CRUSADERS #5
SEPTEMBER 1992
$4

THE CRUSADERS #6
OCTOBER 1992
$4

THE CRUSADERS #7
NOVEMBER 1992
$4

THE CRUSADERS #8
DECEMBER 1992
$4

THE FLY #1
AUGUST 1991
$5

THE FLY #2
SEPTEMBER 1991
$4

THE FLY #3
OCTOBER 1991
$4

THE FLY #4
NOVEMBER 1991
$4

THE FLY #5
DECEMBER 1991
$4

THE FLY #6
JANUARY 1992
$4

THE FLY #7
FEBRUARY 1992
$4

THE FLY #8
MARCH 1992
$4

THE FLY #9
APRIL 1992
$4

THE FLY #10
MAY 1992
$4

THE FLY #11
JUNE 1992
$4

THE FLY #12
JULY 1992
$4

THE FLY #13
AUGUST 1992
$4

THE FLY #14
SEPTEMBER 1992
$4

THE FLY #15
OCTOBER 1992
$4

THE FLY #16
NOVEMBER 1992
$4

THE FLY #17
DECEMBER 1992
$4

THE FLY ANNUAL #1
1992
$5

**IMPACT CHRISTMAS
SPECIAL #1**
1991
$4

THE JAGUAR #1
AUGUST 1991
$4

THE JAGUAR #2
SEPTEMBER 1991
$4

THE JAGUAR #3
OCTOBER 1991
$4

THE JAGUAR #4
NOVEMBER 1991
$4

THE JAGUAR #5
DECEMBER 1991
$4

THE JAGUAR #6
JANUARY 1992
$4

THE JAGUAR #7
MARCH 1992
$4

THE JAGUAR #8
APRIL 1992
$4

THE JAGUAR #9
MAY 1992
$4

THE JAGUAR #10
JUNE 1992
$4

THE JAGUAR #11
JULY 1992
$4

THE JAGUAR #12
AUGUST 1992
$4

THE JAGUAR #13
SEPTEMBER 1992
$4

THE JAGUAR #14
OCTOBER 1992
$4

THE JAGUAR ANNUAL #1
1992
$5

LEGEND OF THE SHIELD #1
JULY 1991
$4

LEGEND OF THE SHIELD #2
AUGUST 1991
$4

LEGEND OF THE SHIELD #3
SEPTEMBER 1991
$4

LEGEND OF THE SHIELD #4
OCTOBER 1991
$4

LEGEND OF THE SHIELD #5
NOVEMBER 1991
$4

LEGEND OF THE SHIELD #6
DECEMBER 1991
$4

LEGEND OF THE SHIELD #7
JANUARY 1992
$4

LEGEND OF THE SHIELD #8
FEBRUARY 1992
$4

LEGEND OF THE SHIELD #9
MARCH 1992
$4

LEGEND OF THE SHIELD #10
APRIL 1992
$4

LEGEND OF THE SHIELD #11
MAY 1992
$4

LEGEND OF THE SHIELD #12
JUNE 1992
$4

LEGEND OF THE SHIELD #13
JULY 1992
$4

LEGEND OF THE SHIELD #14
AUGUST 1992
$4

LEGEND OF THE SHIELD #15
SEPTEMBER 1992
$4

LEGEND OF THE SHIELD #16
OCTOBER 1992
$4

LEGEND OF THE SHIELD ANNUAL #1
1992
$4

THE WEB #1
SEPTEMBER 1991
$5

THE WEB #2
OCTOBER 1991
$5

THE WEB #3
NOVEMBER 1991
$5

THE WEB #4
DECEMBER 1991
$5

THE WEB #5
JANUARY 1992
$5

THE WEB #6
FEBRUARY 1992
$5

THE WEB #7
EARLY APRIL 1992
$5

THE WEB #8
LATE APRIL 1992
$5

THE WEB #9
MAY 1992
$5

THE WEB #10
JUNE 1992
$5

THE WEB #11
JULY 1992
$5

THE WEB #12
AUGUST 1992
$5

THE WEB #13
SEPTEMBER 1992
$5

THE WEB #14
OCTOBER 1992
$5

THE WEB ANNUAL #1
1992
$5

WHO'S WHO IN THE !MPACT UNIVERSE #1
SEPTEMBER 1991
$5

WHO'S WHO IN THE !MPACT UNIVERSE #2
NOVEMBER 1991
$5

WHO'S WHO IN THE !MPACT UNIVERSE #1
MAY 1992
$5

FIFTH UNIVERSE

OCTOBER 2009 — FEBRUARY 2011

THE MIGHTY CRUSADERS SPECIAL #1
JULY 2010
$4

THE MIGHTY CRUSADERS #1
SEPTEMBER 2010
$4

THE MIGHTY CRUSADERS #1
VARIANT COVER
SEPTEMBER 2010
$4

THE MIGHTY CRUSADERS #2
OCTOBER 2010
$4

THE MIGHTY CRUSADERS #3
NOVEMBER 2010
$4

THE MIGHTY CRUSADERS #4
DECEMBER 2010
$4

THE MIGHTY CRUSADERS #5
JANUARY 2011
$4

THE MIGHTY CRUSADERS #6
FEBRUARY 2011
$4

**THE RED CIRCLE
INFERNO #1**
OCTOBER 2009
$5

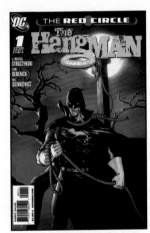

**THE RED CIRCLE
THE HANGMAN #1**
OCTOBER 2009
$5

**THE RED CIRCLE
THE SHIELD #1**
OCTOBER 2009
$5

**THE RED CIRCLE
THE WEB #1**
OCTOBER 2009
$5

THE SHIELD #1
NOVEMBER 2009
$4

THE SHIELD #1
VARIANT COVER
NOVEMBER 2009
$4

THE SHIELD #2
DECEMBER 2009
$4

THE SHIELD #3
JANUARY 2010
$4

THE SHIELD #4
FEBRUARY 2010
$4

THE SHIELD #5
MARCH 2010
$4

THE SHIELD #6
APRIL 2010
$4

THE SHIELD #7
MAY 2010
$4

THE SHIELD #8
JUNE 2010
$4

THE SHIELD #9
JULY 2010
$4

THE SHIELD #10
AUGUST 2010
$4

THE WEB #1
NOVEMBER 2009
$4

THE WEB #1
VARIANT COVER
NOVEMBER 2009
$4

THE WEB #2
DECEMBER 2009
$4

THE WEB #3
JANUARY 2010
$4

THE WEB #4
FEBRUARY 2010
$4

THE WEB #5
MARCH 2010
$4

THE WEB #6
APRIL 2010
$4

THE WEB #7
MAY 2010
$4

THE WEB #8
JUNE 2010
$4

SIXTH
UNIVERSE

OCTOBER 2012
—
SEPTEMBER 2018

(PLUS A FEW
ARCHIE GANG
CROSSOVERS)

THE WEB #9
JULY 2010
$4

THE WEB #10
AUGUST 2010
$4

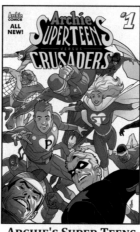

**ARCHIE AND FRIENDS AND
THE SHIELD #1**
HALLOWEEN PROMO • OCTOBER 2002
$4

**ARCHIE'S SUPER TEENS
VERSUS CRUSADERS #1**
AUGUST 2018
$4

**ARCHIE'S SUPER TEENS
VERSUS CRUSADERS #1**
VARIANT COVER • AUGUST 2018
$4

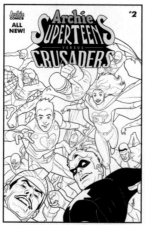

**ARCHIE'S SUPER TEENS
VERSUS CRUSADERS #2**
SEPTEMBER 2018
$4

**ARCHIE'S SUPER TEENS
VERSUS CRUSADERS #2**
VARIANT COVER • SEPTEMBER 2018
$4

**ARCHIE'S SUPER TEENS
VERSUS CRUSADERS #2**
VARIANT COVER • SEPTEMBER 2018
$4

ARCHIE'S WEIRD MYSTERIES #3
APRIL 2000
$4

ARCHIE'S WEIRD MYSTERIES #14
AUGUST 2001
$4

THE BLACK HOOD #1
APRIL 2015
$4

THE BLACK HOOD #1
VARIANT COVER
APRIL 2015
$4

THE BLACK HOOD #1
VARIANT COVER
APRIL 2015
$4

THE BLACK HOOD #1
VARIANT COVER
APRIL 2015
$4

THE BLACK HOOD #1
VARIANT COVER
APRIL 2015
$4

THE BLACK HOOD #2
MAY 2015
$4

THE BLACK HOOD #2
VARIANT COVER
MAY 2015
$4

THE BLACK HOOD #2
VARIANT COVER
MAY 2015
$4

THE BLACK HOOD #3
JUNE 2015
$4

THE BLACK HOOD #3
VARIANT COVER
JUNE 2015
$4

THE BLACK HOOD #3
VARIANT COVER
JUNE 2015
$4

THE BLACK HOOD #3
VARIANT COVER
JUNE 2015
$4

THE BLACK HOOD #4
JULY 2015
$4

THE BLACK HOOD #4
VARIANT COVER
JULY 2015
$4

THE BLACK HOOD #4
VARIANT COVER
JULY 2015
$4

THE BLACK HOOD #4
VARIANT COVER
JULY 2015
$4

THE BLACK HOOD #5
AUGUST 2015
$4

THE BLACK HOOD #5
VARIANT COVER
AUGUST 2015
$4

THE BLACK HOOD #5
VARIANT COVER
AUGUST 2015
$4

THE BLACK HOOD #5
VARIANT COVER
AUGUST 2015
$4

THE BLACK HOOD #5
VARIANT COVER
AUGUST 2015
$4

THE BLACK HOOD #6
DECEMBER 2015
$4

THE BLACK HOOD #6
VARIANT COVER
DECEMBER 2015
$4

THE BLACK HOOD #6
VARIANT COVER
DECEMBER 2015
$4

THE BLACK HOOD #6
VARIANT COVER
DECEMBER 2015
$4

THE BLACK HOOD #7
JANUARY 2016
$4

THE BLACK HOOD #7
VARIANT COVER
JANUARY 2016
$4

THE BLACK HOOD #8
MARCH 2016
$4

THE BLACK HOOD #8
VARIANT COVER
MARCH 2016
$4

THE BLACK HOOD #9
APRIL 2016
$4

THE BLACK HOOD #9
VARIANT COVER
APRIL 2016
$4

THE BLACK HOOD #10
JUNE 2016
$4

THE BLACK HOOD #10
VARIANT COVER
JUNE 2016
$4

THE BLACK HOOD #11
AUGUST 2016
$4

THE BLACK HOOD #11
VARIANT COVER
AUGUST 2016
$4

THE BLACK HOOD VOL. 2 #1
DECEMBER 2016
$4

THE BLACK HOOD VOL. 2 #1
VARIANT COVER
DECEMBER 2016
$4

THE BLACK HOOD VOL. 2 #1
LOCAL COMIC SHOP DAY COVER
DECEMBER 2016
$4

THE BLACK HOOD VOL. 2 #2
FEBRUARY 2017
$4

THE BLACK HOOD VOL. 2 #2
VARIANT COVER
FEBRUARY 2017
$4

THE BLACK HOOD VOL. 2 #3
APRIL 2017
$4

THE BLACK HOOD VOL. 2 #3
VARIANT COVER
APRIL 2017
$4

THE BLACK HOOD VOL. 2 #4
JUNE 2017
$4

THE BLACK HOOD VOL. 2 #4
VARIANT COVER
JUNE 2017
$4

THE BLACK HOOD VOL. 2 #5
AUGUST 2017
$4

THE BLACK HOOD VOL. 2 #5
VARIANT COVER
AUGUST 2017
$4

THE FOX #1
DECEMBER 2013
$3

THE FOX #1
VARIANT COVER
DECEMBER 2013
$3

THE FOX #1
VARIANT COVER
DECEMBER 2013
$3

THE FOX #1
VARIANT COVER
DECEMBER 2013
$3

THE FOX #1
2ND PRINTING
DECEMBER 2013
$3

THE FOX #2
JANUARY 2014
$3

THE FOX #2
VARIANT COVER
JANUARY 2014
$3

THE FOX #3
FEBRUARY 2014
$3

THE FOX #3
VARIANT COVER
FEBRUARY 2014
$3

THE FOX #4
MARCH 2014
$3

THE FOX #4
VARIANT COVER
MARCH 2014
$3

THE FOX #5
APRIL 2014
$3

THE FOX #5
VARIANT COVER
APRIL 2014
$3

THE FOX #5
VARIANT COVER
APRIL 2014
$3

THE FOX #5
VARIANT COVER
APRIL 2014
$3

THE FOX #5
VARIANT COVER
APRIL 2014
$3

THE FOX #5
VARIANT COVER
APRIL 2014
$3

THE FOX VOL. 2 #1
JUNE 2015
$4

THE FOX VOL. 2 #1
VARIANT COVER
JUNE 2015
$4

THE FOX VOL. 2 #1
VARIANT COVER
JUNE 2015
$4

THE FOX VOL. 2 #1
VARIANT COVER
JUNE 2015
$4

THE FOX VOL. 2 #1
VARIANT COVER
JUNE 2015
$4

THE FOX VOL. 2 #2
JULY 2015
$4

THE FOX VOL. 2 #2
VARIANT COVER
JULY 2015
$4

The Fox Vol. 2 #2
Variant cover
July 2015
$4

The Fox Vol. 2 #3
August 2015
$4

The Fox Vol. 2 #3
Variant cover
August 2015
$4

The Fox Vol. 2 #3
Variant cover
August 2015
$4

The Fox Vol. 2 #3
Variant cover
August 2015
$4

The Fox Vol. 2 #4
September 2015
$4

The Fox Vol. 2 #4
Variant cover
September 2015
$4

The Fox Vol. 2 #4
Variant cover
September 2015
$4

The Fox Vol. 2 #4
Variant cover
September 2015
$4

THE FOX VOL. 2 #5
OCTOBER 2015
$4

THE FOX VOL. 2 #5
VARIANT COVER
OCTOBER 2015
$4

THE FOX VOL. 2 #5
VARIANT COVER
OCTOBER 2015
$4

THE FOX VOL. 2 #5
VARIANT COVER
OCTOBER 2015
$4

THE FOX VOL. 2 #5
VARIANT COVER
OCTOBER 2015
$4

FREE COMIC BOOK DAY:
DARK CIRCLE #1
JUNE/JULY 2015
$3

THE HANGMAN #1
DECEMBER 2015
$4

THE HANGMAN #1
VARIANT COVER
DECEMBER 2015
$4

THE HANGMAN #1
VARIANT COVER
DECEMBER 2015
$4

THE HANGMAN #1
VARIANT COVER
DECEMBER 2015
$4

THE HANGMAN #1
LOCAL COMIC SHOP DAY COVER
DECEMBER 2015
$4

THE HANGMAN #2
MARCH 2016
$4

THE HANGMAN #2
VARIANT COVER
MARCH 2016
$4

THE HANGMAN #3
MAY 2016
$4

THE HANGMAN #3
VARIANT COVER
MAY 2016
$4

THE HANGMAN #4
DECEMBER 2016
$4

THE HANGMAN #4
VARIANT COVER
DECEMBER 2016
$4

MIGHTY CRUSADERS #1
JANUARY 2018
$4

MIGHTY CRUSADERS #1
Variant cover
January 2018
$4

MIGHTY CRUSADERS #2
March 2018
$4

MIGHTY CRUSADERS #2
Variant cover
March 2018
$4

MIGHTY CRUSADERS #2
Variant cover
March 2018
$4

MIGHTY CRUSADERS #3
April 2018
$4

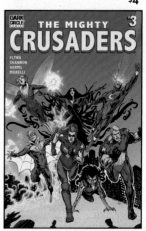

MIGHTY CRUSADERS #3
Variant cover
April 2018
$4

MIGHTY CRUSADERS #3
Variant cover
April 2018
$4

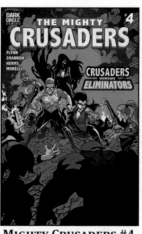

MIGHTY CRUSADERS #4
May 2018
$4

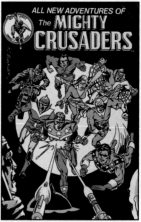

MIGHTY CRUSADERS #4
Variant cover
May 2018
$4

MIGHTY CRUSADERS #4
VARIANT COVER
MAY 2018
$4

NEW CRUSADERS PREVIEW
2012
$3

NEW CRUSADERS #1
OCTOBER 2012
$3

NEW CRUSADERS #1
VARIANT COVER
OCTOBER 2012
$3

NEW CRUSADERS #1
VARIANT COVER
OCTOBER 2012
$3

NEW CRUSADERS #1
VARIANT COVER
OCTOBER 2012
$3

NEW CRUSADERS #2
DECEMBER 2012
$3

NEW CRUSADERS #2
VARIANT COVER
DECEMBER 2012
$3

NEW CRUSADERS #2
VARIANT COVER
DECEMBER 2012
$3

NEW CRUSADERS #3
DECEMBER 2012
$3

NEW CRUSADERS #3
VARIANT COVER
DECEMBER 2012
$3

NEW CRUSADERS #3
VARIANT COVER
DECEMBER 2012
$3

NEW CRUSADERS #4
DECEMBER 2012
$3

NEW CRUSADERS #4
VARIANT COVER
DECEMBER 2012
$3

NEW CRUSADERS #4
VARIANT COVER
DECEMBER 2012
$3

NEW CRUSADERS #5
JANUARY 2013
$3

NEW CRUSADERS #5
VARIANT COVER
JANUARY 2013
$3

NEW CRUSADERS #5
VARIANT COVER
JANUARY 2013
$3

NEW CRUSADERS #6
MARCH 2013
$3

NEW CRUSADERS #6
VARIANT COVER
MARCH 2013
$3

NEW CRUSADERS #6
VARIANT COVER
MARCH 2013
$3

THE SHIELD #1
DECEMBER 2015
$4

THE SHIELD #1
VARIANT COVER
DECEMBER 2015
$4

THE SHIELD #1
VARIANT COVER
DECEMBER 2015
$4

THE SHIELD #1
VARIANT COVER
DECEMBER 2015
$4

THE SHIELD #1
VARIANT COVER
DECEMBER 2015
$4

THE SHIELD #1
LOCAL COMIC SHOP DAY COVER
DECEMBER 2015
$4

THE SHIELD #2
APRIL 2016
$4

THE SHIELD #2
VARIANT COVER
APRIL 2016
$4

THE SHIELD #2
VARIANT COVER
APRIL 2016
$4

THE SHIELD #2
VARIANT COVER
APRIL 2016
$4

THE SHIELD #3
DECEMBER 2016
$4

THE SHIELD #3
VARIANT COVER
DECEMBER 2016
$4

THE SHIELD #3
VARIANT COVER
DECEMBER 2016
$4

THE SHIELD #3
VARIANT COVER
DECEMBER 2016
$4

THE SHIELD #4
JANUARY 2017
$4

THE SHIELD #4
VARIANT COVER
JANUARY 2017
$4

THE SHIELD #4
VARIANT COVER
JANUARY 2017
$4

THE SHIELD #4
VARIANT COVER
JANUARY 2017
$4

INSIDE THE DARK CIRCLE

"I've always loved those characters, so the idea of bringing them back with a more 'network' or genre approach really spoke to me. I'm immensely proud of the stuff that came out of it," said Alex Segura, the former Archie writer and editor, who headed up the company's Dark Circle reboot of the MLJ/Archie superhero characters.

The tough, street-smart realism of the Dark Circle incarnation of *The Black Hood* starts out more in line with writer Duane Swierczynski's novels rather than his previous comic book work, which included *Cable* at Marvel, *Birds of Prey* at DC, *Bloodshot* at Valiant, and *Judge Dredd* at IDW.

In Michael Gaydos (*Alias*), who illustrated the first arc, Swierczynski was matched with an artist for whom "dark and gritty" does not mean poorly drawn as it does for so many. The art is moody and rough, but it does not choose style over substance. Rather, it delivers both.

The story is indeed a rough one, aimed at adults and not kids. Even though it's filled with a difficult subject and coarse language, and even though it might seem bleak, there are some really human elements that shine through.

The tone of the Dean Haspiel-illustrated issues of *The Fox* are a strong counterpoint to *The Black Hood*. In his work, there's a sense of whimsy that harkens back to the earliest days of Spider-Man or the early adventures of Static.

It clearly showed that the plot and the danger the character faces could be either silly or formidable, but the character taking things seriously doesn't mean that he or she won't say or think something funny. Plotter-artist Haspiel and dialoguer Mark Waid captured this idea superbly, and it's highlighted to great effect in *The Fox: Freak Magnet* collected edition.

MLJ Magazines, Inc. began publishing comics in 1939. Founded by Maurice Coyne, Louis Silberkleit, and John L. Goldwater, the company's name came from the initials of its founders' first names. Among its earliest offerings were superhero comics.

To paraphrase Mark Twain, "reports of the MLJ Universe's demise have been greatly exaggerated." In fact, the MLJ heroes have thrived in six different universes interconnected by the "Blue Ribbon," as in *Blue Ribbon Comics*, the first title published by MLJ Comics in 1939. The Blue Ribbon encapsulates the entire MLJ Multiverse.

FIRST UNIVERSE

The original universe encompasses stories printed under the MLJ Comics imprint in the 1940s, also known as the Golden Age of comics. In the Golden Age, Archie Comics was known as MLJ Comics, and they were a full-service comic publisher. Their first superhero, Bob Phantom, premiered in the second issue of the company's flagship title, *Blue Ribbon Comics*, in December 1939.

In a tale written by editor Harry Shorten and drawn by superstar artist Irv Novick, columnist Walter Whitney becomes one of the first citizens to take to the streets and fight crime in the name of vigilante justice. Walter's costumed persona, Bob Phantom, haunted the world of drug dealers and organized crime using an array of

mysterious abilities including teleportation and matter-transforming mists.

The following year, in *Pep Comics* #1 (January 1940), Shorten and Novick reunited to create The Shield, the first patriotic superhero. The Shield was the bestselling character in the MLJ pantheon of heroes. Not only was he the star of *Pep Comics*, but he also had a second title, *Shield-Wizard Comics*.

In the story, Joe Higgins was the son of Thomas Higgins, a government biochemist and member of the Burning Hand, a secret society formed to protect America. Thomas was attempting to recreate the powers of the Shield formula when he was killed by Axis spies. Joe completed his father's research, applied it to himself, and became the Shield.

Pep Comics #1 also saw the debut of the Comet from creator Jack Cole. He would go on to create Plastic Man, and Comet would serve as the inspiration for Marvel Comics' Cyclops. When John Dickering began his scientific experiments, he didn't know at the time that one of those experiments was going to change his life forever. During his experiments, he discovered the formula for a new lighter-than-air gas, but he wasn't sure how humans would be affected by direct contact with the gas. He chose the most unorthodox way of testing the effects of the gas on humans by

Irv Novick's original Page 4 art for *Shield-Wizard #7* (1942), which features The Shield vs. The Hun.
Image courtesy of Heritage Auctions.

injecting himself with it, risking his life in the process. After injecting himself with the gas, he found he was able to leap tremendous distances. Further injections made him buoyant enough that he practically had the power of flight.

There was a major catch to those injections, however: an unforeseen – and very deadly – side effect. The gas had collected in his eyes and threw off two beams. When the beams crossed, they combined to form a deadly energy beam that disintegrated anything he looked at! Discovering that the beam was ineffective against the element Silicon, Dickering formed a protective pair of goggles to protect those around him from being harmed by the deadly eyebeams.

At the height of his popularity, the Comet was the first superhero to die in the line of duty. He was replaced by his brother Bob, who became the Hangman to avenge John's death. Creators Cliff Campbell and George Storm produced one of the most powerful and emotional moments in comics, in *Pep Comics* #17 (July 1941), Bob Dickering vowed "I'll carry on for him… I'll bring his murderers to the hangman! I'll be their hangman!"

The Hangman was a powerful and imposing figure, but the company's only multimedia Golden Age star was Black Hood. The Black Hood was created by Cliff Campbell and Al Camerata. Patrolman Kip Burland, was attacked by the Skull, who framed him for robbing a jewelry store. Burland was discharged from the force. When Burland tried to capture the Skull on his own he was shot and thrown in the woods. A man called the Hermit rescued him and trained him to become the Black Hood. As the Black Hood, Burland was able to clear his name. He now fights crime as both a lawman and a vigilante. The concept was so strong that the Black Hood was featured in comics, pulp magazines, and on the radio.

In what would become commonplace in comics, the Comet came back from his temporary death. As it turned out according to the story, the Comet was struck by a fireball that teleported him to the

planet Altrox, where he had adventures before eventually returning to Earth.

The Golden Age MLJ Comics featured many other great heroes as well, but they all succumbed to the post-war market's turn away from superheroes and MLJ's own success with a teenaged boy named Archie Andrews. Archie was so popular that he took over the starring role in *Pep Comics*… and ultimately, the name of the publisher changed from MLJ Comics to Archie Comics.

The first Crusaders universe ended in January 1948 with *Pep Comics* #65.

SECOND UNIVERSE

It is generally agreed that the Silver Age of comics initially began in 1956 when DC released *Showcase* #4. It wouldn't hit the company that became Marvel for several more years, but Archie Comics decided it was time to revive their line of superheroes in June 1959.

The team of Joe Simon and Jack Kirby came to Archie Comics to relaunch their superheroes in the pages of *The Double Life of Private Strong* with a new version of the Shield and their new character, the Fly.

The new Shield was Roger Fleming. His father, Dr. Malcolm Fleming, raised Roger to use the untapped portions of the human brain, thus making him a superhuman. After communist spies killed Dr. Fleming, the Strongs, a farm couple, raised Roger.

Once he hit his teens, he discovered the truth of his background and his powers. He also learned that his father had created a patriotic costume for him, and this led Roger to embark upon a life of heroics as a new iteration of the Shield.

He soon joined the army, hence his "double life" as both a soldier and a superhero. When DC Comics noticed that Roger was a baby with superpowers raised by a childless farm couple, they considered it too close to their Superman and brought up the

Jack Kirby and Joe Simon's original art for *Adventures of the Fly* #1 Page 13 (1959), which showcases Tommy Troy's transformation into The Fly. Image courtesy of Heritage Auctions.

matter to Archie management, resulting in Archie canceling the title.

The Fly, however, would continue to soar in one form or another from 1959 to 1967. The Fly has an interesting backstory. Young Tommy Troy started his superhero life with the name "Spiderman" with veteran Captain Marvel artist C.C. Beck providing the art. When Joe Simon sold the story to Harvey Comics, he changed the name to the Silver Spider. Harvey failed to publish the comic, so Simon sold the story to Archie Comics changing his name again, this time to the Fly, with artist Jack Kirby redrawing the Beck pages.

During the Silver Age renaissance of superheroes at Archie Comics, when their Mighty Comics Group imprint was in use, virtually all the Golden Age MLJ heroes were revived. Only Red Rube and Mister Satan failed to return. The Wizard and Hangman, who had been stars in the Golden Age, would find themselves in the role of villains as Superman creator Jerry Siegel took over writing the Fly.

Siegel used the exaggerated, comical camp style for his work with these mighty heroes. While many people incorrectly attribute Siegel's use of camp to the popular 1966 *Batman* TV show, his work on these comic books predates the debut of that series.

Others have unfavorably compared Siegel's style to that of Stan Lee. While Lee used a lot of similar hyperbole and was not beyond a pun or character-driven humor, Lee's modus operandi was to contrast extraordinary super-heroics with the often mundane, though no less soap operatic lives of those heroes' very ordinary alter egos. Siegel was aware that he was working for a humor comics publisher, so he deliberately delivered camp versions of the publisher's heroes as a form of humor, as opposed to emulating the Lee style. Especially since the Archie heroes could be seen

regularly in the pages of *Pep Comics* and *Laugh Comics*, both of which were humor titles by the late 1950s and into the '60s.

Speaking of humor, Archie Andrews experienced a tremendous amount of success during the Silver Age. This era saw the greatest expansion of Archie Andrews-related titles in the company's history. With Archie and the gang being cheaper to produce and selling better than the superheroes, the heroes were stuck in the drawer once more, and died a second death.

THIRD UNIVERSE

In 1972, the comic book business was on the cusp of major changes. Phil Seuling founded Sea Gate Distributors and made purchasing arrangements with Archie, DC, Marvel, and Warren, creating the direct market distribution system. The system had a business model opposite to the traditional comics distribution approach. Prior to the direct market, the only avenue publishers had to get their comics to retail stores was newsstand distribution. In newsstand distribution, unsold comics could be returned to publishers after a set period had elapsed, with credits then being made to the distributor and passed on to the retailers for the unsold copies. In the direct sales model, stores (usually hobby shops or shops dedicated exclusively to comic books), would buy the comics from the distributor on a non-returnable basis. It was a guaranteed sale for publishers, in which they cut in the distributor for a percentage of the sale, and it was up to the comic shops to hope they could sell every copy they ordered for clear profit, or to at least make back something down the road with discounted sales.

In 1981, John Carbonaro worked out a deal with Archie owner Richard Goldwater to have Archie Comics print and distribute his JC Comics into the growing direct comics market. In *JCP Features #1* (December 1981), Carbonaro reprinted a Black

Paul Reinman's Page 1 splash from *The Mighty Crusaders #6* (1966) featuring Fly Man and Fly Girl in a story by Superman co-creator Jerry Siegel. Image courtesy of Heritage Auctions.

Hood story by Gray Morrow and Neal Adams. The story was well-received, and Goldwater hired Carbonaro as editor to revive the MLJ heroes for the third time under their Red Circle imprint.

Plans were made for a new comic featuring the Fly, Private Strong, and the Mighty Crusaders. The line had production problems and was late, which led to Goldwater firing Carbonaro before the March 1983 shipping of the new Red Circle line of comics. Carbonaro was replaced as editor by *Mighty Crusaders* writer-artist Rich Buckler.

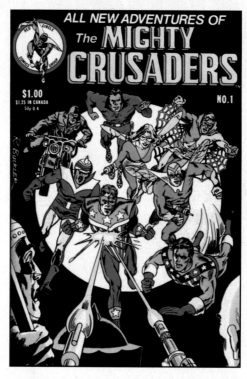

While Buckler was a veteran comic creator, he had not been an editor before, and also fell victim to slow production and missed deadlines. Despite the problems, this is one of the most beloved periods for these heroes. It featured the work of creators Jim Steranko, Alex Toth, Steve Ditko, Rudy Nebres, Alan Weiss, Carmine Infantino, Dick Ayers, John Severin, and Pat Boyette, among others. Despite the love the fans had for these comics, the publisher was very unhappy with the erratic shipping schedule.

Goldwater then asked Bill DuBay to step in and replace Buckler as editor, but DuBay was Buckler's brother-in-law and refused, citing the family issues could arise should he take the role. Instead, the editorial duties were split between them. Unfortunately, the missed deadlines continued. This resulted in an erratic shipping schedule, and the line's audience began to erode.

Both Buckler and DuBay were let go and Victor Gorelick took over as editor. He used a less expensive stable of artists. At the same time, Archie changed the imprint from Red Circle to Archie Adventure Comics and started to distribute them on the newsstands as well as in the direct market. The newsstand audience didn't take to the comics. After suffering heavy returns, the line was canceled, resulting in the heroes' third death.

FOURTH UNIVERSE

As comics experienced a boom the early 1990s, Archie licensed their heroes to DC Comics. The new line was called "Impact! Comics." In general, it was a dark age for the tone and style of many comics, but the Impact line wasn't dark at all. Instead, DC Comics wanted an all-age line to bring in younger readers who they hoped would then "graduate" from Impact to the mainline DC titles as they became older. Mike Gold was to edit the line and he had great fondness for the characters.

This idea was very appealing to Archie's Michael Silberkleit. He saw his company as an entry point for younger readers. There was a slogan at Archie Comics that "Our Comics Are Reader Breeders" because they were proud that children learned to read with Archie. The line was launched in 1991 with four titles: *The Comet* and *The Legend of the Shield* in July, followed by *The Fly* #1 and *Jaguar* #1 in August. While all the characters were updated, the Jaguar was notable because of a gender change from male to female (Archie continued the concept of a female Jaguar in later comics once the licensing deal ended).

The line did well and in September 1991 they added *The Web*, which was the biggest departure from the original concept. While the Comet, Shield, and Fly were reworked updates of the original heroes, and the Jaguar featured a gender swap, the Web had nothing to do with the original character whatsoever. Now the Web was an organization with many members, emulating Marvel's S.H.I.E.L.D.

By December 1991, *The Black Hood* joined the mix, followed in May 1992 with the MLJ heroes united as *The Crusaders*. There was a *Winter Special, Annuals* and even a three-volume *Who's Who* cataloging all the MLJ heroes in their new Impact! roles, edited by Bob Kahan and written by Mark Waid.

Gray Morrow's original art for Page 1 of *The Black Hood* #3 (1983).
Image courtesy of Heritage Auctions.

In February 1993, *The Crucible* miniseries by Waid and Joe Quesada was created to transition the MLJ heroes from an all-ages line into something more in line with DC Comics' older audience under editor Jim Owsley.

As things geared up for this relaunch, there was trouble in paradise. Quesada left the project and Silberkleit didn't like the new direction that Owsley was taking the MLJ Heroes. They were drifting too far away from their Archie roots. As a result, Silberkleit asked for the line to be canceled and returned to Archie. *The Crucible* had to be rewritten mid-series going from a launch pad for Impact! 2.0 to a conclusion of the entire line.

FIFTH UNIVERSE

While *The Crucible* came to an end, that didn't completely spell the end for the MLJ heroes at DC Comics. They were licensed again and came back to DC for a 2009 line of comics with the premise of integrating them with DC's stable of heroes… but not before one false start.

After spending six years writing *Spider-Man*, J. Michael Straczynski headed to DC to write *Batman*. Only he didn't want to deal with DC's continuity. So, it was decided that he would write the *Brave & the Bold* starring Batman teaming up with different MLJ heroes each issue. He described his place in the DC universe as "An apartment just outside DC continuity."

Deals were signed between DC Comics and Archie Comics. There was an announcement at the San Diego Comic-Con with art featuring Batman and the MLJ Heroes. The comics went into production. However, after two issues of *Brave & the Bold* were completed, work on the movie *The Changeling* took Straczynski away from comics. Those issues were never published;

alternate stories featuring DC characters replaced the MLJ relaunch plans. Those plans, though, weren't shelved for long.

Straczynski soon returned to comics, and DC decided to go in another direction with the MLJ Heroes. They launched with a series of one-shots by Straczynski, followed by two series: *The Web* and *The Shield* by young, fresh creators. Straczynski produced a "bible" for the heroes, but his return was short-lived. Both he and Batman left the project. The smaller launch without Batman failed to impress the readers at DC and the two titles were folded into one comic as the new line became the *Mighty Crusaders*. It ended up with a very short life at DC this time. Elements from the *Web* series and the Webhost could later be seen in DC's *Batman, Inc.* where Batman would license his brand the same way the Web had done in this DC incarnation.

SIXTH UNIVERSE

Returning back home to Archie, the MLJ heroes transitioned from the "aughts" to the 2010s by entering "the Dark Circle." It was a slow entry. Starting with young, second generation characters, Archie relaunched the MLJ heroes in a new Red Circle line. *The New Crusaders* met with tremendous critical success, mixing an animated aesthetic with some very serious consequences, including prison riots and heroes who died. However, the critical success did not turn into sales success and the second *New Crusaders* mini-series was canceled before it shipped. In came the Fox, who revived the Red Circle line and embraced Archie's humor as well as the MLJ Comics history. *The Fox* miniseries was successful and a different take on the way serious superheroes blended with humor.

Editorial changes moved the line from Red Circle to Dark Circle. With Dark Circle, the idea was

Tom Lyle's original cover art for *The Comet* #4 (1991). The Comet and other MLJ/Archie superheroes were revived in the Impact line, which was published by DC. Image courtesy of Heritage Auctions.

to remake the heroes in a series of mini-series. First up was *Black Hood*, who went from a happy-go-lucky guy who rode a mechanical horse in the Silver Age to a drug addicted cop with a disfigured face. This was a departure from the original character, but it was also a way of showing that Archie was committed to telling high-quality, hard-hitting stories that were as contemporary as any other publisher.

The Fox had a second miniseries which showed that the Dark Circle line was about putting the right creator with the right character. *The Fox* was comedy and *The Black Hood* was crime drama, both exciting to fans and different than the comics from DC and Marvel.

Next up was a different presentation for the *Shield*. Victoria Adams was the new Shield. A five-issue miniseries was planned but with artistic challenges, the mini-series faced delays and was reduced from five issues to four. Likewise, the new *Hangman* series was shortened to four issues and the *Web* series, although announced, never launched.

The heroes came back together for the launch of another on-going *Mighty Crusaders* monthly comic combining the original versions of the heroes with their *New Crusaders* versions as well as introducing a new update of *Darkling*, the female sorcerous hero last seen in the original Red Circle *Mighty Crusaders*. Shortly after its launch the on-going *Mighty Crusaders* series switched to a mini-series and was compiled into a paperback edition still in print at this time.

Following this was another miniseries in which Archie's Super Teens (the core cast of teens from Riverdale High with their own superpowers,

such as Archie as Pureheart the Powerful, Betty as Super Teen, Jughead as Capt. Hero, etc.) meet the Mighty Crusaders. It is in this mini-series that the MLJ heroes return to their classic form.

Though at times it may be in limbo, or even on life support, one thing the MLJ Universe can never be called is a "Dead Universe." It always has a living, breathing pulse, with a limitless cast of characters and ideas flexible enough to change with the times and mold to editorial needs and interpretations over and over again. It is the ultimate phoenix of comic universes, having been reborn over and over during its 80-year history.

There are very few universes of superheroes that have remained in publication for 80 years, and while it has not been a continuous monthly road for the MLJ heroes, it is only momentary hibernation between each incarnation. We can hardly wait to see what's next for these eternally iconic heroes.

– Rik Offenberger & Paul Castiglia

Rik Offenberger has worked in the comics industry since 1990, serving as Archie Comics' Public Relations Coordinator for a decade. Currently he is the Editor-In-Chief at G-Man Comics and First Comics News. He co-wrote The MLJ Companion *with Paul Castiglia and Jon B. Cooke.*

Paul Castiglia is a veteran comic book writer, editor, promoter, and historian whose work has been published by Archie, DC, Dark Horse and more. With Rik Offenberger and Jon B. Cooke, Castiglia co-wrote and edited The MLJ Companion *from TwoMorrows Publishing.*

Robert Hack's "Movie Poster Throwback" variant cover for *The Fox* #2 (2015), which actually included fold lines in the art (which has not actually been folded). Image courtesy of Heritage Auctions.

Looking Under the Black Hood

Of all the characters in Archie's new Dark Circle line-up, the Black Hood has easily gone through the most changes over the years. The original Hood was a man by the name of Matthew "Kip" Burland who made his debut in MLJ Comics' Top-Notch Comics #9 in October of 1940. Burland had been trained by a hermit to battle evil; an ex-cop, he was framed for larceny and left for dead, and while he eventually cleared his name, he continued to fight crime throughout the Golden Age.

Burland's nephew, Thomas, became the Hood in the 1970s revival under Archie's Red Circle Comics line. This Hood could be seen riding a fancy motorcycle and was armed with custom Pepper-box pistols. He was featured in three issues of his own title in 1983 but most often was featured in The Mighty Crusaders and Archie's Super Hero Comic Digest.

The Black Hood jumped to DC Comics in 1991 when the company began its Impact Comics imprint. Impact was only around from '91 to '93 and featured heroes licensed from Archie Comics, including the Comet and the Shield in addition to the Black Hood. For many, the Impact line ended far too soon, but The Black Hood was definitely a standout. This version of the Hood actually featured three different characters as the vigilante, and the titular hood itself was an executioner's hood that would grant its wearer heightened strength and agility – but would force them to only use these abilities for good.

As The Black Hood celebrated its 75th anniversary and a highly touted new version of the character launched in Spring 2015, Overstreet spoke with artist Rick Burchett and writer Mark Wheatley about their involvement with Impact's Black Hood series.

Overstreet: Did you have any specific story objectives going in?
Rick Burchett (RB): We were to create stories that would be good jumping on points for new comic readers of all ages. Stories that weren't bogged down by decades of continuity and would be complete in a single issue.
Mark Wheatley (MW): I was under orders from Mike Gold to shake things up and ignore everything that had ever been done with The Black Hood. The Impact line of comics was guaranteed three years to establish the stories, characters and commercial viability. So my

objective was to create a set of fascinating characters and a setting that had a deep back story. The plan was to lay the foundation of a major new line of comics. I was weaving a tapestry that would be able to still be paying off stories a decade after our launch.

Overstreet: Do you think you were able to achieve these?
MW: With the help of Rick Burchett and the other artists, I think we managed a near 100 percent of our goals for the first year. I was very pleased and gratified that fan response was so strong, as well. The Black Hood was a hit, with sales growing constantly. I was very excited, anticipating the next two years of the series. The future looked bright for The Black Hood.
RB: I think so, at least in The Black Hood. Some of the rest of the books in the Impact line started that way, but then began to feature continued stories.

Overstreet: The Black Hood you wrote for Impact differed pretty significantly from the previous iterations of the character in Mighty Comics and Red Circle Comics. Why was that the case?
MW: Mike Gold was the mastermind behind Impact. He felt that the character names of the Mighty Crusaders were our major asset. He felt that the actual characters and their back stories were so messy, muddled and largely forgotten, we should concentrate on creating something essentially new. No one was lobbying for a return of these characters. We would have created entirely new characters, but Mike felt that we needed the name recognition factor. And since it also took the Archie company out of the superhero market, that played into the DC strategy.

Overstreet: There were three different Hoods in this series. Did you have a favorite?
MW: Nate was absolutely my favorite. And my long term plan was to have Nate becoming The Black Hood and then abandoning the hood, over and over again. As other people would wear the hood for a while and have their lives shaken up or ended, Nate would be drawn back into the world of crime and superheroes. We would follow Nate as he grew into a man, seeing him struggle to keep his own identity, to have a normal life, to connect with people and family – and then to be dragged back into the fray. That said, the opportunity to cast other people as The Black Hood allowed

Rick Burchett's original art for *The Black Hood* #2 Page 23. Image courtesy of Mark Wheatley.

for the potential of some delightful and extreme characters to be superheroes, people you would not usually expect to see in that role. You know – I think your count is off. There were at least three Hoods in the regular *Black Hood* comics. But I think there were two, maybe three more in the annuals. We had short back-up stories of historical Black Hood characters. This was part of the deep back story I was developing for the series.

RB: Yeah, I liked Nate the best. I'm a sucker for traditional heroes – ordinary people who find themselves in extraordinary situations and rise to the occasion. The first Hood in our series used the hood to serve an agenda, and Hit Coffee was an opportunist, using the hood to further personal gain.

Overstreet: There were a lot of very colorful characters in the book besides the Hood himself. How did you go about designing the look of the book?

RB: I'm a big fan of the early Marvel books and one of the things I loved about them was the way Kirby and Ditko designed the characters. Not everyone looked like they had a lifetime membership to 24 Hour Fitness. Some of the bad guys were stout, some were lanky, many different body types. If you wield a power like Doctor Octopus, you don't need defined musculature. The mechanical arms do all the work. The same with the Vulture. It's probably better if the wings don't have to lift a lot of muscle mass. Different types of figures give the strip visual variety.

Overstreet: The Black Hood series seemed really reflective of societal fears at the time – The G-NE drugs, the ozone-afflicted villain, and so on. How were you able to integrate these issues into the book without seeming as though you were pandering to your audience?

MW: Pandering is exactly what I always avoid in my work. An audience is a moving target. If you aim at where they are, by the time your comic is in their hands six months later, they will have moved on. Pandering is usually wasted effort. I was writing *The Black Hood* based on my own interactions with the world. I was pulling from my own reactions and concerns with society. That's what I always do.

RB: That was Mark's doing, and I think he was just following in the footsteps of those writers who came before. When DC started the Silver Age, science was the underpinning for the characters and the stories. When Stan created the Marvel Universe, the touchstones were Radioactivity and the spread of Communism. All of these things reflected the times in which the stories were written. Comics have always reflected their times. You could put together a pretty good look at America in the 20th century just by reading the comics.

Overstreet: Was there any single stand-out moment or issue in the series for you?

MW: Most of the issues have moments I loved. Rick Burchett is an amazing storyteller. His ability to get the maximum visual impact from what I had written was a real joy for me. There is a three-page sequence in one of the issues where the Hood is trying to climb out of a sewer that just blows me away. Issue #7 is probably my favorite, entire book. "Horton Wears The Hood" was inspired by two sources. First, it was my whimsical effort at telling a crime story in the style of a Doctor Seuss children's book – and I think we managed that very well. Second, the founding of the city was based on my own family history. Weaving details of my first ancestors to arrive in the new world and how they settled on Virginia's Eastern Shore was a sly nod to my roots.

RB: Actually, there are a couple. When Nate is in the tunnels under the city and they begin to flood. That turned out pretty good visually. The other was a quiet moment. Nate is in his room, feeling unsure of himself and he puts the Hood on and it gives him confidence. I started the sequence with the action in the panel tilted and, as he put on the Hood, the panels rotate to a visually more stable composition. I was trying to reach the reader's subconscious by indicating that without the Hood, Nate's emotions were uneasy. With the Hood, he was on firmer ground. I think that worked.

Overstreet: When you started on this project, what was your initial thought on the character and on the Impact line as a whole?

MW: It was a fun experience. I got to work with some of the most talented people working in comics at that time. We had several group retreats and spent a good deal of time cross-pollenating ideas and plans. I remember thinking that it would be an opportunity to do some world building in the same collaborative way that the early Marvel Comics under Lee, Kirby, Ditko, Heck, etc. had done – to be a part of a group of talented creators all working for a common goal.

RB: I thought the Impact line was a great idea, something that was desperately needed in the industry. It was intended to be an entry point for new readers, a way to expand the audience. I was familiar with the MLJ heroes before this, and I always felt there was a charm to them and unlimited potential. It's funny, but the one I gravitated to was the Black Hood. There were great possibilities to the character. When editor Mike Gold called to offer me the job and told me it would be *The Black Hood*, I was thrilled. Given a choice, it was the one I would've picked. What Mark did with the character was brilliant, not unlike the early Spider-Man. It was great fun. To this day Mark Wheatley is still the most creative person I've ever worked with. His influence helped me get better at what I did.

Overstreet: Did those thoughts change once the Black Hood finished?

MW: Well, I did get that creative experience that I was looking for. But the market was in turmoil at the time. And in spite of Mike Gold's best efforts to keep Impact on the rails, we were still hit with last minute changes and some astoundingly bad production problems. One of the issues was published without ANY of the caption boxes included – so the story made only partial sense and had little relation to the story I was actually telling, since the captions were explaining characters' hidden motivations for their actions that were on view in the art. Also, with so many other comics being released at the time from all the publishers, the creative teams were being tempted away by big money and more assured opportunities. I was so fortunate that Rick Burchett stayed with the book as long as he did. And the other artists on the book were turning in amazing work. Ultimately, we had the rug pulled out from under us at the end of the first year. While it was acknowledged that my *Black Hood* was the standout commercial success of the line, for some odd reason, it was decided to throw out the baby with the bath water. *The Black Hood* was cancelled while at a very high and growing circulation, so they could mount a reboot of the entire line. So my three-year plan to pay off the stories and characters had only reached the end of their first act. In many ways we had only scratched the surface of the potential for that title. And the fans loved what we were doing. So, in the end, it was a somewhat frustrating experience.

RB: My thoughts on the Hood didn't change. The Impact line, as a whole, seemed to lose its way and DC stopped promoting it. I'm not sure the reasons behind those changes, but it was a shame. Impact was a noble experiment and I wish it would've been more successful. Its failure doesn't mirror the quality of the work that was done. There were some good comics produced in that short period of time.

Overstreet: When Archie redeveloped the Mighty Crusaders characters as their Dark Circle line, they also made your Black Hood available digitally. What would you tell new readers about your stories?

MW: I think Rick and I managed to create some great characters in *The Black Hood*. They have interesting lives and unexpected things happened to them. In some ways, it was a subversive book. We were creating an anti-vigilante story that featured a prime vigilante. We enjoyed poking at some of the accepted superhero tropes. I think it started as a reaction to the silly elements in other comics. But it actually led us into some serious and fascinating areas of story. Things that usually get passed by while creators and readers all race to the usual super conflicts and complications. I wish I had had a chance to do at least 36 issues of *The Black Hood*. But the 12 issues, annual and short stories that we got done tell a cohesive story.

RB: Those stories were intended to engage the reader and entertain them. They were stories that were meant to be fun and filled with a sense of wonder. I'd just like readers to have a good time and for a few minutes forget that they're looking at pixels on a screen and believe they're watching the lives of real people unfold.

- Carrie Wood

Rick Burchett's original art for *The Black Hood* #2 Page 24. Image courtesy of Mark Wheatley.

A Fox in Archie's Henhouse

ALEX TOTH'S EDGY TAKE ON THE MLJ/RED CIRCLE HERO

It was the late 1980s. I was a year or so out of art school. I knew I didn't have the chops to be a comics artist but I was determined to become a writer and/or editor of comics. I started researching all the nearby companies, including Archie. I bought up a bunch of Archie Comics and digests for reference and was perplexed by a few one-page, full panel drawings contained in some of the digests. The drawings showed superhero characters I hadn't recalled ever seeing before. They weren't doing anything other than touting literacy and their own existence, but that was enough for me – I was entranced and hooked!

Soon thereafter I had an opportunity to visit a store deep in back issues – basically a warehouse with more comics than I'd ever seen before! I sought out the comics featuring the characters I saw in the digest public service announcements and left the store with a precariously bulging armful. Among them were a few issues of a character called The Black Hood. I snatched them up because I recognized the artist's signature on the cover: Alex Toth! While I was disappointed that the title character did not feature in accompanying Toth stories inside the covers, the Golden Age MLJ character The Fox (think a lilywhite version of Marvel's *Black Panther* and you'll get the drift) *did* appear as a backup, resplendent in a fabulous fury of colorful Toth art and prose.

I had been enjoying Toth for years when I was a kid, but I didn't know it. I'd seen his designs in such classic Hanna-Barbera animated fare as the 1967 *Fantastic Four, Space Ghost, Birdman,* and *Super Friends.* As a kid I didn't immediately make the connection that these designs all came from the same artist's pencil. It was in the *Justice League of America Limited Collector's Edition* that I first encountered Toth's name. In addition to classic JLA reprints, the oversized 1976 edition featured *Super Friends* model sheets drawn by Toth himself!

Seeing those model sheets blew my mind, because included in the images were shots of Plastic Man (who made one guest-appearance on *Super Friends*). Even then Plas was my favorite superhero, having been introduced to the looooooooong

arm of the law via Jules Feiffer's essential *Great Comic Book Heroes*… the seminal work that also included Eisner's legendary The Spirit.

If it sounds like I'm backing into some connection between Toth, The Fox, Toth's past work and the work of his influences, you're right.

Toth only did two Fox stories to my knowledge. But what stories!

In the initial, untitled Toth Fox tale from *Black Hood Comics* #2 (released August, 1983), we see both an artist wearing his influences on his sleeves as well as one enjoying the freedom of working on a non-Comics Code title. In the early days of the Red Circle line, the comics were distributed exclusively to comic shops. Eventually the line would be re-christened the Archie Adventure Series and join Riverdale's fabled teens at traditional newsstand outlets.

But in the beginning… well, Toth got to go whole hog on hardboiled yet fun (and naturally funny… not forced) tales. Toth infused as many elements from film noir movies and the classic Cole Plastic Man and Eisner Spirit tales as possible. From a non-Code perspective, he peppered the dialogue with "hells" and "damns" not usually seen in mainstream superhero comics (though never feeling gratuitous) as well as themes more adult (such as adultery) than typically found in standard action-adventure comics fare.

The film noir movie Toth's initial Fox tale most resembles is 1944's *Murder, My Sweet* starring Dick Powell, itself an adaptation of Raymond Chandler's famous Philip Marlowe mystery novel, *Farewell, My Lovely.* The story has proved venerable – two years prior to *Murder, My Sweet* the plot was cherry-picked and shoe-horned into a George Sanders-as-the-Falcon entry called *The Falcon Takes Over*; while a 1975 version starring Robert Mitchum finally used Chandler's original title. In all cases, the stories feature a big lug/ex (possibly current)-felon named Moose Malloy who employs the hero to locate his sweetheart, who may or may not want him back.

The Fox by Alex Toth

In Toth's story, we get Cosmo Gilly, ex-prizefighter with implications of underworld ties. Those implications come clear in a very funny "intro" scene where photo-journalist Paul Patton (secret identity of The Fox) is "welcomed" by Cosmo via a fist to the face, credited by Cosmo as being courtesy of one Petey Bosco "from the Chicago mob Boscos." Cosmo swears no hard (personal) feelings – just that Petey is still plenty sore that Paul's photos helped land Petey in the pen! There are several scenes where Cosmo punches out would-be-assassins, as well as accidentally (and comically) KO'ing Patton an additional time or two.

While the story echoes the Chandler tale in that the hero takes pity on the big lug and agrees to help him, it's the Eisner Spirit and Cole Plastic Man influence that infuses the humorous interactions between Patton and Cosmo, giving their alliance a unique freshness that ultimately ends in friendship. At just eight pages the denouement is easy to telegraph – Cosmo's "brudder" and manager made some healthy investments for the punchy pugilist… and made some unhealthy advances on Cosmo's wife! Needless to say the philandering filly teamed with her conniving brother-in-law/lover to see if they could reap a windfall from Cosmo's life insurance policy. Still, it's the journey that counts here.

In addition to the Chandler/Cole/Eisner story influences, and humor/characterizations owed to Cole and Eisner, this first Fox tale is highly stylized (its exotic Morocco locale in particular putting it in Spirit territory) with terrifically exaggerated caricatures and is gloriously colored in bright color schemes evoking the best of the Spirit and Plastic Man comics.

It's Toth the idealist that turns up in the following issue's Fox tale, *The Most sssssss Man in the World!?* (from *Black Hood* #3, released October, 1983). Those who followed Toth knew that he was an outspoken interview, someone who made his work about the art/story first (and took those fellow practitioners who didn't to task) but who also didn't suffer big business' treatment of "the little guy" kindly, either. It seems only natural that Toth would concoct a tale whose protagonist drew his main influence from Nikola Tesla, the Serbian-American inventor, father of electromagnetics and showman who rivaled Thomas Edison in his day but whose inventions fell into obscurity for many years thereafter, leading to speculation that some may have been suppressed by government agencies or private businesses whose livelihoods could be threatened by the technological advances.

Toth tips his hand from the get-go, starting with the odd title of the story which has an entire, undecipherable word crossed out. He tips it further by presenting his protagonist full-figured on the first page, lanky-armed and lankier-legged, with a long pear-shaped torso, chicken-neck, Ross Perot ears, pursed lips, squinted eyes and furrowed brow. The man is a walking contradiction: he looks frail and ornery all at once, and Toth further confounds his readers' ability to know whether to sympathize with the character or not by saddling him with the name, Otis Dumm.

Toth also makes great use of the Texas "backroads" locales and the colorful locals who populate it to give an extra sense of urgency to the tale while adding an unexpected layer. It's almost as if Toth knew his Dumm character would be

so confusing and polarizing to readers that he had to acquiesce to his choice of locale: though the story was set in the 1940s Texas itself hearkened back to the days where the good guys wore white and the bad guys black… enabling Toth to cast what some readers may consider a reactionary anti-hero in resplendent hero garb and win naysayers over to his (both Toth and Dumm's) cause.

The plot of this one is less involving and more episodic than Cosmo's story, yet also much more action-packed. A chance meeting with Dumm at a gas station puts the paranoid man in Patton's care, and it's a good thing, too as nefarious thugs are after Dumm! Turns out the old man has invented a fuel-less motor that runs on electromagnetics whose very existence would make current motors obsolete! Everyone wants it… so they can bury it and continue to have their businesses prosper! It's a much more densely scripted entry than its predecessor – particularly in the dialogue department – and yet it still works because once everyone's sympathies are with Otis there's no turning back.

While overall Toth's art is less exaggerated this outing, he adds an extra special touch not present in the previous tale: the Fox's totally white eye slits in his mask (nee The Phantom or Batman) are altered as needed to convey expressive reactions. The effect is more akin to the white eyes on Spider-Man's mask leaving the reader to wonder whether they are really "slits" at all. An effective choice that heightens the entertainment value of the story.

While Toth's contribution to the Fox only lasted two stories and a total of 20 pages, the influence of the stories lives on in Archie's new Fox stories published under its modern-day Red Circle imprint. Regular series collaborators Mark Waid and Dean Haspiel, along with such guest cover artists as Paul Pope and Darwyn Cooke haven't been shy in citing Toth's influence on their own Fox work.

Paul Castiglia is a veteran comic book writer, editor and historian who has worked for Archie, DC, Dark Horse and others. A frequent contributor to CBM, Castiglia researched and compiled all 12 editions of the Archie Americana Series over a 20 year span, and is co-writing and co-editing The MLJ Companion with Rik Offenberger for TwoMorrows Press.

The story of Alex Toth at Archie is one of those anomalies fitting of such an enigmatic creator. Starting with the fact that he had two extremely short-lived tenures at Archie a decade apart… and ending with the fact that in each decade he only contributed two complete stories!

Toth's first go-round came courtesy of a horror series that Archie published in the early 1970s. Beginning life as *Sabrina's Chilling Adventures in Sorcery*, it was an uneasy mix of truly horrific tales rendered in typical Dan DeCarlo-esque Archie style! Someone (readers… parents… editorial… management) must have caught on to the incongruity and the title was soon changed (starting with issue #3).

Archie decided they needed a unique name to separate the edgy Sorcery horror title from their squeaky clean teenage humor comics, and (in keeping with the series' various ghosts, vampires and zombies) "resurrected" a name from the past: Red Circle. The name went back to 1931 when future MLJ Comics co-founders Louis Silberkleit and Maurice Coyne were in business with future Timely/Marvel Comics founder Martin Goodman publishing pulps and paperback novels under the moniker.

The legendary Gray Morrow was at the editorial helm of the rechristened Red Circle Sorcery and with him came other legends: Larry Hama, Dick Giordano, Phil Seuling, Howard Chaykin, Bruce Jones, Frank Thorne, Jack Abel, Wally Wood, Doug Wildey, T. Casey Brennan… and Alex Toth. Toth delivered art for two of the series' most notable entries, *The Man Who Tried to Kill Death* (issue #8) and *If I Were King* (issue #9), both penned by Marvin Channing.

Fast-forward to the early 1980s and the dawn of the direct sales market. Archie decides to reboot their superheroes, originally seen in the 1940s, brought back in the late '50s/early '60s, and hibernating throughout the 1970s. John Carbonaro was the initial editor, followed by Rich Buckler, and then Bill DuBay.

Bill DuBay and Alex Toth had a prior working relationship on Warren Publishing's *Creepy* magazine. In an interview with Bradley S. Cobb on www.mightycrusaders.net, Bill DuBay said, "I knew there was one artist I had to have in the book – Alex Toth. I did want to give Alex Toth the opportunity to work on any of the old MLJ characters he pleased. He selected The Fox and it seemed as though it would be the perfect back-up series for The Black Hood."

Researched by Rik Offenberger

MILESTONE MEDIA

Milestone Media was formed by comic book industry veterans Dwayne McDuffie, Denys Cowan, and Michael Davis, and business executive Derek T. Dingle to increase minority representation in comic books. The company arranged a relatively unique deal through which their comics would be published by DC Comics with Milestone retaining full editorial control over the content.

In what would later be dubbed the "Dakotaverse," the main action was set in the fictional midwestern city of Dakota based on an extensive story bible created by McDuffie with character designs by Cowan.

In addition to editor Matt Wayne, Milestone recruited both established and then-up-and-coming talent, including M.D. Bright, Mike Gustovich, Noel Giddings, Robert Washington III, John Paul Leon, Shawn Martinbrough, John Rozum, Christopher Sotomayor, J.H. Williams III, Joseph Illidge, Ivan Velez, Jr., Tommy Lee Edwards, Humberto Ramos, Eric Battle, Prentis Rollins, ChrisCross (Christopher Williams) and J.Scott.J (Jason Scott Jones), among others.

The precipitating event for the arrival of most of the super-powered individuals in Dakota was "The Big Bang," a conflict between rival gangs in which the authorities intervened and used a dangerous gas to control the situation. The unintended consequences were many dead and some transformed. The survivors who manifested powers, "Bang Babies," were not always clearly cut good guys or bad guys.

The company launched its first four titles, *Hardware, Icon, Blood Syndicate* and *Static*, in 1993. At about the same time, the trading card company SkyBox released a card set, *Milestone: The Dakota Universe*, which focused on the characters and creators behind the company.

The non-Bang Baby series, *Icon*, an alien in human form, was written by McDuffie and illustrated by M.D. Bright. The technology-centric action-drama *Hardware* was written by McDuffie and illustrated by Cowan. The fluidity of super-powered gang life, which really explored the gray areas of good guys and bad guys, *Blood Syndicate*, was written by Ivan Velez, Jr. with the early issues illustrated by Trevor von Eeden, James Fry, ChrisCross, and Arvell Jones before settling on ChrisCross.

Static, co-written by McDuffie and Robert Washington III, and illustrated by John Paul Leon, was teenage life and struggles, bullies, popular people, romance, would-be romance, true friends, plenty of jerks, and a witty, brainy kid with newly acquired powers, just brimming with possibilities.

Shadow War, a crossover event that ran through the Milestone titles in early 1994, introduced two new titles, *Shadow Cabinet* and *Xombi*. Later that year, *Kobalt* was rolled out as another new title and the Milestone titles crossed over with the DC Universe in a 14-part event called *Worlds Collide*.

Davis left Milestone in 1995 to found Motown Machine Works, a comic book imprint published through Image Comics. Cowan would soon join him as editor-in-chief.

With the comic market devastated by the speculator boom-and-bust of the mid-'90s, Milestone stopped publishing in 1997.

With *Static Shock* airing as a popular cartoon (September 23, 2000 – May 22, 2004 on Kids' WB), the company released the four-issue mini-series *Static Shock: Rebirth of the Cool* in early 2001. That would be it for Milestone until 2010's two-part *Milestone Forever*, which actually delivered something that most Lost Universes fans never get: an actual conclusion before the characters were merged into the DC Universe for a while.

FIRST PUBLICATION:
Blood Syndicate #1 and *Hardware* #1 (both April 1993)

LAST PUBLICATION:
Hardware #50 (April 1997)

REVIVAL(S):
Static Shock: Rebirth of the Cool #1-4 (2001), *Milestone Forever* #1 (2010). Characters appeared in DCU titles following that. "Milestone 2.0" begins with *Milestone Returns* #0 (2021), *Static Season One, Icon & Rocket Season One*, and *Hardware Season One* (all 2021).

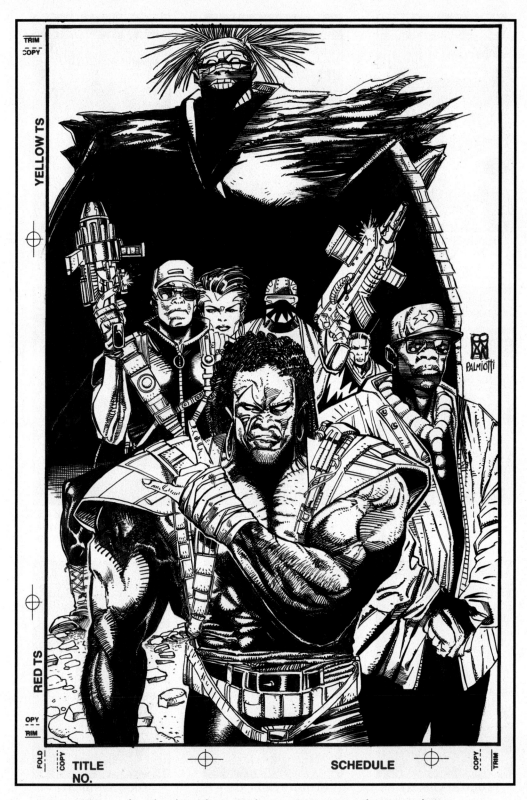

Cover art for *Blood Syndicate* #1 by Denys Cowan and Jimmy Palmiotti.
Image courtesy of Nick Katradis.

BLOOD SYNDICATE #1
Collector's Edition
April 1993
$1 $3 $8

BLOOD SYNDICATE #1
April 1993
$3

BLOOD SYNDICATE #2
May 1993
$3

BLOOD SYNDICATE #3
June 1993
$3

BLOOD SYNDICATE #4
July 1993
$3

BLOOD SYNDICATE #5
August 1993
$3

BLOOD SYNDICATE #6
September 1993
$3

BLOOD SYNDICATE #7
October 1993
$3

BLOOD SYNDICATE #8
November 1993
$3

BLOOD SYNDICATE #9
DECEMBER 1993
$3

BLOOD SYNDICATE #10
JANUARY 1994
$1 $4 $10

BLOOD SYNDICATE #11
FEBRUARY 1994
$3

BLOOD SYNDICATE #12
MARCH 1994
$3

BLOOD SYNDICATE #13
APRIL 1994
$3

BLOOD SYNDICATE #14
MAY 1994
$3

BLOOD SYNDICATE #15
JUNE 1994
$3

BLOOD SYNDICATE #16
JULY 1994
$3

BLOOD SYNDICATE #17
AUGUST 1994
$3

BLOOD SYNDICATE #18
SEPTEMBER 1994
$3

BLOOD SYNDICATE #19
OCTOBER 1994
$3

BLOOD SYNDICATE #20
NOVEMBER 1994
$3

BLOOD SYNDICATE #21
DECEMBER 1994
$3

BLOOD SYNDICATE #22
JANUARY 1995
$3

BLOOD SYNDICATE #23
FEBRUARY 1995
$3

BLOOD SYNDICATE #24
MARCH 1995
$3

BLOOD SYNDICATE #25
APRIL 1995
$4

BLOOD SYNDICATE #26
MAY 1995
$3

BLOOD SYNDICATE #27
JUNE 1995
$3

BLOOD SYNDICATE #28
JULY 1995
$3

BLOOD SYNDICATE #29
AUGUST 1995
$3

BLOOD SYNDICATE #30
SEPTEMBER 1995
$3

BLOOD SYNDICATE #31
OCTOBER 1995
$3

BLOOD SYNDICATE #32
NOVEMBER 1995
$3

BLOOD SYNDICATE #33
DECEMBER 1995
$3

BLOOD SYNDICATE #34
JANUARY 1996
$3

BLOOD SYNDICATE #35
FEBRUARY 1996
$4

DEATHWISH #1
DECEMBER 1994
$3

DEATHWISH #2
JANUARY 1995
$3

DEATHWISH #3
FEBRUARY 1995
$3

DEATHWISH #4
MARCH 1995
$3

HARDWARE #1
COLLECTOR'S EDITION
APRIL 1993
$6

HARDWARE #1
APRIL 1993
$3

HARDWARE #1
PLATINUM EDITION
APRIL 1993
$5 $15 $85

HARDWARE #2
EARLY MAY 1993
$3

HARDWARE #3
LATE MAY 1993
$3

HARDWARE #4
JUNE 1993
$3

HARDWARE #5
JULY 1993
$3

HARDWARE #6
AUGUST 1993
$3

HARDWARE #7
SEPTEMBER 1993
$3

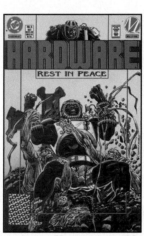

HARDWARE #8
OCTOBER 1993
$3

HARDWARE #9
NOVEMBER 1993
$3

HARDWARE #10
DECEMBER 1993
$3

HARDWARE #11
JANUARY 1994
$3

HARDWARE #12
FEBRUARY 1994
$3

HARDWARE #13
MARCH 1994
$3

HARDWARE #14
APRIL 1994
$3

HARDWARE #15
MAY 1994
$3

HARDWARE #16
JUNE 1994
$4

HARDWARE #17
JULY 1994
$3

HARDWARE #18
AUGUST 1994
$3

HARDWARE #19
SEPTEMBER 1994
$3

HARDWARE #20
OCTOBER 1994
$3

HARDWARE #21
NOVEMBER 1994
$3

HARDWARE #22
DECEMBER 1994
$3

HARDWARE #23
JANUARY 1995
$3

HARDWARE #24
FEBRUARY 1995
$3

HARDWARE #25
MARCH 1995
$4

HARDWARE #26
APRIL 1995
$3

HARDWARE #27
MAY 1995
$3

HARDWARE #28
JUNE 1995
$3

HARDWARE #29
JULY 1995
$3

HARDWARE #30
AUGUST 1995
$3

HARDWARE #31
SEPTEMBER 1995
$3

HARDWARE #32
OCTOBER 1995
$3

HARDWARE #33
NOVEMBER 1995
$3

HARDWARE #34
DECEMBER 1995
$3

HARDWARE #35
JANUARY 1996
$3

HARDWARE #36
FEBRUARY 1996
$3

HARDWARE #37
MARCH 1996
$3

HARDWARE #38
APRIL 1996
$3

HARDWARE #39
MAY 1996
$3

HARDWARE #40
JUNE 1996
$3

HARDWARE #41
JULY 1996
$3

HARDWARE #42
AUGUST 1996
$3

HARDWARE #43
SEPTEMBER 1996
$3

HARDWARE #44
OCTOBER 1996
$3

HARDWARE #45
NOVEMBER 1996
$3

HARDWARE #46
DECEMBER 1996
$3

HARDWARE #47
JANUARY 1997
$3

HARDWARE #48
FEBRUARY 1997
$3

HARDWARE #49
COVER BY MOEBIUS
MARCH 1997
$5 $15 $90

HARDWARE #50
APRIL 1997
$6

HARDWARE: THE MAN IN THE MACHINE TPB
2010
$20

HEROES #1
MAY 1996
$3

HEROES #2
JUNE 1996
$3

HEROES #3
JULY 1996
$3

HEROES #4
AUGUST 1996
$3

HEROES #5
SEPTEMBER 1996
$3

HEROES #6
NOVEMBER 1996
$3

ICON #1
COLLECTOR'S EDITION
MAY 1993
$2 $6 $20

ICON #1
MAY 1993
$1 $4 $10

ICON #2
JUNE 1993
$4

ICON #3
JULY 1993
$4

ICON #4
AUGUST 1993
$4

ICON #5
SEPTEMBER 1993
$4

ICON #6
OCTOBER 1993
$4

ICON #7
NOVEMBER 1993
$4

ICON #8
DECEMBER 1993
$4

ICON #9
JANUARY 1994
$4

ICON #10
FEBRUARY 1994
$4

ICON #11
MARCH 1994
$4

ICON #12
APRIL 1994
$4

ICON #13
MAY 1994
$4

ICON #14
JUNE 1994
$4

ICON #15
JULY 1994
$4

ICON #16
AUGUST 1994
$4

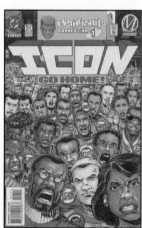

ICON #17
SEPTEMBER 1994
$4

ICON #18
OCTOBER 1994
$4

ICON #19
NOVEMBER 1994
$4

ICON #20
DECEMBER 1994
$4

ICON #21
JANUARY 1995
$4

ICON #22
FEBRUARY 1995
$4

ICON #23
MARCH 1995
$4

ICON #24
APRIL 1995
$4

ICON #25
MAY 1995
$6

ICON #26
JUNE 1995
$4

ICON #27
JULY 1995
$4

ICON #28
AUGUST 1995
$4

ICON #29
SEPTEMBER 1995
$4

ICON #30
OCTOBER 1995
$4

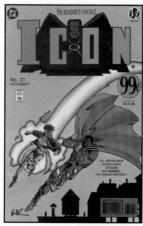

ICON #31
NOVEMBER 1995
$4

ICON #32
DECEMBER 1995
$4

ICON #33
JANUARY 1996
$4

ICON #34
FEBRUARY 1996
$4

ICON #35
MARCH 1996
$4

ICON #36
APRIL 1996
$4

ICON #37
SEPTEMBER 1996
$4

ICON #38
OCTOBER 1996
$4

ICON #39
NOVEMBER 1996
$4

ICON #40
DECEMBER 1996
$4

ICON #41
JANUARY 1997
$4

ICON #42
FEBRUARY 1997
$4

**ICON A HERO'S WELCOME
TPB**
2009
$3 $9 $45

**ICON: MOTHERSHIP
CONNECTION TPB**
MAY 2010
$25

KOBALT #1
JUNE 1994
$3

KOBALT #2
JULY 1994
$3

KOBALT #3
AUGUST 1994
$3

KOBALT #4
SEPTEMBER 1994
$3

KOBALT #5
OCTOBER 1994
$3

KOBALT #6
NOVEMBER 1994
$3

KOBALT #7
DECEMBER 1994
$3

KOBALT #8
JANUARY 1995
$3

KOBALT #9
FEBRUARY 1995
$3

KOBALT #10
MARCH 1995
$3

KOBALT #11
APRIL 1995
$3

KOBALT #12
JUNE 1995
$3

KOBALT #13
EARLY JULY 1995
$3

KOBALT #14
JULY 1995
$3

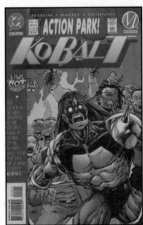

KOBALT #15
AUGUST 1995
$3

KOBALT #16
SEPTEMBER 1995
$3

THE LONG HOT SUMMER #1
JULY 1995
$3

THE LONG HOT SUMMER #2
AUGUST 1995
$3

THE LONG HOT SUMMER #3
SEPTEMBER 1995
$3

MY NAME IS HOLOCAUST #1
MAY 1995
$5

MY NAME IS HOLOCAUST #2
JUNE 1995
$5

MY NAME IS HOLOCAUST #3
JULY 1995
$5

MY NAME IS HOLOCAUST #4
AUGUST 1995
$5

MY NAME IS HOLOCAUST #5
SEPTEMBER 1995
$5

SHADOW CABINET #0
JANUARY 1994
$1 $3 $8

SHADOW CABINET #1
JUNE 1994
$5

SHADOW CABINET #2
JULY 1994
$3

SHADOW CABINET #3
AUGUST 1994
$3

SHADOW CABINET #4
SEPTEMBER 1994
$3

SHADOW CABINET #5
OCTOBER 1994
$3

SHADOW CABINET #6
NOVEMBER 1994
$3

SHADOW CABINET #7
DECEMBER 1994
$3

SHADOW CABINET #8
JANUARY 1995
$3

SHADOW CABINET #9
FEBRUARY 1995
$3

SHADOW CABINET #10
MARCH 1995
$3

SHADOW CABINET #11
APRIL 1995
$3

SHADOW CABINET #12
MAY 1995
$3

SHADOW CABINET #13
JUNE 1995
$3

SHADOW CABINET #14
JULY 1995
$3

SHADOW CABINET #15
AUGUST 1995
$3

SHADOW CABINET #16
SEPTEMBER 1995
$3

SHADOW CABINET #17
OCTOBER 1995
$3

STATIC #1
COLLECTOR'S EDITION
JUNE 1993
$3 $9 $40

STATIC #1
JUNE 1993
$4 $12 $50

STATIC #1
PLATINUM EDITION
JUNE 1993
$10 $30 $200

STATIC #2
JULY 1993
$4

STATIC #3
AUGUST 1993
$4

STATIC #4
SEPTEMBER 1993
$4

STATIC #5
OCTOBER 1993
$4

STATIC #6
NOVEMBER 1993
$4

STATIC #7
DECEMBER 1993
$4

STATIC #8
JANUARY 1994
$4

STATIC #9
FEBRUARY 1994
$4

STATIC #10
MARCH 1994
$4

STATIC #11
APRIL 1994
$4

STATIC #12
MAY 1994
$4

STATIC #13
JUNE 1994
$4

STATIC #14
AUGUST 1994
$6

STATIC #15
SEPTEMBER 1994
$4

STATIC #16
OCTOBER 1994
$4

STATIC #17
NOVEMBER 1994
$4

STATIC #18
DECEMBER 1994
$4

STATIC #19
JANUARY 1995
$4

STATIC #20
FEBRUARY 1995
$4

STATIC #21
MARCH 1995
$4

STATIC #22
APRIL 1995
$4

STATIC #23
JUNE 1995
$4

STATIC #24
EARLY JULY 1995
$4

STATIC #25
LATE JULY 1995
$5

STATIC #26
AUGUST 1995
$4

STATIC #27
SEPTEMBER 1995
$4

STATIC #28
OCTOBER 1995
$4

STATIC #29
NOVEMBER 1995
$4

STATIC #30
DECEMBER 1995
$4

STATIC #31
JANUARY 1996
$4

STATIC #32
FEBRUARY 1996
$4

STATIC #33
MARCH 1996
$4

STATIC #34
APRIL 1996
$4

STATIC #35
MAY 1996
$4

STATIC #36
JUNE 1996
$4

STATIC #37
JULY 1996
$4

STATIC #38
AUGUST 1996
$4

STATIC #39
SEPTEMBER 1996
$4

STATIC #40
OCTOBER 1996
$4

STATIC #41
NOVEMBER 1996
$4

STATIC #42
DECEMBER 1996
$4

STATIC #43
JANUARY 1997
$4

STATIC #44
FEBRUARY 1997
$4

STATIC #45
COVER BY MOEBIUS
MARCH 1997
$300

STATIC: TRIAL BY FIRE TPB
2000
$2   **$6**   **$20**

WISE SON: THE WHITE WOLF #1
NOVEMBER 1996
$1 $4 $10

WISE SON: THE WHITE WOLF #2
DECEMBER 1996
$5

WISE SON: THE WHITE WOLF #3
JANUARY 1997
$5

WISE SON: THE WHITE WOLF #4
FEBRUARY 1997
$5

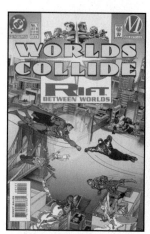

WORLDS COLLIDE #1
JULY 1994
$4

WORLDS COLLIDE #1
POLYBAGGED WITH VINYL CLINGS
JULY 1994
$5

XOMBI #0
JANUARY 1994
$8

XOMBI #1
JUNE 1994
$1 $3 $8

XOMBI #1
PLATINUM EDITION
JUNE 1994
$2 $6 $15

XOMBI #2
JULY 1994
$5

XOMBI #3
AUGUST 1994
$5

XOMBI #4
SEPTEMBER 1994
$5

XOMBI #5
OCTOBER 1994
$5

XOMBI #6
NOVEMBER 1994
$5

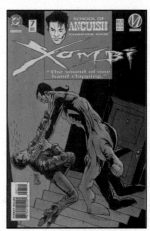

XOMBI #7
DECEMBER 1994
$5

XOMBI #8
JANUARY 1995
$5

XOMBI #9
FEBRUARY 1995
$5

XOMBI #10
MARCH 1995
$5

XOMBI #11
APRIL 1995
$5

XOMBI #12
MAY 1995
$5

XOMBI #13
JUNE 1995
$5

XOMBI #14
JULY 1995
$5

XOMBI #15
AUGUST 1995
$5

XOMBI #16
SEPTEMBER 1995
$5

XOMBI #17
OCTOBER 1995
$5

XOMBI #18
NOVEMBER 1995
$5

XOMBI #19
DECEMBER 1995
$5

XOMBI #20
JANUARY 1996
$5

XOMBI #21
FEBRUARY 1996
$5

STATIC SHOCK: REBIRTH OF THE COOL #1
JANUARY 2001
$5 $15 $85

STATIC SHOCK: REBIRTH OF THE COOL #2
FEBRUARY 2001
$4 $12 $60

STATIC SHOCK: REBIRTH OF THE COOL #3
MAY 2001
$3 $9 $40

STATIC SHOCK: REBIRTH OF THE COOL #4
SEPTEMBER 2001
$3 $9 $40

STATIC SHOCK: REBIRTH OF THE COOL TPB
2009
$20

MILESTONE FOREVER #1
APRIL 2010
$2 $6 $15

MILESTONE FOREVER #2
MAY 2010
$6

ELECTRIFYING!

AN ISSUE-BY-ISSUE TOUR THROUGH THE INCREDIBLE FIRST YEAR OF STATIC

In the early 1990s, the comic book market was flooded with new titles, new characters, new publishers and new superhero universes. Many of them are gone and perhaps best forgotten, but among the standouts was high school student Virgil Hawkins, who became much more than a electrifying young hero anew to the comics scene. In the eyes of many critics and large number of fans, the hero Static became Milestone Media's thematic analog to the energy, relationship angst, feelings and trepidations of the earliest days of Stan Lee and Steve Ditko's Amazing Spider-Man *at Marvel.*

With a quick-witted big mouth and originally not much to back it up, the intelligent, opinionated Hawkins was caught up in the Big Bang, the event that transformed a number of citizens of the fictional city of Dakota into super-powered beings and Hawkins into the electromagnetic-powered Static.

Produced by writers Dwayne McDuffie & Robert L. Washington III and artists John Paul Leon, Steve Mitchell & Shawn C. Martinbrough, the young superhero helped make his city safe from the likes of Hotstreak and Holocaust, but the comic book Static *was more than just about super-powers. It focused on kids growing up and the issues that were important for the time – and for all times. It went deeper than many other super-hero titles in that era, and gave the reader his or her money's worth with every issue.*

The first year of the title, some have asserted, was the best monthly superhero comic book on the market at that time. Join us for this tour of Static *#1-12 and we'll show you why.*

Static #1
DC Comics; Milestone Media; June 1993
Trial by Fire Part One – Burning Sensation

"You don't start none there won't be none" is scrawled on the forefront of the premiere issue's front cover, and that's just about the high level of bravado that Virgil Hawkins gets up to when he's the hero Static.

Inside the comic, in his identity as Static, he's trying to protect an arcade that Frieda Goren, a young schoolmate who he's got a crush on, frequents. Suddenly, a group of gangbangers who work for a heavy named Hotstreak go after Frieda, and that's when Static enters the scene.

Taking out the "trash" like an electrically charged Spider-Man, he saves the day while reminding himself that as Static, he's not supposed to know his potential "girlfriend" while bidding her adieu.

The scene then changes to Static returning home as Virgil, where the reader meets his strong-willed mother and his overbearing sister, Sharon. After brief banter, he heads up to his bedroom to talk to Frieda on the phone, who has called to tell him how the hero Static saved her life.

The next day, Hawkins meets up with his friends at school – the ultra-cool Larry Wade and the overly sensitive ballet dancer Rick Stone – as well as Hotstreak's boys. Given the task to round up Frieda for Hotstreak, the toughs intimidate the students, with one of Hotstreak's thugs pulling out a gun.

Leaving the scene, Virgil transforms into Static, and he finds Frieda coming face-to-face with her pursuer, the mysterious Hotstreak. Super powers collide as Static and Hotstreak go head to head, with our hero getting the upper hand by binding a metal chain around the villain.

Then, as Hotstreak melts his bindings, Static recognizes his opponent as Biz Money B, a thug who bullied him at school. Falling to the ground after multiple punches, Static is defeated by Hotstreak, unintentionally shedding his mask and revealing his secret identity to his beloved Frieda while saying, "You don't understand. I can't fight him. I can't beat him. I can't… I can't…"

Not bad for a first issue, huh?

Static #2
DC Comics; Milestone Media; July 1993
Trial by Fire Part Two – Everything But the Girl

Static's origin issue opens up a little time after the end of the exciting series premiere, with Hawkins and Frieda discussing the climactic events of the first issue. This melds into a flashback of Hawkins' first meeting with Biz Money B, where he gets beaten up by the thug for attempting to defend Frieda's honor in school.

Flash forward to the present where Hawkins, crying and revealing his insecure side to Frieda, continues his story by describing the events that transpired on Paris Island on the night of the Big Bang – the genesis event that caused a number of Dakota's citizens to become super-powered.

With a gun that he acquired from his friend Larry firmly in hand, Hawkins was preparing himself to have his revenge on Biz Money B. While telling himself that he is not "a walking bullseye" and "a loser," he also comes to the sober conclusion that more importantly, he's not a killer either. This epiphany serves to reinforce Hawkins' character

and shows the reader just what kind of hero he really is, and he makes no bones about it.

Just as he's dumping the gun into the river, though, Hawkins gets caught up in the gas of the Big Bang. Laid unconscious for some time, Hawkins awakens to see Biz Money B down on the ground and mistakenly considered dead, and then looks up to find super-powered people flying toward the city. Then, Hawkins finds himself the target of the mysterious "Indigo Base" authorities, which prompts him to first use his electromagnetic powers to defend himself.

His first show of force works, and he flies out of Paris Island no longer Hawkins – but now the super-hero Static. Coming back to the present, Hawkins tells Frieda that "so a legend was born," and chronicles the time it took to practice his skills, so he could bust up crack houses, street thugs, and fight other crime – victories that stopped when he met Biz Money B again. Realizing what he had to do, he sets out to face Hotstreak once more – and this time, to the reader's surprise, there's little or no resistance from the super-powered bully.

Triumphantly returning to Frieda's house where he stands floating just outside her upstairs window, Static learns to his displeasure that she only thinks of him as a friend. Meanwhile, he's caught the eye of another, Holocaust, who wants Static to either work for him . . . or die.

Static #3

DC Comics; Milestone Media; August 1993

Trial by Fire Part Three – Pounding the Pavement

"Pounding the Pavement" starts off with lots of action – and lots of sparks! Static spends the first several pages of the issue saving armies of victims from near disaster using a combination of his superhuman abilities and the lessons he learned from his Chemistry One class.

Then, after all the excitement, we see him at his part-time job, performing mundane tasks like washing dishes. It's through this plot point that

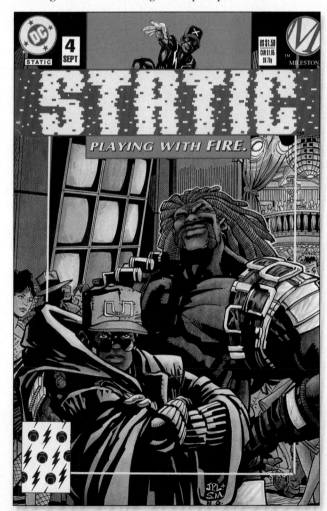

we see another of Hawkins' impressive traits: modesty. It's also at this time that he receives a phone call at work from Frieda, who informs him that some "terminator guy" is after Static.

Hawkins immediately tells his boss, Ms. Ervin, that he's got to go and that it's an emergency – whether she decides to fire him or not. Fast forward to Static in downtown Dakota, where he learns that his pursuer is named Tarmack. After acquiring this knowledge, Static returns home and prepares for school the next day.

It's at school that he learns that Tarmack is nearby, and a battle between the two soon takes place. The fight turns out to be a draw, when suddenly, Tarmack throws a car on an innocent bystander and demands that he and Static settle their differences once and for all in Bradshaw's Parking Lot at midnight.

After the fight – and after school – Hawkins and his friends are taking the subway home and talking about the big fight between Static and Tarmack. It's during this exchange that Frieda tells Hawkins and the others that Tarmack is older and bigger, and that Static should leave him to the more powerful Milestone character, Icon.

Before leaving the train, Hawkins whispers to Frieda that he has two things for the upcoming fight that Tarmack doesn't – a brain and a plan. Later, outside of Bradshaw's, Static meets up with Tarmack for a fight to the finish.

But after a relatively one-sided battle where Static is winning, the hero finally takes Holocaust's soldier down for the count…but not without Holocaust bringing the fight to Static.

Static #4

DC Comics; Milestone Media; September 1993

Trial by Fire Part Four – Playing with Fire

Picking up where the last issue left off, Static talks with Holocaust. On the surface, it seems that Holocaust wants Static to understand that he either takes or "he'll be took," that the rich are only rich because of their "birthright" and luck, not because of brains or talent.

It comes down to one thing: Holocaust wants Static to watch his back. To that end, Holocaust shows Static his gratitude by introducing him to his women, and presenting a life that the young hero could have.

The next panel finds Static (flying) and Holocaust (relaxing in his limo) entering Don Giacomo Cornelius' mansion at 1:15 in the morning. Holocaust starts using his fire powers on the thugs, before Static interrupts and says he'll take care of them (in a more humane way). Holocaust then screams that Cornelius family got most of their wealth "off the backs of my people."

After leaving the compound in flames, Static makes his way to Frieda's home, where he finds her in the arms of his friend, Larry. After blowing up at his discovery, he leaves while remarking that he can't "trust anyone else around here."

The next day, Hawkins is woken up and confronted by his mom and his sister about losing his job. To his surprise, his mom has Sharon take over his job and informs him that if he finds "something to do with himself, to let her know."

Hawkins then hangs out with his friends and finds out that Larry and Frieda have been an item even before they met – and that everybody knew but him. The scene then changes to Hawkins' bedroom, where he gets a call from Frieda trying to explain herself, which pushes him over the edge.

On the way out of the house, he tells his mom that he's going to see a man about "a real job." Next, we find Static next to Holocaust's SUV, where he is taking care of business and laying waste to mobsters everywhere. Once they get inside Don Cornelius' mansion, Holocaust decides to hurt the mobster's young son – at least that's the intent until Static steps in, saves the day, and says his piece.

After a less-than-friendly send off by Holocaust, he then talks to Larry in his bedroom, who tells him that he doesn't have to lose his friendship with Frieda because of the couple.

Meanwhile, as he picks up the phone – it's Frieda – his mom asks him whether

the job he talked about earlier was "no hoodlum kind of job." He says no, and she replies: "Good, we raised you better than that."

Static #5
DC Comics; Milestone Media; October 1993
Louder Than a Bomb Chapter One – Megablast

Page one finds Hawkins right smack dab in the middle of a race riot between blacks and Jews. While trying to separate the warring parties, he creates a repulsion field to keep everybody away from each other until they calm down.

Flashback to Hawkins at his favorite comic book store playing a role-playing game with friends when one of them remembers that he has a date with Daisy Watkins. After saying that he didn't remember any date, Daisy walks in, confronts Hawkins, and leaves in tears. Processing that she really wanted a date with him, Hawkins then hears about the riot at Temple Beth Ad and, next

thing he knows, he's running crowd control – super-powers style.

Fast-forward to a Jewish rabbi and a black pastor holding hands, jointly lecturing and pointing out the uselessness of continued violence. Afterward, the rabbi and the pastor meet with Static and ask him to speak at an assembly against Commando X and his recent bombings – the reason for the riot. Static at first doesn't know what to say – then accepts.

Segue way to Hawkins in school, where after some small talk between Larry and Frieda, our hero uses his electromagnetic powers to activate the sprinkler system after Commando X attacked his school. Later, at a restaurant, Hawkins and his friends debate Commando X and his tactics, when he tells Frieda and everybody else that Static will be at the peace rally on Saturday.

Finally, the big day comes, and Static gets ready for his big speech, when all of a sudden Commando X makes himself heard at the assembly – putting Static on the defensive. Then, Commando X unleashes a plethora of bombs on the peace rally – leaving Static seemingly helpless!

Static #6
DC Comics; Milestone Media; November 1993
Louder Than a Bomb Chapter Two – War at 30 Frames Per Second

As Static fights to save the people assembled at the peace rally from Commando X, he remarks: "Listen X, we came here to get a little peace – not wind up in little pieces." He then uses his electromagnetism to have the stadium chairs scoop up the bombs and move them safely away. Static then chases after Commando X – until he loses his magnetic field after Commando X touched something that just blew up (that's his power).

Static then flies atop the loud speaker and says: "Commando X! I don't care if you can hear me or not -- we are at war! Armageddon is in effect! There will be no late pass! Whatever it takes, you're going down!"

Then, at the Dakota Library, Hawkins and Frieda talk about the peace rally and the fact that a lot of people would have been hurt if not for Static. Hawkins also finds out that Commando X is a black militant zealot named Howell X, and that he's been sending op-ed letters to both of Dakota's newspapers, *The Chronicle* and *The North Star*. Hawkins also learns that Howell X had a public access TV show, and calls the cable company to get a tape.

At home, he watches the tape to get leads on Commando X's next target. On the tape, he finds one show referencing "pigs" – so he knows he's after the S.H.R.E.D. and anti-gang unit, G.R.I.N.D., at the old downtown precinct. Getting into costume, Hawkins becomes Static and heads towards trouble. Near the precinct, he finds some cop effigies that are set to explode. He then sends them flying and the bombs safely explode several stories higher in the air above the cops.

The next day at school, Hawkins, Frieda and Rick talk about the success found in both the Jewish and black communities. Hawkins and Rick also talk about what happened to Daisy, and how our hero should apologize – and he does, while also inviting her to a matinee. And as luck would have it, she agrees to the date.

Later, at home, Hawkins discovers that the tapes were made at the Rockdale Housing Apartments – or better known as the Rock. At the complex, he comes across Howell X, and pretends to be a fan. Hawkins learns that Commando X has planted some more bombs, and is offered the chance to get out all the statements to the media. The last image is Howell X offering Hawkins the phone.

Static #7

DC Comics; Milestone Media; December 1993
Louder Than a Bomb Chapter Three – You're Gonna Get Yours

The first page picks up right where we left off on *Static* #6, with Howell X (a.k.a. Commando X) offering Hawkins the chance to call the media. Through coming up with distractions (excuses for going to the bathroom, getting change for

phone calls, getting gas), he heads to City Hall, where he finds the hidden bomb in a van parked in the garage. Drawing enough power to shoot the van into the air, it explodes harmlessly over City Hall.

Hawkins then returns home to find his mom and dad (first appearance) waiting up to talk to him about the militant "Malcolm 10" program he was using for his investigation of Howell X.

Meanwhile at Frieda's house, her father and mother are talking to Frieda about the Jews easier integration into American society because they are white, and how racism, sadly, works both ways for them. Right afterward, Hawkins and Frieda call each other on the phone, and decide that they both have a lot to talk about. At the same time, they try to figure out Commando X's next target – and they come up with WDKA Studios.

Much later, Static finds his quarry on the studio's grounds. Commando X tries to take Static out of the way by exploding gasoline, but he gets away and wraps Commando X – and his bombs – up in wire. And by wrapping Commando X's hands, prevents the militant from using his power.

Returning late at home with his mom and dad still awake, he's left to climb his wall and get to bed. In the morning, Frieda calls him up and tells Hawkins that Static is famous and running on Channel 11. Our hero – fighting the good fight no matter what!

Static #8

DC Comics; Milestone Media; January 1994
Shadow War Crossover – Needless to Say, The Party Broke Up

Featuring a cover by comics legend Walter Simonson, this issue starts with Static versus a villain by the name of the Botanist, who has the unlikely power of making plants grow. After defeating him, the comic segues to members of the Shadow Cabinet – Dharma and Plus – discussing Static, with Plus calling him "talky but huggable." She is reminded that Static is important to both the Shadow Cabinet . . . and the world.

Meanwhile, Frieda is buying snacks for Hawkins and his friends, and talking about the role-playing games she *won't* be playing with them, as well as the house party that they all have to attend (her parents are gone for three weeks, after all).

Then, when he's off on his own and going to his secret garage headquarters, Static runs into Funyl, a member of the Shadow Cabinet who "funnels" him to the top of the Eiffel Tower in Paris, France. After they agree to talk, Funyl transports them both back to the garage, where Hawkins learns about the Shadow Cabinet – and their place for him.

After saying that he'd join the Shadow Cabinet, he heads out to Frieda's house for the party. There, he meets Plus, who comes at an inconvenient time. (Daisy comes up to see Hawkins when he's "alone" . . . and then subsequently turns around and leaves.) Then, Funyl comes out of nowhere and, with Plus, tells Hawkins that some gangbangers are moving against him. Hawkins – who wants nothing to happen to Frieda's house or his friends – turns into Static, and with Plus' help, take down the bad guys.

Funyl comes back to get Static and Plus – only to let slip that they had a homing device in Static's badge, and that's how they were able to keep tabs on him. With Funyl leaving, Plus takes Static to a dark closet – and they both disappear to the amazement of the partygoers.

The action then continues in *Shadow Cabinet* #0.

Static #9
DC Comics; Milestone Media; February 1994
Static Needs a New Pair of Shoes (In which our fab phenom finds fashionable form-fitting footwear fit for foe-fighting)

Static starts things off by leaping into action in the mall, chasing down a shoplifting operation. He unarms the would-be felons and reverses their polarity so they are stuck to the ground, ready for mall security.

Flashback to Hawkins riding the train downtown with Frieda, who is surprised to learn that he wants to spend his last dollar buying "fighting" shoes for his Static costume. As he says, he hasn't had a decent pair of shoes since he fought Tarmack in issue #3. When he gets to the store, though, he realizes a theft is taking place – by little "hardened criminals." Transforming back into Static, he confronts one of the thieves, who says, "Mamma's sick, she's been in the basement too long. I gotta get stuff. Lemme go!"

In the middle of that, the little guy drops some gold rings and runs off with his twin. Hawkins, changed back to his normal self, finds Frieda and they head off the jewelry store to return the rings. They do just that, but the store manager thinks they were part of the operation and calls security. Suddenly,

the manager sees micro-versions of the thieves running around the jewelry display case and picking up pricey trinkets for themselves. Hawkins scoops them up with his hat, and finds himself chased by the rest of the thieves, all identical except for their varying sizes.

Trying to find a place to change (again), Hawkins climbs down an elevator shaft and becomes Static. Then the little thieves fall down around him, transforming into a single enemy named Virus, who's out to protect a mannequin he calls Mamma. After a fierce battle, where the mannequin catches on fire, Static learns Virus' "origin" and wants to help out the teenager. He makes him a bike, makes the big juvenile promise not to steal again, and then flies him over to St. Peter's Mission.

When all is said and done, Hawkins catches up with Frieda and misses out on his shoes – or does he..? The store manager of the shoe store recognizes Hawkins as the kid who stopped the earlier robbery, opens up the store, and says there's a "special discount for junior crime stoppers." Frieda, on the other hand sees the hero's reward as another reason for Hawkins to play super-hero – and she thinks that's one thing that should be stopped now.

Static #10

DC Comics; Milestone Media; March 1994
Escort Etiquette for Guyz Chapter One – Mystery Date

The comic starts out with a bang, as Static and Frieda fly out of the page and into the story. Static is giving Frieda the thrill ride of her life, when suddenly he remembers – via flashback – that he, Rick, Felix, and Frieda were playing a role-playing game (Frieda beats Hawkins, for shame, and gave her the right to wear a t-shirt that would say "I Beat Virgil O. Hawkins on His Best Day"), when suddenly the boys show her their self-made comic book, *Captain Lightning.*

Afterward, and with some polite words concerning the comic book, Frieda is confronted by Hawkins, who says he'd do anything if not for the t-shirt. And thus, the joyride begins. Then, Frieda jumps off Static's back and points out a car theft in progress. Static comes in and saves the day, and tracks the stolen car and gets it to the cops. He then picks up Frieda – who's impressed – and finishes up the joyride.

At his secret garage headquarters, he changes while talking to Frieda about Daisy. The next day at school, Hawkins tells Daisy that the Indian super-hero girl who appeared and disappeared at Frieda's party was looking for Static, and there was nothing to it. Daisy ponders it and says with a giggle that maybe she'll call Hawkins later.

Happy, Hawkins then comes across his old friend, Larry, who is dating Frieda. Making up, the two friends wander down the school hallway when another friend comes up to Hawkins and talks about how his cousin is in love with Static.

After stopping by the Fish Shack to harass his sister, he heads to the Tab to meet Puff, a girl who seems to have a serious crush on him. After passing her flowers in mid-air, she wants to get physical. When Static tries to slow things down, she turns violent – revealing that like Static, she too is a Bang Baby.

In response to this, he realizes that "gas girl" just ate through a concrete piling. A battle ensues and it looks like Static is going to get away, except he gets wrapped in chain by Coil – and things don't even begin to look good!

Static #11

DC Comics; Milestone Media; April 1994
Escort Etiquette for Guyz Chapter Two – Double Date

Picking up where the last issue left off, Coil tells Static that he's been set up and the flowers that he brought will be put on his grave. Puff poses with a strung up Static for a picture. Then, Static swings his chain into the Puff's lingering acid cloud and

breaks loose from his femmes fatale. Static asks if they are trying to use this attack on him as a way to get in good with a gang. They reply that they want all the gangs, and that the girls are going to run Dakota. Finally, he gets away – but they say they've still got the photo of Static tied up.

After the super-powered battle, he heads by the Fish Shack to see if he can get his old job back. And after an impassioned appeal for the job, he succeeds. The next day at school, the usual bickering is going on (Rick takes serious offense when his friend calls his shirt "fruit-flavored"), and Daisy and Hawkins have a chat (Hawkins forgets the date that he promised last issue). So, he either fights the supervillains or has a date with Daisy. Following his gut reaction to treat life like an *Archie* comic, he chooses both.

After choosing his proper attire – both civilian and super-hero – he meets up with Larry's car, and goes to the concert with his friends . . . and Daisy. At 6:45, Hawkins makes his move, telling everybody he's going to the concession stand, when actually he turns into Static and searches for Coil and Puff. Finding Puff's acid cloud, the brawl begins.

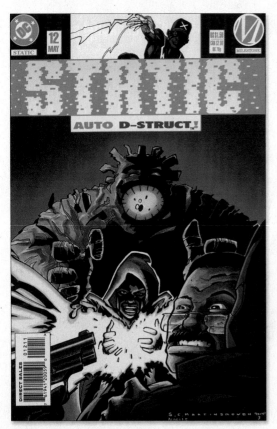

Static splashes her with water, diluting her acid and, paraphrasing our hero, bringing her "acid reign" to an end. And with all the water she absorbed, Hawkins made Puff fat. He then goes back to the concert and brings the food back to his friends, He gives the food to Frieda, and says he's going to go into the t-shirt line – when he's off to fight Coil. He challenges her inside Bradshaw's, where she can't control anything outside. He uses his force field, breaks out of his chains, and gives her a kiss – as well as takes a picture of her defeat.

Back at the concert, he gets Daisy a t-shirt and learns that Frieda covered for him – he supposedly had digestive-trouble from eating Indian food.

Static #12
DC Comics; Milestone Media; May 1994
Getting Out

The end of the series' first year begins with Static on patrol, when all of a sudden, a Buick flies out from nowhere and almost hits him. The culprit was D-Struct Briggs, another Bang Baby, who is jealous of Static. And when some thugs take D-Struct's father and say they'll kill him if he doesn't kill Static, then he knows what he has to do.

But that also leaves Static to think of a way to save his own butt. So, when D-Struct comes into school, Hawkins transforms into Static and confronts his new nemesis. He tells him that by working together, they'll save his dad – and that he has a plan.

While D-Struct takes pot shots at him, Hawkins gives him a grand tour of Sadler and the other neighborhoods of Dakota. The last location is where D-Struct's dad is being held, and they literally crash the party. As D-Struct goes after Static, he's taking out one gangster after another – to the point that the thugs think they're working together. As Static joins in and kicks major booty, D-Struct finds his father . . . safe and sound.

Segue to D-Struct meeting Static and telling him he and his father are leaving Dakota. In D-Struct's words, he doesn't want to be a super-hero or a super-villain, he just wants to go to college.

And at the end, he tells Static that he hopes he and the Superman-esque hero Icon and the others keep fighting, because some day he wants to come home.

John Paul Leon and Steve Mitchell's original art for *Static* #6 Page 20.
Image courtesy of Heritage Auctions.

NEW UNIVERSE (MARVEL)

To celebrate the 25th anniversary of Marvel Comics, the company launched the New Universe. While behind the scenes budgets were being axed, what readers saw was a different approach. The New Universe was designed to be separate from the existing Marvel Universe and provide a setting in which superheroes were previously nonexistent and events moved much closer to real time than in standard comics.

Along with Editor-in-Chief Jim Shooter, creators Archie Goodwin, Eliot R. Brown, Mark Gruenwald, John Morelli, Tom DeFalco, and Michael Higgins played significant roles in developing the line's original eight titles. Shooter described the universe as "Simply deciding to use a universe hitherto unused in comics. Our own. No repulsors. No unstable molecules. In fact, no fantasy or fantastic elements at all except for the very few we introduce. Carefully. Does it make sense? You bet!"

It began with the "White Event," which took place in *Star Brand* #1. Created by Shooter and illustrated by John Romita, Jr. and Al Williamson, the story set in motion events that led to the creation of humans with paranormal abilities. The Star Brand is a black, star-shaped tattoo-like mark that provides infinite, god-like powers to the person branded with the mark. In this case, Ken Connell of Pittsburgh. The original wielder of the Star Brand, known as the Old Man, transferred the power to Ken Connell. Although the title was demoted to bimonthly after Shooter left Marvel, it remained the key to the New Universe and is the concept most revisited in the years since.

D.P. 7 (Displaced Paranormals) is tied for the New Universe's longest running title and was the most stable in terms of its creative team. It ran a total of 32 regular issues and one annual. Writer Mark Gruenwald, penciler Paul Ryan, and colorist Paul Becton were on for the entire run, with inker Danny Bulanadi on board for #10-32. The title featured seven main characters that received paranormal abilities thanks to the White Event.

FIRST PUBLICATION:
Star Brand #1 (October 1986)

LAST PUBLICATION:
The War #4 (March 1990)

REVIVAL(S):
Untold Tales of the New Universe one-shots (2006), *newuniversal* mini-series and one-shots (2007), *Starbrand and Nightmask* mini-series (2016), and multiple appearances in the Marvel Universe.

Psi-Force, which also ran 32 regular issues and one annual, was one of the more popular of the New Universe titles with favorable reviews making comparisons to the X-Men. The comic focused on a group of adolescents who had developed psionic powers following the White Event. Created by Archie Goodwin and Walter Simonson, creators who worked on the book included writer Fabian Nicieza (#9, 13, 16-32), artist Ron Lim (#16-22), and writer Danny Fingeroth (#3-15). Artists Mark Texeira and Bob Hall also contributed.

The balance of the original line-up included *Kickers, Inc.*, *Mark Hazzard: Merc*, *Justice*, *Nightmask*, and *Spitfire and the Troubleshooters*. Perhaps the title most in search of an identity, *Spitfire* had three different titles during a 13-issue run. The initial title ran seven issues before changing to *Spitfire*, followed three issues later by *Codename: Spitfire* for its final four.

Kickers, Inc., *Mark Hazzard: Merc*, *Nightmask*, and *Codename: Spitfire* were canceled at the one-year mark or immediately thereafter. The May 1988 cover-dated issues of the remaining original series, *Star Brand* #13, *D.P. 7* #19, *PSI-Force* #19, and *Justice* #19, increased cover prices from 75¢ to $1.25 and page counts from 22 to 28 editorial pages. They also became Direct Market only offerings at that point.

Continuing events from *Star Brand* #12 (trying to rid himself of the Star Brand, Ken Connell unleashed power, which became known as the Black Event), a series of graphic novels – *The Pitt* (March 1998), *The Draft* (November 1988), and *The War* #1 (October 1989), #2 (November 1989), and #3 (December 1989) – brought the original incarnation of the New Universe to a close in *The War* #4 (March 1990).

This, of course, makes it one of the few lost universes to get a firm conclusion, but that doesn't mean that diehard fans ever lost interest. There have been several revivals over the years.

– Charles S. Novinskie

Co-creator Paul Ryan's original cover art for *D.P. 7 #2*. Image courtesy of the Estate of Paul Ryan. Special thanks to Jason Versaggi.

D.P. 7 #1
NOVEMBER 1986
$3

D.P. 7 #2
DECEMBER 1986
$3

D.P. 7 #3
JANUARY 1987
$3

D.P. 7 #4
FEBRUARY 1987
$3

D.P. 7 #5
MARCH 1987
$3

D.P. 7 #6
APRIL 1987
$3

D.P. 7 #7
MAY 1987
$3

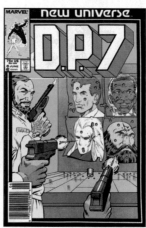

D.P. 7 #8
JUNE 1987
$3

D.P. 7 #9
JULY 1987
$3

D.P. 7 #10
AUGUST 1987
$3

D.P. 7 #11
SEPTEMBER 1987
$3

D.P. 7 #12
OCTOBER 1987
$3

D.P. 7 #13
NOVEMBER 1987
$3

D.P. 7 #14
DECEMBER 1987
$3

D.P. 7 #15
JANUARY 1988
$3

D.P. 7 #16
FEBRUARY 1988
$3

D.P. 7 #17
MARCH 1988
$3

D.P. 7 #18
APRIL 1988
$3

D.P. 7 #19
MAY 1988
$3

D.P. 7 #20
JUNE 1988
$3

D.P. 7 #21
JULY 1988
$4

D.P. 7 #22
AUGUST 1988
$4

D.P. 7 #23
SEPTEMBER 1988
$4

D.P. 7 #24
OCTOBER 1988
$4

D.P. 7 #25
NOVEMBER 1988
$4

D.P. 7 #26
DECEMBER 1988
$4

D.P. 7 #27
JANUARY 1989
$4

D.P. 7 #28
FEBRUARY 1989
$4

D.P. 7 #29
MARCH 1989
$4

D.P. 7 #30
APRIL 1989
$4

D.P. 7 #31
MAY 1989
$4

D.P. 7 #32
JUNE 1989
$4

D.P. 7 ANNUAL #1
NOVEMBER 1987
$4

THE DRAFT #1
NOVEMBER 1988
$4

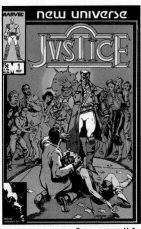

JUSTICE #1
NOVEMBER 1986
$3

JUSTICE #2
DECEMBER 1986
$3

JUSTICE #3
JANUARY 1987
$3

JUSTICE #4
FEBRUARY 1987
$3

JUSTICE #5
MARCH 1987
$3

JUSTICE #6
APRIL 1987
$3

JUSTICE #7
MAY 1987
$3

JUSTICE #8
JUNE 1987
$3

JUSTICE #9
JULY 1987
$3

JUSTICE #10
AUGUST 1987
$3

JUSTICE #11
SEPTEMBER 1987
$3

JUSTICE #12
OCTOBER 1987
$3

JUSTICE #13
NOVEMBER 1987
$3

JUSTICE #14
DECEMBER 1987
$3

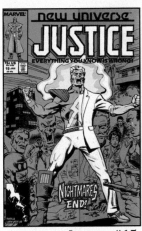

JUSTICE #15
JANUARY 1988
$3

JUSTICE #16
FEBRUARY 1988
$3

JUSTICE #17
MARCH 1988
$3

JUSTICE #18
APRIL 1988
$3

JUSTICE #19
MAY 1988
$3

JUSTICE #20
JUNE 1988
$3

JUSTICE #21
JULY 1988
$3

JUSTICE #22
AUGUST 1988
$3

JUSTICE #23
SEPTEMBER 1988
$3

JUSTICE #24
OCTOBER 1988
$3

JUSTICE #25
NOVEMBER 1988
$3

JUSTICE #26
DECEMBER 1988
$3

JUSTICE #27
JANUARY 1989
$3

JUSTICE #28
FEBRUARY 1989
$3

JUSTICE #29
MARCH 1989
$3

JUSTICE #30
APRIL 1989
$3

JUSTICE #31
MAY 1989
$3

JUSTICE #32
JUNE 1989
$3

KICKERS INC. #1
NOVEMBER 1986
$6

KICKERS INC. #2
DECEMBER 1986
$4

KICKERS INC. #3
JANUARY 1987
$4

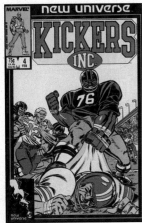

KICKERS INC. #4
FEBRUARY 1987
$4

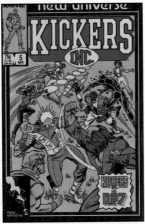

KICKERS INC. #5
MARCH 1987
$4

KICKERS INC. #6
APRIL 1987
$4

KICKERS INC. #7
MAY 1987
$4

KICKERS INC. #8
JUNE 1987
$4

KICKERS INC. #9
JULY 1987
$4

KICKERS INC. #10
AUGUST 1987
$4

KICKERS INC. #11
SEPTEMBER 1987
$4

KICKERS INC. #12
OCTOBER 1987
$4

MARK HAZZARD: MERC #1
NOVEMBER 1986
$5

MARK HAZZARD: MERC #2
DECEMBER 1986
$3

MARK HAZZARD: MERC #3
JANUARY 1987
$3

MARK HAZZARD: MERC #4
FEBRUARY 1987
$3

MARK HAZZARD: MERC #5
MARCH 1987
$3

MARK HAZZARD: MERC #6
APRIL 1987
$3

MARK HAZZARD: MERC #7
MAY 1987
$3

MARK HAZZARD: MERC #8
JUNE 1987
$3

MARK HAZZARD: MERC #9
JULY 1987
$3

MARK HAZZARD: MERC #10
AUGUST 1987
$3

MARK HAZZARD: MERC #11
SEPTEMBER 1987
$3

MARK HAZZARD: MERC #12
OCTOBER 1987
$3

**MARK HAZZARD: MERC
ANNUAL #1**
NOVEMBER 1987
$4

NIGHTMASK #1
NOVEMBER 1986
$3

NIGHTMASK #2
DECEMBER 1986
$3

NIGHTMASK #3
JANUARY 1987
$3

NIGHTMASK #4
FEBRUARY 1987
$3

NIGHTMASK #5
MARCH 1987
$3

NIGHTMASK #6
APRIL 1987
$3

NIGHTMASK #7
MAY 1987
$3

NIGHTMASK #8
JUNE 1987
$3

NIGHTMASK #9
JULY 1987
$3

NIGHTMASK #10
AUGUST 1987
$3

NIGHTMASK #11
SEPTEMBER 1987
$3

NIGHTMASK #12
OCTOBER 1987
$3

THE PITT #1
MARCH 1988
$4

PSI-FORCE #1
NOVEMBER 1986
$3

PSI-FORCE #2
DECEMBER 1986
$3

PSI-FORCE #3
JANUARY 1987
$3

PSI-FORCE #4
FEBRUARY 1987
$3

PSI-FORCE #5
MARCH 1987
$3

PSI-FORCE #6
APRIL 1987
$3

PSI-FORCE #7
MAY 1987
$3

PSI-FORCE #8
JUNE 1987
$3

PSI-FORCE #9
JULY 1987
$3

PSI-FORCE #10
AUGUST 1987
$3

PSI-FORCE #11
SEPTEMBER 1987
$3

PSI-FORCE #12
OCTOBER 1987
$3

PSI-FORCE #13
NOVEMBER 1987
$3

PSI-FORCE #14
DECEMBER 1987
$3

PSI-FORCE #15
JANUARY 1988
$3

PSI-FORCE #16
FEBRUARY 1988
$3

PSI-FORCE #17
MARCH 1988
$3

PSI-FORCE #18
APRIL 1988
$3

PSI-FORCE #19
MAY 1988
$3

PSI-FORCE #20
JUNE 1988
$3

PSI-FORCE #21
JULY 1988
$3

PSI-FORCE #22
AUGUST 1988
$3

PSI-FORCE #23
SEPTEMBER 1988
$3

PSI-FORCE #24
OCTOBER 1988
$3

PSI-FORCE #25
NOVEMBER 1988
$3

PSI-FORCE #26
DECEMBER 1988
$3

PSI-FORCE #27
JANUARY 1989
$3

PSI-FORCE #28
FEBRUARY 1989
$3

PSI-FORCE #29
MARCH 1989
$3

PSI-FORCE #30
APRIL 1989
$3

PSI-FORCE #31
MAY 1989
$3

PSI-FORCE #32
JUNE 1989
$3

PSI-FORCE ANNUAL #1
OCTOBER 1987
$4

**SPITFIRE AND THE
TROUBLESHOOTERS #1**
OCTOBER 1986
$3

**SPITFIRE AND THE
TROUBLESHOOTERS #2**
NOVEMBER 1986
$3

**SPITFIRE AND THE
TROUBLESHOOTERS #3**
DECEMBER 1986
$3

**SPITFIRE AND THE
TROUBLESHOOTERS #4**
JANUARY 1987
$6

**SPITFIRE AND THE
TROUBLESHOOTERS #5**
FEBRUARY 1987
$3

**SPITFIRE AND THE
TROUBLESHOOTERS #6**
MARCH 1987
$3

**SPITFIRE AND THE
TROUBLESHOOTERS #7**
APRIL 1987
$3

SPITFIRE #8
MAY 1987
$3

SPITFIRE #9
JUNE 1987
$3

CODENAME SPITFIRE #10
JULY 1987
$3

CODENAME SPITFIRE #11
AUGUST 1987
$3

CODENAME SPITFIRE #12
SEPTEMBER 1987
$3

CODENAME SPITFIRE #13
OCTOBER 1987
$3

STAR BRAND #1
OCTOBER 1986
$3

STAR BRAND #2
NOVEMBER 1986
$3

STAR BRAND #3
DECEMBER 1986
$3

STAR BRAND #4
JANUARY 1987
$3

STAR BRAND #5
FEBRUARY 1987
$3

STAR BRAND #6
MARCH 1987
$3

STAR BRAND #7
MAY 1987
$3

STAR BRAND #8
JULY 1987
$3

STAR BRAND #9
SEPTEMBER 1987
$3

STAR BRAND #10
NOVEMBER 1987
$3

STAR BRAND #11
JANUARY 1988
$3

STAR BRAND #12
MARCH 1988
$3

STAR BRAND #13
MAY 1988
$3

STAR BRAND #14
JULY 1988
$3

STAR BRAND #15
SEPTEMBER 1988
$3

STAR BRAND #16
NOVEMBER 1988
$5

STAR BRAND #17
JANUARY 1989
$5

STAR BRAND #18
MARCH 1989
$5

STAR BRAND #19
MAY 1989
$5

STAR BRAND ANNUAL #1
OCTOBER 1987
$4

THE WAR #1
OCTOBER 1989
$5

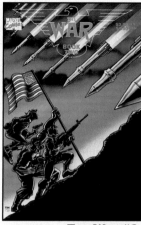

THE WAR #2
NOVEMBER 1989
$5

THE WAR #3
DECEMBER 1989
$5

THE WAR #4
MARCH 1990
$5

PROMOTING THE NEW UNIVERSE

MARVEL AGE #44
NOVEMBER 1986
$4

MARVEL AGE #47
FEBRUARY 1987
$4

MARVEL AGE #50
MAY 1987
$4

THE END OF THE NEW UNIVERSE

The Draft leads up to the reinstatement of the draft in the United States. This one-shot story deals primarily with the recruitment of paranormals into the military for special missions and the perceived coming war with the Soviet Union, which the government believed to be the cause of the Black Event. Following that, *The War* was a four-issue series of graphic novels designed to wrap up the New Universe. With the world on the brink of total annihilation, all weapons are rendered inert by the Star Child, the offspring of Ken Connell and Madelyne Felix. The Star Child issued a warning to all mankind – to live in peace – or else!

– *Charles S. Novinskie*

In 2006, 20 years after the demise of the New Universe, Marvel decided to test the waters with a series of five, new one-shots and a series of three short stories rolled into *Untold Tales of the New Universe*. The short stories consisted of Kickers, Inc. appearing in *New Avengers* #16, Mark Hazzard: Merc in *Amazing Fantasy* #18, and Spitfire in *Amazing Fantasy* #19. Five one-shot titles were also published under the title *Untold Tales of the New Universe*: *Star Brand*, *Nightmask*, *Justice*, *D.P. 7*, and *Psi-Force*. All the tales take place before the Black Event or destruction of Pittsburgh by the Star Brand. The reintroduction of a reimagined New Universe from writer Warren Ellis came in the form of *Newuniversal* (beginning February 2007). The series consisted of *Newuniversal* #1-6 by Ellis and Salvador Larroca, two issues of *Newuniversal: Shockfront*, and one-shots of *Newuniversal: 1959* and *Newuniversal: Conquerer*.

– Charles S. Novinskie

UNTOLD TALES OF THE NEW UNIVERSE: D.P. 7
MAY 2006
$3

UNTOLD TALES OF THE NEW UNIVERSE: JUSTICE
MAY 2006
$3

UNTOLD TALES OF THE NEW UNIVERSE: NIGHTMASK
MAY 2006
$3

UNTOLD TALES OF THE NEW UNIVERSE: PSI-FORCE
MAY 2006
$3

UNTOLD TALES OF THE NEW UNIVERSE: STAR BRAND
MAY 2006
$3

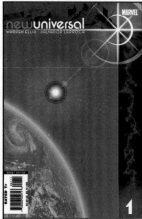

NEWUNIVERSAL #1
FEBRUARY 2007
$3

NEWUNIVERSAL #2
FEBRUARY 2007
$3

NEWUNIVERSAL #3
APRIL 2007
$3

NEWUNIVERSAL #4
MAY 2007
$3

NEWUNIVERSAL #5
JUNE 2007
$3

NEWUNIVERSAL #6
JULY 2007
$3

NEWUNIVERSAL:
CONQUERER
OCTOBER 2008
$4

NEWUNIVERSAL: 1959
SEPTEMBER 2008
$4

NEWUNIVERSAL:
SHOCKFRONT #1
JULY 2008
$3

NEWUNIVERSAL:
SHOCKFRONT #2
AUGUST 2008
$3

**STARBRAND AND
NIGHTMASK #1**
FEBRUARY 2016
$4

**STARBRAND AND
NIGHTMASK #2**
MARCH 2016
$4

**STARBRAND AND
NIGHTMASK #3**
APRIL 2016
$4

**STARBRAND AND
NIGHTMASK #4**
MAY 2016
$4

**STARBRAND AND
NIGHTMASK #5**
JUNE 2016
$4

**STARBRAND AND
NIGHTMASK #6**
JULY 2016
$4

NOT IN THIS UNIVERSE?

In a response to a question raised in the letter column of *D.P. 7*'s final issue (#32), it was stated, "There are absolutely no plans to have the New Universe cross over into the Marvel Universe. We feel that such a move would only compromise the integrity of both universes."

Times change and eventually the New Universe did indeed become part of the Marvel Universe. An alternate version of Spitfire was recruited by Quentin Quire as part of Quire's version of The Exiles, in which the team helped the surviving heroes battle the Annihilation Wave.

In 1993, Peter David introduced a version of Justice in *Spider-Man 2099* as the Net Prophet, the prophet of Thor.

In *Quasar* #31 (February 1992), Mark Gruenwald sent Quasar to the New Universe, allowing the D.P. 7 crew to appear in that issue. The Star Brand also appeared in 2013's *Avengers Infinity* and is playing a pivotal role in the current *Avengers* series.

These are just a few examples. What follows is a checklist of New Universe character appearances in the Marvel Universe.

• POST NEW UNIVERSE APPEARANCES •

Other than the reboots such as *Untold Tales of the New Univese*, *newuniversal*, and *Starbrand and Nightmask*, there have been appearances by the characters in both the regular Marvel Universe and the Ultimate Marvel universe.

1990s
Quasar in New Universe

Quasar travels to the New Universe in #31 & uses the Star Brand to travel back to the 616 universe. Further plots sporadically involve appearances of one mini-antibody & the eventual revelation that character Kayla Ballantine has the Star Brand.
Quasar #31-53

Starblast Crossover (1994)

Fantastic Four #385-386
Namor the Sub-Mariner #46-48
Quasar #54-58, 60
Secret Defenders #11
Starblast #1-4

Justice in 2099 (1993-1996)

A character named The Net Prophet is eventually revealed near the end of the series to be John Tensen, a.k.a. Justice
Spider-Man 2099 #12-14, #25, #41, 42, 44
Spider-Man 2099 Annual #1

2000-2010

Exiles (2005) #72-75
World Tour storyline features alternate versions of D.P.7, Justice, Star Brand and Nightmask characters.

Gambit #19 (2000)
Ken Connell Star Brand cameo.

Fantastic 4 (vol.1 - 2009) #570-572, 583
Alternate version of Reed Richards from an unknown galaxy appears in the "Interdimensional Council Of Reeds" with the Star Brand.

2011 – 2021

Amazing Spider-Man (vol. 4 2016) #4
Blur in Squadron Supreme, cameo

Avengers (vol. 5 2013) #1, 2, 3, 5, 6
"Adam Blackveil" appearances – revealed in #6 as a 616 version of Nightmask.

Avengers (vol. 5 2013) #7-9, 12, 16, 17, 19, 20, 23, 24.NOW, 28, 32, 34, 34.2, 36, 38
Kevin Connor, a 616 version of Starbrand, &/or Adam Blackveil Nightmask.

Avengers (vol. 6 2015) #0
Blur of DP7 is in Squadron Supreme.

QUASAR #31
FEBRUARY 1992

EXILES #73
FEBRUARY 2006

AVENGERS (2013) #9
JUNE 2013

Avengers (vol. 8 2018) #1, 4, 5, 6, 10, 13
Savage Starbrand minor appearances

Avengers (vol. 8 2018) #26-30
Starbrand Reborn part 1-4, new Starbrand host –
Suzanne Selby followed by her baby, Brandy Selby

Avengers (vol. 8 2018) #32, 34-38, 44, 46
Brandy Selby

Avengers Assemble (vol. 2 2012) #18, 19
Kevin Connor Starbrand, Adam Blackveil Nightmask

Avengers FCBD 2018, 2019
Savage Starbrand appearances

Avengers World (2014) #1, 4, 8, 12, 14, 18, 19, 21
Kevin Connor Starbrand, Adam Blackveil Nightmask

Avengers & X-Men: AXIS (2014) #5
Kevin Connor Starbrand

Captain America (vol. 7 2013) #25
Kevin Connor Starbrand, Adam Blackveil Nightmask

Captain America: Steve Rogers #14
Kevin Connor Starbrand

Captain Marvel (vol. 7 2012) #15, 16
Kevin Connor Starbrand, Adam Blackveil Nightmask

Guardians Team-Up (2015) #1, 2
Kevin Connor Starbrand

Heroes Reborn (2021) #1, #4
Brandy Selby Starbrand

Heroes Return (2021) #1
Brandy Selby Starbrand

Hyperion (2016) #4
Blur in Squadron Supreme, cameo

Infinity (2013) #1, 3, 5, 6
Kevin Connor Starbrand, Adam Blackveil Nightmask

King Thor (2019) #4
Savage Starbrand minor appearance

Marvel Comics (2019) #1001
One-page Kickers, Inc. story, Starbrand, Spitfire,
Nightmask, PSI_Hawk cameos

Marvel Legacy #1 (2017)
Modern 616 Starbrand, Savage Starbrand

Marvel's Voices: Pride (2021) #1
Savage Starbrand

New Avengers (vol. 3 2013) #27, 31, 32
Kevin Connor Starbrand, Adam Blackveil Nightmask

Original Sin [2014] #0
Kevin Connor Starbrand cameo

Secret Empire (2017) #3, 7, 9
Kevin Connor Starbrand, Adam Blackveil Nightmask

AVENGERS (2018) #30
May 2020

AVENGERS WORLD #4
May 2014

NEW AVENGERS (2013) #32
May 2015

Secret Empire: Brave New World (2017) #3
Kevin Connor Starbrand

Secret Warps: Ghost Panther Annual (2019) #1
New U appearance on final page

Secret Warps: Arachnight (2019) Annual #1
Alternate amalgamated New Universe
characters

Secret Warps: Iron Hammer (2019) Annual #1
Alternate amalgamated New Universe
characters

Secret Wars: FCBD 2015 issue

S.H.I.E.L.D. (vol. 3 2014) #1
Adam Blackveil Nightmask

Squadron Sinister (2015) #1-4
Alternate versions of Merc, Kickers, Spitfire, and
Starbrand

Squadron Supreme (2016) #1-15
Blur of DP7 on team

Thunderbolts (vol. 3 2016) #4
Blur in Squadron Supreme, cameo

Ultimates (vol. 3 – 2015) #8-10, 12
Alternate 616 version of Philip Nelson Vogt &
"Troubleshooters" unit appearances

Ultimates 2 (2016) #2-6, 100
Alternate 616 characters in "Troubleshooters"
unit

U.S.Avengers (2017) #7, 8, 9
Various members of "Troubleshooters" unit cameos, mentions

Wolverines (2014) #13
Kevin Connor Starbrand

In addition to the various trade paperback collections of stories from the series above, New Universe characters also appeared *The Official Handbook of the Marvel Universe: Alternate Universes* (2005), *All-New Official Handbook of the Marvel Universe A to Z #6* (2006, Justice), *All-New Official Handbook of the Marvel Universe A to Z: Update #1* (2007, Merc), *All-New Official Handbook of the Marvel Universe A to Z: Update #2* (2007, All-American), *All-New Official Handbook of the Marvel Universe A to Z: Update #3* (2007, Chrome), *All-New Official Handbook of the Marvel Universe A to Z: Update #4* (2010, Star Brand), *Marvel Legacy: The 1980s Handbook* one-shot (2006, D.P.7, Nightmask, PSI-Force), *Avengers NOW! Handbook* (2015) #1, and *Marvel Avengers: The Ultimate Character Guide* (DK Hardcover – 2015) #2.

– Josh Deck, Lee Seitz and Mark Davis

SECRET WARS #0 FCBD
MAY 2015

SQUADRON SUPREME #5
MAY 2016

U.S.AVENGERS #9
OCTOBER 2017

SANDY PLUNKETT • Writer/Artist

In the 1970s, early in his career, Sandy Plunkett assisted the Crusty Bunkers at Continuity Studios. His first credited work was a one-page illustration in Marvel's Savage Tales *#11 (July 1975). From there he would go on to work for Marvel, DC, and Gold Key, among others. In addition to his New Universe work, he teamed with writer Mike W. Barr on* Marvel Fanfare *#6's acclaimed Spider-Man/Scarlet Witch story. His credits extend from comics to posters, album covers, and political cartoons.*

Overstreet: Your style is very evocative of the best fantasy art. Talk a little about your early influences and your training honing your craft under Neal Adams.
Sandy Plunkett (SP): Well, I appreciate the compliment. I was probably picking up early influences all over the place as a kid – the Marvel comics I read, the early Disney cartoons I watched on TV, the diorama art at the New York Museum of Natural History. But when I finally rediscovered comics around 1970-1971, I was immediately smitten by the new artists DC was taking on board, particularly Bernie Wrightson and Mike Kaluta, and their work on the mystery books. A while later I discovered comic fanzines and comic conventions and another, huge world opened up to me. I started seeing the work of Al Williamson, Roy Krenkel, and Frank Frazetta and realized how influential these guys were on the artists I was admiring over at DC. And it didn't take too long after that to trace their influences to Hal Foster and Alex Raymond. All those artists had a tremendous influence on me. Neal Adams gave me a very nice reception when

Written by Sandy Plunkett, illustrated by Mark Bagley, and inked by Ernie, *Nightmask* #9 featured a cover by Plunkett and Charles Vess.

I took my work up to Continuity, and he was instrumental in helping me get my foot in the door at DC. As much as I enjoyed and admired his work, I was a bit of a fish out of water at Continuity. The other guys working there, all just getting their careers started, were able to take his style on board very successfully, slowly developing their own approach. Any time I tried an overtly Adams' approach, it was a disaster.

Overstreet: What stories and creators influenced you and your work? Was there a genre that you gravitated to?
SP: Actually, I don't think I've ever received that great an influence from other comic book storytellers. When I was asked many years ago what has influenced my writing and the type of stories I try to tell, I realized that music and novels have had the greatest impact. When I've written and drawn comic stories for my own pleasure, I can almost always trace the influence to a particular piece of music that's been important to me. My favorite author is William Faulkner and I've tried, more than once, to capture the same ambience he creates with his descriptions of the South in the early 1900s.

Overstreet: How did your relationship with Marvel begin?
SP: That's pretty easy to answer. I attended college as a fine art student for one year and left, feeling I'd already made up my mind about the direction I wanted to go, and it wasn't too hard to determine that they couldn't offer me any classes that could help me get there. I dropped out, spent about a

Original cover art for *Nightmask #9* by Sandy Plunkett and Charles Vess.
Image courtesy of Sandy Plunkett.

month drawing up samples and on the advice of my friend Larry Ivie, gave Archie Goodwin a call and arranged an appointment. He was at Marvel at the time, sharing an office with Marv Wolfman, editing the black and white line. He seemed impressed with my work, offered me a job in the bullpen which, foolishly or not, I turned down. But he also gave me my first assignment: a pin-up for their zombie book (I've forgotten the title).

Overstreet: How did your work for Marvel's New Universe imprint come about?

SP: I'm a little sketchy on that. The New Universe line had been introduced maybe a year before and wasn't selling as well as their other books. I'd been wanting to try my hand at writing and figured that since these were lower profile books, ones other writers were less eager to work on, I might have a better chance in convincing an editor to let me take a shot as a writer. I think the first editor I approached was Mike Higgins, and he seemed fine with the idea.

Overstreet: Writing and illustrating New Universe stories, who was your favorite character to write and draw?

SP: The character I gravitated to was Nightmask. I definitely think he was the character with the greatest potential. I actually played around with a couple other plots that I never submitted that would have taken Nightmask into territory that Neil Gaiman eventually explored with Sandman – Jungian ideas of the collective conscience and architypes that appear in dreams.

Each cover sprang from the content of the stories. My approach to these was similar to the way I approached the other covers I drew for Marvel: I simply fiddled around with thumbnails until I came up with a compelling image (or at least one that felt compelling to me). In one case, the Nightmask cover which Charles Vess was kind enough to ink,

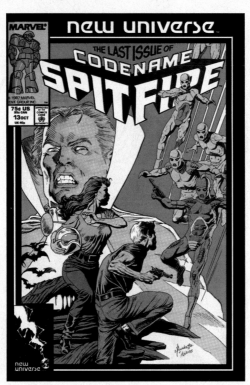

Written by Sandy Plunkett, illustrated by Plunkett and Dave Hoover, and inked by Tony DeZuniga, *Codename Spitfire* #13 featured a cover by Plunkett and Alan Weiss.

you definitely spot an Alphonse Mucha influence. On the *Spitfire* cover, I signed my name "Plunketta" since the piece was such an obvious homage to Frazetta.

As to those covers having the feel of movie posters. Well, like most comic artists, I'm a great movie fan and I love the movie posters from the bygone era of Hollywood. But there wasn't any conscious attempt to infuse my covers with a sensibility derived from that particular art style.

Overstreet: While short-lived, the New Universe does have a devoted following. Were there any untold tales of the New Universe line you had hoped to get to tell?

SP: Boy, I wish there were. I enjoyed doing the books. I worked under three different editors, all of whom were great. So fond memories of that period, but no untold stories. Perhaps I can make a confession: I did thumbnail layouts for all the stories I wrote. I believe, for the most part, the artists illustrating the plots followed them faithfully. In retrospect, I think that the approach was a mistake, that it might have inhibited their own creativity. But I learned a fair amount about storytelling in the process, and the pay for those thumbnails was pretty good!

Overstreet: If you had the opportunity to reboot the New Universe line what character or characters would you want to create stories for?

SP: I'll go back to Nightmask again, since I believe he was the one with the greatest potential. But Spitfire certainly had potential. Come to think about it, it would be fun to reboot that title, setting it in the present, since technology has advanced so much in the interim. All sorts of directions you can take it.

– Jason Versaggi

Original cover art for *Nightmask* #11 by Sandy Plunkett and Alan Weiss.
Image courtesy of Sandy Plunkett.

PAUL RYAN • D.P. 7

D.P. 7, or Displaced Paranormals ran a total of 32 regular issues and one annual, which made it – along with *Psi-Force* – the longest running New Universe title. It was also the only New Universe series that maintained a high level of consistency with its creative team over its whole original existence.

Co-creators writer Mark Gruenwald and penciler Paul Ryan, joined by colorist Paul Becton, produced the entire run. After the first nine issues, they were joined by inker Danny Bulanadi for *D.P. 7* #10-32, which further added to the stability of the look of the book.

The title featured seven main characters that received paranormal abilities thanks to the White Event:

· Randy O'Brien, or Antibody, was a medical resident who could project a dark, intangible image of himself and could fly. He could also transfer memories from one person to another with contact.

· David Landers, nicknamed Mastodon, gained incredible strength and was able to lift over 15 tons.

· Jeff Walters, known as Blur, could vibrate so fast that he appeared as a blur. He consumed vast amounts of food to maintain his accelerated metabolism and could move at superhuman speed. Post-New Universe, Blur appeared as a member of the Squadron Supreme.

· Charlotte Beck, a dance student, acquired the power to make herself, or anything she touched, friction-free. Nicknamed Friction, she also learned to increase an object's friction.

· Dennis "Scuzz" Cuzinski was a troubled teenager who could create a corrosive substance from his skin. He could increase his skin's production of the chemical to burn through just about any object.

· Stephanie Harrington, referred to as Glitter, was a housewife who could heal and energize others by physical contact. The use of her power produces the appearance of twinkling stars.

· Lenore Fenzl, or Twilight, produced a bioluminescence that could paralyze or render individuals unconscious.

Another of the line's titles was related to *D.P. 7* in an interesting way. Perhaps the New Universe title most in search of an identity was *Spitfire and The Troubleshooters*. It had three different titles during its 13-issue run. *Spitfire and The Troubleshooters* ran seven issues before it was changed to *Spitfire*. Three issues later, the *Spitfire* book changed names again to *Codename: Spitfire* for its final four issues.

The series followed the exploits of the title character and a group of brilliant college students as they used high-tech exoskeletons to combat the mysterious terrorist organization known only as The Club.

Created by Eliot R. Brown and Jack Morelli, the idea was that the Spitfire technology would be a more reality-based version of Iron Man's armor. Unlike *D.P. 7*, it was plagued with a number of creative teams over its short, 13-issue run.

Once the series was cancelled, Professor Swensen, Spitfire, became the armor-skinned paranormal Chrome, and was a regular in *D.P. 7*.

Several years before his untimely passing, our *Comic Book Marketplace* asked *D.P. 7* artist Paul Ryan, who was widely known for his work on *Fantastic Four* and other Marvel Universe titles, what his favorite creative moment was in his then-30-year career at Marvel.

"Favorite creative moment? That's an easy one," Ryan said. "Sitting down with Mark Gruenwald and coming up with the look for *D.P. 7*. At Mark's direction, we "cast" our characters based on real people. This is something that I still do when confronted with new characters. When given a description of character by the writer, I look through various magazines for just the right look."

As his work in *D.P. 7* will attest, he almost always succeeded in that.

– Charles S. Novinskie and Jason Versaggi

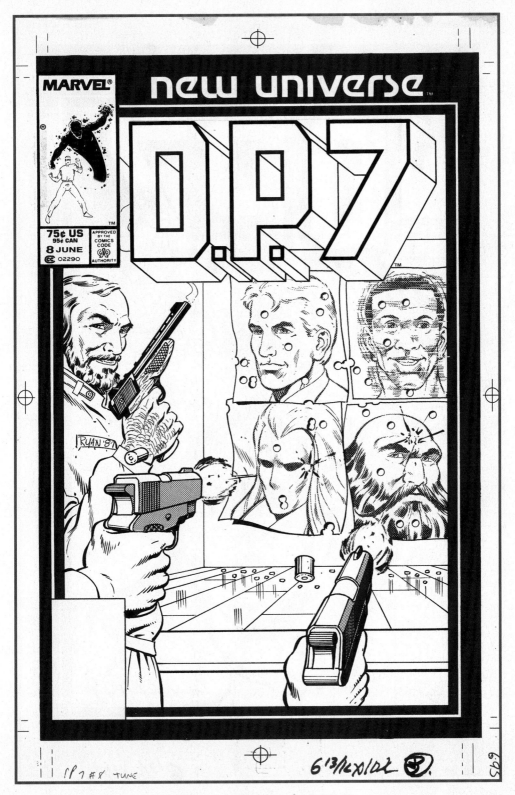

Paul Ryan's original cover for D.P. 7 #8.
Image courtesy of the Estate of Paul Ryan. Special thanks to Jason Versaggi.

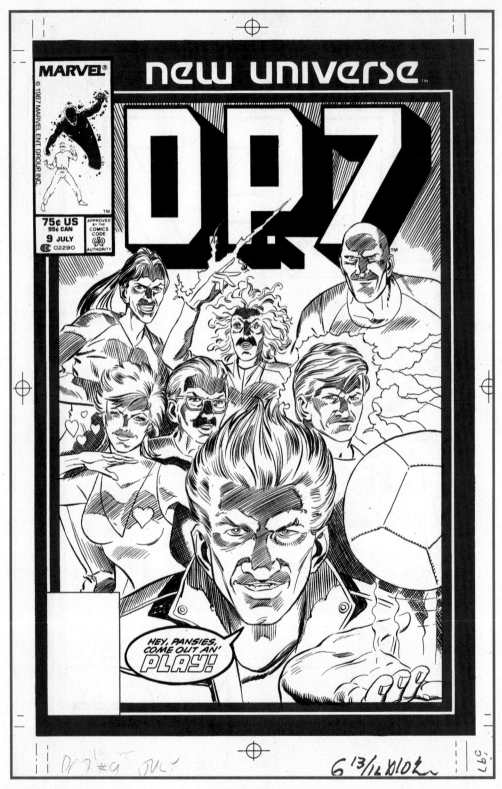

Paul Ryan's original cover for D.P. 7 #9.
Image courtesy of the Estate of Paul Ryan. Special thanks to Jason Versaggi.

Paul Ryan's original Page 1 splash for *D.P. 7 #16*.
Image courtesy of the Estate of Paul Ryan. Special thanks to Jason Versaggi.

I started in on reading/collecting the New Universe with *Spitfire* #2 and *Nightmask* #2. I was immediately hooked on those titles, and shortly after discovered *D.P. 7* and *Star Brand*, too. A younger cousin of mine, who lived down the street from me, was into *Justice* and *Kickers, Inc.* We would read all of each other's comics. But we hadn't even found out that comic shops existed at that point, so our collections were sparse as we had to fight over what we could find in nearby convenience store newsstands.

I got in trouble with my parents the following year over something and as a result I was not allowed to buy comics for a few months. When I came back to them, I was sad to see that some of the New Universe titles had been cancelled. Especially my favorite one, *Spitfire*. I kept up with *D.P. 7* into the early 20s, but couldn't afford the higher price tag once they became direct editions (I was still just a teen working minimal hours after school for minimum wage at that time). That higher price kind of kept me away from the line up through to its unfortunate cancellation, but I did raid bargain bins thereafter to fill in whatever I could find from my very favorite series. I never quite had the urge to collect every single issue in the original imprint until about 15 years ago (around the time that Marvel released the *newuniversal* reboot, and the new *Untold Tales* one-shots), and even then it took me up until three or four years ago to finally find all 174 New Universe comics released between 1986-1990. Through all that time, I have always remained a huge fan of the New U even when not specifically collecting the books.

Josh Deck with some of his New Universe collection.
Photo courtesy of Josh Deck.

When it comes to collecting original art, I only started about three years ago, and it was with two pages by Ron Wagner from *Spitfire* #3. I think I first saw those in a link to an eBay listing shared on the New Universe Fan Page (on Facebook). When I got those two pages in hand, I got bit hard by the art collecting bug. I was immediately and thoroughly enamored with seeing the work up close, and at the original size. What a thrill to compare the art to the printed page side-by-side! I am an artist myself, and it was an absolute revelation to see not only the powerful energy in it firsthand, but also the tiny imperfections and corrections, the editorial markups and side notes, and the hand lettering. All of it provided a massive surge of inspiration to me. I really appreciate every line and every decision behind every line that the pros make. I used to draw plenty of inspiration from the printed pages of my favorite comics, but this was a whole new next-level experience. I wish I had started collecting comic art sooner, but up to that point I guess I just expected that original art was a thing I would never be able to afford to collect, and it stayed off my radar. I'm glad that it was artwork from my favorite New U series that started me down that path of discovery.

It's actually tough for me to distill only a few favorite pieces of art out of my New U collection as I really do love it all, but I guess I'd have to go with the following: two John Romita, Jr. pages from *Star Brand* - one from #1 (part of his origin story receiving the Brand from the Old Man) and another from #4 (a great action page of Ken facing some random strange paranormals in a forest. I love that part of that issue).

The original cover art for *Justice #6* by Geof Isherwood.
Image courtesy of Josh Deck.

I have John Byrne's opening splash page 1 from *Star Brand* #11 (his first page of sequential art from his run on the series, showing the new costume he created for the first time). I am beyond pleased to have a Todd McFarlane page from *Spitfire* #4 that is quite special to me. I never expected to be able to own any original work by him (and it's a great scene between Jenny in the damaged MAX armor vs. the terrorist Arun Bahkti).

I also love a Marshall Rogers page I own from *Spitfire* #10 featuring more MAX armors on one single page than any other from the entire series, as well as another pair of Spitfire pages by Dave Hoover from #13 - both featuring a battle between Jenny in the Mk. IV armor vs. a strange "cybernetic" enemy. I used to draw all the various MAX suits quite obsessively as a kid (and often incorporated their look into my own childhood comic creations), but the one from #13 was a particularly unique and intriguing design to me as it only appeared in that single issue.

And finally, I have the cover art for *Justice* #6 by Geof Isherwood. I love that piece not just for the fine work itself (I am a big fan of all Geof's issues on the series), but for the fond memories I have of reading my cousin's copy of that particular issue when we were kids, long before I got my own. It was a particular thrill to share that piece with my cousin when I acquired it directly from Geof; he was floored!

As a general comment here, I feel it's important to mention that as an artist and an art collector I have come to appreciate the talent behind these books ever more so as I grow older. I have original artwork in my collection by the likes of John Romita, Jr., John Byrne, Todd McFarlane, Gray Morrow, Joe Sinnott, Al Williamson, Tom Palmer, Tom Morgan, Mark Texiera, Geof Isherwood, Mark Bagley, Herb Trimpe, Ron Lim, Ernie Chan, Keith Giffen, Marshall Rogers, Tony DeZuniga, and more... all legends of the industry who happened to grace the pages of New U comics with their talents. It's just incredible how many of these tremendous artists actually worked on the New U line!

When Stan Lee and Jack Kirby began to build the Marvel universe proper in 1961, they were adding a new level of realism and characterization within a really imaginative, fantastic setting that just wasn't there in other comics of that time. I think Jim Shooter's concept for the New Universe line tried to take that same storytelling perspective to a whole new level, making the core setting and characters even more relatable to the reader than in the original Marvel universe by aiming to keep it really close to the world outside your window. I love reading about Ken Connell not having the slightest real clue what to do with all that cosmic power and ending up worrying more about how to juggle sleeping around on his girlfriend than figuring out what to do with himself, while a crazy Old Man with the same power keeps coming around and threatening him and everyone around him. I applaud the courage of telling a more human story like that in a comic instead of something tropey that had already been done to death. That would be a great premise for a creator-owned comic series, or even a strange TV show, right now. It is wonderfully different.

I also still feel the influence from these comics on me to this very day, as I tend to stray off the beaten path of standard superhero fare in my present comic reading tastes. New U comics helped teach me that great comics could literally be about anything, encompass any genre, and not just be restricted to the activities of heroes in tights (that's not a knock against superhero comics, they are great fun). I also consider some of the New Universe comics to be among the deepest sources of influence on my tastes in pop culture in general. I love the escapism element of entertainment, but my favorite kind of escapism is that which finely crafts the least need for suspension of disbelief within something fantastical. I want to be fully absorbed in the imaginative

The original art for *Star Brand* #1 Page 7 by John Romita, Jr. and Al Williamson.
Image courtesy of Josh Deck.

Spitfire all told stories about real, sometimes average people who have something truly extraordinary thrust upon them unbidden. It is the exploration of the repercussions of how that would really play out in our own world that always grabs me.

Not everyone in the real world reads comics or has any awareness of, or interest in, typically "nerdy" things like sci-fi, etc. If a random real person like that was suddenly given a bizarre paranormal ability or the Star Brand for example, they would not automatically adjust to that strangeness and embrace it. They would not necessarily decide to start acting like a superhero and go on crazy adventures, they wouldn't even know what that means . . . so to see the best of these New Universe stories play out in that vein with much more realistic characters is a rewarding reading experience to me.

I admit that nostalgia plays a factor as well, as I was only 12 when the New Universe launched. Reading them now brings me back to that happy place when I was just beginning to really develop my lifelong passion for comics in general. I had no preconceived notions of what should and should not be taking place in a comic book back then, no metric to judge the contents of New Universe comics against accepted norms. I found that I could relate to the characters reactions to their newly found odd circumstances. I wasn't even aware of any of the sales hype of the industry at that point. I was buying these comics alongside other more typical superhero comics off newsstands in corner stores for the first time. I discovered *Spitfire* and *Iron Man* at the same time. It was all equally compelling to me.

fiction that I engage with. I don't need it to be simple adventure escapism. I really think that I developed that sensibility in part from reading New Universe comics during my formative years. They are not always well executed, but when they are at their best, they present you with a story that you could project yourself into and wonder how you would handle the unreality that the characters face. And that makes it all the more fun and entertaining for me to read and re-read them all these years later.

It all comes down to that "world outside your window" concept that encompasses the line. These comics attempted to tell stories set in the real world while exploring a controlled number of fantastical elements. The level of realism is a concept that was largely ahead of its time in comics in 1986, but something we praise now in modern era publications. Rather than assuming typical superhero tropes for all the main characters, the best books like *D.P. 7, Star Brand* or

I am a big fan of the *newuniversal* reboot from 2007. Warren Ellis revised the core concept of New Universe in that separate, stand-alone series. He introduced some great abstract sci-fi multiversal elements that provided a new explanation for the nature of the White Event and where the power and purpose of the Starbrand came from. The artwork by Salvador Larroca in that mini-series is top-notch excellence.

Jonathan Hickman's now classic *Avengers* run is also another highlight – he clearly took some inspiration and influence from ideas in *newuniversal* and used that as a basis to create very cool new versions of Starbrand and Nightmask that exist for the first time in the main 616 Marvel Universe and fight alongside the Avengers across multiple storylines.

There was a *Starbrand & Nightmask* mini-series that spun out of those stories at one point, which I have never been too excited about, but it was just meant for a younger audience than me and I don't really criticize it for that. [Editor's note: Marvel's logo stylization of *Star Brand* changed from two words to one word, *Starbrand*, with this mini-series.]

I have also been keeping an eye on Jason Aaron's current run on *Avengers*, as he has developed some further new spins on Starbrand. He has introduced a new current host for the Starbrand, a very young girl named Brandy Selby. He also wrote a rather daring tale of a White Event that happened millions of years ago, wherein a "dinosaur" was actually given the power of Starbrand. That essentially places a Starbrand host as the very earliest super-hero to exist in the Marvel 616 universe. I kind of raise an eyebrow at that one, and yet it is exciting in general to see these elements of the New Universe live on in modern comics to this very day.

I have never had a chance to meet Jim Shooter, but if I did, I would certainly love to ask him some questions about the New Universe. I think he drew on his experiences of creating that independent shared universe when he later moved on to form Valiant, DEFIANT, and Broadway Comics. With Valiant in particular, there are some very similar concepts and characters that echo New Universe titles.

I am proud to say that years ago, I collaborated on a Valiant comics fan-based art print project with JayJay Jackson (she colored a piece of art I drew for it), and she was able to get Shooter to sign all the copies we made. It's a thrill to think that he has seen and held artwork of mine in his hands once.

- Josh Deck

Josh Deck lives just outside of Hamilton ON, Canada. He is a lifelong fan of comic books and it has always been his dream job to be a comic artist. He studied Illustration in college and has done some freelance professional art. While he never made it big, he has done some short stories and cover art at the indie comics level. He has an endless well of passion for the New Universe in particular (they were among his favorite comics growing up and still are to this day). He also helps co-run the Nukin' New U Fan page dedicated to the line on Facebook alongside its founder, Mark Davis.

T.H.U.N.D.E.R. AGENTS (Tower)

It was an era of high-tech espionage. James Bond was fighting the forces of S.P.E.C.T.R.E. on the big screen, while on the small screen The Man From U.N.C.L.E. battled the machinations of THRUSH, and in comics Nick Fury, Agent of S.H.I.E.L.D. took on all comers.

At the same time, the superhero comic book revival was in full swing, with Marvel in the ascendency, so it might have been inevitable that someone was going to put the two genres together in a big way.

The ones who did it were writer Len Brown and artist Wally Wood, who developed The T.H.U.N.D.E.R. Agents for Tower Comics. "T.H.U.N.D.E.R." stood for The Higher United Nations Defense Enforcement Reserves, which served as the springboard for all of the adventures. Unlike many start-ups, there was no problem attracting talent.

The roster of A-list creators who worked alongside Brown and Wood included Larry Ivie, Reed Crandall, Gil Kane, George Tuska, Mike Esposito, Mike Sekowsky, Frank Giacoia, Dan Adkins, Dick Ayers, Joe Orlando, Steve Skeates, Steve Ditko, Ralph Reese, Chic Stone, and Joe Giella, among others. Artists and writers such as Paul Reinman, Ray Bailey, Sheldon Moldoff, John Giunta, Manny Stallman, Ogden Whitney, and Jack Abel also worked on the series.

Agents Dynamo, NoMan, and Menthor debuted in *T.H.U.N.D.E.R. Agents* #1 (November 1965) in a 64-page, 25¢ format when most comics were 32 pages for 12¢. In those pages, multiple stories showcased the individual team members and then the team as a whole.

In an original twist, not only did their powers come from scientific devices, but the technology also took a physical and mental toll on the agents who used it. Another change of pace came via the

character of John Janus, Menthor, whose mental powers come from the Menthor helmet. Janus is actually a double-agent working for The Warlord, T.H.U.N.D.E.R.'s foe. However, he turns to the side of good before eventually dying (permanently) in *T.H.U.N.D.E.R. Agents* #7. This was still a rarity in comics at the time (and of course the character staying dead continues to be a rarity to this day).

Additional agents including Raven, Lightning (a speedster whose suit aged him prematurely), Vulvan, Undersea Agent, and the T.H.U.N.D.E.R. Squad, as well as a couple of new Menthors were introduced as the series progressed.

Dynamo, NoMan and Undersea Agent all had their own short-lived series as well. In 1966, Tower also released four paperback reprint collections: Dynamo, NoMan, Menthor, and The Terrific Trio (which featured NoMan, Dynamo, and Menthor).

Paralleling the boom and bust of the spy craze of that era (and very similar to the ups and downs of Batmania), the ride at Tower came to an end with *T.H.U.N.D.E.R. Agents* #20 (November 1969) when the company folded.

Since then, there have been many revivals. These efforts included issues produced by JC Comics, Texas Comics, Deluxe Comics, Solson, Penthouse Comics, DC Comics, and IDW Publishing. Some of these have been one-and-done, and one never even was released, but the DC and IDW periods added new material to the characters' legend.

Of these post-Tower efforts, all are worth noting for diehard T.H.U.N.D.E.R. Agents fans, but the multi-volume hardcover reprint collection from DC, *The T.H.U.N.D.E.R. Agents Archives* command the most attention, followed by Deluxe's talent-packed *Wally Wood's T.H.U.N.D.E.R. Agents* series.

FIRST PUBLICATION:
T.H.U.N.D.E.R. Agents #1 (November 1965)

LAST PUBLICATION:
T.H.U.N.D.E.R. Agents #20 (November 1969)

REVIVAL(S):
JC Comics, Texas Comics (*Justice Machine Annual* #1), Deluxe Comics, Solson, Penthouse Comics, DC Comics, and IDW Publishing

---

Reed Crandall's original art for Page 2 of the NoMan story from
T.H.U.N.D.E.R. Agents #1. Image courtesy of Heritage Auctions.

DYNAMO #1
AUGUST 1966
$8 $24 $160

DYNAMO #2
OCTOBER 1966
$5 $15 $90

DYNAMO #3
MARCH 1967
$5 $15 $90

DYNAMO #4
JUNE 1967
$5 $15 $90

NOMAN #1
NOVEMBER 1966
$9 $27 $165

NOMAN #2
MARCH 1967
$5 $15 $90

T.H.U.N.D.E.R. AGENTS #1
NOVEMBER 1965
$18 $54 $440

T.H.U.N.D.E.R. AGENTS #2
JANUARY 1966
$9 $27 $195

T.H.U.N.D.E.R. AGENTS #3
MARCH 1966
$7 $21 $135

T.H.U.N.D.E.R. Agents #4
April 1966
$7 **$21** **$135**

T.H.U.N.D.E.R. Agents #5
June 1966
$7 **$21** **$135**

T.H.U.N.D.E.R. Agents #6
July 1966
$6 **$18** **$100**

T.H.U.N.D.E.R. Agents #7
August 1966
$6 **$18** **$100**

T.H.U.N.D.E.R. Agents #8
September 1966
$6 **$18** **$100**

T.H.U.N.D.E.R. Agents #9
October 1966
$6 **$18** **$100**

T.H.U.N.D.E.R. Agents #10
November 1966
$6 **$18** **$100**

T.H.U.N.D.E.R. Agents #11
March 1967
$5 **$15** **$90**

T.H.U.N.D.E.R. Agents #12
April 1967
$5 **$15** **$90**

T.H.U.N.D.E.R. Agents #13
JUNE 1967
$5 $15 $90

T.H.U.N.D.E.R. Agents #14
JULY 1967
$5 $15 $90

T.H.U.N.D.E.R. Agents #15
SEPTEMBER 1967
$5 $15 $90

T.H.U.N.D.E.R. Agents #16
OCTOBER 1967
$5 $15 $85

T.H.U.N.D.E.R. Agents #17
DECEMBER 1967
$5 $15 $85

T.H.U.N.D.E.R. Agents #18
SEPTEMBER 1968
$5 $15 $85

T.H.U.N.D.E.R. Agents #19
NOVEMBER 1968
$5 $15 $85

T.H.U.N.D.E.R. Agents #20
NOVEMBER 1969
$4 $12 $60

UNDERSEA AGENT #1
JANUARY 1966
$8 $24 $140

UNDERSEA AGENT #2
APRIL 1966
$5 $15 $85

UNDERSEA AGENT #3
JUNE 1966
$5 $15 $85

UNDERSEA AGENT #4
AUGUST 1966
$5 $15 $85

UNDERSEA AGENT #5
OCTOBER 1966
$5 $15 $85

UNDERSEA AGENT #6
MARCH 1967
$5 $15 $85

LEN BROWN: DID YOU KNOW...?

In addition to co-creating the *T.H.U.N.D.E.R. Agents* with artist Wally Wood and having T.H.U.N.D.E.R. Agent Dynamo's alter ego named after him, did you know that writer Len Brown had earlier played a major role in the development of *Mars Attacks*? While working at Topps in 1962, Brown was inspired by Wood's now-classic cover for EC's *Weird Science* #16 and pitched the idea of *Mars Attacks* to department head Woody Gelman. Bob Powell provided the pencil art, and Norman Saunders painted the now-highly-collectible original 55-card set. The project would, of course, go on to inspire comic books and the 1996 feature film.

TRIUMPHANT

Triumphant was a science fiction/action-adventure universe with an emphasis on continuity within title and across the whole line. Billed as "The Collector's Universe," the individual comics were given a unique edition number.

I always loved comics. The first one I published at 16 (back in 1986) was *GI Jackrabbits*, an animal parody of *GI Joe*. Triumphant grew out of the contacts and network we established with Personality and Spoof Comics two years prior to the launch. We were publishing biography comics, spoof comics, a female parody of mainstream superheroes (with some great name covers by Adam Hughes, Kelley Jones, Dave Johnson, and others). Through the success of Personality Comics, we established an in-house art studio, had in-house writers and production people and many freelance contacts. We had 20-plus studio seats alone, it was great.

Inspired by Valiant, I wanted to take on publishing with an integrated universe with strong continuity and ongoing monthly titles. This was a much larger editorial commitment than the comics we'd produced before, but we did have some prior experience putting out books and the resources to get it going.

Triumphant was me, my business partner at the time, Eric Shefferman, and Kirk Lindo. Kirk was a force of nature, really talented and passionate, a creative and business person. He hired, trained and managed the guys in the studio and could implement almost any idea I could come up with for comics projects.

READ, SAVE, COLLECT. That was the three-word mantra for Triumphant. I came up with the idea, and it resonated with many fans. The individual numbering made each physical comic book unique, and it only cost about 2¢ per issue. We'd been doing limited editions for many of our Personality Comics titles,

FIRST PUBLICATION:
The Chromium Man #1 (August 1993)

LAST PUBLICATION:
The Chromium Man #11, *Scavengers* #10 (both May 1994)

REVIVAL(S):
None to date

where the books would have a bound-in, signed, serially numbered card. One example: John Tartaglione on our Babe Ruth biography comic. I haven't seen anyone do the individual numbering since. I loved it, thought it was a privilege to figure out a way to make every number unique for the reader. Fans liked it, some people were turned off to reference to the collectability, but they seemed to be the same kind of people that weren't interested in buying them!

We had Adam Pollina's first published professional comics work, as far as I know. Adam is a super-talent. We also had Franchesco on *Scavengers* for the first few issues. He was always a dynamic and hard-working talent. He worked from home like a traditional freelancer.

Among our high points was the *Triumphant Unleashed* crossover, which was great. We sold many comics, and they were well received. After the success of the *Triumphant Unleashed* crossover, though, we didn't really have a great plan to maintain interest in the ongoing titles. There was more and more competition in publishing, and more and more stores were struggling. Launching a universe of ongoing monthly titles is tremendously ambitious and ultimately was too ambitious for the time and our resources.

These days there are so many more resources for publishers, such as crowdfunding, digital distribution, and multiple printing options we never had access to in the 1990s. I'm making plans now to launch a new universe with tight continuity starting with standalone graphic novels through crowdfunding. People can find out more about what I'm doing at my YouTube channel, adampostspeaks.com. Two of my current graphic novel projects are at collegeofthedead.com and epicmermaids.com.

– Adam Post

Adam Pollina's original art for *The Chromium Man* #1 Page 4.
Image courtesy of James Bella.

THE CHROMIUM MAN #1
AUGUST 1993
$3

THE CHROMIUM MAN #2
SEPTEMBER 1993
$3

THE CHROMIUM MAN #3
OCTOBER 1993
$3

THE CHROMIUM MAN #4
NOVEMBER 1993
$3

THE CHROMIUM MAN #5
NOVEMBER 1993
$3

THE CHROMIUM MAN #6
JANUARY 1994
$3

THE CHROMIUM MAN #7
FEBRUARY 1994
$3

THE CHROMIUM MAN #8
MARCH 1994
$3

THE CHROMIUM MAN #9
APRIL 1994
$3

THE CHROMIUM MAN #0
APRIL 1994
$3

THE CHROMIUM MAN #0
RED LOGO EDITION
APRIL 1994
$3

THE CHROMIUM MAN #0
PURPLE LOGO LIMITED EDITION
APRIL 1994
$3

THE CHROMIUM MAN #0
BLUE LOGO LIMITED EDITION
APRIL 1994
$3

THE CHROMIUM MAN #10
MAY 1994
$3

**THE CHROMIUM MAN:
VIOLENT PAST #1**
JANUARY 1994
$3

**THE CHROMIUM MAN:
VIOLENT PAST #2**
JANUARY 1994
$3

DOCTOR CHAOS #1
NOVEMBER 1993
$3

DOCTOR CHAOS #2
NOVEMBER 1993
$3

DOCTOR CHAOS #3
JANUARY 1994
$3

DOCTOR CHAOS #4
FEBRUARY 1994
$3

DOCTOR CHAOS #5
MARCH 1994
$3

DOCTOR CHAOS #6
MARCH 1994
$3

PRINCE VANDAL #1
NOVEMBER 1993
$3

PRINCE VANDAL #2
NOVEMBER 1993
$3

PRINCE VANDAL #3
JANUARY 1994
$3

PRINCE VANDAL #4
FEBRUARY 1994
$3

PRINCE VANDAL #5
MARCH 1994
$3

PRINCE VANDAL #6
APRIL 1994
$3

RIOT GEAR #1
ASHCAN EDITION
1993
$3

RIOT GEAR #1
SEPTEMBER 1993
$3

RIOT GEAR #2
OCTOBER 1993
$3

RIOT GEAR #3
NOVEMBER 1993
$3

RIOT GEAR #4
NOVEMBER 1993
$3

RIOT GEAR #5
JANUARY 1994
$3

RIOT GEAR #6
FEBRUARY 1994
$3

RIOT GEAR #7
MARCH 1994
$3

RIOT GEAR #8
APRIL 1994
$3

RIOT GEAR: VIOLENT PAST #1
FEBRUARY 1994
$3

RIOT GEAR: VIOLENT PAST #2
MARCH 1994
$3

SCAVENGERS #1
JULY 1993
$3

SCAVENGERS #1
SECOND EDITION
JULY 1993
$3

SCAVENGERS #1
B&W COVER
JULY 1993
$3

SCAVENGERS #2
AUGUST 1993
$3

SCAVENGERS #3
SEPTEMBER 1993
$3

SCAVENGERS #4
OCTOBER 1993
$3

SCAVENGERS #5
NOVEMBER 1993
$3

SCAVENGERS #6
NOVEMBER 1993
$3

SCAVENGERS #7
JANUARY 1994
$3

SCAVENGERS #8
FEBRUARY 1994
$3

SCAVENGERS #9
MARCH 1994
$3

SCAVENGERS #0
MARCH 1994
$3

SCAVENGERS #0
BLUE LOGO EDITION
MARCH 1994
$3

SCAVENGERS #0
RED LOGO EDITION
MARCH 1994
$3

SCAVENGERS #0
FREE EDITION
MARCH 1994
$3

SCAVENGERS #10
APRIL 1994
$3

SCAVENGERS #11
MAY 1994
$3

TRIUMPHANT UNLEASHED #1
NOVEMBER 1993
$3

TRIUMPHANT UNLEASHED #1
NOVEMBER 1993
$3

XIMOS: VIOLENT PAST #1
MARCH 1994
$3

XIMOS: VIOLENT PAST #2
MARCH 1994
$3

THE TRIUMPHANT/DEFIANT NON-CROSSOVER CROSSOVER

Overstreet: What was the non-crossover with DEFIANT and how did it come to happen?

Adam Post: This was a two-page spread across all the *Triumphant Unleashed* titles for two months where we met Jim Shooter's characters from DEFIANT, his new company at the time. Jim and I met when he left Valiant and was looking for funding for his next venture. Jim gave us some great advice on publishing a universe of comics, and came out to our studio office a few times to check us out. Ultimately Jim put a deal together with the backers for DEFIANT before we could sort out what we may be able to do together.

Adam Post, circa 1990s

ULTRAVERSE (MALIBU)

Backed by Scott Mitchell Rosenberg of Sunrise Distributors, Malibu Comics was launched in 1986 by Dave Olbrich and Tom Mason. Chris Ulm would join the company the following year. It grew at least in part out of a web of other small comic publishers. Eternity Comics, Amazing Comics, Wonder Comics, and Imperial Comics all had been financed by Rosenberg. Eternity was retained as imprint of Malibu, which later added Adventure and Aircel as other imprints.

The company's roster was a blend of licensed properties and creator-owned titles. Its offerings ranged from newspaper strip reprints to original material, chiefly in black and white formats. Eventually their titles included *Planet of the Apes*, *Alien Nation*, *Men in Black*, *Ninja High School*, *Ex-Mutants*, and *Dinosaurs For Hire*, among others.

In 1992 the company was also the home for the first year of Image Comics. After the Image founders left Marvel, Malibu was able to offer its services and distribution network to the start-up. After that year, Malibu needed to replace the significant revenue that Image had generated.

Along with Olbrich, Mason, and Ulm, the company recruited writers Mike W. Barr, Steve Englehart, Steve Gerber, James D. Hudnall, Gerard Jones, James Robinson, and Len Strazewski, as well as science fiction novelist Larry Niven and filmmaker Wes Craven to develop a new superhero universe. (Craven eventually declined, citing a scheduling conflict.) With tight continuity and innovative promotions including TV ads, the Ultraverse debuted in June 1993.

Their initial titles included *The Exiles*, *Firearm*, *Freex*, *Hardcase*, *Mantra*, *The Night Man*, *Prime*, *Prototype*, *Sludge*, *Solitaire*, and *The Strangers*, as well as the mini-series *Break-Thru* and the flip-book series *Ultraverse Premiere*. *The Exiles* deserve a special note as the entire team was killed off in *Exiles* #4, though bogus solicitations had been offered for subsequent issues (this was not done again until Robert Kirkman's *The Walking Dead* #193 surprised fans in similar fashion in 2019).

FIRST PUBLICATION:
Hardcase #1, *Prime* #1,
The Strangers #1 (all June 1993)

LAST PUBLICATION:
Ultraverse: Future Shock #1
(February 1997)

REVIVAL(S):
Rune HeroClix figure (June 2019)

Prime, illustrated by Norm Breyfogle, became the unofficial pillar of the Ultraverse, and Steve Englehart's *The Night Man* was adapted by *Battlestar Galactica* creator Glen A. Larson into the syndicated *Night Man* television series. The show ran two seasons from September 15, 1997 through May 17, 1999

The initial comic book line-up was followed in 1994 by *Elven*, *Rune*, *Warstrike*, and *Wrath*, as well as the team book *UltraForce*, which would eventually become a cartoon series.

Malibu was not immune to the market forces at work at the time. As the speculator boom faded, sales continued to drop. Courted by DC which had made an offer to buy Malibu, the company was purchased by Marvel Comics on November 3, 1994. Malibu's *Godwheel* mini-series included a high-profile appearance by Thor. It would not be the last crossover between the two universes.

In September 1995, Malibu canceled the remaining Ultraverse line and with Marvel's support re-launched a small number of its most popular titles in an event called *Black September*. The story pitted Loki and an entity called Nemesis against UltraForce and the Avengers in a battle to possess the Infinity Gems.

The "volume 2" series each started with "#∞" (infinity) issues, the first of many moves in that era seemingly designed only to punish the kind-hearted people who publish price guides. They also added a full slate of crossovers, including *Rune/Silver Surfer*, *Conan vs. Rune*, *Avengers/UltraForce* (and *UltraForce/Avengers*), *Rune vs. Venom*, *UltraForce/Spider-Man*, and *Prime/Captain America*.

The new, truncated Ultraverse lasted less than a year. It ended with its last release, *Ultraverse: Future Shock* #1, in February 1997. Since then, despite at least toying with the idea, Marvel has steadfastly declined to bring back the characters, although Topaz from *UltraForce* appeared in *Thor: Ragnarok* in 2017 and a Rune figure was included in the WizKid's HeroClix game in 2018.

Barry Windsor-Smith's original art for the cover of *Rune #5*.
Image courtesy of Heritage Auctions.

ALL NEW EXILES INFINITY
SEPTEMBER 1995
$3

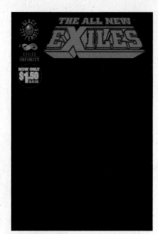

ALL NEW EXILES INFINITY
BLACK VARIANT COVER
SEPTEMBER 1995
$3

ALL NEW EXILES INFINITY
JUGGERNAUT VARIANT COVER
SEPTEMBER 1995
$3

ALL NEW EXILES #1
OCTOBER 1995
$4

ALL NEW EXILES #1
PAINTED VARIANT COVER
OCTOBER 1995
$4

ALL NEW EXILES #1
VARIANT COVER
OCTOBER 1995
$4

ALL NEW EXILES #2
FLIP BOOK WITH PHOENIX RESURRECTION
NOVEMBER 1995
$3

ALL NEW EXILES #3
DECEMBER 1995
$3

ALL NEW EXILES #4
JANUARY 1996
$3

ALL NEW EXILES #5
FEBRUARY 1996
$4

ALL NEW EXILES #6
MARCH 1996
$3

ALL NEW EXILES #7
APRIL 1996
$3

ALL NEW EXILES #8
MAY 1996
$3

ALL NEW EXILES #9
JUNE 1996
$3

ALL NEW EXILES #10
JULY 1996
$3

ALL NEW EXILES #11
AUGUST 1996
$3

**ALL NEW EXILES
VS. THE X-MEN #0**
OCTOBER 1995
$1 $4 $10

ANGELS OF DESTRUCTION #1
OCTOBER 1996
$3

AVENGERS/ULTRAFORCE #1
OCTOBER 1995
$4

**BATTLEZONES:
DREAM TEAM² #1**
MARCH 1996
$3

**BLACK SEPTEMBER
ASHCAN #1**
1995
$3

**BLACK SEPTEMBER
INFINITY**
1995
$3

**BLACK SEPTEMBER
INFINITY**
1995
$3

BREAK-THRU #1
DECEMBER 1993
$4

BREAK-THRU #2
JANUARY 1994
$4

CODENAME: FIREARM #0
JUNE 1995
$3

CODENAME: FIREARM #1
JUNE 1995
$3

CODENAME: FIREARM #2
JULY 1995
$3

CODENAME: FIREARM #3
JULY 1995
$3

CODENAME: FIREARM #4
AUGUST 1995
$3

CODENAME: FIREARM #5
AUGUST 1995
$3

CONAN #4
NOVEMBER 1995
$3

CONAN VS. RUNE #1
NOVEMBER 1995
$4

CURSE OF RUNE #1
MAY 1995
$3

CURSE OF RUNE #1
MAY 1995
$3

CURSE OF RUNE #2
JUNE 1995
$3

CURSE OF RUNE #3
JULY 1995
$3

CURSE OF RUNE #4
AUGUST 1995
$3

DREAM TEAM #1
JULY 1995
$5

ELIMINATOR #0
APRIL 1995
$3

ELIMINATOR #1
MAY 1995
$3

ELIMINATOR #1
BLACK COVER EDITION
MAY 1995
$4

ELIMINATOR #2
JUNE 1995
$3

ELIMINATOR #3
JULY 1995
$3

ELVEN #0
OCTOBER 1994
$3

ELVEN #1
FEBRUARY 1995
$3

ELVEN #1
LIMITED FOIL EDITION
FEBRUARY 1995
$4

ELVEN #2
MARCH 1995
$3

ELVEN #3
APRIL 1995
$3

ELVEN #4
MAY 1995
$3

EXILES #1
AUGUST 1993
$3

EXILES #2
SEPTEMBER 1993
$3

EXILES #3
FLIP BOOK WITH RUNE COVER/STORY
OCTOBER 1993
$5

EXILES #4
NOVEMBER 1993
$3

FIREARM #0
BAGGED WITH VIDEOTAPE OF STORY PRELUDE
NOVEMBER 1993
$15

FIREARM #1
SEPTEMBER 1993
$3

FIREARM #2
FLIP BOOK WITH RUNE COVER/STORY
OCTOBER 1993
$4

FIREARM #3
NOVEMBER 1993
$3

FIREARM #4
DECEMBER 1993
$3

FIREARM #5
JANUARY 1994
$3

FIREARM #6
FEBRUARY 1994
$3

FIREARM #7
MARCH 1994
$3

FIREARM #8
MAY 1994
$3

FIREARM #9
JUNE 1994
$3

FIREARM #10
JULY 1994
$3

FIREARM #11
FLIP BOOK WITH ULTRAVERSE PREMIERE #5
JULY 1994
$4

FIREARM #12
AUGUST 1994
$3

FIREARM #13
SEPTEMBER 1994
$3

FIREARM #14
NOVEMBER 1994
$3

FIREARM #15
DECEMBER 1994
$3

FIREARM #16
JANUARY 1995
$3

FIREARM #17
FEBRUARY 1995
$3

FIREARM #18
MARCH 1995
$4

FLOOD RELIEF #1
JANUARY 1994
$4

FOXFIRE #1
GLENN FABRY COVER
FEBRUARY 1996
$3

FOXFIRE #1
STEVE LIGHTLE COVER
FEBRUARY 1996
$3

FOXFIRE #2
MARCH 1996
$3

FOXFIRE #3
APRIL 1996
$3

FOXFIRE #4
MAY 1996
$3

FREEX #1
JULY 1993
$3

FREEX #1
ULTRA 5000 LIMITED EDITION
JULY 1993
$5

FREEX #2
AUGUST 1993
$3

FREEX #3
SEPTEMBER 1993
$3

FREEX #4
FLIP BOOK WITH RUNE COVER/STORY
OCTOBER 1993
$4

FREEX #5
NOVEMBER 1993
$3

FREEX #6
DECEMBER 1993
$3

FREEX #7
JANUARY 1994
$3

FREEX #8
FEBRUARY 1994
$3

FREEX #9
MARCH 1994
$3

FREEX #10
APRIL 1994
$3

FREEX #11
MAY 1994
$3

FREEX #12
JUNE 1994
$3

FREEX #13
SEPTEMBER 1994
$3

FREEX #14
OCTOBER 1994
$3

FREEX #15
FLIP BOOK WITH ULTRAVERSE PREMIERE #9
JANUARY 1995
$3

FREEX #16
JANUARY 1995
$3

FREEX #17
FEBRUARY 1995
$3

FREEX #18
MARCH 1995
$3

GIANT SIZE FREEX #1
JULY 1994
$3

GODWHEEL #0
FLIP COVER
JANUARY 1995
$3

GODWHEEL #0
FLIP COVER
JANUARY 1995
$3

GODWHEEL #1
FLIP COVER
JANUARY 1995
$3

GODWHEEL #1
FLIP COVER
JANUARY 1995
$3

GODWHEEL #2
FLIP COVER
FEBRUARY 1995
$3

GODWHEEL #2
FLIP COVER
FEBRUARY 1995
$3

GODWHEEL #3
FLIP COVER
FEBRUARY 1995
$3

GODWHEEL #3
FLIP COVER
FEBRUARY 1995
$3

HARDCASE
PREMIUM EDITION #0
JULY 1993
$3

HARDCASE #1
JUNE 1993
$4

HARDCASE #1
ULTRA 5000 LIMITED EDITION
JUNE 1993
$6

HARDCASE #2
JULY 1993
$3

HARDCASE #3
AUGUST 1993
$3

HARDCASE #4
SEPTEMBER 1993
$3

HARDCASE #5
FLIP BOOK WITH RUNE COVER/STORY
OCTOBER 1993
$4

HARDCASE #6
NOVEMBER 1993
$3

HARDCASE #7
DECEMBER 1993
$3

HARDCASE #8
JANUARY 1994
$3

HARDCASE #9
FEBRUARY 1994
$3

HARDCASE #10
MARCH 1994
$3

HARDCASE #11
APRIL 1994
$3

HARDCASE #12
MAY 1994
$3

HARDCASE #13
JUNE 1994
$3

HARDCASE #14
JULY 1994
$3

HARDCASE #15
AUGUST 1994
$3

HARDCASE #16
FLIP BOOK WITH ULTRAVERSE PREMIERE #7
OCTOBER 1994
$4

HARDCASE #17
NOVEMBER 1994
$3

HARDCASE #18
DECEMBER 1994
$3

HARDCASE #19
JANUARY 1995
$3

HARDCASE #20
FEBRUARY 1995
$4

HARDCASE #21
MARCH 1995
$4

HARDCASE #22
APRIL 1995
$4

HARDCASE #23
MAY 1995
$4

HARDCASE #24
JUNE 1995
$4

HARDCASE #25
JULY 1995
$4

HARDCASE #26
AUGUST 1995
$4

HOSTILE TAKEOVER ASHCAN
SEPTEMBER 1994
$3

JUMP START EFFECT #1
OCTOBER 1994
$3

LORD PUMPKIN #0
OCTOBER 1994
$3

LORD PUMPKIN #0
FEBRUARY 1995
$3

LORD PUMPKIN #1
FLIP BOOK WITH NECROMANTRA #1
APRIL 1995
$3

LORD PUMPKIN #2
FLIP BOOK WITH NECROMANTRA #2
MAY 1995
$3

LORD PUMPKIN #3
FLIP BOOK WITH NECROMANTRA #3
JUNE 1995
$3

LORD PUMPKIN #4
FLIP BOOK WITH NECROMANTRA #4
JULY 1995
$3

**MALIBU ASHCAN:
RAFFERTY #1**
NOVEMBER 1994
$4

MANTRA #1
JULY 1993
$3

MANTRA #2
AUGUST 1993
$3

MANTRA #3
SEPTEMBER 1993
$3

MANTRA #4
FLIP BOOK WITH RUNE COVER/STORY
OCTOBER 1993
$4

MANTRA #5
DIRECT EDITION
NOVEMBER 1993
$3

MANTRA #5
NEWSSTAND EDITION
NOVEMBER 1993
$3

MANTRA #6
DECEMBER 1993
$3

MANTRA #7
JANUARY 1994
$3

MANTRA #8
DIRECT EDITION
FEBRUARY 1994
$3

MANTRA #8
NEWSSTAND EDITION
FEBRUARY 1994
$3

MANTRA #9
MARCH 1994
$3

MANTRA #10
FLIP BOOK WITH ULTRAVERSE PREMIERE #2
APRIL 1994
$4

MANTRA #11
MAY 1994
$3

MANTRA #12
JUNE 1994
$3

MANTRA #13
AUGUST 1994
$3

MANTRA #13
VARIANT COVER
AUGUST 1994
$3

MANTRA #14
SEPTEMBER 1994
$3

MANTRA #15
OCTOBER 1994
$3

MANTRA #16
NOVEMBER 1994
$3

MANTRA #17
DECEMBER 1994
$3

MANTRA #18
FEBRUARY 1995
$3

MANTRA #19
MARCH 1995
$3

MANTRA #20
APRIL 1995
$3

MANTRA #21
MAY 1995
$3

MANTRA #22
JUNE 1995
$3

MANTRA #23
JULY 1995
$3

MANTRA #24
AUGUST 1995
$3

GIANT SIZE MANTRA #1
JULY 1994
$4

MANTRA INFINITY
SEPTEMBER 1995
$3

MANTRA INFINITY
BLACK COVER
SEPTEMBER 1995
$3

MANTRA VOL. 2 #1
OCTOBER 1995
$3

MANTRA VOL. 2 #1
PAINTED VARIANT COVER
OCTOBER 1995
$3

MANTRA VOL. 2 #2
FLIP BOOK WITH PHOENIX RESURRECTION
NOVEMBER 1995
$3

MANTRA VOL. 2 #3
DECEMBER 1995
$3

MANTRA VOL. 2 #4
JANUARY 1996
$3

MANTRA VOL. 2 #5
FEBRUARY 1996
$3

MANTRA VOL. 2 #6
MARCH 1996
$3

MANTRA VOL. 2 #7
APRIL 1996
$3

MANTRA:
SPEAR OF DESTINY #1
APRIL 1995
$3

MANTRA:
SPEAR OF DESTINY #2
MAY 1995
$3

MUTANTS VS. ULTRAS:
FIRST ENCOUNTERS #1
NOVEMBER 1995
$7

NECROMANTRA #1
FLIP BOOK WITH LORD PUMPKIN #1
APRIL 1995
$3

NECROMANTRA #2
FLIP BOOK WITH LORD PUMPKIN #2
MAY 1995
$3

NECROMANTRA #3
FLIP BOOK WITH LORD PUMPKIN #3
JUNE 1995
$3

NECROMANTRA #4
FLIP BOOK WITH LORD PUMPKIN #4
JULY 1995
$3

THE NIGHT MAN #1
FLIP BOOK WITH RUNE COVER/STORY
OCTOBER 1993
$5

THE NIGHT MAN #2
NOVEMBER 1993
$4

THE NIGHT MAN #3
DECEMBER 1993
$4

THE NIGHT MAN #4
JANUARY 1994
$4

THE NIGHT MAN #5
FEBRUARY 1994
$4

THE NIGHT MAN #6
MARCH 1994
$4

THE NIGHT MAN #7
APRIL 1994
$4

THE NIGHT MAN #8
MAY 1994
$4

THE NIGHT MAN #9
JUNE 1994
$4

THE NIGHT MAN #10
JULY 1994
$4

THE NIGHT MAN #11
FLIP BOOK WITH ULTRAVERSE PREMIERE #11
AUGUST 1994
$4

THE NIGHT MAN #12
SEPTEMBER 1994
$4

THE NIGHT MAN #13
OCTOBER 1994
$4

THE NIGHT MAN #14
NOVEMBER 1994
$4

THE NIGHT MAN #15
DECEMBER 1994
$4

THE NIGHT MAN #16
FLIP BOOK WITH ULTRAVERSE PREMIERE #11
JANUARY 1995
$5

THE NIGHT MAN #17
FEBRUARY 1995
$4

THE NIGHT MAN #18
MARCH 1995
$4

THE NIGHT MAN #19
APRIL 1995
$4

THE NIGHT MAN #20
MAY 1995
$4

THE NIGHT MAN #21
JUNE 1995
$4

THE NIGHT MAN #22
JULY 1995
$4

THE NIGHT MAN #23
AUGUST 1995
$4

THE NIGHT MAN INFINITY
SEPTEMBER 1995
$4

THE NIGHT MAN INFINITY
BLACK COVER
SEPTEMBER 1995
$4

THE NIGHT MAN VOL. 2 #1
NEWSSTAND EDITION
OCTOBER 1995
$3

THE NIGHT MAN VOL. 2 #1
DIRECT EDITION
OCTOBER 1995
$3

THE NIGHT MAN VOL. 2 #2
FLIP BOOK WITH PHOENIX RESURRECTION
NOVEMBER 1995
$3

THE NIGHT MAN VOL. 2 #3
DECEMBER 1995
$3

THE NIGHT MAN VOL. 2 #4
DECEMBER 1995
$3

THE NIGHT MAN/GAMBIT #1
DIETRICH COVER
MARCH 1996
$3

THE NIGHT MAN/GAMBIT #1
HOTZ COVER
MARCH 1996
$3

THE NIGHT MAN/GAMBIT #2
APRIL 1996
$3

THE NIGHT MAN/GAMBIT #3
MAY 1996
$3

**THE NIGHT MAN:
THE PILGRIM CONUNDRUM
SAGA #1**
JANUARY 1995
$5

**THE NIGHT MAN
VS. WOLVERINE #0**
1995
$1 $4 $10

PHOENIX RESURRECTION
FLIP BOOK WITH PRIME VOL. 2 #2
CHAPTER ONE • NOVEMBER 1995
$3

PHOENIX RESURRECTION
FLIP BOOK WITH NIGHT MAN VOL. 2 #2
CHAPTER TWO • NOVEMBER 1995
$3

PHOENIX RESURRECTION
FLIP BOOK WITH SIREN #2
CHAPTER THREE • NOVEMBER 1995
$3

PHOENIX RESURRECTION
FLIP BOOK WITH MANTRA VOL. 2 #2
CHAPTER FOUR • NOVEMBER 1995
$3

PHOENIX RESURRECTION
FLIP BOOK WITH ALL NEW EXILES #2
CHAPTER FIVE • NOVEMBER 1995
$3

PHOENIX RESURRECTION
FLIP BOOK WITH RUNE VOL. 2 #2
CHAPTER SIX • NOVEMBER 1995
$3

PHOENIX RESURRECTION
FLIP BOOK WITH ULTRAFORCE VOL. 2 #2
CHAPTER SEVEN • NOVEMBER 1995
$3

PHOENIX RESURRECTION
GENESIS #1
DECEMBER 1995
$5

PHOENIX RESURRECTION
REVELATIONS #1
DECEMBER 1995
$5

PHOENIX RESURRECTION AFTERMATH #1
JANUARY 1996
$5

PHOENIX RESURRECTION #0
MAY 1996
$4

THE POWER OF PRIME #1
JULY 1995
$3

THE POWER OF PRIME #2
AUGUST 1995
$3

THE POWER OF PRIME #3
AUGUST 1995
$3

THE POWER OF PRIME #4
SEPTEMBER 1995
$3

PRIME #1/2
APRIL 1994
$3

PRIME #1
JUNE 1993
$4

PRIME #2
JULY 1993
$3

PRIME #3
AUGUST 1993
$3

PRIME #4
SEPTEMBER 1993
$3

PRIME #5
FLIP BOOK WITH RUNE COVER/STORY
OCTOBER 1993
$4

PRIME #6
NOVEMBER 1993
$3

PRIME #7
DECEMBER 1993
$3

PRIME #8
JANUARY 1994
$3

PRIME #9
FEBRUARY 1994
$3

PRIME #10
MARCH 1994
$3

PRIME #11
APRIL 1994
$3

PRIME #12
FLIP BOOK WITH ULTRAVERSE PREMIERE #3
MAY 1994
$4

PRIME #13
JULY 1994
$4

PRIME #13
VARIANT COVER
JULY 1994
$4

PRIME #14
SEPTEMBER 1994
$3

PRIME #15
OCTOBER 1994
$3

PRIME #16
NOVEMBER 1994
$3

PRIME #17
DECEMBER 1994
$3

PRIME #18
DECEMBER 1994
$3

PRIME #19
JANUARY 1995
$3

PRIME #20
MARCH 1995
$3

PRIME #21
APRIL 1995
$3

PRIME #22
MAY 1995
$3

PRIME #23
JUNE 1995
$3

PRIME #24
JUNE 1995
$3

PRIME #25
JULY 1995
$3

PRIME #26
AUGUST 1995
$3

PRIME ASHCAN
AUGUST 1994
$3

**PRIME: GROSS AND
DISGUSTING #1**
OCTOBER 1994
$4

PRIME INFINITY
SEPTEMBER 1995
$3

PRIME INFINITY
BLACK COVER
SEPTEMBER 1995
$3

PRIME VOL. 2 #1
OCTOBER 1995
$3

PRIME VOL. 2 #1
PAINTED VARIANT COVER
OCTOBER 1995
$3

PRIME VOL. 2 #2
FLIP BOOK WITH PHOENIX RESURRECTION
NOVEMBER 1995
$3

PRIME VOL. 2 #3
DECEMBER 1995
$3

PRIME VOL. 2 #4
JANUARY 1996
$3

PRIME VOL. 2 #5
FEBRUARY 1996
$3

PRIME VOL. 2 #6
MARCH 1996
$3

PRIME VOL. 2 #7
APRIL 1996
$3

PRIME VOL. 2 #8
MAY 1996
$3

PRIME VOL. 2 #9
JUNE 1996
$3

PRIME VOL. 2 #10
JULY 1996
$3

PRIME VOL. 2 #11
AUGUST 1996
$3

PRIME VOL. 2 #12
SEPTEMBER 1996
$3

PRIME VOL. 2 #13
OCTOBER 1996
$3

PRIME VOL. 2 #14
NOVEMBER 1996
$3

PRIME VOL. 2 #15
DECEMBER 1996
$3

PRIME/CAPTAIN AMERICA #1
MARCH 1996
$5

PRIME VS. THE INCREDIBLE HULK #1
LIMITED PREMIUM EDITION • 1995
$10

PRIME VS. THE INCREDIBLE HULK #1
LIMITED SUPER PREMIUM EDITION • 1995
$15

PROTOTYPE #0
AUGUST 1994
$4

PROTOTYPE #1
AUGUST 1993
$4

PROTOTYPE #1
ULTRA LIMITED EDITION
AUGUST 1993
$6

PROTOTYPE #2
SEPTEMBER 1993
$3

PROTOTYPE #3
FLIP BOOK WITH RUNE COVER/STORY
OCTOBER 1993
$4

PROTOTYPE #4
NOVEMBER 1993
$3

PROTOTYPE #5
DECEMBER 1993
$3

PROTOTYPE #6
JANUARY 1994
$3

PROTOTYPE #7
FEBRUARY 1994
$3

PROTOTYPE #8
MARCH 1994
$3

PROTOTYPE #9
APRIL 1994
$3

PROTOTYPE #10
MAY 1994
$3

PROTOTYPE #11
JUNE 1994
$3

PROTOTYPE #12
JULY 1994
$3

PROTOTYPE #13
FLIP BOOK WITH ULTRAVERSE PREMIERE #6
AUGUST 1994
$3

PROTOTYPE #14
OCTOBER 1994
$3

PROTOTYPE #15
NOVEMBER 1994
$3

PROTOTYPE #16
DECEMBER 1994
$3

PROTOTYPE #17
JANUARY 1995
$3

PROTOTYPE #18
FEBRUARY 1995
$3

GIANT SIZE PROTOTYPE #1
OCTOBER 1994
$4

RIPFIRE #0
JANUARY 1995
$3

RUNE ASHCAN #1
FLIP BOOK WITH WRATH #1
JANUARY 1994
$3

RUNE #0
JANUARY 1994
$1 **$4** **$10**

The cover for January 1994's *Rune* #0 was previewed with these 9 interlocking images, all flip books from Ultraverse's October 1993 issues: *Exiles* #3, *Firearm* #2, *Freex* #4, *Hardcase* #5, *Mantra* #4, *The Night Man* #1, *Prime* #5, *Prototype* #3, and *The Strangers* #5. Each of these issues, plus *Sludge* #1 and *The Solution* #2, had 3 pages from a serialized story revealing the origin of the vampire Rune, with story and art by Barry Windsor-Smith.

RUNE #1
JANUARY 1994
$3

RUNE #1
ULTRA LIMITED EDITION
JANUARY 1994
$6

RUNE #2
FEBRUARY 1994
$3

RUNE #3
FLIP BOOK WITH ULTRAVERSE PREMIERE #1
MARCH 1994
$4

RUNE #4
JUNE 1994
$3

RUNE #5
SEPTEMBER 1994
$3

RUNE #6
DECEMBER 1994
$3

RUNE #7
JANUARY 1995
$3

RUNE #8
FEBRUARY 1995
$3

RUNE #9
APRIL 1995
$3

GIANT SIZE RUNE #1
JANUARY 1995
$4

RUNE VOL. 2 INFINITY
SEPTEMBER 1995
$3

RUNE VOL. 2 INFINITY
BLACK VARIANT COVER
SEPTEMBER 1995
$3

RUNE VOL. 2 #1
OCTOBER 1995
$3

RUNE VOL. 2 #2
FLIP BOOK WITH PHOENIX RESURRECTION
NOVEMBER 1995
$3

RUNE VOL. 2 #3
DECEMBER 1995
$3

RUNE VOL. 2 #4
JANUARY 1996
$3

RUNE VOL. 2 #5
FEBRUARY 1996
$3

RUNE VOL. 2 #6
MARCH 1996
$3

RUNE VOL. 2 #7
APRIL 1996
$3

RUNE: HEARTS OF DARKNESS #1
FLIP BOOK • SEPTEMBER 1995
$3

RUNE: HEARTS OF DARKNESS #1
FLIP BOOK • SEPTEMBER 1995
$3

RUNE: HEARTS OF DARKNESS #2
FLIP BOOK • OCTOBER 1995
$3

RUNE: HEARTS OF DARKNESS #2
FLIP BOOK • OCTOBER 1995
$3

RUNE: HEARTS OF DARKNESS #3
FLIP BOOK • NOVEMBER 1995
$3

RUNE: HEARTS OF DARKNESS #3
FLIP BOOK • NOVEMBER 1995
$3

RUNE/SILVER SURFER #1
NEWSSTAND EDITION
APRIL 1995
$3

RUNE/SILVER SURFER #1
DIRECT MARKET EDITION
APRIL 1995
$6

RUNE/SILVER SURFER #1
COLLECTOR'S LIMITED EDITION
APRIL 1995
$6

**RUNE THE SPIN
SPECIAL EDITION #1**
SEPTEMBER 1994
$3

RUNE VS. VENOM #1
DECEMBER 1995
$4

SIREN INFINITY
SEPTEMBER 1995
$3

SIREN INFINITY
BLACK VARIANT COVER
SEPTEMBER 1995
$3

SIREN #1
OCTOBER 1995
$3

SIREN #2
FLIP BOOK WITH PHOENIX RESURRECTION
NOVEMBER 1995
$3

SIREN #3
DECEMBER 1995
$3

SIREN SPECIAL #1
FEBRUARY 1996
$3

SLUDGE #1
FLIP BOOK WITH RUNE COVER/STORY
OCTOBER 1993
$4

SLUDGE #2
NOVEMBER 1993
$3

SLUDGE #3
DECEMBER 1993
$3

SLUDGE #4
JANUARY 1994
$3

SLUDGE #5
FEBRUARY 1994
$3

SLUDGE #6
MARCH 1994
$3

SLUDGE #7
JUNE 1994
$3

SLUDGE #8
JULY 1994
$3

SLUDGE #9
SEPTEMBER 1994
$3

SLUDGE #10
OCTOBER 1994
$3

SLUDGE #11
NOVEMBER 1994
$3

SLUDGE #12
FLIP BOOK WITH ULTRAVERSE PREMIERE #8
DECEMBER 1994
$4

SLUDGE: RED X-MAS #1
DECEMBER 1994
$4

SOLITAIRE #1
BLACK BAGGED WITH PLAYING CARD
NOVEMBER 1993
$4

SOLITAIRE #1
NOVEMBER 1993
$3

SOLITAIRE #2
DECEMBER 1993
$3

SOLITAIRE #3
FEBRUARY 1994
$3

Solitaire #4
March 1994
$3

Solitaire #5
April 1994
$3

Solitaire #6
May 1994
$3

Solitaire #7
September 1994
$3

Solitaire #8
September 1994
$3

Solitaire #9
September 1994
$3

Solitaire #10
October 1994
$3

Solitaire #11
November 1994
$3

Solitaire #12
December 1994
$3

THE SOLUTION #0
JANUARY 1994
$5

THE SOLUTION #1
SEPTEMBER 1993
$3

THE SOLUTION #2
FLIP BOOK WITH RUNE COVER/STORY
OCTOBER 1993
$4

THE SOLUTION #3
NOVEMBER 1993
$3

THE SOLUTION #4
DECEMBER 1993
$3

THE SOLUTION #5
JANUARY 1994
$3

THE SOLUTION #6
FEBRUARY 1994
$3

THE SOLUTION #7
MARCH 1994
$3

THE SOLUTION #8
APRIL 1994
$3

THE SOLUTION #9
JUNE 1994
$3

THE SOLUTION #10
JULY 1994
$3

THE SOLUTION #11
AUGUST 1994
$3

THE SOLUTION #12
OCTOBER 1994
$3

THE SOLUTION #13
OCTOBER 1994
$3

THE SOLUTION #14
DECEMBER 1994
$3

THE SOLUTION #15
JANUARY 1995
$3

THE SOLUTION #16
FLIP BOOK WITH ULTRAVERSE PREMIERE #10
JANUARY 1995
$4

THE SOLUTION #17
FEBRUARY 1995
$3

THE STRANGERS #1
JUNE 1993
$3

THE STRANGERS #1
ULTRA LIMITED EDITION
JUNE 1993
$3

THE STRANGERS #2
JULY 1993
$3

THE STRANGERS #3
AUGUST 1993
$3

THE STRANGERS #4
SEPTEMBER 1993
$3

THE STRANGERS #5
FLIP BOOK WITH RUNE COVER/STORY
OCTOBER 1993
$4

THE STRANGERS #6
NOVEMBER 1993
$3

THE STRANGERS #7
DECEMBER 1993
$3

THE STRANGERS #8
JANUARY 1994
$3

THE STRANGERS #9
FEBRUARY 1994
$3

THE STRANGERS #10
MARCH 1994
$3

THE STRANGERS #11
APRIL 1994
$3

THE STRANGERS #12
MAY 1994
$3

THE STRANGERS #13
FLIP BOOK WITH ULTRAVERSE PREMIERE #4
JUNE 1994
$4

THE STRANGERS #14
JULY 1994
$3

THE STRANGERS #15
AUGUST 1994
$3

THE STRANGERS #16
SEPTEMBER 1994
$3

THE STRANGERS #17
OCTOBER 1994
$3

THE STRANGERS #18
NOVEMBER 1994
$3

THE STRANGERS #19
DECEMBER 1994
$3

THE STRANGERS #20
JANUARY 1995
$3

THE STRANGERS #21
FEBRUARY 1995
$3

THE STRANGERS #22
MARCH 1995
$3

THE STRANGERS #23
APRIL 1995
$3

THE STRANGERS #24
MAY 1995
$3

**THE STRANGERS: THE
PILGRIM CONUNDRUM #1**
JANUARY 1995
$4

**ULTRAFORCE
MALIBU ASHCAN**
1994
$3

ULTRAFORCE ASHCAN #0A
JUNE 1994
$3

ULTRAFORCE ASHCAN #0B
JULY 1994
$3

ULTRAFORCE #0
SEPTEMBER 1994
$4

ULTRAFORCE #1
AUGUST 1994
$4

ULTRAFORCE #1
ULTRA LIMITED EDITION
AUGUST 1994
$1 $3 $8

ULTRAFORCE #2
OCTOBER 1994
$3

ULTRAFORCE #2
LIMITED SPECIAL EDITION
OCTOBER 1994
$4

ULTRAFORCE #3
NOVEMBER 1994
$3

ULTRAFORCE #4
JANUARY 1995
$3

UltraForce #5
FEBRUARY 1995
$3

UltraForce #6
MARCH 1995
$3

UltraForce #7
APRIL 1995
$3

UltraForce #8
MAY 1995
$3

UltraForce #9
JUNE 1995
$3

UltraForce #10
JULY 1995
$3

UltraForce Infinity
SEPTEMBER 1995
$3

UltraForce Infinity
BLACK VARIANT COVER
SEPTEMBER 1995
$3

UltraForce Vol. 2 #1
OCTOBER 1995
$3

ULTRAFORCE VOL. 2 #2
FLIP BOOK WITH PHOENIX RESURRECTION
NOVEMBER 1995
$3

ULTRAFORCE VOL. 2 #3
DECEMBER 1995
$3

ULTRAFORCE VOL. 2 #4
JANUARY 1996
$3

ULTRAFORCE VOL. 2 #5
FEBRUARY 1996
$3

ULTRAFORCE VOL. 2 #6
MARCH 1996
$3

ULTRAFORCE VOL. 2 #7
APRIL 1996
$3

ULTRAFORCE VOL. 2 #8
MAY 1996
$3

ULTRAFORCE VOL. 2 #9
JUNE 1996
$3

ULTRAFORCE VOL. 2 #10
JULY 1996
$3

ULTRAFORCE VOL. 2 #11
AUGUST 1996
$3

ULTRAFORCE VOL. 2 #12
SEPTEMBER 1996
$3

ULTRAFORCE VOL. 2 #13
OCTOBER 1996
$3

ULTRAFORCE VOL. 2 #14
NOVEMBER 1996
$3

ULTRAFORCE VOL. 2 #15
DECEMBER 1996
$3

**ULTRAFORCE/AVENGERS
PRELUDE #1**
AUGUST 1995
$3

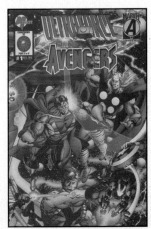

ULTRAFORCE/AVENGERS #1
FALL 1995
$4

ULTRAFORCE/SPIDER-MAN #1A
JANUARY 1996
$4

ULTRAFORCE/SPIDER-MAN #1B
JANUARY 1996
$4

**ULTRAVERSE
DOUBLE FEATURE #1**
Flip book • January 1995
$4

**ULTRAVERSE
DOUBLE FEATURE #1**
Flip book • January 1995
$4

**ULTRAVERSE:
FUTURE SHOCK #1**
February 1997
$3

Ultraverse Origins #1
January 1994
$3

Ultraverse Premiere #0
November 1993
$5

Ultraverse Premiere #1
Flip book with Rune #3
March 1994
$4

Ultraverse Premiere #2
Flip book with Mantra #10
April 1994
$4

Ultraverse Premiere #3
Flip book with Prime #12
May 1994
$4

Ultraverse Premiere #4
Flip book with The Strangers #13
June 1994
$4

ULTRAVERSE PREMIERE #5
FLIP BOOK WITH FIREARM #11
JULY 1994
$4

ULTRAVERSE PREMIERE #6
FLIP BOOK WITH PROTOTYPE #13
AUGUST 1994
$4

ULTRAVERSE PREMIERE #7
FLIP BOOK WITH HARDCASE #16
OCTOBER 1994
$4

ULTRAVERSE PREMIERE #8
FLIP BOOK WITH SLUDGE #12
DECEMBER 1994
$4

ULTRAVERSE PREMIERE #9
FLIP BOOK WITH FREEX #15
JANUARY 1995
$4

ULTRAVERSE PREMIERE #10
FLIP BOOK WITH THE SOLUTION #16
JANUARY 1995
$4

ULTRAVERSE PREMIERE #11
FLIP BOOK WITH THE NIGHT MAN #16
JANUARY 1995
$5

ULTRAVERSE UNLIMITED #1
JUNE 1995
$3

ULTRAVERSE UNLIMITED #2
SEPTEMBER 1995
$3

ULTRAVERSE YEAR ONE
1994
$5

ULTRAVERSE YEAR TWO
AUGUST 1995
$5

**ULTRAVERSE: YEAR ZERO
THE DEATH OF THE SQUAD #1**
APRIL 1995
$3

**ULTRAVERSE: YEAR ZERO
THE DEATH OF THE SQUAD #2**
MAY 1995
$3

**ULTRAVERSE: YEAR ZERO
THE DEATH OF THE SQUAD #3**
JUNE 1995
$3

**ULTRAVERSE: YEAR ZERO
THE DEATH OF THE SQUAD #4**
JULY 1995
$3

WARSTRIKE #1
MAY 1994
$3

WARSTRIKE #1
WALT SIMONSON COVER
MAY 1994
$3

WARSTRIKE #1
ULTRA LIMITED EDITION
MAY 1994
$6

WARSTRIKE #2
JUNE 1994
$3

WARSTRIKE #3
JULY 1994
$3

WARSTRIKE #4
AUGUST 1994
$3

WARSTRIKE #5
SEPTEMBER 1994
$3

WARSTRIKE #6
OCTOBER 1994
$3

WARSTRIKE #7
NOVEMBER 1994
$3

GIANT SIZE WARSTRIKE #1
DECEMBER 1994
$3

WITCH HUNTER #1
APRIL 1996
$3

WRATH ASHCAN #1
FLIP BOOK WITH RUNE ASHCAN #1
JANUARY 1994
$3

WRATH #1
JANUARY 1994
$3

WRATH #1
ULTRA LIMITED EDITION
JANUARY 1994
$4

WRATH #2
FEBRUARY 1994
$3

WRATH #3
MARCH 1994
$3

WRATH #4
APRIL 1994
$3

WRATH #5
MAY 1994
$3

WRATH #6
JUNE 1994
$3

WRATH #7
JULY 1994
$3

WRATH #8
OCTOBER 1994
$3

WRATH #9
DECEMBER 1994
$3

GIANT SIZE WRATH #1
AUGUST 1994
$3

Rick Hoberg's original cover art for *The Strangers* #1 depicts team members Atom Bob, Grenade, Yrial, Lady Killer, Zip-Zap, Electrocute, and Spectral. Along with *Hardcase* #1 and *Prime* #1, the debut of the Ultraverse and this team of superheroes came in June 1993. The series would run for 24 issues with creator/writer Steve Englehart on board for all of them and artist Rick Hoberg present for the majority of them. This ink over graphite piece of original art has an image area of 10.5" x 15.75" on DC Comics DC Bristol. Image courtesy of Heritage Auctions.

VALIANT

Former Marvel Comics Editor-in-Chief Jim Shooter, entertainment lawyer Steven J. Massarsky and a group of investors, after coming in second to financier Ronald O. Perelman in an attempt to purchase Marvel in 1988, formed Voyager Communications in 1989. Perelman would go on to bankrupt Marvel, while Voyager launched the VALIANT imprint.

While the company became known for its superhero line, they were not the company's first offerings. Utilizing many of the same creators who would soon define their better-selling efforts, VALIANT produced *Adventures of Super Mario Bros.*, *Legend of Zelda*, *Captain N: The Game Master*, and others under a Nintendo license, and *WWF Battlemania*. These comics have appeal to VALIANT completists and fans of the specific characters, but they have no bearing on the superhero universe that was to follow or the later iterations of it.

FIRST PUBLICATION:
Magnus Robot Fighter #1 (May 1991)

LAST PUBLICATION:
X-O Manowar #68 (September 1996)

REVIVAL(S):
Acclaim VH2 reboot (1996), Valiant Entertainment collected editions (2007, 2008), new comics beginning with *X-O Manowar* #1 (May 2012).

Magnus Robot Fighter #1 (May 1991) saw the debut of that universe. The character had originally appeared in *Magnus Robot Fighter 4000 A.D.* #1 from Gold Key (February 1963). Shooter and company had licensed Magnus, Solar, and Turok from Gold Key's parent, Western Publishing, on terms that Shooter has described as "a sweetheart deal." They would pay off for the new publisher.

After that, the fabric of the universe was woven quickly and convincingly, with alien and man-made threats, technology, circumstances, and tone linking the titles together. *Solar, Man of the Atom* #1 debuted in September 1991. *Magnus Robot Fighter* #5 (October 1991) kicked off a four-issue arc that turned the series into a flip-book with *Rai*, the company's first original title. *Solar, Man of the Atom* #3 (September 1991) included the first appearance of Toyo Harada and the Harbinger Foundation. *Magnus Robot Fighter* #5 (December 1991) saw the introduction of the X-O Commando armor and the Spider aliens. *Harbinger* #1 (January 1992)

became their second original title. It was followed by *X-O Manowar* #1 (February 1992). A new, standalone *Rai* #1 (March 1992) solidified the character's position after his flipbook appearances in Magnus. *Shadowman* #1 debuted in May 1992, the same month that saw Turok, the last of the three characters licensed from Western Publishing, appear in *Magnus Robot Fighter* #12. *Harbinger* #6, which featured the completion of the first story arc and the death of Torque, and *Solar, Man of the Atom* #10, which concluded the serialized origin story "Alpha and Omega," appeared in June 1992. *Archer & Armstrong* #0 hit stands in July 1992, and the table was set.

The tightly written continuity had led the stories inexorably to *Unity*, an event that ran through all of the company's titles for two months, and firmly established the VALIANT universe. During the Unity event, *Eternal Warrior* #1 (August 1992) established the company's eighth regular monthly title.

With the company on an upward trajectory, Shooter was forced out, Bob Layton took over as Editor-in-Chief, and new titles continued to roll out, including *H.A.R.D. Corps* #1 (December 1992), *Bloodshot* #1 (February 1993), and *Turok Dinosaur Hunter* #1 (July 1993). As the 1990s comic book boom accelerated, the company was sold to video game maker Acclaim Entertainment for a reported $65 million.

The company continued to ride the boom, selling by some estimates half of the comics it sold during its original incarnation in 1993. While there were many strong individual efforts during this period, there were also initiatives such as "Birthquake" that did not have any lasting impact. The boom was, perhaps not surprisingly, followed by a bust, and VALIANT was hit hard by it. The last original Valiant issue was *X-O Manowar* #68 (September 1996), but a major reboot would soon follow.

Barry Windsor-Smith and Bob Layton's original art of *Solar, Man of the Atom: Alpha and Omega* Chapter Three, Page 1. Image courtesy of Dan Moler.

ARCHER & ARMSTRONG #0
JUNE 1992
$1 $4 $10

ARCHER & ARMSTRONG #0
GOLD LOGO VARIANT
JUNE 1992
$6 $18 $100

ARCHER & ARMSTRONG #1
AUGUST 1992
$5

ARCHER & ARMSTRONG #2
SEPTEMBER 1992
$5

ARCHER & ARMSTRONG #3
OCTOBER 1992
$4

ARCHER & ARMSTRONG #4
NOVEMBER 1992
$4

ARCHER & ARMSTRONG #5
DECEMBER 1992
$4

ARCHER & ARMSTRONG #6
JANUARY 1993
$4

ARCHER & ARMSTRONG #7
FEBRUARY 1993
$4

ARCHER & ARMSTRONG #8
MARCH 1993
$5

ARCHER & ARMSTRONG #9
APRIL 1993
$3

ARCHER & ARMSTRONG #10
MAY 1993
$3

ARCHER & ARMSTRONG #11
JUNE 1993
$3

ARCHER & ARMSTRONG #12
JULY 1993
$3

ARCHER & ARMSTRONG #13
AUGUST 1993
$3

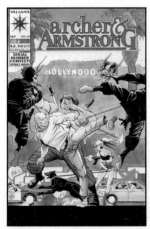

ARCHER & ARMSTRONG #14
SEPTEMBER 1993
$3

ARCHER & ARMSTRONG #15
OCTOBER 1993
$3

ARCHER & ARMSTRONG #16
NOVEMBER 1993
$3

ARCHER & ARMSTRONG #17
DECEMBER 1993
$3

ARCHER & ARMSTRONG #18
JANUARY 1994
$3

ARCHER & ARMSTRONG #19
FEBRUARY 1994
$3

ARCHER & ARMSTRONG #20
MARCH 1994
$3

ARCHER & ARMSTRONG #21
APRIL 1994
$3

ARCHER & ARMSTRONG #22
MAY 1994
$3

ARCHER & ARMSTRONG #23
JUNE 1994
$3

ARCHER & ARMSTRONG #24
AUGUST 1994
$3

ARCHER & ARMSTRONG #25
SEPTEMBER 1994
$3

ARCHER & ARMSTRONG #26
OCTOBER 1994
$3

ARMORINES #0
FEBRUARY 1994
$34

ARMORINES #0
GOLD LOGO VARIANT
FEBRUARY 1994
$28

ARMORINES #1
JULY 1994
$4

ARMORINES #2
AUGUST 1994
$3

ARMORINES #3
SEPTEMBER 1994
$3

ARMORINES #4
OCTOBER 1994
$3

ARMORINES #5
NOVEMBER 1994
$3

ARMORINES #6
DECEMBER 1994
$3

ARMORINES #7
JANUARY 1995
$3

ARMORINES #8
FEBRUARY 1995
$3

ARMORINES #9
MARCH 1995
$3

ARMORINES #10
APRIL 1995
$3

ARMORINES #11
MAY 1995
$3

ARMORINES #12
JUNE 1995
$5

BLOODSHOT #0
MARCH 1994
$5

BLOODSHOT #0
GOLD LOGO VARIANT
MARCH 1994
$40

BLOODSHOT #1
FEBRUARY 1993
$2 $6 $12

BLOODSHOT #2
MARCH 1993
$4

BLOODSHOT #3
APRIL 1993
$4

BLOODSHOT #4
MAY 1993
$4

BLOODSHOT #5
JUNE 1993
$4

BLOODSHOT #6
JULY 1993
$2 $6 $12

BLOODSHOT #7
AUGUST 1993
$2 $6 $12

BLOODSHOT #8
SEPTEMBER 1993
$4

BLOODSHOT #9
OCTOBER 1993
$4

BLOODSHOT #10
NOVEMBER 1993
$4

BLOODSHOT #11
DECEMBER 1993
$4

BLOODSHOT #12
JANUARY 1994
$4

BLOODSHOT #13
FEBRUARY 1994
$4

BLOODSHOT #14
MARCH 1994
$4

BLOODSHOT #15
APRIL 1994
$3

BLOODSHOT #16
MAY 1994
$3

BLOODSHOT #17
JUNE 1994
$3

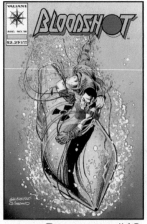

BLOODSHOT #18
AUGUST 1994
$3

BLOODSHOT #19
SEPTEMBER 1994
$3

BLOODSHOT #20
OCTOBER 1994
$3

BLOODSHOT #21
NOVEMBER 1994
$3

BLOODSHOT #22
DECEMBER 1994
$3

BLOODSHOT #23
JANUARY 1995
$3

BLOODSHOT #24
FEBRUARY 1995
$3

BLOODSHOT #25
MARCH 1995
$3

BLOODSHOT #26
APRIL 1995
$3

BLOODSHOT #27
MAY 1995
$3

BLOODSHOT #28
MAY 1995
$3

BLOODSHOT #29
JUNE 1995
$3

BLOODSHOT #30
JULY 1995
$3

BLOODSHOT #31
JULY 1995
$3

BLOODSHOT #32
AUGUST 1995
$3

BLOODSHOT #33
AUGUST 1995
$3

BLOODSHOT #34
SEPTEMBER 1995
$3

BLOODSHOT #35
SEPTEMBER 1995
$3

BLOODSHOT #36
OCTOBER 1995
$3

BLOODSHOT #37
OCTOBER 1995
$3

BLOODSHOT #38
NOVEMBER 1995
$3

BLOODSHOT #39
NOVEMBER 1995
$3

BLOODSHOT #40
DECEMBER 1995
$3

BLOODSHOT #41
DECEMBER 1995
$3

BLOODSHOT #42
JANUARY 1996
$3

BLOODSHOT #43
JANUARY 1996
$3

BLOODSHOT #44
FEBRUARY 1996
$3

BLOODSHOT #45
MARCH 1996
$3

BLOODSHOT #46
APRIL 1996
$3

BLOODSHOT #47
MAY 1996
$3

BLOODSHOT #48
MAY 1996
$3

BLOODSHOT #49
JUNE 1996
$3

BLOODSHOT #50
JULY 1996
$3

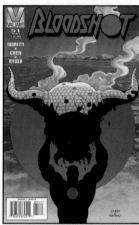

BLOODSHOT #51
AUGUST 1996
$4 $12 $55

BLOODSHOT SPECIAL #1
MARCH 1994
$12

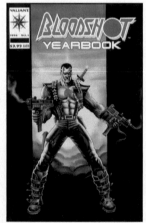

BLOODSHOT YEARBOOK #1
1994
$4

**CAPTAIN JOHNER &
THE ALIENS #1**
MAY 1995
$3

**CAPTAIN JOHNER &
THE ALIENS #2**
MAY 1995
$3

THE CHAOS EFFECT ALPHA
1994
$4

THE CHAOS EFFECT ALPHA
RED LOGO VARIANT
1994
$5

THE CHAOS EFFECT OMEGA
1994
$3

THE CHAOS EFFECT OMEGA
GOLD LOGO VARIANT
1994
$1 $3 $10

**THE CHAOS EFFECT:
EPILOGUE PART 1**
1994
$3

**THE CHAOS EFFECT:
EPILOGUE PART 2**
1994
$3

DEATHMATE PREVIEW
ADVANCE COMICS EDITION
JULY 1993
$1 $4 $10

DEATHMATE PREVIEW
COMIC DEFENSE SYSTEM EDITION
JULY 1993
$1 $4 $10

DEATHMATE PREVIEW
PREVIEWS ORANGE EDITION
AUGUST 1993
$4 $12 $50

DEATHMATE PREVIEW
PREVIEWS PINK EDITION
AUGUST 1993
$2 **$6** **$15**

DEATHMATE PROLOGUE
SEPTEMBER 1993
$3

DEATHMATE PROLOGUE
GOLD EDITION
SEPTEMBER 1993
$3 **$9** **$28**

DEATHMATE BLACK
SEPTEMBER 1993
$6

DEATHMATE BLACK
GOLD EDITION
SEPTEMBER 1993
$7

DEATHMATE YELLOW
OCTOBER 1993
$5

DEATHMATE YELLOW
GOLD EDITION
OCTOBER 1993
$6

DEATHMATE BLUE
OCTOBER 1993
$5

DEATHMATE BLUE
GOLD EDITION
OCTOBER 1993
$6

DEATHMATE RED
NOVEMBER 1993
$3

DEATHMATE RED
GOLD EDITION
NOVEMBER 1993
$4

DEATHMATE EPILOGUE
FEBRUARY 1994
$3

DEATHMATE EPILOGUE
GOLD EDITION
FEBRUARY 1994
$3

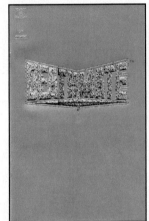

DEATHMATE TOURBOOK
1993
$3

DESTROYER #0
APRIL 1995
COVER PRICE $2.95 - $2 $6 $15
COVER PRICE $2.50 - $4

ETERNAL WARRIOR #1
AUGUST 1992
$2 $6 $12

ETERNAL WARRIOR #1
GOLD LOGO VARIANT
AUGUST 1992
$3 $9 $28

ETERNAL WARRIOR #1
GOLD LOGO ON EMBOSSED COVER VARIANT
AUGUST 1992
$4 $12 $55

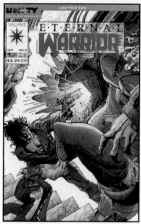

ETERNAL WARRIOR #2
SEPTEMBER 1992
$4

ETERNAL WARRIOR #3
OCTOBER 1992
$4

ETERNAL WARRIOR #4
NOVEMBER 1992
$3 $9 $38

ETERNAL WARRIOR #5
DECEMBER 1992
$4

ETERNAL WARRIOR #6
JANUARY 1993
$4

ETERNAL WARRIOR #7
FEBRUARY 1993
$4

ETERNAL WARRIOR #8
MARCH 1993
$4

ETERNAL WARRIOR #9
APRIL 1993
$3

ETERNAL WARRIOR #10
MAY 1993
$3

ETERNAL WARRIOR #11
JUNE 1993
$3

ETERNAL WARRIOR #12
JULY 1993
$3

ETERNAL WARRIOR #13
AUGUST 1993
$3

ETERNAL WARRIOR #14
SEPTEMBER 1993
$3

ETERNAL WARRIOR #15
OCTOBER 1993
$3

ETERNAL WARRIOR #16
NOVEMBER 1993
$3

ETERNAL WARRIOR #17
DECEMBER 1993
$3

ETERNAL WARRIOR #18
JANUARY 1994
$3

ETERNAL WARRIOR #19
FEBRUARY 1994
$3

ETERNAL WARRIOR #20
MARCH 1994
$3

ETERNAL WARRIOR #21
APRIL 1994
$3

ETERNAL WARRIOR #22
MAY 1994
$3

ETERNAL WARRIOR #23
JUNE 1994
$3

ETERNAL WARRIOR #24
AUGUST 1994
$3

ETERNAL WARRIOR #25
SEPTEMBER 1994
$3

ETERNAL WARRIOR #26
OCTOBER 1994
$4

ETERNAL WARRIOR #27
NOVEMBER 1994
$3

ETERNAL WARRIOR #28
DECEMBER 1994
$3

ETERNAL WARRIOR #29
JANUARY 1995
$3

ETERNAL WARRIOR #30
FEBRUARY 1995
$3

ETERNAL WARRIOR #31
MARCH 1995
$3

ETERNAL WARRIOR #32
APRIL 1995
$3

ETERNAL WARRIOR #33
MAY 1995
$3

ETERNAL WARRIOR #34
JUNE 1995
$3

ETERNAL WARRIOR #35
OUTER COVER

ETERNAL WARRIOR #35
"GRAPHIC" INNER COVER
JULY 1995
$3

ETERNAL WARRIOR #36
JULY 1995
$3

ETERNAL WARRIOR #37
AUGUST 1995
$3

ETERNAL WARRIOR #38
AUGUST 1995
$3

ETERNAL WARRIOR #39
SEPTEMBER 1995
$3

ETERNAL WARRIOR #40
SEPTEMBER 1995
$3

ETERNAL WARRIOR #41
OCTOBER 1995
$3

ETERNAL WARRIOR #42
OCTOBER 1995
$3

ETERNAL WARRIOR #43
NOVEMBER 1995
$3

ETERNAL WARRIOR #44
NOVEMBER 1995
$3

ETERNAL WARRIOR #45
DECEMBER 1995
$3

ETERNAL WARRIOR #46
DECEMBER 1995
$3

ETERNAL WARRIOR #47
JANUARY 1996
$3

ETERNAL WARRIOR #48
JANUARY 1996
$3

ETERNAL WARRIOR #49
FEBRUARY 1996
$3

ETERNAL WARRIOR #50
MARCH 1996
$3

**ETERNAL WARRIOR
SPECIAL #1**
FEBRUARY 1996
$3

**ETERNAL WARRIOR
YEARBOOK #1**
1993
$4

**ETERNAL WARRIOR
YEARBOOK #2**
1994
$4

**ETERNAL WARRIOR:
FIST AND STEEL #1**
MAY 1996
$4

**ETERNAL WARRIOR:
FIST AND STEEL #2**
JUNE 1996
$4

GEOMANCER #1
NOVEMBER 1994
$5

GEOMANCER #2
DECEMBER 1994
$4

GEOMANCER #3
JANUARY 1995
$4

GEOMANCER #4
FEBRUARY 1995
$4

GEOMANCER #5
MARCH 1995
$4

GEOMANCER #6
APRIL 1995
$4

GEOMANCER #7
MAY 1995
$4

GEOMANCER #8
JUNE 1995
$4

HARBINGER #0
FEBRUARY 1993
$5   **$15**   **$75**

HARBINGER #0
2ND PRINTING
1993
$1   **$4**   **$10**

HARBINGER #1
JANUARY 1992
$7   **$21**   **$120**

HARBINGER #2
FEBRUARY 1992
$3   **$9**   **$24**

HARBINGER #3
MARCH 1992
$3   **$9**   **$24**

HARBINGER #4
APRIL 1992
$3   **$9**   **$24**

HARBINGER #5
MAY 1992
$2   **$6**   **$15**

HARBINGER #6
JUNE 1992
$2   **$6**   **$15**

HARBINGER #7
JULY 1992
$1   **$3**   **$8**

HARBINGER #8
AUGUST 1992
$1 $3 $8

HARBINGER #9
SEPTEMBER 1992
$1 $3 $8

HARBINGER #10
OCTOBER 1992
$1 $3 $8

HARBINGER #11
NOVEMBER 1992
$4

HARBINGER #12
DECEMBER 1992
$4

HARBINGER #13
JANUARY 1993
$4

HARBINGER #14
FEBRUARY 1993
$4

HARBINGER #15
MARCH 1993
$4

HARBINGER #16
APRIL 1993
$4

HARBINGER #17
MAY 1993
$4

HARBINGER #18
JUNE 1993
$4

HARBINGER #19
JULY 1993
$4

HARBINGER #20
AUGUST 1993
$4

HARBINGER #21
SEPTEMBER 1993
$4

HARBINGER #22
OCTOBER 1993
$4

HARBINGER #23
NOVEMBER 1993
$4

HARBINGER #24
DECEMBER 1993
$4

HARBINGER #25
JANUARY 1994
$5

HARBINGER #26
FEBRUARY 1994
$4

HARBINGER #27
MARCH 1994
$4

HARBINGER #28
APRIL 1994
$4

HARBINGER #29
MAY 1994
$4

HARBINGER #30
JUNE 1994
$4

HARBINGER #31
AUGUST 1994
$4

HARBINGER #32
SEPTEMBER 1994
$4

HARBINGER #33
OCTOBER 1994
$4

HARBINGER #34
NOVEMBER 1994
$4

HARBINGER #35
DECEMBER 1994
$4

HARBINGER #36
JANUARY 1995
$4

HARBINGER #37
FEBRUARY 1995
$4

HARBINGER #38
MARCH 1995
$4

HARBINGER #39
APRIL 1995
$4

HARBINGER #40
MAY 1995
$4

HARBINGER #41
JUNE 1995
$4

HARBINGER FILES #1
AUGUST 1994
$4

HARBINGER FILES #2
FEBRUARY 1995
$4

THE H.A.R.D. CORPS #1
DECEMBER 1992
$5

THE H.A.R.D. CORPS #1
GOLD LOGO VARIANT
DECEMBER 1992
$15

THE H.A.R.D. CORPS #2
JANUARY 1993
$3

THE H.A.R.D. CORPS #3
FEBRUARY 1993
$3

THE H.A.R.D. CORPS #4
MARCH 1993
$3

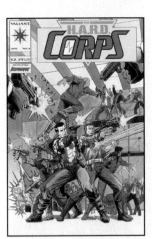

THE H.A.R.D. CORPS #5
APRIL 1993
$3

THE H.A.R.D. CORPS #5
COMIC DEFENSE SYSTEM VARIANT
APRIL 1993
$3

THE H.A.R.D. CORPS #6
MAY 1993
$3

THE H.A.R.D. CORPS #7
JUNE 1993
$3

THE H.A.R.D. CORPS #8
JULY 1993
$3

THE H.A.R.D. CORPS #9
AUGUST 1993
$3

THE H.A.R.D. CORPS #10
SEPTEMBER 1993
$3

THE H.A.R.D. CORPS #11
OCTOBER 1993
$3

THE H.A.R.D. CORPS #12
NOVEMBER 1993
$3

THE H.A.R.D. CORPS #13
DECEMBER 1993
$3

THE H.A.R.D. CORPS #14
JANUARY 1994
$3

THE H.A.R.D. CORPS #15
FEBRUARY 1994
$3

THE H.A.R.D. CORPS #16
MARCH 1994
$3

The H.A.R.D. Corps #17
APRIL 1994
$3

The H.A.R.D. Corps #18
MAY 1994
$3

The H.A.R.D. Corps #19
JUNE 1994
$3

The H.A.R.D. Corps #20
AUGUST 1994
$3

The H.A.R.D. Corps #21
SEPTEMBER 1994
$3

The H.A.R.D. Corps #22
OCTOBER 1994
$3

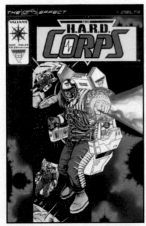

The H.A.R.D. Corps #23
NOVEMBER 1994
$3

The H.A.R.D. Corps #24
DECEMBER 1994
$3

The H.A.R.D. Corps #25
JANUARY 1995
$3

THE H.A.R.D. CORPS #26
FEBRUARY 1995
$3

THE H.A.R.D. CORPS #27
MARCH 1995
$3

THE H.A.R.D. CORPS #28
APRIL 1995
$3

THE H.A.R.D. CORPS #29
MAY 1995
$3

THE H.A.R.D. CORPS #30
JUNE 1995
$3

MAGNUS ROBOT FIGHTER #0
1992
$3 $9 $40

MAGNUS ROBOT FIGHTER #1
MAY 1991
$3 $9 $24

MAGNUS ROBOT FIGHTER #2
JULY 1991
$1 $4 $10

MAGNUS ROBOT FIGHTER #3
AUGUST 1991
$1 $4 $10

MAGNUS ROBOT FIGHTER #4
SEPTEMBER 1991
$1 $4 $10

MAGNUS ROBOT FIGHTER #5
FLIP BOOK WITH RAI MINI-SERIES #1
OCTOBER 1991
$3 $9 $30

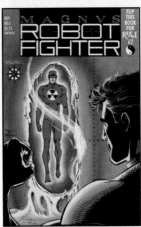

MAGNUS ROBOT FIGHTER #6
FLIP BOOK WITH RAI MINI-SERIES #2
NOVEMBER 1991
$1 $4 $10

MAGNUS ROBOT FIGHTER #7
FLIP BOOK WITH RAI MINI-SERIES #3
DECEMBER 1991
$2 $6 $20

MAGNUS ROBOT FIGHTER #8
FLIP BOOK WITH RAI MINI-SERIES #4
JANUARY 1992
$1 $4 $10

MAGNUS ROBOT FIGHTER #9
FEBRUARY 1992
$6

MAGNUS ROBOT FIGHTER #10
MARCH 1992
$6

MAGNUS ROBOT FIGHTER #11
APRIL 1992
$6

MAGNUS ROBOT FIGHTER #12
MAY 1992
$3 $9 $35

MAGNUS ROBOT FIGHTER #13
JUNE 1992
$4

MAGNUS ROBOT FIGHTER #14
JULY 1992
$4

MAGNUS ROBOT FIGHTER #15
AUGUST 1992
$4

MAGNUS ROBOT FIGHTER #16
SEPTEMBER 1992
$4

MAGNUS ROBOT FIGHTER #17
OCTOBER 1992
$4

MAGNUS ROBOT FIGHTER #18
NOVEMBER 1992
$4

MAGNUS ROBOT FIGHTER #19
DECEMBER 1992
$4

MAGNUS ROBOT FIGHTER #20
JANUARY 1993
$4

MAGNUS ROBOT FIGHTER #21
FEBRUARY 1993
$4

MAGNUS ROBOT FIGHTER #21
GOLD LOGO VARIANT
FEBRUARY 1993
$2 $6 $20

MAGNUS ROBOT FIGHTER #22
MARCH 1993
$4

MAGNUS ROBOT FIGHTER #23
APRIL 1993
$4

MAGNUS ROBOT FIGHTER #24
MAY 1993
$4

MAGNUS ROBOT FIGHTER #25
JUNE 1993
$5

MAGNUS ROBOT FIGHTER #26
JULY 1993
$4

MAGNUS ROBOT FIGHTER #27
AUGUST 1993
$4

MAGNUS ROBOT FIGHTER #28
SEPTEMBER 1993
$4

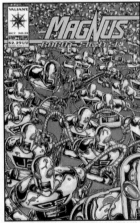

MAGNUS ROBOT FIGHTER #29
OCTOBER 1993
$4

MAGNUS ROBOT FIGHTER #30
NOVEMBER 1993
$4

MAGNUS ROBOT FIGHTER #31
DECEMBER 1993
$4

MAGNUS ROBOT FIGHTER #32
JANUARY 1994
$4

MAGNUS ROBOT FIGHTER #33
FEBRUARY 1994
$4

MAGNUS ROBOT FIGHTER #34
MARCH 1994
$4

MAGNUS ROBOT FIGHTER #35
APRIL 1994
$4

MAGNUS ROBOT FIGHTER #36
MAY 1994
$4

MAGNUS ROBOT FIGHTER #37
JUNE 1994
$4

MAGNUS ROBOT FIGHTER #38
AUGUST 1994
$4

MAGNUS ROBOT FIGHTER #39
SEPTEMBER 1994
$4

MAGNUS ROBOT FIGHTER #40
OCTOBER 1994
$4

MAGNUS ROBOT FIGHTER #41
NOVEMBER 1994
$4

MAGNUS ROBOT FIGHTER #42
DECEMBER 1994
$4

MAGNUS ROBOT FIGHTER #43
JANUARY 1995
$4

MAGNUS ROBOT FIGHTER #44
FEBRUARY 1995
$4

MAGNUS ROBOT FIGHTER #45
MARCH 1995
$4

MAGNUS ROBOT FIGHTER #46
APRIL 1995
$4

MAGNUS ROBOT FIGHTER #47
MAY 1995
$4

MAGNUS ROBOT FIGHTER #48
JUNE 1995
$4

MAGNUS ROBOT FIGHTER #49
JULY 1995
$4

MAGNUS ROBOT FIGHTER #50
JULY 1995
$4

MAGNUS ROBOT FIGHTER #51
AUGUST 1995
$4

MAGNUS ROBOT FIGHTER #52
AUGUST 1995
$4

MAGNUS ROBOT FIGHTER #53
SEPTEMBER 1995
$4

MAGNUS ROBOT FIGHTER #54
SEPTEMBER 1995
$4

MAGNUS ROBOT FIGHTER #55
OCTOBER 1995
$4

MAGNUS ROBOT FIGHTER #56
OCTOBER 1995
$4

MAGNUS ROBOT FIGHTER #57
NOVEMBER 1995
$4

MAGNUS ROBOT FIGHTER #58
NOVEMBER 1995
$4

MAGNUS ROBOT FIGHTER #59
DECEMBER 1995
$4

MAGNUS ROBOT FIGHTER #60
DECEMBER 1995
$4

MAGNUS ROBOT FIGHTER #61
JANUARY 1996
$4

MAGNUS ROBOT FIGHTER #62
JANUARY 1996
$4

MAGNUS ROBOT FIGHTER #63
FEBRUARY 1996
$4

MAGNUS ROBOT FIGHTER #64
FEBRUARY 1996
$2   **$6**   **$20**

**MAGNUS ROBOT FIGHTER
YEARBOOK #1**
1994
$8

**MAGNUS ROBOT FIGHTER/
NEXUS PREVIEW**
1993
$4

**MAGNUS ROBOT FIGHTER/
NEXUS #1**
DECEMBER 1993
$4

**MAGNUS ROBOT FIGHTER/
NEXUS #2**
APRIL 1994
$4

NINJAK #0
JUNE 1995
$3

NINJAK #00
JUNE 1995
$3

NINJAK #1
FEBRUARY 1994
$6

NINJAK #1
GOLD LOGO VARIANT
FEBRUARY 1994
$3 $9 $40

NINJAK #2
MARCH 1994
$4

NINJAK #3
APRIL 1994
$4

NINJAK #4
MAY 1994
$4

NINJAK #5
JUNE 1994
$4

NINJAK #6
AUGUST 1994
$4

NINJAK #7
SEPTEMBER 1994
$4

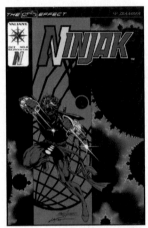

NINJAK #8
OCTOBER 1994
$4

NINJAK #9
NOVEMBER 1994
$4

NINJAK #10
DECEMBER 1994
$4

NINJAK #11
JANUARY 1995
$4

NINJAK #12
FEBRUARY 1995
$4

NINJAK #13
MARCH 1995
$4

NINJAK #14
APRIL 1995
$3

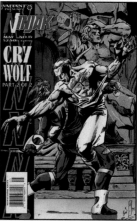

NINJAK #15
MAY 1995
$3

NINJAK #16
JUNE 1995
$3

NINJAK #17
JULY 1995
$3

NINJAK #18
JULY 1995
$3

NINJAK #19
AUGUST 1995
$3

NINJAK #20
SEPTEMBER 1995
$3

NINJAK #21
SEPTEMBER 1995
$3

NINJAK #22
SEPTEMBER 1995
$3

NINJAK #23
OCTOBER 1995
$3

NINJAK #24
OCTOBER 1995
$3

NINJAK #25
NOVEMBER 1995
$3

NINJAK #26
NOVEMBER 1995
$3

NINJAK YEARBOOK #1
1994
$4

**THE ORIGINAL DOCTOR SOLAR,
MAN OF THE ATOM #1**
APRIL 1995
$4

**THE ORIGINAL MAGNUS
ROBOT FIGHTER #1**
APRIL 1995
$5

**THE ORIGINAL TUROK
SON OF STONE #1**
APRIL 1995
$4

**THE ORIGINAL TUROK
SON OF STONE #2**
MAY 1995
$4

THE OUTCAST #1
DECEMBER 1995
$3

**PREDATOR VS. MAGNUS
ROBOT FIGHTER #1**
OCTOBER 1992
$5

**PREDATOR VS. MAGNUS
ROBOT FIGHTER #1**
PLATINUM EDITION • OCTOBER 1992
$10

**PREDATOR VS. MAGNUS
ROBOT FIGHTER #2**
1993
$5

PSI-LORDS #1
SEPTEMBER 1994
$5

PSI-LORDS #1
GOLD LOGO VARIANT
SEPTEMBER 1994
$8

PSI-LORDS #2
OCTOBER 1994
$3

PSI-LORDS #3
NOVEMBER 1994
$3

PSI-LORDS #4
DECEMBER 1994
$3

PSI-LORDS #5
JANUARY 1995
$3

PSI-LORDS #6
FEBRUARY 1995
$3

PSI-LORDS #7
MARCH 1995
$3

PSI-LORDS #8
APRIL 1995
$3

PSI-LORDS #9
MAY 1995
$3

PSI-LORDS #10
JUNE 1995
$3

PUNX #1
NOVEMBER 1995
$3

PUNX #2
DECEMBER 1995
$3

PUNX #3
JANUARY 1996
$3

PUNX SPECIAL #1
MARCH 1996
$3

RAI (MINI-SERIES) #1
FLIP BOOK WITH MAGNUS R.F. #5
OCTOBER 1991
$3 $9 $30

RAI (MINI-SERIES) #2
FLIP BOOK WITH MAGNUS R.F. #6
NOVEMBER 1991
$1 $4 $10

RAI (MINI-SERIES) #3
FLIP BOOK WITH MAGNUS R.F. #7
DECEMBER 1991
$2 $6 $20

RAI (MINI-SERIES) #4
FLIP BOOK WITH MAGNUS R.F. #8
JANUARY 1992
$1 $4 $10

RAI #0
NOVEMBER 1992
$4 $12 $50

RAI #1
MARCH 1992
$3 $9 $24

RAI #2
APRIL 1992
$2 $6 $20

RAI #3
MAY 1992
$2 $6 $20

RAI #4
JUNE 1992
$2 $6 $20

RAI #5
JULY 1992
$2 $6 $20

RAI #6
AUGUST 1992
$6

RAI #7
SEPTEMBER 1992
$6

RAI #8
OCTOBER 1992
$6

**RAI AND
THE FUTURE FORCE #9**
MAY 1993
$6

**RAI AND
THE FUTURE FORCE #9**
GOLD LOGO VARIANT • MAY 1993
$6

**RAI AND
THE FUTURE FORCE #10**
JUNE 1993
$6

RAI AND
THE FUTURE FORCE #11
JULY 1993
$4

RAI AND
THE FUTURE FORCE #12
AUGUST 1993
$4

RAI AND
THE FUTURE FORCE #13
SEPTEMBER 1993
$4

RAI AND
THE FUTURE FORCE #14
OCTOBER 1993
$4

RAI AND
THE FUTURE FORCE #15
NOVEMBER 1993
$4

RAI AND
THE FUTURE FORCE #16
DECEMBER 1993
$4

RAI AND
THE FUTURE FORCE #17
JANUARY 1994
$4

RAI AND
THE FUTURE FORCE #18
FEBRUARY 1994
$4

RAI AND
THE FUTURE FORCE #19
MARCH 1994
$4

**RAI AND
THE FUTURE FORCE #20**
APRIL 1994
$4

**RAI AND
THE FUTURE FORCE #21**
MAY 1994
$4

**RAI AND
THE FUTURE FORCE #22**
JUNE 1994
$4

**RAI AND
THE FUTURE FORCE #23**
JULY 1994
$4

RAI #24
SEPTEMBER 1994
$4

RAI #25
OCTOBER 1994
$4

RAI #26
NOVEMBER 1994
$4

RAI #27
DECEMBER 1994
$4

RAI #28
JANUARY 1995
$4

RAI #29
FEBRUARY 1995
$4

RAI #30
MARCH 1995
$4

RAI #31
APRIL 1995
$4

RAI #32
MAY 1995
$4

RAI #33
JUNE 1995
$4

RAI COMPANION #1
DECEMBER 1993
$4

**THE SECOND LIFE OF
DOCTOR MIRAGE #1**
NOVEMBER 1993
$3

**THE SECOND LIFE OF
DOCTOR MIRAGE #1**
GOLD VARIANT • NOVEMBER 1993
$2 $6 $15

**THE SECOND LIFE OF
DOCTOR MIRAGE #2**
DECEMBER 1993
$3

THE SECOND LIFE OF
DOCTOR MIRAGE #3
JANUARY 1994
$3

THE SECOND LIFE OF
DOCTOR MIRAGE #4
FEBRUARY 1994
$3

THE SECOND LIFE OF
DOCTOR MIRAGE #5
MARCH 1994
$3

THE SECOND LIFE OF
DOCTOR MIRAGE #6
APRIL 1994
$3

THE SECOND LIFE OF
DOCTOR MIRAGE #7
MAY 1994
$3

THE SECOND LIFE OF
DOCTOR MIRAGE #8
JUNE 1994
$3

THE SECOND LIFE OF
DOCTOR MIRAGE #9
AUGUST 1994
$3

THE SECOND LIFE OF
DOCTOR MIRAGE #10
SEPTEMBER 1994
$3

THE SECOND LIFE OF
DOCTOR MIRAGE #11
OCTOBER 1994
$3

THE SECOND LIFE OF DOCTOR MIRAGE #12
NOVEMBER 1994
$3

THE SECOND LIFE OF DOCTOR MIRAGE #13
DECEMBER 1994
$3

THE SECOND LIFE OF DOCTOR MIRAGE #14
JANUARY 1995
$3

THE SECOND LIFE OF DOCTOR MIRAGE #15
FEBRUARY 1995
$3

THE SECOND LIFE OF DOCTOR MIRAGE #16
MARCH 1995
$3

THE SECOND LIFE OF DOCTOR MIRAGE #17
APRIL 1995
$3

THE SECOND LIFE OF DOCTOR MIRAGE #18
MAY 1995
$3

SECRET WEAPONS #1
SEPTEMBER 1993
$4

SECRET WEAPONS #2
OCTOBER 1993
$4

SECRET WEAPONS #3
NOVEMBER 1993
$**4**

SECRET WEAPONS #4
DECEMBER 1993
$**4**

SECRET WEAPONS #5
JANUARY 1994
$**4**

SECRET WEAPONS #6
FEBRUARY 1994
$**4**

SECRET WEAPONS #7
MARCH 1994
$**4**

SECRET WEAPONS #8
APRIL 1994
$**4**

SECRET WEAPONS #9
MAY 1994
$**4**

SECRET WEAPONS #10
JUNE 1994
$**4**

SECRET WEAPONS #11
AUGUST 1994
$**5**

SECRET WEAPONS #12
SEPTEMBER 1994
$4

SECRET WEAPONS #13
OCTOBER 1994
$4

SECRET WEAPONS #14
NOVEMBER 1994
$4

SECRET WEAPONS #15
DECEMBER 1994
$4

SECRET WEAPONS #16
JANUARY 1995
$4

SECRET WEAPONS #17
FEBRUARY 1995
$4

SECRET WEAPONS #18
MARCH 1995
$4

SECRET WEAPONS #19
APRIL 1995
$4

SECRET WEAPONS #20
MAY 1995
$4

SECRET WEAPONS #21
MAY 1995
$4

SHADOWMAN #0
APRIL 1994
$6

SHADOWMAN #0
CHROMIUM COVER VARIANT
APRIL 1994
$1 $3 $8

SHADOWMAN #0
GOLD LOGO VARIANT
APRIL 1994
$20

SHADOWMAN #1
MAY 1992
$3 $9 $30

SHADOWMAN #2
JUNE 1992
$5

SHADOWMAN #3
JULY 1992
$5

SHADOWMAN #4
AUGUST 1992
$5

SHADOWMAN #5
SEPTEMBER 1992
$5

SHADOWMAN #6
OCTOBER 1992
$4

SHADOWMAN #7
NOVEMBER 1994
$4

SHADOWMAN #8
DECEMBER 1992
$2 **$6** **$14**

SHADOWMAN #9
JANUARY 1993
$4

SHADOWMAN #10
FEBRUARY 1993
$4

SHADOWMAN #11
MARCH 1993
$4

SHADOWMAN #12
APRIL 1993
$4

SHADOWMAN #13
MAY 1993
$4

SHADOWMAN #14
JUNE 1993
$4

SHADOWMAN #15
JULY 1993
$4

SHADOWMAN #16
AUGUST 1993
$4

SHADOWMAN #17
SEPTEMBER 1993
$4

SHADOWMAN #18
OCTOBER 1993
$4

SHADOWMAN #19
NOVEMBER 1993
$4

SHADOWMAN #20
DECEMBER 1993
$4

SHADOWMAN #21
JANUARY 1994
$4

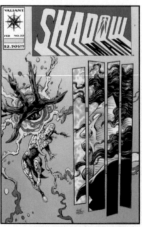

SHADOWMAN #22
FEBRUARY 1994
$4

SHADOWMAN #23
MARCH 1994
$4

SHADOWMAN #24
APRIL 1994
$4

SHADOWMAN #25
MAY 1994
$4

SHADOWMAN #26
JUNE 1994
$4

SHADOWMAN #27
AUGUST 1994
$4

SHADOWMAN #28
SEPTEMBER 1994
$4

SHADOWMAN #29
OCTOBER 1994
$4

SHADOWMAN #30
NOVEMBER 1994
$4

SHADOWMAN #31
DECEMBER 1994
$4

SHADOWMAN #32
JANUARY 1995
$4

SHADOWMAN #33
FEBRUARY 1995
$4

SHADOWMAN #34
MARCH 1995
$4

SHADOWMAN #35
APRIL 1995
$4

SHADOWMAN #36
MAY 1995
$4

SHADOWMAN #37
JUNE 1995
$4

SHADOWMAN #38
JULY 1995
$4

SHADOWMAN #39
AUGUST 1995
$4

SHADOWMAN #40
SEPTEMBER 1995
$4

SHADOWMAN #41
OCTOBER 1995
$4

SHADOWMAN #42
NOVEMBER 1995
$4

SHADOWMAN #43
DECEMBER 1995
$1 $4 $10

SHADOWMAN YEARBOOK #1
DECEMBER 1994
$5

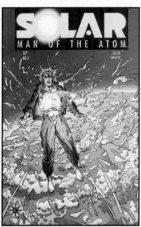

SOLAR #1
SEPTEMBER 1991
$3 $9 $25

SOLAR #2
OCTOBER 1991
$1 $4 $10

SOLAR #3
NOVEMBER 1991
$4 $12 $50

SOLAR #4
DECEMBER 1991
$1 $4 $10

SOLAR #5
JANUARY 1992
$1 $4 $10

SOLAR #6
FEBRUARY 1992
$1 $4 $10

SOLAR #7
MARCH 1992
$1 $4 $10

SOLAR #8
APRIL 1992
$1 $4 $10

SOLAR #9
MAY 1992
$1 $4 $10

SOLAR #10
JUNE 1992
$4 $12 $55

SOLAR #10
SECOND PRINTING
JUNE 1992
$6

SOLAR #11
JULY 1992
$5

SOLAR #12
AUGUST 1992
$5

SOLAR #13
SEPTEMBER 1992
$5

SOLAR #14
OCTOBER 1992
$5

SOLAR #15
NOVEMBER 1992
$5

SOLAR #16
DECEMBER 1992
$4

SOLAR #17
JANUARY 1993
$4

SOLAR #18
FEBRUARY 1993
$4

SOLAR #19
MARCH 1993
$4

SOLAR #20
APRIL 1993
$4

SOLAR #21
MAY 1993
$4

SOLAR #22
JUNE 1993
$4

SOLAR #23
JULY 1993
$4

SOLAR #24
AUGUST 1993
$4

SOLAR #25
SEPTEMBER 1993
$4

SOLAR #26
OCTOBER 1993
$4

SOLAR #27
NOVEMBER 1993
$4

SOLAR #28
DECEMBER 1993
$4

SOLAR #29
JANUARY 1994
$4

SOLAR #30
FEBRUARY 1994
$4

SOLAR #31
MARCH 1994
$4

SOLAR #32
APRIL 1994
$4

SOLAR #33
MAY 1994
$4

SOLAR #34
JUNE 1994
$4

SOLAR #35
AUGUST 1994
$4

SOLAR #36
SEPTEMBER 1994
$4

SOLAR #37
OCTOBER 1994
$4

SOLAR #38
NOVEMBER 1994
$4

SOLAR #39
DECEMBER 1994
$4

SOLAR #40
JANUARY 1995
$4

SOLAR #41
FEBRUARY 1995
$4

SOLAR #42
MARCH 1995
$4

SOLAR #43
APRIL 1995
$4

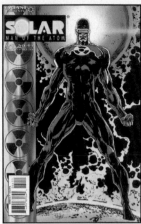

SOLAR #44
MAY 1995
$4

SOLAR #45
JUNE 1995
$4

SOLAR #46
JULY 1995
$4

SOLAR #47
AUGUST 1995
$4

SOLAR #48
SEPTEMBER 1995
$4

SOLAR #49
SEPTEMBER 1995
$4

SOLAR #50
OCTOBER 1995
$4

SOLAR #51
NOVEMBER 1995
$4

SOLAR #52
NOVEMBER 1995
$4

SOLAR #53
DECEMBER 1995
$4

SOLAR #54
DECEMBER 1995
$4

SOLAR #55
JANUARY 1996
$4

SOLAR #56
JANUARY 1996
$4

SOLAR #57
FEBRUARY 1996
$4

SOLAR #58
FEBRUARY 1996
$4

SOLAR #59
MARCH 1996
$4

SOLAR #60
APRIL 1996
$4

TIMEWALKER #0
MARCH 1996
$3

TIMEWALKER #1
JANUARY 1995
$3

TIMEWALKER #2
FEBRUARY 1995
$3

TIMEWALKER #3
MARCH 1995
$3

TIMEWALKER #4
APRIL 1995
$3

TIMEWALKER #5
APRIL 1995
$3

TIMEWALKER #6
MAY 1995
$3

TIMEWALKER #7
JUNE 1995
$3

TIMEWALKER #8
JULY 1995
$3

TIMEWALKER #9
JULY 1995
$3

TIMEWALKER #10
AUGUST 1995
$3

TIMEWALKER #11
AUGUST 1995
$3

TIMEWALKER #12
SEPTEMBER 1995
$3

TIMEWALKER #13
SEPTEMBER 1995
$3

TIMEWALKER #14
OCTOBER 1995
$3

TIMEWALKER #15
OCTOBER 1995
$3

**TIMEWALKER
YEARBOOK #1**
MAY 1995
$3

TUROK, DINOSAUR HUNTER #0
NOVEMBER 1995
$3

TUROK, DINOSAUR HUNTER #1
JULY 1993
$4

TUROK, DINOSAUR HUNTER #1
GOLD LOGO VARIANT • JULY 1993
$20

TUROK, DINOSAUR HUNTER #2
AUGUST 1993
$3

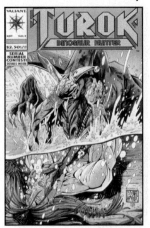

TUROK, DINOSAUR HUNTER #3
SEPTEMBER 1993
$3

TUROK, DINOSAUR HUNTER #4
OCTOBER 1993
$3

TUROK, DINOSAUR HUNTER #5
NOVEMBER 1993
$3

TUROK, DINOSAUR HUNTER #6
DECEMBER 1993
$3

TUROK, DINOSAUR HUNTER #7
JANUARY 1994
$3

TUROK,
DINOSAUR HUNTER #8
FEBRUARY 1994
$3

TUROK,
DINOSAUR HUNTER #9
MARCH 1994
$3

TUROK,
DINOSAUR HUNTER #10
APRIL 1994
$3

TUROK,
DINOSAUR HUNTER #11
MAY 1994
$3

TUROK,
DINOSAUR HUNTER #12
JUNE 1994
$3

TUROK,
DINOSAUR HUNTER #13
AUGUST 1994
$3

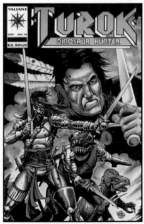

TUROK,
DINOSAUR HUNTER #14
SEPTEMBER 1994
$3

TUROK,
DINOSAUR HUNTER #15
OCTOBER 1994
$3

TUROK,
DINOSAUR HUNTER #16
OCTOBER 1994
$3

**TUROK,
DINOSAUR HUNTER #17**
NOVEMBER 1994
$3

**TUROK,
DINOSAUR HUNTER #18**
DECEMBER 1994
$3

**TUROK,
DINOSAUR HUNTER #19**
JANUARY 1995
$3

**TUROK,
DINOSAUR HUNTER #20**
FEBRUARY 1995
$3

**TUROK,
DINOSAUR HUNTER #21**
MARCH 1995
$3

**TUROK,
DINOSAUR HUNTER #22**
APRIL 1995
$3

**TUROK,
DINOSAUR HUNTER #23**
MAY 1995
$3

**TUROK,
DINOSAUR HUNTER #24**
JUNE 1995
$3

**TUROK,
DINOSAUR HUNTER #25**
JULY 1995
$3

TUROK, DINOSAUR HUNTER #26
JULY 1995
$3

TUROK, DINOSAUR HUNTER #27
AUGUST 1995
$3

TUROK, DINOSAUR HUNTER #28
AUGUST 1995
$3

TUROK, DINOSAUR HUNTER #29
SEPTEMBER 1995
$3

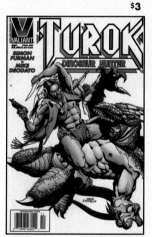

TUROK, DINOSAUR HUNTER #30
SEPTEMBER 1995
$3

TUROK, DINOSAUR HUNTER #31
OCTOBER 1995
$3

TUROK, DINOSAUR HUNTER #32
OCTOBER 1995
$3

TUROK, DINOSAUR HUNTER #33
NOVEMBER 1995
$3

TUROK, DINOSAUR HUNTER #34
NOVEMBER 1995
$3

**TUROK,
DINOSAUR HUNTER #35**
NOVEMBER 1995
$3

**TUROK,
DINOSAUR HUNTER #36**
DECEMBER 1995
$3

**TUROK,
DINOSAUR HUNTER #37**
JANUARY 1996
$3

**TUROK,
DINOSAUR HUNTER #38**
JANUARY 1996
$3

**TUROK,
DINOSAUR HUNTER #39**
FEBRUARY 1996
$3

**TUROK,
DINOSAUR HUNTER #40**
MARCH 1996
$3

**TUROK,
DINOSAUR HUNTER #41**
APRIL 1996
$3

**TUROK,
DINOSAUR HUNTER #42**
APRIL 1996
$3

**TUROK,
DINOSAUR HUNTER #43**
MAY 1996
$3

**TUROK,
DINOSAUR HUNTER #44**
MAY 1996
$3

**TUROK,
DINOSAUR HUNTER #45**
JUNE 1996
$3

**TUROK,
DINOSAUR HUNTER #46**
JULY 1996
$3

**TUROK,
DINOSAUR HUNTER #47**
AUGUST 1996
$3

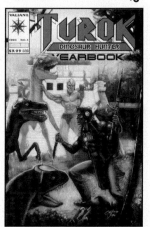

**TUROK, DINOSAUR
HUNTER YEARBOOK #1**
1994
$4

TUROK THE HUNTED #1
MARCH 1996
$4

TUROK THE HUNTED #2
MARCH 1996
$4

UNITY #0
AUGUST 1992
$1 $4 $10

UNITY #0
RED LOGO VARIANT
AUGUST 1992
$5 $15 $70

UNITY #1
1992
$5

UNITY #1
GOLD LOGO VARIANT
1992
$2 $6 $15

UNITY #1
PLATINUM LOGO VARIANT
1992
$2 $6 $15

**UNITY:
THE LOST CHAPTER #1**
FEBRUARY 1995
$6

VINTAGE MAGNUS #1
JANUARY 1992
$3

VINTAGE MAGNUS #2
FEBRUARY 1992
$3

VINTAGE MAGNUS #3
MARCH 1992
$3

VINTAGE MAGNUS #4
APRIL 1992
$3

THE VISITOR #1
APRIL 1995
$3

THE VISITOR #2
MAY 1995
$3

THE VISITOR #3
JUNE 1995
$3

THE VISITOR #4
JULY 1995
$3

THE VISITOR #5
JULY 1995
$3

THE VISITOR #6
AUGUST 1995
$3

THE VISITOR #7
AUGUST 1995
$3

THE VISITOR #8
SEPTEMBER 1995
$3

THE VISITOR #9
SEPTEMBER 1995
$3

THE VISITOR #10
OCTOBER 1995
$3

THE VISITOR #11
OCTOBER 1995
$3

THE VISITOR #12
NOVEMBER 1995
$3

THE VISITOR #13
NOVEMBER 1995
$3

**THE VISITOR VS.
THE VALIANT UNIVERSE #1**
FEBRUARY 1995
$3

**THE VISITOR VS.
THE VALIANT UNIVERSE #2**
MARCH 1995
$3

X-O DATABASE #1
1993
$3

X-O MANOWAR #0
AUGUST 1993
$8

X-O MANOWAR #0
GOLD LOGO VARIANT
AUGUST 1993
$3 $9 $45

X-O MANOWAR #1
FEBRUARY 1992
$3 $9 $45

X-O MANOWAR #2
MARCH 1992
$2 $6 $12

X-O MANOWAR #3
APRIL 1992
$2 $6 $12

X-O MANOWAR #4
MAY 1992
$4 $12 $50

X-O MANOWAR #5
JUNE 1992
$1 $3 $8

X-O MANOWAR #6
JULY 1992
$1 $3 $8

X-O MANOWAR #7
AUGUST 1992
$4

X-O MANOWAR #8
SEPTEMBER 1992
$4

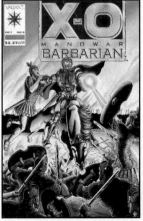

X-O MANOWAR #9
OCTOBER 1992
$4

X-O MANOWAR #10
NOVEMBER 1992
$4

X-O Manowar #11
DECEMBER 1992
$4

X-O Manowar #12
JANUARY 1993
$4

X-O Manowar #13
FEBRUARY 1993
$4

X-O Manowar #14
MARCH 1993
$4

X-O Manowar #15
APRIL 1993
$4

X-O Manowar #15
PINK LOGO VARIANT
APRIL 1993
$1 $4 $10

X-O Manowar #16
MAY 1993
$3

X-O Manowar #17
JUNE 1993
$3

X-O Manowar #18
JULY 1993
$3

X-O MANOWAR #19
AUGUST 1993
$3

X-O MANOWAR #20
SEPTEMBER 1993
$3

X-O MANOWAR #21
OCTOBER 1993
$3

X-O MANOWAR #22
NOVEMBER 1993
$3

X-O MANOWAR #23
DECEMBER 1993
$3

X-O MANOWAR #24
JANUARY 1994
$3

X-O MANOWAR #25
FEBRUARY 1994
$4

X-O MANOWAR #26
MARCH 1994
$3

X-O MANOWAR #27
APRIL 1994
$3

X-O Manowar #28
MAY 1994
$3

X-O Manowar #29
JUNE 1994
$3

X-O Manowar #30
AUGUST 1994
$3

X-O Manowar #31
SEPTEMBER 1994
$3

X-O Manowar #32
OCTOBER 1994
$3

X-O Manowar #33
NOVEMBER 1994
$3

X-O Manowar #34
DECEMBER 1994
$3

X-O Manowar #35
JANUARY 1995
$3

X-O Manowar #36
FEBRUARY 1995
$3

X-O MANOWAR #37
MARCH 1995
$3

X-O MANOWAR #38
MARCH 1995
$3

X-O MANOWAR #39
MARCH 1995
$3

X-O MANOWAR #40
MARCH 1995
$3

X-O MANOWAR #41
APRIL 1995
$3

X-O MANOWAR #42
MAY 1995
$3

X-O MANOWAR #43
JUNE 1995
$3

X-O MANOWAR #44
JULY 1995
$3

X-O MANOWAR #45
JULY 1995
$3

X-O Manowar #46
August 1995
$3

X-O Manowar #47
August 1995
$3

X-O Manowar #48
September 1995
$3

X-O Manowar #49
September 1995
$3

X-O Manowar #50-X
October 1995
$3

X-O Manowar #50-O
October 1995
$3

X-O Manowar #51
November 1995
$3

X-O Manowar #52
November 1995
$3

X-O Manowar #53
December 1995
$3

X-O MANOWAR #54
DECEMBER 1995
$3

X-O MANOWAR #55
JANUARY 1996
$3

X-O MANOWAR #56
JANUARY 1996
$3

X-O MANOWAR #57
FEBRUARY 1996
$3

X-O MANOWAR #58
FEBRUARY 1996
$3

X-O MANOWAR #59
MARCH 1996
$3

X-O MANOWAR #60
MARCH 1996
$3

X-O MANOWAR #61
APRIL 1996
$3

X-O MANOWAR #62
APRIL 1996
$3

X-O Manowar #63
May 1996
$3

X-O Manowar #64
May 1996
$3

X-O Manowar #65
June 1996
$3

X-O Manowar #66
July 1996
$3

X-O Manowar #67
August 1996
$1 $3 $8

X-O Manowar #68
September 1996
$3 $9 $30

**X-O Manowar
Yearbook #1**
April 1995
$3

**X-O Manowar
Wizard #1/2**
1994
$6

**X-O Manowar
Wizard #1/2**
Gold logo variant • 1994
$20

MAGNUS ROBOT FIGHTER #0: TWO VERSIONS

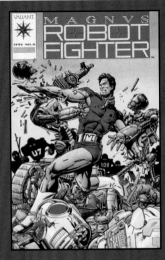

There has been some confusion regarding the two versions of *Magnus Robot Fighter* #0. This issue was supposed to be available as a mail-in/send away only for those who redeemed coupons from *Magnus Robot Fighter* #1-8. Approximately 9,400 copies were redeemed.

However, VALIANT also produced copies of *Magnus Robot Fighter* #0 as giveaways for comic book dealers. One copy of *Magnus Robot Fighter* #0 was given to dealers for every 10 copies of *Magnus Robot Fighter* #1 they had ordered months earlier. Since #1 was the first VALIANT superhero book in 1991 (following the Nintendo and wrestling titles), many stores had not ordered 10 or more copies, so they did not receive the issue. Approximately 8,900 copies were printed as dealer incentives through this program.

The difference between the coupon/send away version and the retailer incentive version is that the retailer version did not contain the bound-in card illustrated by Barry Windsor-Smith. There are no other differences in the two versions of *Magnus Robot Fighter* #0.

It could be argued that the send away version could be worth more than the retailer version due to the presence of the card, just as it could be suggested that the retailer version is scarcer and could correspondingly be worth more. The card itself has little value when removed from the issue.

The send away version may bring slightly more than the retailer version, but over a protracted period, the two versions have generally been bought and sold at the same or very similar prices.

– *Greg Holland*

X-O MANOWAR/OVERSTREET

In *Overstreet's FAN* #19 (January 1997) readers were offered a chance to jump onto VH2 early in the process with *X-O Manowar FAN Edition* #1 (*Wizard* had gotten upset when we did *Witchblade* #1/2, so we switched to *FAN Edition* #1s instead).

The issue tied directly into the first story arc in VH2's *X-O Manowar* Vol. 2 #1-4, which was written by Mark Waid and Brian Augustyn, penciled by Sean Chen, inked by Tom Ryder, and colored by Atomic Paintbrush.

For *X-O Manowar FAN Edition* #1, Augustyn handled the script, Mike McKone penciled, Andy Lanning inked, and Atomic Paintbrush provided the colors. The story includes the first VH2 appearances of the Armorines and HARD Corps.

This page in *Overstreet's FAN* #19 (January 1997) featured a coupon for *X-O Manowar FAN Edition* #1. The coupon offer is no longer valid, but for those interested - as of the printing of this publication - we do have some copies remaining on www.gemstonepub.com.

When the original VALIANT (all caps, as it was stylized) sold to Acclaim Entertainment, comics were selling huge – and as it turned out, unsupportable – numbers. After trying to reboot their titles as the VH2 universe and even taking a much more low-key approach to a second reboot, Acclaim itself went out of business, casting the properties into a bankruptcy auction.

During these dark times, many dumped their VALIANT collections in 50¢ boxes. A hardy few, however, knew that no one ever really got tired of great comics and started buying all the high-grade copies, talking to other diehard fans, and fighting the good fight.

ValiantFans.com became an outpost for such fans, and Greg Holland became a major facilitator of the ongoing conversations. Among the many ways he's encouraged his fellow fans was the creation of a chronological list to introduce new readers to the universe.

A Guided Tour of Pre-Unity VALIANT, May 1991 to July 1992

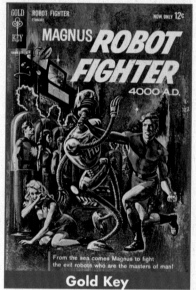

May 1991

Gold Key

The **VALIANT UNIVERSE** began in the early 1990s with a revival of the 1963 Gold Key title Magnus Robot Fighter 4000 AD.

The first comic in the Valiant Universe was **Magnus Robot Fighter #1**, with a cover date of May 1991.

Valiant

Another Gold Key character *Doctor Solar, Man of the Atom* from 1962 was reimagined in *Solar, Man of the Atom* #1 for September 1991.

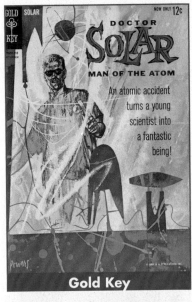

Gold Key

September 1991

flipbook

October 1991

Valiant

The first original VALIANT universe character was **Rai**, first appearing on the flipside of *Magnus Robot Fighter #5* as a *Rai #1* mini-series cover. Rai is the earliest original Valiant character included in the current Valiant universe.

flipbook

September 1991

Solar, Man of the Atom #3 introduced **Toyo Harada** and the **Harbinger Foundation**.

December 1991

Magnus Robot Fighter #7 showed the first X-O Commando armor, worn by the first Spider-Alien shown with four fingers on each hand. X-O Commando armor is a lower class than the X-O Manowar armor.

January 1992

Harbinger #1 was the first original Valiant universe title, introducing five teen Harbinger renegades: Peter, Kris, Faith, Charlene (Flamingo), and Torque.

February 1992

X-O Manowar #1 followed as the second original Valiant title with the first appearance of **Aric of Dacia** and the first appearance of the X-O Manowar armor.

March 1992

Rai #1 was the third regular series Valiant title, following the *Rai* four-issue mini-series published as the flip-side of *Magnus Robot Fighter* #5-8

***Shadowman* #1** presented Jack Boniface as Shadowman, the same month as his brief appearance as a jazz musican in ***X-O Manowar* #4**.

May 1992

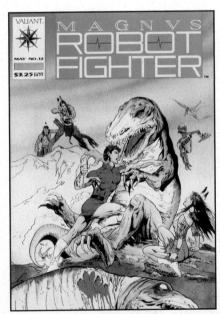

***Magnus Robot Fighter* #12** re-introduced Turok, first appearing in *Four Color* #596 from Dell Publishing in 1954.

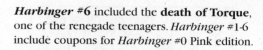

Harbinger #6 included the **death of Torque**, one of the renegade teenagers. *Harbinger* #1-6 include coupons for *Harbinger* #0 Pink edition.

June 1992

Solar, Man of the Atom #10 introduced the **Eternal Warrior** (Gilad) and **Geomancers** Buck and Geoff McHenry. The issue had a second printing six months later. The solid black cover is embossed, and the second printing has Roman numeral II.

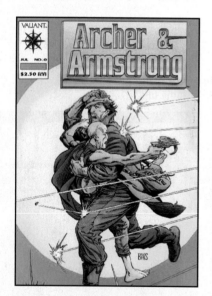

July 1992

Archer & Armstrong #0 is the first issue and the first appearance of Obadiah **Archer** and **Armstrong** (Aram Anni-Padda). A gold edition of 5,000 copies was also released as the earliest-dated VALIANT retailer premium.

VALIANT comics with cover dates through July 1992 are **Pre-*Unity* Valiant**, indicating their publication prior to the Unity crossover storyline. A complete set of Pre-Unity Valiant comics is 54 issues.

In alphabetical order:
Archer & Armstrong #0
Harbinger #1-7
Magnus Robot Fighter #1-14
Rai #1-5
Shadowman #1-3
Solar, Man of the Atom #1-11
Vintage Magnus #1-4
X-O Manowar #1-6

Harbinger #1-6 and *Magnus Robot Fighter* #1-8 included coupons for sendaway comics (*Harbinger* #0 and *Magnus* #0), so those issues often have the coupons cut out of their interiors. Without the coupons, the issues are considered damaged/incomplete and are less valuable than intact copies.

The 51 comics noted above were released prior to the *Unity* storyline beginning with VALIANT comics dated August 1992. Three additional limited edition comics were written prior to *Unity*, but were released later with special distribution. These three are usually included in the Pre-*Unity* list of 54 comics.

Magnus #0 exists with and without a trading card insert. The trading card was included in the sendaway edition of *Magnus* #0, and the retailer edition of *Magnus* #0 does not contain the trading card. The version including the trading card has higher average sale prices.

Harbinger #0 was reprinted later with a different cover featuring dark blue clouds and the title "HARBINGER" written in red. Despite also stating "1992" on the cover, the blue clouds version is a more common reprint from mid-1993 and not a Pre-*Unity* comic. The original 1992 *Harbinger* #0 sendaway edition has pink clouds and the title "HARBINGER" written in blue on the cover.

The only difference between *Archer & Armstrong* #0 (regular edition) and *Archer & Armstrong* #0 Gold edition is the upper left information box on the front cover with the gold background.

– Greg Holland

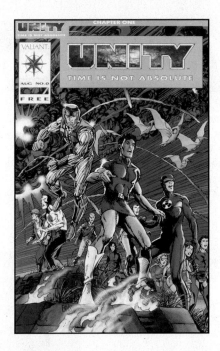

Following the Pre-Unity issues was, of course, Unity, *an 18-chapter crossover that brought the full VALIANT universe together for the first time.* Unity *started in* Unity *#0, a giveaway comic, and continued in each of the company's regular titles for May and June 1992 before concluding in* Unity *#1.*

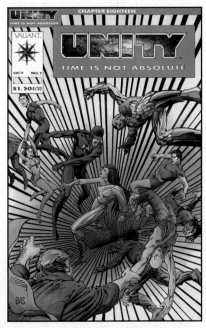

VH2 (Acclaim Comics)

The story of the VH2/Acclaim Comics incarnation of Valiant actually begins before the end of the original VALIANT. In June 1994, Voyager Communications was sold to videogame company Acclaim Entertainment for a reported $65 million. Acclaim intended to develop videogames based on the comic book properties.

Almost as the ink was drying on the deal, however, the market for new comic books, which had been booming, started contracting. Among the factors were speculators, many of whom had migrated to comic books after devastating the trading card market. They bought and sold huge numbers of comics with the promise that comic values would only continue their rapid ascent. However, when demand decreased, market forces took over. From their post-*Unity* highs, print runs on the original VALIANT titles continue decreasing until even their longest-running series were canceled by September 1996.

That same month, though, the company teamed up with Marvel Comics for a two-part mini-series featuring X-O Manowar and Iron Man. *X-O Manowar/ Iron Man in Heavy Metal* #1 (published by Acclaim) *and Iron Man/X-O Manowar in Heavy Metal* #1 (published by Marvel) were both written by Fabian Nicieza. Based on an Acclaim video game of the same name, the story involved fragments of the reality-altering Cosmic Cube. In one altered reality, the mini-series ended up giving readers their first glimpse of the VH2 universe.

As Senior Vice-President and Editor-in-Chief of Valiant (and later President and Publisher), Nicieza would be the prime architect of the VH2 universe (for "Valiant Heroes 2" based on the logo and the fan interpretation of it), which saw the retooling of *Magnus Robot Fighter, Solar, Turok, X-O Manowar, Shadowman, Ninjak,* and *Bloodshot.* It also combined *Eternal Warrior* and *Archer & Armstrong* into a new take, single series, *Eternal Warriors.* Harbinger was basically ignored until the one-shot *Harbinger: Acts of God* #1 (January 1998). In addition to revamping the company's established characters, Nicieza and

company introduced new properties such as *N.I.O., Trinity Angels, Troublemakers,* and VH2's breakout series, *Quantum & Woody.*

The comic book market continued to contract, and parent company Acclaim was faced with mounting problems. The VH2 comic book line was ended as they were told to focus on tie-ins to Acclaim's video games. *Shadowman* #20 and *X-O Manowar* #21 (June 1998), *Doctor Tomorrow* #12 (August 1998), *Bloodshot* #16 (October 1998), and *Turok/Shadowman* #1 (February 1999) represented the last of VH2. Following staff and budget cuts, Nicieza left the company in 1999. Acclaim Comics limped along under a new logo, shedding the Valiant identity for which they had paid so much. Some collectors refer to the period that followed as "VH3" or simply "Acclaim Comics" to differentiate it from VH2 continuity.

There was a last hurrah still to come for VH2, however. That same year, they brough back *Quantum & Woody* (starting with #32, the issue they would have reached if it had been published continuously) before resuming with #18. They also launched new volumes of *Armorines* and *Shadowman.*

The biggest effort was *Unity 2000,* a six-part story designed to unify the original VALIANT and VH2 universes. Scripted by original VALIANT founder Jim Shooter and illustrated by Jim Starlin and Joe Rubenstein, six issues were plotted and illustrated, five were scripted, four were inked, and three had been released when mounting losses in the videogame industry caused Acclaim to pull the plug. The finished mini-series would have combined the best of both universes into a single new Valiant universe. It was not to be.

By 2003, Acclaim Entertainment allowed Valiant's sweetheart licenses on Magnus Robot Fighter and Solar: Man of the Atom to lapse, keeping only Turok for video games. In 2004, the company was forced into bankruptcy. The assets were sold at auction in 2005 to Valiant Entertainment.

FIRST PUBLICATION:
X-O Manowar Vol. 2 #1 (February 1997)

LAST PUBLICATION:
Turok Evolution #1 (August 2002)

REVIVAL(S):
Valiant Entertainment collected editions (2007, 2008), new comics beginning with X-O Manowar #1 (May 2012).

Scott Eaton and Don Hudson's original art for Page 21 of *X-O Manowar Vol. 2 #21*, the last page of the last issue of the VH2 run. Image courtesy of Dan Moler.

ACCLAIM ADVENTURE ZONE #1
DIGEST SIZE • 1997
$3 $9 $40

ACCLAIM ADVENTURE ZONE #1
DIGEST SIZE • 1997
$1 $4 $10

ACCLAIM ADVENTURE ZONE #1
DIGEST SIZE • 1997
$4.50

ARMORINES VOL. 2 #1
OCTOBER 1999
$6

ARMORINES VOL. 2 #2
NOVEMBER 1999
$4

ARMORINES VOL. 2 #3
DECEMBER 1999
$4

ARMORINES VOL. 2 #4
MARCH 2000
$60

BLOODSHOT VOL. 2 #1
RETAILER REVIEW COPY
MARCH 1997
$3

BLOODSHOT VOL. 2 #1
JULY 1997
$3

BLOODSHOT VOL. 2 #1
VARIANT COVER
JULY 1997
$3

BLOODSHOT VOL. 2 #2
AUGUST 1997
$3

BLOODSHOT VOL. 2 #3
SEPTEMBER 1997
$2 **$6** **$12**

BLOODSHOT VOL. 2 #4
OCTOBER 1997
$3

BLOODSHOT VOL. 2 #5
NOVEMBER 1997
$3

BLOODSHOT VOL. 2 #6
DECEMBER 1997
$3

BLOODSHOT VOL. 2 #7
JANUARY 1998
$3

BLOODSHOT VOL. 2 #8
FEBRUARY 1998
$3

BLOODSHOT VOL. 2 #9
MARCH 1998
$3

BLOODSHOT VOL. 2 #10
April 1998
$3

BLOODSHOT VOL. 2 #11
May 1998
$3

BLOODSHOT VOL. 2 #12
June 1998
$3

BLOODSHOT VOL. 2 #13
July 1998
$3

BLOODSHOT VOL. 2 #14
August 1998
$3

BLOODSHOT VOL. 2 #15
September 1998
$6

BLOODSHOT VOL. 2 #16
October 1998
$6

**CONCRETE JUNGLE: THE LEGEND
OF THE BLACK LION #1**
Retailer Review Copy • 1998
$3

**CONCRETE JUNGLE: THE LEGEND
OF THE BLACK LION #1**
April 1998
$3

DARQUE PASSAGES #1
APRIL 1998
$3

DARQUE PASSAGES #2
APRIL 1998
$3

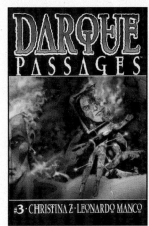

DARQUE PASSAGES #3
APRIL 1998
$3

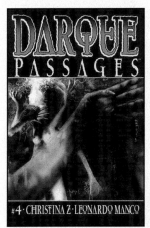

DARQUE PASSAGES #4
APRIL 1998
$3

DEADSIDE #1
FEBRUARY 1999
$3

DEADSIDE #2
MARCH 1999
$3

DEADSIDE #3
APRIL 1999
$3

DOCTOR TOMORROW #1
SEPTEMBER 1997
$4

DOCTOR TOMORROW #2
OCTOBER 1997
$4

DOCTOR TOMORROW #3
NOVEMBER 1997
$4

DOCTOR TOMORROW #4
DECEMBER 1997
$4

DOCTOR TOMORROW #5
JANUARY 1998
$4

DOCTOR TOMORROW #6
FEBRUARY 1998
$4

DOCTOR TOMORROW #7
MARCH 1998
$4

DOCTOR TOMORROW #8
APRIL 1998
$4

DOCTOR TOMORROW #9
MAY 1998
$4

DOCTOR TOMORROW #10
JUNE 1998
$4

DOCTOR TOMORROW #11
JULY 1998
$4

DOCTOR TOMORROW #12
AUGUST 1998
$4

**ETERNAL WARRIORS:
ARCHER & ARMSTRONG #1**
DECEMBER 1997
$4

**ETERNAL WARRIORS:
BLACKWORKS #1**
MARCH 1998
$4

**ETERNAL WARRIORS:
DIGITAL ALCHEMY VOL. 2 #1**
SEPTEMBER 1997
$4

**ETERNAL WARRIORS:
MOG #1**
MARCH 1998
$4

**ETERNAL WARRIORS:
THE IMMORTAL ENEMY #1**
JUNE 1998
$4

**ETERNAL WARRIORS:
TIME AND TREACHERY #1**
RETAILER REVIEW COPY • 1998
$4

**ETERNAL WARRIORS:
TIME AND TREACHERY #1**
JUNE 1997
$4

**ETERNAL WARRIORS:
TIME AND TREACHERY #1**
VARIANT COVER • JUNE 1997
$4

THE GOAT: H.A.E.D.U.S. #1
1998
$3

**HARBINGER:
ACTS OF GOD #1**
JANUARY 1998
$4

**MAGNUS ROBOT FIGHTER
VOL. 2 #1**
RETAILER REVIEW COPY • 1997
$3

**MAGNUS ROBOT FIGHTER
VOL. 2 #1**
MAY 1997
$4

**MAGNUS ROBOT FIGHTER
VOL. 2 #1**
VARIANT COVER • MAY 1997
$4

**MAGNUS ROBOT FIGHTER
VOL. 2 #2**
JUNE 1997
$4

**MAGNUS ROBOT FIGHTER
VOL. 2 #3**
JULY 1997
$4

**MAGNUS ROBOT FIGHTER
VOL. 2 #4**
AUGUST 1997
$4

**MAGNUS ROBOT FIGHTER
VOL. 2 #5**
SEPTEMBER 1997
$4

MAGNUS ROBOT FIGHTER
VOL. 2 #6
OCTOBER 1997
$4

MAGNUS ROBOT FIGHTER
VOL. 2 #7
NOVEMBER 1997
$4

MAGNUS ROBOT FIGHTER
VOL. 2 #8
DECEMBER 1997
$4

MAGNUS ROBOT FIGHTER
VOL. 2 #9
JANUARY 1998
$4

MAGNUS ROBOT FIGHTER
VOL. 2 #10
FEBRUARY 1998
$4

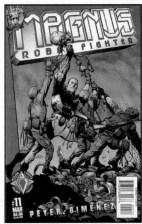

MAGNUS ROBOT FIGHTER
VOL. 2 #11
MARCH 1998
$4

MAGNUS ROBOT FIGHTER
VOL. 2 #12
APRIL 1998
$4

MAGNUS ROBOT FIGHTER
VOL. 2 #13
JANUARY 1998
$4

MAGNUS ROBOT FIGHTER
VOL. 2 #14
FEBRUARY 1998
$4

MAGNUS ROBOT FIGHTER
VOL. 2 #15
MARCH 1998
$4

MAGNUS ROBOT FIGHTER
VOL. 2 #16
APRIL 1998
$4

MAGNUS ROBOT FIGHTER
VOL. 2 #17
MAY 1998
$4

MAGNUS ROBOT FIGHTER
VOL. 2 #18
JUNE 1998
$4

MASTER DARQUE #1
RETAILER REVIEW COPY
1997
$3

MASTER DARQUE #1
FEBRUARY 1998
$4

NINJAK VOL. 2 #1
RETAILER REVIEW COPY
1997
$3

NINJAK VOL. 2 #1
MARCH 1997
$2 $6 $15

NINJAK VOL. 2 #1
VARIANT COVER
MARCH 1997
$2 $6 $15

NINJAK VOL. 2 #2
APRIL 1997
$3

NINJAK VOL. 2 #3
MAY 1997
$3

NINJAK VOL. 2 #4
JUNE 1997
$3

NINJAK VOL. 2 #5
JULY 1997
$3

NINJAK VOL. 2 #6
AUGUST 1997
$3

NINJAK VOL. 2 #7
SEPTEMBER 1997
$3

NINJAK VOL. 2 #8
OCTOBER 1997
$3

NINJAK VOL. 2 #9
NOVEMBER 1997
$3

NINJAK VOL. 2 #10
DECEMBER 1997
$3

NINJAK VOL. 2 #11
JANUARY 1998
$3

NINJAK VOL. 2 #12
FEBRUARY 1998
$3

N.I.O. #1
NOVEMBER 1998
$3

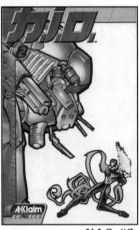

N.I.O. #2
DECEMBER 1998
$3

N.I.O. #3
JANUARY 1999
$3

N.I.O. #4
FEBRUARY 1999
$3

**OPERATION:
STORMBREAKER #1**
AUGUST 1997
$5

QUANTUM & WOODY #0
NOVEMBER 1997
$3

QUANTUM & WOODY #1
RETAILER REVIEW COPY
1997
$3

QUANTUM & WOODY #1
JUNE 1997
$1 $3 $8

QUANTUM & WOODY #1
VARIANT COVER
JUNE 1997
$2 $6 $15

QUANTUM & WOODY #2
JULY 1997
$3

QUANTUM & WOODY #3
AUGUST 1997
$2 $6 $20

QUANTUM & WOODY #4
SEPTEMBER 1997
$3

QUANTUM & WOODY #5
OCTOBER 1997
$3

QUANTUM & WOODY #6
NOVEMBER 1997
$3

QUANTUM & WOODY #7
DECEMBER 1997
$3

QUANTUM & WOODY #8
JANUARY 1998
$3

QUANTUM & WOODY #9
FEBRUARY 1998
$3

QUANTUM & WOODY #10
MARCH 1998
$3

QUANTUM & WOODY #11
APRIL 1998
$3

QUANTUM & WOODY #12
JANUARY 1998
$3

QUANTUM & WOODY #13
FEBRUARY 1998
$3

QUANTUM & WOODY #14
MARCH 1998
$3

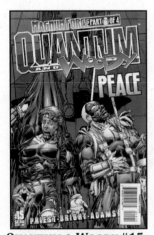

QUANTUM & WOODY #15
APRIL 1998
$3

QUANTUM & WOODY #16
MAY 1998
$3

QUANTUM & WOODY #17
JUNE 1998
$3

QUANTUM & WOODY #32
Numbering jumps to #32
September 1999
$3

QUANTUM & WOODY #18
Numbering reverts to #18
October 1999
$3

QUANTUM & WOODY #19
November 1999
$3

QUANTUM & WOODY #20
January 2000
$3

QUANTUM & WOODY #21
February 2000
$3

SHADOWMAN VOL. 2 #1
Retailer Review Copy
1997
$3

SHADOWMAN VOL. 2 #1
March 1997
$1 $3 $8

SHADOWMAN VOL. 2 #1
Variant cover
March 1997
$1 $3 $8

SHADOWMAN VOL. 2 #2
April 1997
$3

SHADOWMAN VOL. 2 #3
MAY 1997
$3

SHADOWMAN VOL. 2 #4
JUNE 1997
$3

SHADOWMAN VOL. 2 #5
1997
$3

SHADOWMAN VOL. 2 #5
JULY 1997
$3

SHADOWMAN VOL. 2 #6
AUGUST 1997
$3

SHADOWMAN VOL. 2 #7
SEPTEMBER 1997
$3

SHADOWMAN VOL. 2 #8
OCTOBER 1997
$3

SHADOWMAN VOL. 2 #9
NOVEMBER 1997
$3

SHADOWMAN VOL. 2 #10
DECEMBER 1997
$3

SHADOWMAN VOL. 2 #11
JANUARY 1998
$3

SHADOWMAN VOL. 2 #12
FEBRUARY 1998
$3

SHADOWMAN VOL. 2 #13
MARCH 1998
$3

SHADOWMAN VOL. 2 #14
APRIL 1998
$3

SHADOWMAN VOL. 2 #15
JANUARY 1998
$3

SHADOWMAN VOL. 2 #16
SEPTEMBER 1998
$3

SHADOWMAN VOL. 2 #16
FEBRUARY 1998
$3

SHADOWMAN VOL. 2 #16
GLOW IN THE DARK VARIANT COVER
FEBRUARY 1998
$3

SHADOWMAN VOL. 2 #17
MARCH 1998
$3

SHADOWMAN VOL. 2 #18
APRIL 1998
$3

SHADOWMAN VOL. 2 #19
MAY 1998
$3

SHADOWMAN VOL. 2 #20
JUNE 1998
$3

**SHADOWMAN SPECIAL
EDITION #1**
VIDEO GAME TIE-IN • 1998
$20

SHADOWMAN VOL. 3 #1
JULY 1999
$1 $3 $8

SHADOWMAN VOL. 3 #1
VARIANT COVER
JULY 1999
$2 $6 $12

SHADOWMAN VOL. 3 #1
RETAILER INCENTIVE COVER
JULY 1999
$2 $6 $12

SHADOWMAN VOL. 3 #2
AUGUST 1999
$3

SHADOWMAN VOL. 3 #2
RETAILER INCENTIVE COVER
AUGUST 1999
$3

SHADOWMAN VOL. 3 #3
FLIP BOOK WITH UNITY 2000 TIE-IN
SEPTEMBER 1999
$3

SHADOWMAN VOL. 3 #4
FLIP BOOK WITH UNITY 2000 TIE-IN
OCTOBER 1999
$3

SHADOWMAN VOL. 3 #5
NOVEMBER 1999
$3

SHADOWMAN VOL. 3 #6
DECEMBER 1999
$3

**SOLAR, MAN OF THE ATOM
VOL. 2 #1**
RETAILER REVIEW COPY • 1997
$3

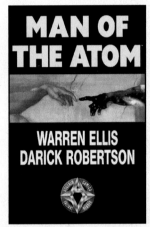

**SOLAR, MAN OF THE ATOM
VOL. 2 #1**
MAY 1997
$4

**SOLAR, MAN OF THE ATOM:
HELL ON EARTH #1**
JANUARY 1998
$3

**SOLAR, MAN OF THE ATOM:
HELL ON EARTH #2**
FEBRUARY 1998
$3

**SOLAR, MAN OF THE ATOM:
HELL ON EARTH #3**
MARCH 1998
$3

**SOLAR, MAN OF THE ATOM:
HELL ON EARTH #4**
APRIL 1998
$3

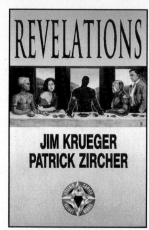

**SOLAR, MAN OF THE ATOM:
REVELATIONS #1**
NOVEMBER 1997
$5

TRINITY ANGELS #1
RETAILER REVIEW COPY
1997
$3

TRINITY ANGELS #1
JULY 1997
$3

TRINITY ANGELS #1
VARIANT COVER
JULY 1997
$3

TRINITY ANGELS #2
AUGUST 1997
$3

TRINITY ANGELS #3
SEPTEMBER 1997
$3

TRINITY ANGELS #4
OCTOBER 1997
$3

TRINITY ANGELS #5
NOVEMBER 1997
$3

TRINITY ANGELS #6
DECEMBER 1997
$3

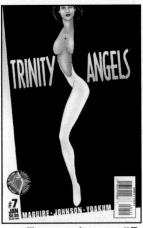

TRINITY ANGELS #7
JANUARY 1998
$3

TRINITY ANGELS #8
FEBRUARY 1998
$3

TRINITY ANGELS #9
MARCH 1998
$3

TRINITY ANGELS #10
APRIL 1998
$3

TRINITY ANGELS #11
MAY 1998
$3

TRINITY ANGELS #12
JUNE 1998
$3

TROUBLEMAKERS #1
RETAILER REVIEW COPY
1996
$3

TROUBLEMAKERS #1
APRIL 1997
$3

TROUBLEMAKERS #1
VARIANT COVER
APRIL 1997
$3

TROUBLEMAKERS #2
MAY 1997
$3

TROUBLEMAKERS #3
JUNE 1997
$3

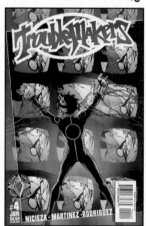

TROUBLEMAKERS #4
JULY 1997
$3

TROUBLEMAKERS #5
AUGUST 1997
$3

TROUBLEMAKERS #6
SEPTEMBER 1997
$3

TROUBLEMAKERS #7
OCTOBER 1997
$3

TROUBLEMAKERS #8
NOVEMBER 1997
$3

TROUBLEMAKERS #9
DECEMBER 1997
$3

TROUBLEMAKERS #10
JANUARY 1998
$3

TROUBLEMAKERS #11
FEBRUARY 1998
$3

TROUBLEMAKERS #12
MARCH 1998
$3

TROUBLEMAKERS #13
APRIL 1998
$3

TROUBLEMAKERS #14
JANUARY 1998
$3

TROUBLEMAKERS #15
FEBRUARY 1998
$3

TROUBLEMAKERS #16
MARCH 1998
$3

TROUBLEMAKERS #17
APRIL 1998
$3

TROUBLEMAKERS #18
MAY 1998
$3

TROUBLEMAKERS #19
JUNE 1998
$3

TUROK #1
MARCH 1998
$4

TUROK #2
APRIL 1998
$4

TUROK #3
MAY 1998
$4

TUROK #4
JUNE 1998
$4

TUROK, CHILD OF BLOOD #1
JANUARY 1998
$6

TUROK EVOLUTION #1
AUGUST 2002
$24

TUROK, REDPATH #1
OCTOBER 1997
$4

TUROK/SHADOWMAN #1
FEBRUARY 1999
$12

TUROK: SPRING BREAK IN THE LOST LAND #1
JULY 1997
$4

TUROK: TALES OF THE LOST LAND #1
APRIL 1998
$4

TUROK: TALES OF THE LOST LAND #1
NO PRICE VARIANT COVER • APRIL 1998
$4

TUROK: THE EMPTY SOULS #1
RETAILER REVIEW COPY • APRIL 1997
$4

TUROK: THE EMPTY SOULS #1
APRIL 1997
$4

TUROK: THE EMPTY SOULS #1
NO PRICE VARIANT COVER • APRIL 1997
$4

TUROK: THE EMPTY SOULS #1
VARIANT COVER • APRIL 1997
$4

TUROK, TIMEWALKER #1
AUGUST 1997
$4

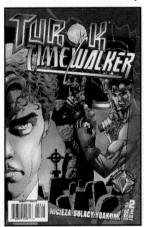

TUROK, TIMEWALKER #2
SEPTEMBER 1997
$4

TUROK 2: ADON'S CURSE
VIDEOGAME MAGAZINE
OCTOBER 1998
$8

TUROK 2: SEEDS OF EVIL
VIDEOGAME MAGAZINE
OCTOBER 1998
$8

TUROK 3: SHADOWS OF OBLIVION
VIDEOGAME MAGAZINE
SEPTEMBER 2000 • $10

UNITY 2000 PREVIEW BOOK
2000
$3

UNITY 2000 #1
NOVEMBER 1999
$3

UNITY 2000 #1
VARIANT COVER
NOVEMBER 1999
$3

UNITY 2000 #2
DECEMBER 1999
$3

UNITY 2000 #3
JANUARY 2000
$3

THE VALIANT DEATHS OF JACK BONIFACE ALPHA
FLIP BOOK WITH SHADOWMAN V3 #3
SEPTEMBER 1999 • $3

THE VALIANT DEATHS OF JACK BONIFACE OMEGA
FLIP BOOK WITH SHADOWMAN V3 #4
OCTOBER 1999 • **$3**

X-O MANOWAR VOL. 2 #1
RETAILER REVIEW COPY
1996
$3

X-O MANOWAR VOL. 2 #1
FEBRUARY 1997
$3

X-O MANOWAR VOL. 2 #1
VARIANT COVER
FEBRUARY 1997
$3

X-O MANOWAR VOL. 2 #2
MARCH 1997
$3

X-O MANOWAR VOL. 2 #3
APRIL 1997
$3

X-O MANOWAR VOL. 2 #4
MAY 1997
$3

X-O MANOWAR VOL. 2 #5
JUNE 1997
$3

X-O MANOWAR VOL. 2 #6
JULY 1997
$3

X-O Manowar Vol. 2 #7
AUGUST 1997
$3

X-O Manowar Vol. 2 #8
SEPTEMBER 1997
$3

X-O Manowar Vol. 2 #9
OCTOBER 1997
$3

X-O Manowar Vol. 2 #10
NOVEMBER 1997
$3

X-O Manowar Vol. 2 #11
DECEMBER 1997
$3

X-O Manowar Vol. 2 #12
JANUARY 1998
$3

X-O Manowar Vol. 2 #13
FEBRUARY 1998
$3

X-O Manowar Vol. 2 #14
MARCH 1998
$3

X-O Manowar Vol. 2 #15
APRIL 1998
$3

X-O Manowar Vol. 2 #16
JANUARY 1998
$3

X-O Manowar Vol. 2 #17
FEBRUARY 1998
$3

X-O Manowar Vol. 2 #18
MARCH 1998
$3

X-O Manowar Vol. 2 #19
APRIL 1998
$3

X-O Manowar Vol. 2 #20
MAY 1998
$3

X-O Manowar Vol. 2 #21
JUNE 1998
$3

**X-O Manowar
FAN Edition #1**
OBTAINED THROUGH MAIL-IN OFFER FROM
OVERSTREET'S FAN MAGAZINE #19
FEBRUARY 1997 • $5

**X-O Manowar/Iron Man:
In Heavy Metal #1**
PART 1 OF MARVEL/VALIANT CROSSOVER
SEPTEMBER 1996 • $5

**Iron Man/X-O Manowar:
In Heavy Metal #1**
PART 2 OF MARVEL/VALIANT CROSSOVER
SEPTEMBER 1996 • $4

DAN MOLER Collecting Valiant Original Art

In the years after the last Valiant comics were published by Acclaim and before the first issues were released by Valiant Entertainment, a cadre of loyal enthusiasts kept the flames of fandom alive. Dan Moler was one of those fans. In the late 1990s, his Valiant collecting habits expanded to include original comic art.

Overstreet: How did you become a fan of Valiant originally?

Dan Moler (DM): I grew up in the '80s reading Spider-Man and then the X-Men. In the early '90s my tastes started to change and I wasn't enjoying that stuff as quite as much. I remember seeing an advertisement for *Archer & Armstrong* in *Wizard* that was drawn by Barry Windsor-Smith. I always liked those X-Men books he did, so I was intrigued. When some of the Valiant titles finally started to show up on the newsstand in the small town I lived in, I had to check them out. I was hooked! I liked how in *Harbinger* they talked about Magnus, and in *Eternal Warrior* you'd have Bloodshot show up. The characters were new and interesting. They interacted with each other in a shared universe outside your window.

Overstreet: When did your Valiant collecting turn toward art?

DM: I think it was in 1998 or so. Acclaim/ Valiant, like much of the industry, had scaled back in publishing and print runs were diminishing. I was busy tracking down some of the harder to find books that had eluded me before.

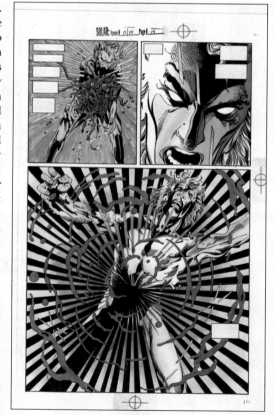

Books like *Harbinger* #1, *Rai* #3 and #4, and *Magnus* #12 were all of a sudden more affordable. Around this time I realized that original art pages were obtainable as well. During this time more and more people began corresponding via the internet and email. I got in touch with as many creators as possible and would inquire about availability of pages.

Overstreet: What was the first piece of Valiant art you purchased?

DM: Again back in 1998, I won a limited print from a contest from a Valiant fan site, but it arrived damaged. The site administrator felt bad about it and sent me the original cover to *Bloodshot* Volume 2 #10 by Sal Velluto and Bob Almond instead. I was blown away by the detail. Little did I know at the time it had started my obsession with collecting Valiant art. I think some of the pages I picked up after that were from *Shadowman* by David Lapham and *H.A.R.D. Corps* by Mike Leeke.

Overstreet: What do you look for in a piece of original comic art?

DM: A variety of factors come into play. Who's the artist? Does the page tell a story? How relevant is it in the development of the series or character? Is it cool or interesting to look at? I also enjoy pages that feature a guest star or characters from another title. Origins, flash-

Magnus Robot Fighter #2, Page 20 by Art Nichols and Bob Layton.

backs, and pages that have prominent events are also always on my radar.

Overstreet: In the years before the new Valiant started publishing, did your enthusiasm for the universe fade or did you stay enthusiastic for it?

DM: I've been an enthusiastic collector of Valiant the whole time. I continued to buy art, hoard books and track down anything related to Valiant. I made lasting friendships with other Valiant fans. I kept updated on how things developed over the years. I was optimistic that a return would eventually happen. I had high hopes and was thrilled my expectations were exceeded! The books now are accessible to new readers and yet have a lot of throwbacks and nods to the original continuity.

Overstreet: Has the degree of difficulty in getting good pieces changed since the new Valiant brought the characters back or are things just about the same?

DM: It has gotten increasingly more challenging to find key pieces or nice covers on a budget. Much of the early stuff or key pieces are tucked away in collections. At the same time though there's been some really nice stuff that has hit the market recently as a result of the characters returning to prominence.

I buy sell trade original Valiant art so I enjoy sharing tips and getting in touch with other collectors.

Overstreet: Do you collect original art from the new Valiant universe or do you just stick with the original?

DM: I collect Valiant art from all eras and enjoy having work by many other artists who

Rai #0 Page 15 pencils by David Lapham and inks by Tom Ryder (top) with colors by Dave Chlystek (bottom)

worked on the Valiant properties over the years. I especially like pre-*Unity*/*Unity* pages from the original Valiant along with covers from their peak in popularity. I'm always glad when I can add work by David Lapham, Bob Hall, Bob Layton, BWS, Don Perlin, Bernard Chang, Sean Chen, among others, to my collection. There's some stuff from the Acclaim era I enjoyed as well, especially their versions of Turok, Shadowman and Bloodshot.

With the new Valiant it's nice to be back on the ground floor so to speak. I was able to pick up *Eternal Warrior* (2013) #1 page 1 by Trevor Hairsine. It was cool getting the first page of the new series. *Harbinger* is probably my favorite so I like any and all pages from that title. With the proliferation of variant covers I think it's nice to be able to have more choices on getting a cover from a favorite book. Valiant has done a real nice job showcasing their magnificent roster of characters rendered by a variety of talented artists. I particularly like the recent work by Lewis LaRosa, CAFU, Cary Nord, Clayton Henry, Riley Rossmo, Brian Level, and Stefano Gaudiano.

Overstreet: What would you consider the crown jewel of your collection at this point?
DM: There's a lot of pieces in my collection that I admire. I have to say my favorite piece though is the *Solar Man of the Atom* #11 cover art. It has a nice pre-*Unity* classic composition and pencils by Don Perlin and then inked by the super talented, Bob Layton. It features Solar vs. Harada's Eggbreakers while the Eternal Warrior rushes in. It really emphasizes the shared universe concept brilliantly. For the new stuff, the *Harbinger* #0 trifold variant cover by Lewis LaRosa is one of my all-time favorites!

(top) *Solar: Man of the Atom* #11 cover by Bob Layton and Don Perlin

(bottom) Early Harbinger promotional art by David Lapham and (perhaps) John Dixon.

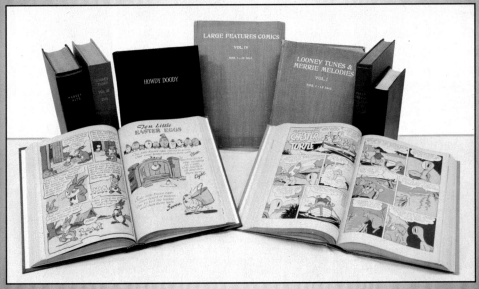

NOW AVAILABLE!
VISIT YOUR LOCAL COMIC BOOK RETAILER TODAY!

$24.95 SC NOV211456
$34.95 HC JAN211365

$19.95 SC SEP131204

$12.95 SC AUG131333

$20.00 SC JUN201130

$15.00 SC JUN201131

$15.00 SC JUN201129

$19.95 SC JUL191947

$15.00 SC JUN201133

$15.00 SC SEP151411

www.gemstonepub.com

COMIC SHOP LOCATOR SERVICE
comicshoplocator.com
888-COMIC-BOOK

The DEFIANT Ones

At the DEFIANT booth at Comic-Con International: San Diego 1994 (from left to right), Len Wein, David Lapham, Joe James, Charles Yoakum, Keith (KEZ) Wilson, and Art Holcomb. Photo courtesy of Brady Darvin.

"Ah, what might have been…" That's the melancholy-infused fragrant breeze of possibilities contained in this book, isn't it? No matter which of our lost universes you love, it's bittersweet to let your imagination run wild with that particular "What if…?" or "If only…"

Just about any of the companies or imprints featured in this first edition of *The Overstreet Comic Book Price Guide To Lost Universes* would have made for a great subject of our "Deep Dive" section, but there are a few good reasons we decided to take this particular deep dive "beyond the imaginary limits" with DEFIANT.

First, most of the key players are still alive and many of them are active in comics. This is not a must for documenting comics history, of course, but it does make it easier to get as many first-hand experiences down in interviews without having to seek out previously published materials (This, however, is not to say that all are still with us. Len Wein and Greg Boone are just two who have passed).

Second, Jim Shooter is a key figure in a wide swath of comics history. Whether for his work as a teen writing DC's Legion of Super-Heroes, his tenure as Marvel's Editor-in-Chief, or as the founder of a set of creative companies, his name attracts attention.

Never a bad thing when trying to sell a book.

Third, no one has done a particularly great job of covering the company. There have been some solid articles, to be sure, but who else is going to spend the time and effort to document to this extent a company that existed for a couple of years a quarter of a century ago?

Fourth, I've been covering this particular lost universe since before it was lost, almost from the company's earliest days. DEFIANT's Clark Smith even introduced me to Bob and Carol Overstreet, as well as their then-Editor Gary M. Carter. That, a few months later, led me to Gemstone Publishing, where I've been ever since. In this one case, I stake no claim to serious objectivity other than a professional's eye, the passage of time, and the willingness to ask questions fairly and listen to the answers.

Before I got to Gemstone, though, I had freelanced for Bob's original company, Overstreet Publications. Clark set me up to do an article I called "Everything's Been Leading Up To This" about *Schism* for *Overstreet's Comic Book Monthly* #16. I chose the title because it's a familiar hype phrase, but in the case of *Schism*, everything really *had* been leading up to it. I interviewed JayJay Jackson for the piece. She sent me the plot beats and walked

DEFIANT's JayJay Jackson shared the basic plot of *Schism* in "Everything's Been Leading Up To This" in *Overstreet's Comic Book Monthly* #16 (August 1994).

me through some of what was coming. It *sounded* amazing. It *read* amazing. To this day, I really think it would have *been* amazing.

The *Schism* article, one of my first two published pieces in comics, came out right before Comic-Con International: San Diego 1994, which was the first San Diego I attended. Clark had arranged for there to be copies of the issue at the DEFIANT booth for me to sign. I ended up sitting next to *Dogs of War* writer Art Holcomb, a friend ever since, signing copies and giving them to fans. For a budding freelancer, it was a heady experience!

At the DEFIANT booth, I also got to talk with Pauline Weiss, Peter Gyrich, inker Charles Yokum, and several creators and editors who floated in and out. I got to know DEFIANT Sales Associate Brady Darvin a bit more as well.

When I first joined the staff at Gemstone, not only did that mean I worked just down the corridor from Bob, but also that I worked with co-author Scott Braden, and with Brady, who by then worked there. Scott and I peppered him with DEFIANT questions over lunches until he stopped eating with us.

Even when Scott left Gemstone after a of couple years, we would talk regularly. If the conversation went on long enough, sooner or later the topic would inevitably turn to DEFIANT.

In the days between then and now, Scott became one of the most knowledgeable people outside of the original DEFIANT team on *Schism*, and has continued a career in comics journalism with *Tripwire* and other outlets. Getting him to come back for this one did not take a lot of persuasion.

As with all of the other sections in this book, I would like to thank everyone who participated and helped make this possible. Bob, Scott, and I, along with Steve Geppi and the entire Gemstone team, hope that our efforts will encourage other enthusiasts to continue documenting the history of this wonderful medium.

– J.C. Vaughn

P.S. I stole my most-used catch phrase, "In my copious free time…" from DEFIANT's Pauline Weiss. I think of her every time I say it.

Former DC Comics President and Publisher Paul Levitz, Gemstone Publishing's J.C. Vaughn, Geppi Family Enterprises Chairman Steve Geppi, and Jim Shooter (left to right) at Geppi's 70th birthday party.
Photo by Rosina Ally.

It's difficult to write something about Jim Shooter that hasn't been written. He first hit the comic book world as a teenager writing for DC. Among his other work there, he penned Legion of Super-Heroes *stories that are still fan-favorites. He moved to Marvel and began to make his mark as Associate Editor before becoming Editor-in-Chief.*

During his tenure, Walter Simonson's Thor, *Frank Miller and Klaus Janson's* Daredevil, *Chris Claremont and Bill Sienkiewicz's* New Mutants, *John Byrne's* Fantastic Four, *and, Frank Miller and David Mazzuchelli's* Daredevil, *among others, shook up the superhero status quo.*

During that same time, Marvel published a string of Moebius *graphic novels, launched the New Universe and the Marvel Graphic Novel series, and improved creator rights. Shooter himself*

wrote an exalted run on The Avengers *as well as* Marvel Superheroes: Secret Wars, *which along with DC's* Crisis on Infinite Earths *ushered in the concept of the big "event" in comics.*

Following his departure from Marvel, Shooter assembled a team that attempted to purchase the firm. Falling just short – that in itself is another story – he co-founded VALIANT. As the firm was experiencing the early tastes of success, he was ousted from it. We asked him about this since it was particularly germane to the launch of DEFIANT, his next company.

Overstreet: After your last day at Valiant, how much time passed before you started DEFIANT? What went on during that time? Were you restricted by a non-compete in your contract or were you just shell-shocked from how that went down?

David Lapham's unpublished *Schism* #1 cover (seen in some DEFIANT ads).
Art from Scott Braden's collection.

Jim Shooter (JS): I left VALIANT in June of 1992. My contract remained in effect until October. The evil people who stole VALIANT kept it in effect, rather than settle or terminate, to keep me under rules of fiduciary responsibility. Fiduciary responsibility prohibited me from working elsewhere, raising money, recruiting talent, and/or saying or doing anything that might negatively impact VALIANT. It also kept me homebound, because, by contract, I was required to appear at board meetings on 24 hours' notice. If I were not available, they could convene the board, enact whatever atrocities they wished, against me or to favor themselves, with impunity, and cite me for non-appearance. Triumph Capital, that is, Melanie Okun and Michael Nugent, principals, Fred Pierce, lackey, and my once-alleged partner, Steve Massarsky (who'd married Melanie – what else do you need to know?) threatened to sue me if I violated fiduciary responsibility. It was not an idle threat. They, in fact, sued me for my contractual personal guarantee, payable if the company defaulted on its loan. I spent $70,000 defending against a $50,000 claim. They spent over $300,000 prosecuting it. The real issue was the value of the stock. If they won, it validated their claim that the company was in default, therefore my stock was worthless, therefore they owed me nothing. Then, rid of me, they could take steps to sell the company for its true value and keep all the money. They lost that case, but long story short, they found other ways to screw me and they eventually wound up with everything, according to my unimpeachable sources well over $100 million, and I got nothing.

Then what? What else, start again. You may remember the DEFIANT motto, "Just Don't Quit." It took me till early 1993 to raise the money and gather talent. We started work, I believe in January. I remember that we closed our financing deal during my investment banking firm's Christmas party. McFarland Dewey & Co. was the firm, great people.

Overstreet: What was the first thing you created for DEFIANT and what was the spark for it?
JS: Long story. Back in 1987, while I was still Editor-in-Chief at Marvel, Marvel had a joint venture deal to co-create a boys' toy property with industry giant TCFC (Those Characters From Cleveland – Care Bears, Strawberry Shortcake, Holly Hobby and many more). It was a dream scenario: super-successful TCFC, a division of giant American Greetings, 50/50 partners with relatively tiny Marvel? A home run.

At a meeting in La Jolla with President and head creative guy at TCFC, Ralph Schaffer, several other TCFC'ers, Tom DeFalco, Sid Jacobson, Mike Hobson and me, we started working on ideas. I was blown away by Schaffer, one of the most brilliant-minded creators I ever encountered. I had to bear down and try my best to keep up, but he liked what I had to say.

Shortly thereafter, Marvel fired me. When some Marvel exec, Joe Calamari, I believe, informed Schaffer that DeFalco was now EIC and that I had been let go, Schaffer terminated the agreement. He later told me his exact words: "You no longer have any creative people we're interested in working with."

I did not contact TCFC or seek to pursue some deal with them on my own, because, of course, I knew famously-litigious Marvel *very* well from the inside, and I knew they would sue me in a heartbeat.

However, I started developing a property by myself that was, I hoped, both good in general and "toyetic," as they say in the trade. I created the basis for PLASM.

Years passed. Two or three times, I ran into Ralph Schaffer at Toy Fair. We had dinner at the Palm Too a couple of times. We did not talk about working together. He knew as well as I did that Marvel would sue. He did not have a high opinion of Marvel around that time.

More years passed. It was 1993. I had started DEFIANT. I intended to use *PLASM* as our first and centerpiece property.

Sometime before Toy Fair (which is in mid-February) Ralph called and we made plans for a dinner at Palm Too.

We talked business, his and mine, just catching up. I told him about *PLASM*. Ralph loved the concept. I proposed a deal in which TCFC would do toy development and licensing and we'd do everything else. Six years after Marvel, I figured, why not? He asked, "Standard terms?" I said 50/50. I told him the education he gave me about toyetics in one short meeting was a lot of the inspiration for *PLASM*. So, we started.

The first *PLASM* product was a trading card set for the River Group, which, by the way, funded DEFIANT. It was a tremendous success. Meanwhile, TCFC was developing prototypes.

DEFIANT "advertorial" promotional page illustrated by David Lapham.
Art from Scott Braden's collection.

Ralph and I decided to try Mattel first, reasoning that Mattel had the greatest need for a strong boys' toy. Both of us had a good relationship with Jill Barrad, Mattel CEO. We were granted the opportunity to pitch. We pitched to Jill herself, and her entire boys' toy executive staff. I did the pitch. When I was done, Jill said, "Here's the deal...." Named the terms. Briefly, it guaranteed us $9 million, but she said, "It'll be a lot more than that." Then she said, I remember this all like yesterday, "You and Schaffer get out of here. Leave your business guy."

So, we thought we won, and we were on top of the world.

One of Ralph Schaffer's early jobs at American Greetings was running their studio card shop. One of his employees was R. Crumb. Ralph told me many tales.

Then Marvel, yes, six years later, sued DEFIANT for infringement and intellectual property rights, claiming we'd stolen them. They lost. Our tough, super-smart layer, Marya Lenn-Yee, beat the stuffing out of Marvel's six lawyers. Judge (and future Attorney General of the U.S.) Michael B. Mukasey ruled emphatically in our favor. He also warned Marvel's lawyers, quote, "If you ever use my court as a business weapon again, you will sincerely regret it."

"Winning" cost DEFIANT $300,000 and delayed our deal with Mattel long enough so we missed our window. Project cancelled. So, really, Marvel won. They effectively put us out of business, which was their only goal.

Overstreet: How much of the concept for DEFIANT's universe did you have at the start?
JS: All of it, though of course, things grow and develop as you go along. I had from July 1992 through January 1993 to think about it.

Overstreet: After you got the funding, who were the first folks you hired?
JS: Winston Fowlkes, CFO, Debbie Fix, who was the administrative linchpin at VALIANT, JayJay Jackson, artful art production person and technical expert, J. Clark Smith, marketing master, and David Lapham.

Overstreet: DEFIANT had both new and established creators. Focusing on the up-and-coming talent, who was on your roster and what did you think they brought to the table?
JS: We found some great talent. Artist J.G. Jones was a miraculous find. Joe James, who came to us from Milestone, quickly turned into a star, first as

an artist, later as a writer. JayJay spread her wings and developed as a writer. Inker Mike Witherby was terrific. Although not a creator in the art and writing sense, Brady Darvin, who was Clark Smith's marketing assistant, was outstanding in general and great help with things creative. For instance, when I was writing the first story for *Dark Dominion*, Brady, on his own, talked the people at Con Edison into giving him a tour of the spooky labyrinths under Grand Central Terminal, where Brady, an excellent photographer took lots of reference photos.

Overstreet: David Lapham might have been in-between those two groups. He wasn't a newbie anymore after Valiant and he wasn't yet the guy who would do *Stray Bullets*. What did you think of what he was doing at the time? At what point was his talent obvious to you?
JS: Early on at VALIANT I knew David was an amazing talent. In all my years, only Frank Miller had ever made giant leaps so rapidly. David followed me to DEFIANT and got better, it seemed, minute by minute. He's one of the best. Ever. I don't say that lightly, and remember, I've worked with, and known well many all-time greats.

Overstreet: Among the more established creators, you had Len Wein, Chris Claremont, Steve Ditko, Alan Weiss, JayJay... What did they (and any others you care to mention) add to the mix?
JS: Everyone you named and more besides (outstanding production manager Ron Zalme, for instance) contributed a great deal, as one would expect. What I was asking creators to do was not easy. It was essential to have some seasoned pros.

If we'd had more time and more money, if the market hadn't crashed due to DC, Marvel, Image and others running the speculator business into the ground, if Marvel hadn't sued us and cost our small start-up $300,000 in legal fees, if Marvel's suit hadn't caused us to miss our window on the toy deal we had with Mattel, which had a $9 million guarantee (which, Jill Barad assured me, would be a fraction of the revenues), if the investors who financed us hadn't gotten greedy and killed a $9 million buy-in offer from New Line Cinema AND a subsequent $11 million buy-in offer from Savoy Pictures, if I had been smarter, wiser, stronger, able to stay awake longer, etc., with our old pros and talented kids, I believe we had a chance.

Overstreet: Why didn't Marvel have to pay any damages? Was it that under New York law it would have required a separate trial?

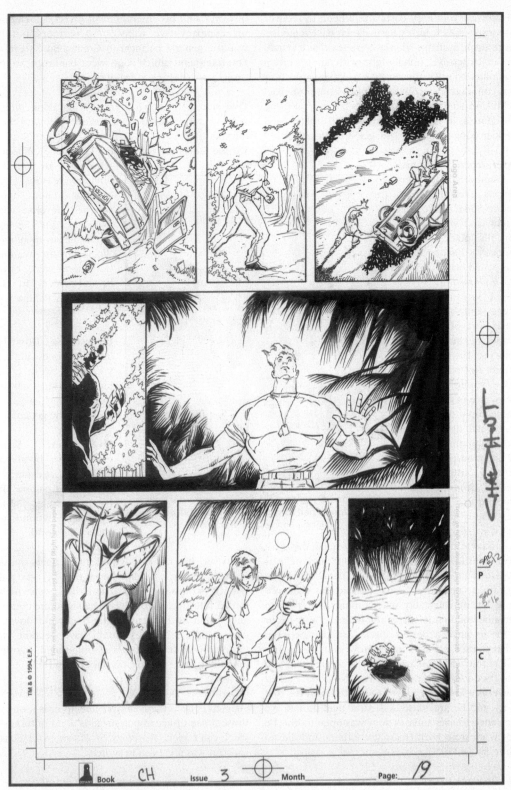

Adam Pollina and Chad Hunt's original art for *Charlemagne* #3 Page 19.
Art from Scott Braden's collection.

JS: In New York legal costs are difficult to recover. Other states, New Jersey, for instance, have remedies more easily available. Our lawyers felt that it would be an expensive, uphill fight with an uncertain outcome. Isn't that amazing? Marvel's suit against us was completely and obviously bogus, Judge Michael B. Mukasey reprimanded Marvel's lawyers for using his court as a "business weapon," and still, in New York, making them pay damages was iffy at best.

Overstreet: We've had a number of conversations over the years about Steve Ditko, his talent, and your regard for his place in our industry's history. What happened with him on *Dark Dominion*?

JS: I sat down with Steve and asked him what sort of thing he would be interested in drawing. He gave me a number of particulars – no costume, self-made hero, able to do whatever he could do because of mental discipline or unlocking potentialities of the mind, plus several more. I custom-created *Dark Dominion* for Steve. At first, he seemed very happy with it. Then, halfway through the origin issue, he told me he couldn't finish the book because the concept was "Platonic" and he was "Aristotelian." I said, "You're going to have to explain that one to me, Steve." He did. He said Plato believed in a conceptual reality where things that we can imagine but do not exist in the here and now occur – for instance a perfect circle. Aristotle believed what you see is what you get. Steve said, "This series is Platonic and I am Aristotelian." I argued that you can't see viruses, but they're real. No good. I asked Steve, as a friend, as a favor to me, to finish the first story, and he graciously did. After that, though we remained friends and our door was open to him, he got work from Dark Horse and others, and did no more for DEFIANT.

P.S. He came to see me later, at Broadway Comics, and we made an agreement for Broadway to publish new Mr. A stories by Steve. Lorne Michaels,

Jim Shooter, colorist Tim Perkins, and artist/editor Joe James (left to right) in the DEFIANT offices. Image courtesy of Tim Perkins.

however sold his entertainment division, including my company (we were 50/50 partners, but he was the general partner) to Golden Books Family Entertainment, which soon went bankrupt, so the project never reached fruition.

Overstreet: As things were moving along, which creators surprised you in a positive way with their efforts?

JS: Joe James proved to be a Godsend. Jeff Jones, who goes by J.G. for obvious reasons, was another talent you watched develop with awe and joy. Several others began to bloom. I'm losing my memory, but there were other up-and-comers in the crew. Adam Pollina was one.

Overstreet: How far into the process did you know you were building toward the "Schism" storyline?

JS: From the get-go.

Overstreet: What would have been the results of that event?

JS: For the first time, the bad guys win. Chasm essentially wound up ruling the world.

However, his control would have been subtle. Regular people wouldn't know that he was pulling the strings, or even that strings were being pulled, but Chasm would have had absolute control, and would have been leading the world down a dark path. The heroes would have become the underground resistance, way outgunned, fighting incredible odds to stave off impending Hell.

Overstreet: Do you have any personal favorite characters from the DEFIANT line-up or is it one of those "I can't pick among my kids" kind of things?

JS: I can't pick. *Warriors of Plasm*, with David Lapham was great fun to write.

This interview was conducted via email.
©2019, 2021 J.C. Vaughn. Used by permission.
All rights reserved.

Plasm promotional cards uncut sheet from *Overstreet's Comic Book Monthly #4* (1993). Sheet gives the proportions of the differently colored cards. Only known example.

Jim Shooter, David Lapham, and JayJay Jackson (left to right) at Clark Smith's Manhattan residence, which served as a meeting space before DEFIANT's offices were open. Photo courtesy of Jim Shooter.

For one of her earliest efforts in comics, Janet "JayJay" Jackson started Texas Comics with her friends Bill Willingham and Keith Wilson. The company only published one comic, Justice Machine Annual #1, *which turned out to be the first appearance of The Elementals. When they decided to host comic conventions, Jackson met Jim Shooter, then Editor-in-Chief of Marvel Comics. Having seen some of her technical illustrations, Shooter asked her to provide drawings of pens, pencils, and paints for* The Marvel Try-Out Book. *A collaboration that would span decades was born.*

She initially worked as a graphic designer at Marvel, producing Marvel Age *and* Doctor Who Magazine, *and began expanding her skillset to include advertising, marketing, coloring, and illustration. She would go on to add writing and editing to her resume, as well as co-creating the Eternal Warrior for Valiant. Her experience made her a perfect candidate for another start-up.*

"I like to be useful, so I became a jack of all trades. I learned to be useful so I could do what I was doing. And everything I did was linked; it was definitely all linked," Jackson said.

After Valiant and just prior to launching DEFIANT, she had teamed with Shooter to consult for then-start-up Milestone Media.

"We helped a lot in setting up their systems, their ways of doing things. I taught their production people the way to do production. I also showed them our coloring system, which they adapted. That was the coloring system that I developed at Valiant. I think I colored their first issues. I colored the cover of *Static* #1, and I colored the first couple issues of *Blood Syndicate*," she said.

At DEFIANT, she led a team of colorists to develop and implement a painted art style that printers wouldn't have been able to handle even just a few years earlier. *Warriors of Plasm*, *Dark Dominion*, and *War Dancer* are probably the best expressions of her system's potential. She said the working arrangements contributed to the team spirit at DEFIANT.

"It was very creative. It was a very creative environment. It was different than when we started Valiant. First off, we had offices, where at Valiant we just had a massive open space. Anybody could chime in, but it was more than a bullpen because everyone other than Steve Massarsky was in one massive space," she said.

"So, in Valiant, people would just chime in. It made people feel very, very involved. At DEFIANT, there was a big open space in the middle that was surrounded by offices. And the office doors were generally kept open. So, it was kind of like Valiant, but not quite. There was definitely an atmosphere of fun," she said.

"JayJay is a Jackson of all trades and a master of all. She's an expert at art production, printing production, graphic design, photography, technical drawing, drawing of all kinds. Need a cover with embossing, debossing, foil stamping, die cuts, spot vanish and a fifth color? No problem. Need someone to go to the plant and press check a job? Need trade dress or a logo designed? Need photos taken? Need an illo for a poster? Need a technical drawing? Need *anything?* She can probably do that," Jim Shooter said.

"She inspires, she teaches, she helps in so many ways, she works hard and cares passionately about the work," he said. "Specifically at DEFIANT, she was involved from the beginning and provided great input on many things from concept to finish. Need a map of the world you're building? Need a floorplan for a location, so you always get the entrances and exits correct? Oh, yeah, and fashion design from grunge to couture. Oh, yeah, and costumes, let's not forget costumes. JayJay is a *creator* in every sense."

JayJay Jackson's original colors over Alan Weiss War Dancer art. Jackson developed VALIANT's, Milestone's, and DEFIANT's coloring processes in a period of just a few years.

A lifelong bass player, guitar player and singer, Joe James performed with the New York City Youth Chorus from age 9 to age 21. After attending the High School of Art and Design, Joe's first job (at the age of 19) was for DC's Who's Who, for which he drew Alfred, The Riddler, Scarecrow and Ra's al Gul. His DEFIANT tenure, which is remembered by many fans for his work illustrating Dark Dominion, was bookended by stints at Milestone, and then Broadway Comics, where he created and wrote Knights on Broadway.

Following the demise of Broadway Comics, he worked in toy design for ToyBiz. He began to design displays and point of purchase products for several prominent New York ad agencies. As he moved on to drawing storyboards, he kept a hand in comics from time to time with Lazer Wars #0 (Toy Island, 1998, a promotional comic packaged with a line of toys), Galactica: The New Millennium #1 (Realm Press, 2000), and Bedtime Stories For Impressionable Children #1 (American Mythology, 2017, on which he worked once again with Jim Shooter).

These days, through his Saint James Studios, he's best known for providing storyboards, treatments, and custom illustrations (among many other things) for top commercial and creative directors. Working in commercials (he frequently has multiple commercials during each Super Bowl), TV, and film, he is very much in demand as a creator. He worked on two Academy Award-winning short films, and he even appeared in one commercial he storyboarded. In comics, he's presently at work (with Framestore Ventures) on Nixon's Demons, a compelling graphic novel released on the Madefire platform take on the demons – and

angels – that drove America's 37th President to his greatest successes and failures.

Overstreet: Before you worked at DEFIANT, you were at Milestone. How did you get to that point?
Joe James (JJ): I was assisting Denys Cowan by doing background work and layouts on Deathlock, Green Arrow, FoolKiller among other things, when I was asked if I was interested in joining Milestone Media.

At that point the key players had several meetings at Denys' studio so I had a sense something was cooking. I came into MM in production capacity under Editor-in-Chief Dwayne McDuffie, who basically taught me my job. He was such a good manager. He'd make suggestions and engaged you in conversation about whatever you were working on and suddenly you were learning.

Joe James (with Jim Shooter, right) at his surprise 50th birthday party. Photo by J.C. Vaughn.

While there I did logo design, I also illustrated concept designs for the Dakota Universe like exteriors of the city, Hardware's lab, that went into the Milestone Media Universe Bible. I also did some inking and penciling for their trading cards. On any given day I was working across various disciplines, we were all hands-on deck trying to get those first issues out the door. Those were the fun days.

Overstreet: While you were there, if I remember it correctly, Jim and JayJay were there doing some consulting during the start-up. Is that right? How did you interact with them during that period?
JJ: Jim Shooter and Janet Jackson came to Milestone to consult on their color process. If you remember Valiant comics were hand painted. Dwayne decided he wanted to use that look for the Milestone line, so he asked Jim and JayJay to come in and teach us the process. That's the first time I'd met Jim and JayJay.

Joe James' *Dark Dominion* #0 Page 1 from the unpublished original graphic novel version of the trading card set story. Image courtesy of Joe James.

Overstreet: How did you end up at DEFIANT after that?

JJ: JayJay became aware of some of the logos I'd done for MM and asked me to pitch in on some of the early work for DEFIANT logos. That led to penciling some trading cards.

Overstreet: How much had they put together before you came on board?

JJ: I believe the main body of the universe was up and running; *Warriors of Plasm* by Shooter and David Lapham, and the *Dark Dominion* trading card set illustrated by Steve Ditko were fully underway, and I believe *War Dancer* was in the development stage. By the time I got involved, they were creating the logos and the trade dress.

Overstreet: When you originally joined, were you going to exclusively be an artist or were there already editorial duties in the mix?

JJ: JayJay brought me in as a designer and then I was offered some trading cards that went on to be a part of the *Dark Dominion* trading card book. I really enjoyed working creatively with the team. I saw my involvement as a real opportunity to learn from one of the masters of comics, so I jumped at the chance to be involved with DEFIANT in any capacity they would have me.

Overstreet: How would you describe working at the DEFIANT offices at that point?

JJ: Fancy. They had a neat midsized office on Madison Avenue with a patio that had a view of the Empire State Building. And I mean an unobstructed view. Very impressive. And there was a really good vibe: professional, polite, funny, respectful, interaction was encouraged, ideas — just a real nice place.

Overstreet: Who were the people with whom you really enjoyed interacting?

JJ: Peter Lucic (our designer), Barbra Morcerf, George Roberts (our letterer), Rob La Quinta, Debbie Fix, Deborah Purcell, Ed Polgardy, Brady Darvin. That was during the day shift. At night it was a menagerie of artists and lots of Chinese food. It was early in everyone's careers, so there was a sense of adventure and excitement at meeting

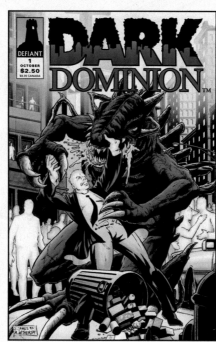

kindred spirits and trying to do good work and wanting to support one another. That's what I meant about a good vibe, there was a genuine feeling of comradery which, really, Jim encouraged.

The longer I was there, the more I saw that this sense of interaction and good feeling came right from the top.

Overstreet: What was your first gig for the company?

JJ: I drew trading card art for the back of the *Dark Dominion* cards. Then after a San Diego Comic Con I was asked if I wanted to draw *Dark Dominion*. I believe I was asked to draw a cover first, which was needed for an ad for the *Comics Buyer's Guide*.

I agreed and read the script several times over on the red eye back to New York, went into the office the next morning and drew the cover. I remember reading the script over and over and doodling thumb sketches in the margins. Dream come true, really.

Overstreet: What did you think when you found out you were going to be illustrating *Dark Dominion*?

JJ: Steve Ditko really did that Spider-Man thing with his hands, you know. You had to see it to believe it. I saw it. I believe it. Anyway….

I was working on staff in production at that point – everything from paste-up to drawing to book design. Good times. One day I was called into Jim's office and informed that Steve Ditko was not going to draw the ongoing series and I was offered penciling duties on the book.

Then I was also told that it had to be completed in two weeks.

After about a minute I accepted.

I mentioned that we had a terrific balcony at the DEFIANT offices with a magnificent view of the Empire State Building? I remember going out to the balcony after accepting the assignment and staring

Within the image: "TM & © 1994, E.P." and "Book D.D. Issue #0 Month Page: 13"

Dark Dominion #0 Page 13 from the unpublished original graphic novel version of the trading card set story.
Image courtesy of Joe James.

Joe James, Jim Shooter, Debbie Fix and JayJay Jackson (left to right) at Joe James' 50th birthday party.
Photo by J.C. Vaughn.

at the skyline and letting it sink in. I remember calling my mom. I was nervous, the book had been promoted as by Steve Ditko, but he left after drawing issue #0. So, I was stepping into his world as it were.

Two weeks. Madness.

I wasn't sure I could do it but I knew I had enough experience to possibly make it happen. Basically, I locked myself in a room at the DEFIANT offices with Tim Perkins, the colorist, and got to it.

Overstreet: What did you think of your collaborators on that book?
JJ: Len Wein? The creator of Wolverine and a mensch? What's not to love? He was extremely encouraging and so helpful and patient.

Don't get me started on Tim. He was an amazing partner on that book, an amazing source of energy to work with, just tons of experience, a fantastic painter and a good pal. Also, he was very patient with my choices of music, I am a Steely Dan fan and, well, many people have suffered due to my compulsive need to listen to their music for months at a time.

Overstreet: On those issues, if I remember correctly, you had a team of inkers – Charles Yoakum, Bob Downs and Mike Barreiro – on the first issue, Steve Leialoha on the second, Bob Downs on the third, and then Mike Witherby on #6. I thought the look on #2 was the best, but it's your art... What did you think?
JJ: Good guys all! Each of them brought their own flair to the book and it was great to work with each of them. I had developed a friendship with Mike Witherby, he was such a fine inker and had a great sense of humor. And, of course, I was a long-time fan

of Leialoha, whose inks just surprised me, freaked me out, brought me back, and then blew me away again.

Overstreet: You did the first three issues and then returned for *Dark Dominion* #6. What was going on that it was scheduled like that?
JJ: Like I said, two weeks, madness. I drew issues #1-3 at a breakneck pace. Tim and I literally sat in a room for weeks and weeks drawing, painting, listening to music, and talking about life. He was so incredibly helpful. It was my first real comic book assignment, and his humor and experience helped me through it. Then of course there was the writer, Len was just the best guy to be in the trenches with.

So, to answer your question, in order to maintain the publishing schedule and live, we had fill-in artists. One of whom is pretty famous nowadays (I'm looking at you J.G. Jones!).

Overstreet: What precipitated the change from penciling to editing?
JJ: I don't just draw, I write, and I'm fascinated by the process of making comics, so I wanted to do it all. Jim was a great mentor and allowed me to explore the various avenues of being a comic book creator. Basically, when the opportunity arose to be an editor, he gave me a choice: draw the book or edit the book.

Overstreet: What kind of changes did that entail for you?
JJ: It was nice to get out of the room, but it was fun to have some creative influence in the direction that the books were taking. I got to plot an issue of *Charlemagne*, I got to work with artists and writers like Alan Weiss, Jim Fern. I got to learn about the craft of storytelling from both the writing and

Joe James and Steve Leialoha's original art for *Dark Dominion* #2 Page 5.
Image courtesy of Joe James.

drawing perspectives. I got to manage the color process, deal with printers.

I was the one who suggested we use Digital Chameleon in Canada, which saved both time and money. I had great help there from their production manager, Jolene Thomas.

You go from a very insular place of just you and the pencil and the paper and maybe one or two collaborators to having to manage three creative teams, get a book to the printer, and not overspend. I'm not sure I was all that good at it, but I was learning.

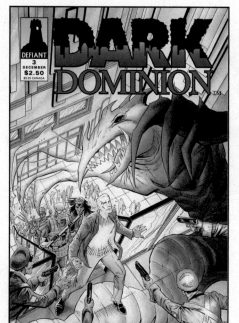

Overstreet: The original version of *Dark Dominion* #0 was created and issued as a trading card set. In talking with Jim Shooter, Clark Smith, and others over the years, it seemed like it Steve Ditko decided he didn't want to do the book, Jim got him to finish, and then he departed. How did the idea to do a new version of it as a graphic novel come about, and how did you get the assignment?

JJ: When I left the monthly book and slipped into editing, Jim was kind enough to offer me the graphic novel as a long-term project.

Overstreet: You were essentially replacing Steve Ditko (again). How much pressure did you feel?
JJ: An immense amount. But you know what? My peers were so supportive, and frankly I didn't have too much time to worry about it. It was a great opportunity.

Overstreet: Were you working from the same original script from Jim or was it different?
JJ: Same script I believe. One of those great, epic, Shooter scripts.

Overstreet: How far along were you when the plug was pulled?
JJ: Somewhere in the mid-teens when I came into the office and was given the bad news. Awful day. I went to the movies and saw *Corrina Corrina* with JayJay. Definitely picked up my mood.

Overstreet: Looking back, what was your favorite part of DEFIANT?
JJ: For me it was a place where I was able to engage in the deep learning of my craft in an environment that was safe and encouraging.

I have a bunch of fond memories of the place; for example, we had a wall in production where Jim hung up all the books that had just been printed. It was fun to see the progress month after month of all those covers.

I remember an occasion where we had to send Robert LaQuinta to the printing plant in Canada to deliver an issue and he got stranded there during a snowstorm. He was like a spy on a mission and when he finally came back it was to thunderous applause.

All in all, imagine a place where you could meet other artists, show off your work, get a critique, grab a Coke, interact with people, chat with the boss, sit and work at an artist's table, mix with editors, finance people… We had that at DEFIANT, and it was amazing while it lasted.

Overstreet: What was the thing that you liked the least?
JJ: Having to meet with artists every week like Grey, David Lapham, J.G. Jones, Greg Boone, Mike Whiterby, Marcus David, Alan Weiss, Adam Pollina, Jim Fern, Frank McLaughlin, and Robert Downs, who had the nerve to come in and show you what real comic-art looks like. Ugh. Totally annoying. And don't get me started on the writers.

Overstreet: You've gone on to an amazing career in storyboarding and development. What are you working on now?
JJ: In terms of comics, I finished writing and drawing *Nixons Demons'* for Framestore Ventures and the Madefire App. In terms of other venues, I'm *always* working.

This interview was conducted via email June 1-6, 2019. ©2019, 2021 J.C. Vaughn. Used by permission. All rights reserved.

Joe James and Steve Leialoha's original art for *Dark Dominion* #2 Page 13.
Image courtesy of Joe James.

Jim Shooter, David Lapham, JayJay Jackson, and Clark Smith (left to right) confer at Smith's Manhattan residence prior to DEFIANT moving into their offices. Photo courtesy of Jim Shooter.

Before signing up with DEFIANT, Clark Smith came from a business background and had previously teamed up with Jim Shooter as part of Shooter's effort to acquire Marvel Comics. That didn't happen, but they stayed in touch and after Valiant, Shooter came knocking again on Smith's door.

Overstreet: You were initially involved in Jim Shooter's effort to purchase Marvel Comics. How did you meet him and how did that come about?

J. Clark Smith (JCS): Two separate answers to this question. I met Jim when he was editor in chief at Marvel through a mutual friend Max O'Neal. Max had done some video work for Marvel that Jim was happy with, and I had recently joined Max to form a computer animation company called Maxamation. Jim was helping with creative decisions for the animation company and so we met–probably around 1985. For some reason we liked each other and over time became very good friends. A few years later, Jim told me that Marvel was going up for sale. I was friends with the head of entertainment lending at Chase Bank and thought they should meet each other to see if there was a possible mutual interest in Marvel; there was. I also had a cousin who had been the Treasurer of Time, Inc. but had recently retired. It occurred to me that Jim would need a solid finance guy. I introduced them and they decided to partner up.

Overstreet: You weren't particularly a fan of superhero comics as a kid. What was it about this venture that caught your attention?

JCS: I loved comics as a kid–I still have over 600 Archie Comics and hundreds of *Sgt. Rock* and *Sgt. Fury and His Howling Commandos*. I had read some Marvel and DC super-hero comics and just could not figure out what was going on. It seemed like you had to have years of story line to understand what was happening. By the way, Jim fixed most of that problem at Marvel, but that was after I had moved on to Hardy Boys books.

I am a believer in Jim, in his ability to create characters and turn out compelling stories. He very nicely sent me all the Valiant Comics each month (a perk of being his friend), and I fell in love with them. The day the package of comics came each month was like Christmas for me.

So, when Jim called me to tell me he was starting DEFIANT and asked if I would consider joining in a marketing capacity, there was no question that I would accept. I just knew this new universe was going to be a fun ride. And it was.

Overstreet: What were you doing before being offered the position of Vice President of Marketing and Development at Enlightened Entertainment?

JCS: I was working for an entertainment service company called Cinequest Entertainment. We

This DEFIANT "advertorial" illustrated by Georges Jeanty appeared in *Comics Buyer's Guide* #1080.
Image courtesy of Georges Jeanty.

David Hillman's colors for *War Dancer* #5 Page 25.
Image courtesy of David Hillman.

helped independent film producers get distribution deals and then pre-sell them to get bank finance among other things. I had learned a lot about how the entertainment business worked so part of my agreement with Jim was to be very involved with the film and television careers of the new DEFIANT characters.

Overstreet: What intrigued you enough about the opportunity to switch careers?
JCS: Wouldn't you want to work with Jim Shooter and help create a new universe of heroes? For me, this was the offer of a lifetime.

Overstreet: You oversaw the marketing in the incredibly successful first year that saw DEFIANT shoot up to being the fourth largest comic book publisher. What was that year like for you?
JCS: My learning curve was about 90 degrees. I had pretty good instincts about marketing, but I had a secret weapon: Jim Shooter. Anytime I had some harebrained idea of what we might do, I would walk across the floor to Jim's office and pitch

my idea. Jim had decades of knowledge of what worked and what didn't. So, he would listen and then give me a history on the subject; sometimes my idea was worthy and sometimes not. He was an incredible boss in that there was never a bad idea, just ideas that might not work because they had been tried before and failed.

I was also given a true gift — the ability to hire a couple of assistants. Brady [Darvin] and Dorian [Tenore-Bartilucci] were the perfect people for me. They made me look good. Brady was so detail-oriented that I used to tell him I paid him the big bucks to get nervous for me. We also hired "Cousin Pete" as our Conventions and trade show manager. Peter Gyrich, Jim's cousin from Pittsburgh [who inspired the name of a longtime Avengers headache], and you will never meet a nicer or better man. And very talented and creative. We always looked great at the various cons because of Pete. We all worked long hours, Saturdays included, and loved every minute of it.

Overstreet: What were some of the products and ideas you helped DEFIANT develop?
JCS: Jim was kind enough at the beginning to let me "pretend" to help with the creation of some of the early titles. As I said before, there is never a bad idea in a meeting with Jim. So, there are probably a few tidbits here and there that I might have helped out with on the creative side, but just being in the room with Jim, JayJay, and the gang was a blast.

Overstreet: What did you enjoy the most about your time working with DEFIANT?
JCS: The creative spirit was amazing. And it's all top-down. But just being around a room of artists and writers was fantastic, and they were literally all over the place. And everyone got along with each other too. No acrimony, just good old fashioned creative work. I also enjoyed my time at trade shows and conventions meeting store owners and fans. I would come back from an event with dozens – if not hundreds – of cards with addresses of people I had spoken to. I tried my best to send each one a personal note, and if they asked for something specific I'd do my best to get it for them.

Overstreet: What was your favorite DEFIANT title or project?
JCS: That's a hard question as I liked them all. If I had to pick one it would probably be *The Good*

Guys, as I had a lot of responsibilities with its development. My office put together the contest for the kids who became superheroes and then we all went to California for the wish bomb explosion at Mile High Comics in Anaheim.

Warriors of Plasm is dear to me as well. While Jim had already plotted the first four issues prior to founding DEFIANT, there was a lot of development work done in my New York apartment on that title before we moved to our offices on Madison Avenue. We met for several months every day at my apartment and had wonderful plotting sessions. Every day, Jim would come prepared with an agenda; he was so darned organized that way. I'll never forget one day when he announced it was naming day. He then proceeded to start listing literally hundreds of names that he had compiled through the years for properties that had not been created yet. So, for that entire day we just lobbed out names to add to his list.

Overstreet: It appeared that sales had stabilized when DEFIANT ran out of money. Do you think things might have been shut down prematurely? Were there other options that would have kept the doors open or had all options been exhausted?
JCS: Unfortunately, there was no way to keep the doors open longer than we did. Jim had raised $2 million in venture money and one of the first things that happened was our being sued by Marvel for copyright infringement. We won the suit completely, but it cost us almost $400,000 and lots of time. *Warriors of Plasm* #1 sold very well, as did *Dark Dominion* #1 and *Good Guys* #1, but we launched DEFIANT just as the entire comics business was in freefall. If you look at a sales chart, it looks like the white cliffs of Dover, straight down.

Even with the crash, Jim and I had taken meetings with New Line Cinema in California, where the owners, Lynne and Shaye, knew Jim from previous business. They made a very generous offer to buy the company, put lots of cash into it and to work towards making movies from the properties. Sadly, the leader of the venture capital group that had invested the funds into DEFIANT turned the deal down and Jim was powerless to override them. Then, of all things, Jim received an even richer deal offer from Victor Kaufman and our idiot investor turned that down as well. At that point Jim knew he had enough cash on hand to make one last payroll, and so had to declare bankruptcy. To this day, I hope that investor (He who shall not be named) realizes how stupid he was.

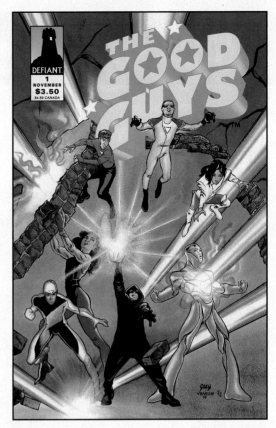

Overstreet: Who were some of your favorite co-workers at DEFIANT?
JCS: Honestly, I loved them all. Each was special in their own way.

Overstreet: Looking back, what is your personal takeaway from your time at DEFIANT?
JCS: I suppose it would be that just because you are good, creative, honest, hardworking there are no guarantees for success. I personally grew tremendously during that time in my life. I became more confident in who I was and what I was capable of doing. I learned teamwork — and am very grateful for that opportunity.

Overstreet: What are you doing today?
JCS: I work for a consulting company called Diversified Growth Solutions. We specialize in helping our commercial real estate clients place variable bonds into the market that gets them a lower cost of borrowing with more flexible terms. We also have a specialty in financing life insurance premiums. Pretty boring after working at DEFIANT.

– Mark F. Davis

BRADY DARVIN • Sales Administrator

If you check out his official bio, you'll quickly learn that Brady Darvin has been studying consumers across a variety of industries for over 18 years. Before founding Darvin Research & Consulting in February 2016, he was Manager of Consumer Intelligence for Kia Motors America, and before then he spent almost 11 years working for Strottman International, a leading youth and family promotions agency. It's before that, though, that puts him on our DEFIANT radar. Brady Darvin was the company's Sales Administrator, and he had a wide range of duties.

Overstreet: How did you get involved with DEFIANT?

Brady Darvin (BD): In the Spring of 1993 I was getting ready to graduate from the University of Virginia. The UVA Career Center had signup sheets for interviews for various companies, and I saw one somewhat cryptic job posting for "a new comic book publishing company based in New York City," and thought that sounded interesting, so I submitted my resume and shortly thereafter got a phone call from some guy named Clark Smith, who was himself a UVA alum and had decided to look for his "right-hand man" from UVA. I was Clark's sixth and final interview of the day. The interview went great, and we went out to dinner afterwards and Clark said he was going to recommend me to the head of the company, a Jim Shooter.

Some weeks passed, I graduated in mid-May, and a week or so afterwards Clark called and asked how quickly I could get up to New York for an interview with Jim Shooter and the Publisher, an man named J. Winston Fowlkes.

I took a Greyhound bus up from my parents' house in Northern Virginia three days later, interviewed

Brady Darvin at the DEFIANT booth at the Philadelphia Comicfest (October 1993). Photo courtesy of Brady Darvin.

with Clark, Winston, and Jim (I'm 5'2" so Jim Shooter seemed like a giant!), and was offered the job on the spot with the condition I could start in exactly one week! I had not expected that, so upon exiting the building after the interview, I realized I had to find an apartment to live in before I got the bus back to my parents' house that evening.

I had only been to New York once before. Then I did the following (and I'm not exaggerating): I looked around and saw a subway stop. I bought a token, got on the first train that came into the station, rode the train for a few stops and then got off where it seemed like a lot of other people were getting off (it was the 4 train and I exited at 86th Street). As I came up to street level, I immediately saw a storefront sign that said "Apartment Finder Service." I went in and said I needed an apartment as cheap as possible in the area. The guy literally handed me a bunch of keys with addresses on them and told me to go look at them by myself and come back and tell him which one I wanted.

Three hours later, I'd selected a studio apartment on First Avenue between 87th & 88th Street and signed a lease. My father had to wire me money through Western Union for the first month's rent and security deposit. Six days later I arrived in Manhattan in a U-Haul with all my stuff, moved in, and my first day at the DEFIANT office was the next day!

Overstreet: What did your role there involve?

BD: As Sales Administrator, my job included liaising with all the distributors to make sure we received their purchase orders each month on time, estimating what the total print run for each issue of each title needed to be to fulfill all the orders (oftentimes using just the quantity from Diamond

DEFIANT's Brady Darvin, Tim Perkins, Dave Hillman, Charlie Adlard, and Peter Lukic (left to right) in October 1993. Photo courtesy of Brady Darvin.

or Capital City to estimate what all the other orders would total before we actually knew them) and communicating those quantities to our reps at the printer, Quebecor in Montreal, purchasing full-page advertisements in the Diamond and Capital City catalogs, as well as in *Wizard* and *Hero Illustrated* magazines, and working with our in-house art department to get the ads designed and approved and getting the electronic files for the ads – which we sent via FedEx on SyQuest cartridges (the 1993 equivalent of today's portable hard drives) – to the distributor's and magazine's advertising departments on time, helping to do editorial reference research and photography (I was a professional photojournalist and wedding photographer while in college) that Jim or any of the writers or artists needed (example below), going with Clark to meetings with potential partners, as well as with artists and writers, coordinating all of our trade show attendance, from reserving booth space to having props/graphics for the booth produced, to booking plane tickets and autograph signings for the artists/writers that were coming with us, to getting the booth set up at the convention centers, and doing miscellaneous tasks for Jim Shooter and Winston Fowlkes.

Overstreet: What did you perceive as the ups and downs of working at DEFIANT?
BD: I was so young and inexperienced. There were no downs (until the sudden end about a year and half later). I was having a blast and just thought everything about working there and living in New York was cool. Between my $950/month rent and

other expenses, I was actually in the red a couple hundred dollars a month and using credit cards to make up the difference, but I didn't care. I thought all the people there were cool and interesting. We frequently went out to bars after work, and Clark would take me to the exclusive Racquet & Tennis Club to which he belonged and introduce me to various bigwigs.

Overstreet: What would you call some of your personal successes while you worked there?
BD: It was my first real job, so I felt like everything was a success. Getting the DEFIANT trade show display built and set up at our first big show complete with custom 3D sculptures of some creatures from *Warriors of Plasm*, was a huge accomplishment. But my biggest sense of accomplishment came when Jim Shooter, Len Wein, and Joe James called me into Jim's office and explained to me that they wanted DEFIANT's second title, *Dark Dominion*, to take place below New York City. Specifically, they wanted the first issue to take place in the network of steam tunnels that ran underneath Grand Central Station. They wanted the setting to be as realistic as possible, but had no idea what those steam tunnels and the various junctions and steam valve rooms looked like, or how extensive they really were. They wanted me to get photographs of everything down there so they could make it truly based on reality.

I spent a week walking around Grand Central Station talking to various employees who thought I was some crazy guy who wanted to go in the steam tunnels until I finally was brought to a very senior administrator that was in charge of, among many other things, the maintenance of the underground steam tunnels.

After some initial skepticism, I convinced him to get a worker to give me a tour of the underground tunnels. I showed up at the appointed time the next day, stupidly wearing an almost brand new pair of leather Docksider shoes, and – after signing about five different waiver forms that seemed to say if I fell and got injured I was on my own – was taken by a maintenance worker with all my camera equipment down into the tunnels.

It was literally 120 degrees down there, with puddles of rancid water everywhere. To make a long story short, it was an incredible maze of hot tunnels, steam pipes, and giant, hissing valves. I had to climb up ladders wearing gloves because the heat

Cathy Christian, Harris Comics' first Vampirella model, and Brady Darvin at the New York Comic Book Spectacular, Javits Center (February 1994). Photo courtesy of Brady Darvin.

from the steam made the metal too hot to touch. My Docksiders were completely ruined in the first ten minutes.

But I got tons of photographs---from the tunnels themselves to the rats and millipedes that lived down there, and even some evidence of people who had been living in the cooler parts of the tunnels. Jim, Len, and Joe were thrilled with the photos, and if you look in *Dark Dominion* #1 and the other issues, the look of that whole underground world was based on the photos I took.

Overstreet: With the great drama of getting those photos for Dark Dominion, was that your favorite of the DEFIANT titles or did you like one of the others more?
BD: *Warriors of Plasm* was my favorite. The fact that *Dark Dominion* superimposed an unseen reality on regular life on earth was cool, but to create an entirely new world from scratch, where virtually everything was alive, was truly magical.

Overstreet: Who were your favorite people to interact with at the company?
BD: Besides Jim Shooter and Clark Smith, I was friendly with artists Tim Perkins and Charlie Adlard (yes, the same Charlie Adlard who went on to illustrate *The Walking Dead!*), and I was in awe of the creative talents of Janet Jackson, David Lapham, and the other artists, but virtually everyone there was a pleasure to interact with.

Overstreet: To many fans, it felt like the company was really just hitting its stride when it was shut down. Did it feel that way to you and other employees or was it obvious that something negative was going to happen?

Brady Darvin at his desk in the DEFIANT offices.
Photo courtesy of Brady Darvin.

Clockwise from top, left: *Warriors of Plasm* #1 signed by David Lapham, a stack of a dozen uncut copies of *Plasm* #0, *Charlemagne* #0, *Charlemagne* #1 signed by Adam Pollina, *The Good Guys* #1 signed by Jan Childress, an unopened, shrinkwrapped case of *Warriors of Plasm* trading cards, a complete album of *Plasm* #0 trading cards, a complete album of *Dark Dominion* #0 trading cards, *Dark Dominion* #1 signed by Joe James, and *War Dancer* #1 signed by Alan Weiss. Photo courtesy of Brady Darvin.

BD: It felt like that to all the employees of DEFIANT, too! The bad times came very suddenly and as a shock. I knew the company didn't have a lot of money to spare, but also knew we were close to a development deal with a major motion picture studio. I remember Jim and Winston had "a very important" meeting with that studio's execs one day. When they returned, Jim looked pale and upset. I think it was the very next day they told us that the studio deal had fallen apart, the company was out of money, and they were shutting everything down and we should look for another job. I was truly stunned and heartbroken.

Overstreet: What would you single out as your best take away from your DEFIANT experience?
BD: DEFIANT was my first exposure to the world of business and entertainment. I learned how business worked, and how creative people and less-creative, more practical business people often had conflicting personalities. My experience at DEFIANT led to my next job at Gemstone Publishing, and a few years later, to my moving to California to accept a job offer from Stan Lee himself as Research Manager of Stan Lee Media, and after that, as Research Manager of Columbia Tristar Home Entertainment, where I worked on the marketing of the 2002 *Spider-Man* movie.

Overstreet: When DEFIANT ended, did you ever imagine you'd be talking about it more than a quarter of a century later or did you think it would end up a forgotten chapter in comics history?
BD: I was absolutely certain it *was* a forgotten chapter in comics history. Honestly, having spent almost two years working side-by-side with Stan Lee only a few years after DEFIANT, and working at Sony Pictures in the years after that, it was a forgotten memory even for me!

Overstreet: What are you doing these days?
BD: After my time at Sony Pictures, I acted as a one-man research department for a kids and family promotions agency for 11 years, where our primary business was designing and manufacturing the kids meal toys for Wendy's, Taco Bell, Chick-fil-A, and several other restaurants. In 2013, I took a research role in the automotive industry at Kia Motors America, and just 18 months ago, I left Kia Motors to start my own market research consultancy, where I specialize in online survey design and project management, and focus group moderation, for a wide variety of clients.

This interview was conducted via email September 8-10, 2017. ©2017, 2021 J.C. Vaughn. Used by permission. All rights reserved.

ED POLGARDY • Senior Editor

Emmy-award-winning writer-producer-director Ed Polgardy, the President of Black Hat Magic Productions, has had a successful career in television and feature films, but chances are good that if you're reading this publication, you know him for his work in comic books.

As a Senior Editor for DEFIANT, he worked with Len Wein and Joe James on Dark Dominion *and with a whole host of contributors on* The Good Guys, *among other projects. After his stint with Jim Shooter and company, he landed at BIG Entertainment, which he not only rode herd on their celebrity-created concepts, but also wrote their adaptation of* From Dusk 'Til Dawn, *which was drawn by Trevor Von Eeden. He eventually became the company's Editor-in-Chief.*

Charlie Adlard, Debbie Fix, and Ed Polgardy in the DEFIANT offices. Photo courtesy of Tim Perkins.

After his tenure in comics, he has developed a host of properties, often but not exclusively skewing toward the horror genre. He talked with us about the camaraderie and education he enjoyed in his DEFIANT days, how it stuck with him, and what he's up to now.

Overstreet: Your projects at DEFIANT and at BIG Entertainment don't immediately suggest a bias toward one type of comic book or another. What types or genres, if any, were you into before you went to work at DEFIANT?

Ed Polgardy (EP): Definitely horror. I loved EC Comics, the Marvel Monsters from the '70s, especially *Werewolf By Night*, and the black-and-white Skywald Horror-Mood magazines that were overseen by Archaic Alan Hewitson. In 1991, I co-created a vampire comic book series with artist

Jim Balent called *From The Darkness* (published by Malibu's Adventure Comics line) and a sequel to that limited series called *From The Darkness: Blood Vows* (published by Cry For Dawn Publications), and from there I edited the *Comic Book Week* tabloid newspaper and *Comic Talk* magazine for Fred Greenberg.

Overstreet: How did you find out about DEFIANT and what attracted you to it?

EP: My work with Fred Greenberg led to a chance meeting with Deborah Purcell and the DEFIANT gang at a Great Eastern Convention in New York City (before any DEFIANT product had been released), and Deborah asked me if I would be interested in helping her edit some books for them. When I went into the DEFIANT office and saw (Spider-Man co-creator) Steve Ditko and some of his original artwork, I knew I wanted to be involved. It felt like I had been plunged into a dream world with Ditko and Shooter, and I couldn't wait to start working there! Then when Jim had a talk with me during that initial meeting at DEFIANT, and he told me about the upcoming DEFIANT books, and I could see how unique and exciting they were, I was hooked.

Overstreet: Who was already on board when you joined the company?

EP: Shooter, JayJay Jackson, David Lapham, Joe James, Deborah Purcell, Rob LaQuinta, Clark Smith, Design Director Pete Lukic, General Manager Debbie Fix, and publisher Winston Fowlkes.

Overstreet: How did you get along with the people there?

EP: We were like family. It was an extremely comfortable working environment, like I knew these people for way longer than I actually did, especially in the beginning. And I never wanted the workday to end, never wanted to go home. In fact, I commuted into Manhattan on a bus from Easton, Pennsylvania, and when there were snowstorms that made travel difficult, Jim would let me stay in an empty apartment he had in the city. The job felt like an adventure with exciting events around every corner. And Shooter made you feel like you were an integral part of the team.

Overstreet: As a senior editor there, what were your specific assignments?

EP: I was the editor of *Dark Dominion* and *The Good Guys*, I co-wrote *The Great Grimmax* #0 with Jim Shooter, and I participated in the bullpen sessions in Jim's office where the artists, writers and editorial team came up with the storylines and marketing ideas for all of the titles. I believe one of the things I thought up during those sessions, was doing those comic book versions of our bullpen meetings to give fans an inside view of the creative process there. Some of the people I worked closely with at DEFIANT were Len Wein, D.G. Chichester, Dave Cockrum, Grey, and Greg Boone. Chris Claremont worked with me on a few things. I was also in charge of finding new talent from the submissions pile. I actually gave J.G. Jones his first comic book job in *Dark Dominion* #7, but I think Jim might have met J.G. first at a comic book convention.

Overstreet: In hindsight, that's an amazing line-up of talent. Could you see any hints in J.G. Jones' work of him becoming the J.G. Jones we know today or was that still a way off?

EP: I knew he was a terrific find right from the get-go, and Jim wanted to put him to work as soon as we had an opening. His trademark style was there in the beginning, and it was pretty obvious he was someone who was going to make a mark.

Overstreet: Did editing one of those titles excite you more than the others or was it pretty much just a general feeling about working in that atmosphere?

EP: Working on *The Good Guys* was very exciting. It was always a rush to the finish line to meet our deadlines with that title. There were a lot of people who had to jump in at the last minute to finish the inking and coloring on a lot of the early issues. It was a group effort that sometimes involved all-night coloring sessions. Thank God the colorists we had were team players who loved the book and what they were doing on it. Most of them worked out of our office, so it was like a sleepover event. Lots of long-term friendships evolved. Tim Perkins from the U.K. was there lending a hand, and some of our colorist trainees, like Benjamin Jung and Su McTeigue, got their start on that book.

Overstreet: As you were getting started, were the creative teams still being assembled or were they set?

EP: I believe most of the teams for the first run of titles were set. Joe James and Len Wein were already on *Dark Dominion*. Grey and Jan Childress were set for *The Good Guys* (I helped with the first issue of *TGG*, uncredited, but officially started editing it with #2).

Overstreet: What was an average day like there, if there was such a thing?

EP: Every day was different, but usually included checking up on how all of the writers and artists were doing on their deadlines (Len Wein was notoriously late most of the time!), new art submissions, bullpen sessions, etc. We were always developing new talent for inking and coloring our books. Storytelling was paramount; using line weights and the placement of blacks in the inks and separating the planes to establish depth in the coloring to help lead the eye in each panel and enhance the artwork. The James Gurney/*Dinotopia* model was used as an example. JayJay Jackson and Jim Shooter live by this method. And I learned so much from them about art and what makes it work in the storytelling medium while I was at DEFIANT, techniques that I still use when I create pitch boards for my movie projects today. It was an incredible time of my life, one that will never be forgotten.

Overstreet: Do any particular stories stand out or was that just the everyday creative atmosphere that had the most impact on you?

EP: One thing that really stands out for me is the launch of *The Good Guys* book in Anaheim, CA. A number of the DEFIANT creatives traveled to this event; Shooter, Deborah Purcell, Grey, Jan Childress and I were all there, and possibly Debbie Fix. We had cool satin-like Good Guys jackets that we were wearing, and the crowd went wild. It felt like we were rock stars meeting our fans. There was a lot of excitement surrounding this, and people came out in droves.

Ed Polgardy grabs some lunch at DEFIANT HQ.
Photo courtesy of Tim Perkins.

Overstreet: Which DEFIANT properties did you think had the most potential?

EP: I really loved all of them, but had a real soft spot for *Dark Dominion*. It was the book I was most involved with, and I thought the concept and characters were incredibly strong. I had a blast working with Len Wein and Joe James on the series, helped write some of the storylines, and was completely happy with the look and feel of the book (It had a dark side that appealed to my horror movie roots!).

Overstreet: You mentioned a lot of great creators both on staff and who you worked with as editors. Were there any you were particularly close with? Who were the best to work with?

EP: I really enjoyed working with Len Wein and miss his sly humor and creative mind. Len was a real character, and I'm so grateful I had a chance to brainstorm with him on *Dark Dominion*. Grey and Greg Boone were good friends of mine. And, of course, Tim Perkins, JayJay Jackson and Joe James. Like I mentioned before, it was like a big family of artists and writers who all enjoyed working together.

Overstreet: What led you to leave DEFIANT?
EP: An offer to be the Executive Editor at BIG Entertainment/TeknoComix that paid way more than I was making in New York. I had a long talk with Shooter about this when it happened, and it was a salary he couldn't match. I was sick to my stomach over having to make that decision, but Jim totally understood I had a family to raise and I just couldn't turn it down at that point in time. There wasn't any bad blood between us, and we're still friends to this day. Funny story, Jim actually called me after I left to say he was going to nuke Boca Raton, Florida (where the office of BIG Entertainment was located) in *Schism*, and he wanted me to know that it wasn't a personal jab at me, they just wanted to destroy BIG! LOL

Overstreet: While you were at TeknoComics/BIG Entertainment, you got to work with a lot of big names. What did you think of the final products you produced there?

EP: I eventually became the editor-in-chief at BIG, but it was a struggle from Day One. The company was run by two people who didn't really understand the comic book marketplace and didn't have any real love for the medium. They just wanted to create a mass media empire. And they thought the way to do that was turning all of the intellectual properties into Image-type comics, which were the rage at the time. Neil Gaiman concepts. Concepts by Mickey Spillane and John Jakes. It was a nightmare. I had Moebius lined up to do covers for *Mr. Hero*, a steam-driven robot story created by Neil Gaiman, and the two powers-that-be told me they didn't like his art. Moebius, one of the all-time greats in the industry, who would have killed-it on a steam-driven anything. Those two executives tampered with most of the books without any understanding of what would make them appeal to actual comic book fans.

But there were a few of the titles that they didn't care so much about that escaped their editorial bullying. *Neil Gaiman's Teknophage* was one they pretty much ignored, and it still holds up. And

Mickey Spillane refused to let them destroy *Mike Danger*. He actually told me he wanted to come down to Florida and have a Mike-Hammer-style talk with the two BIG executives! It was a crazy time, but I had a terrific comic book staff working with me on those projects, including Christopher Mills, James Chambers, Martin Powell, Julie Vigil, and Larry Bogad, who helped me maintain a certain level of quality and keep my sanity.

Overstreet: Considering your post-DEFIANT comic book work, any favorite projects or moments stand out?
EP: I enjoyed working on *Teknophage* with Rick Veitch, Bryan Talbot, Angus McKie and David Pugh. I also wrote the comic book adaptation of Quentin Tarantino's *From Dusk Till Dawn* at BIG. That was a lot of fun.

Overstreet: Following your stint there, you branched into television and film. How did that come about?
EP: I actually started in film and television. I sold my first screenplay, a horror movie I co-wrote in the early '80s when I was 24-years-old, and when it went into development but never got made, I decided to try my hand at comics, which resulted in the *From The Darkness* comic book series, which led to my editorial work in comics. That sidetracked me for over 10 years, until I came full circle and got back into the motion picture industry in 2002.

Overstreet: How did your career develop from there?
EP: I produced my first feature in 2003 and currently have over 18 films and television series under my belt as a producer. My latest movie, *The Wretched*, premiered at the Fantasia Film Festival and was picked up for U.S. theatrical distribution by IFC Midnight, then went on to become the number one movie in America for six weeks straight in the summer of 2020. I also produced *Oh Jerome, No*, a short-form television series of eight 12-minute episodes that aired on "Cake" on Disney's FXX Network, which garnered a Best Actor Emmy Award nomination for its star Mamoudou Athie, so I've been very busy here in Hollywood.

Overstreet: What are you working on at the moment?
EP: I have a couple of feature film screenplays that I co-wrote and have been developing to direct, including a horrific crime thriller called *Kill Everything* that I'm really excited about. I spend most of my time now creating and developing film

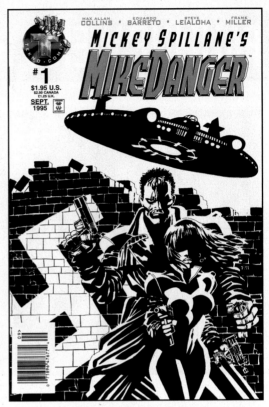

MAX ALLAN COLLINS • EDUARDO BARRETO • STEVE LEIALOHA • FRANK MILLER

MICKEY SPILLANE'S **MikeDanger**

#1
$1.95 U.S.
$2.90 CANADA
£1.25 U.K.
SEPT. 1995

After leaving DEFIANT, Ed Polgardy became Executive Editor of BIG Entertainment's Tekno•Comix before eventually returning to the film industry.

and television ideas at Black Hat Magic Productions, Inc., a development, production and licensing company that I founded in 2010.

Overstreet: Looking back at your time at DEFIANT, what really leaps out at you?
EP: All of the terrific friendships that resulted from me working there. And the incredible lessons I learned from Jim Shooter. It was and still is the most creative time of my life, and I feel blessed that I had the chance to participate in something that people still remember and cherish. Jim created a stellar comic book line at DEFIANT that had the potential to really make a mark in the industry, until Marvel bullied the company into a premature death. I would love to see Jim revisit these characters and concepts someday. Maybe there's a *Dark Dominion* or *Warriors of Plasm* movie waiting to happen! Wouldn't that be cool?!!

PAULINE WEISS • Editor

Pauline Weiss at the DEFIANT booth at
Comic-Con International: San Diego, 1994. Photo by J.C. Vaughn

Pauline Weiss has a reputation for being "a person who figures out how to do stuff." She has worked for comic book superstars throughout her career, and used the skillsets she learned from them to rise to the position of Director of Information Technology Operations at FCB Global. But once upon a time, she was a mover and shaker in the DEFIANT Universe.

"I have had some really good mentors, and some of them had been a little bit rough. Still, I wouldn't have achieved some of the success I earned in my later career without my learning from creative people. In my field, which is technology, communications aren't as valued as technological skills are, right? So, I found myself in a community where the people are really, really brilliant, but not great communicators. I was able to take what I learned working for Jim Steranko and Jim Shooter and working with [her husband] Alan, who is a font of stories and talks about stories all the livelong day. So, you learn a lot by being around good storytellers. That is probably the secret of my success: it's always about the story," Weiss said.

"When Jim came calling for DEFIANT, I was in a really, really good position in the ad agency I was in at the time. We were on the verge of winning the IBM account. We were literally on the verge of winning the biggest account in the history of the agency. I told myself that if I don't take this offer to be creative, I am going to regret it for the rest of my life. So, I spun into that, and even though it didn't turn out to be my career - working in comics - it was a valuable experience, and it formed my professional life forever," she said.

"Jim and Alan had put together a beat outline for *War Dancer* #2. I noticed that what was used in the plotting session didn't make it into the issue. I said, 'Wouldn't it be nice to capture all the fun stuff you guys said during the plotting session, like the pieces of dialogue you came up with or observations of what's going to go into the comic?'"

It was then that she made one of her earliest contributions to DEFIANT, her unique approach to the blocking of a comic book story at the script stage.

"One column was the plot itself, and on the other side was all the color. For example, any visual clues that were put into the comic book. It was my little contribution. I don't want to maximize it too much, but I don't want to minimize it either. It seemed to help and move the needle a little bit how we moved the story along," she said

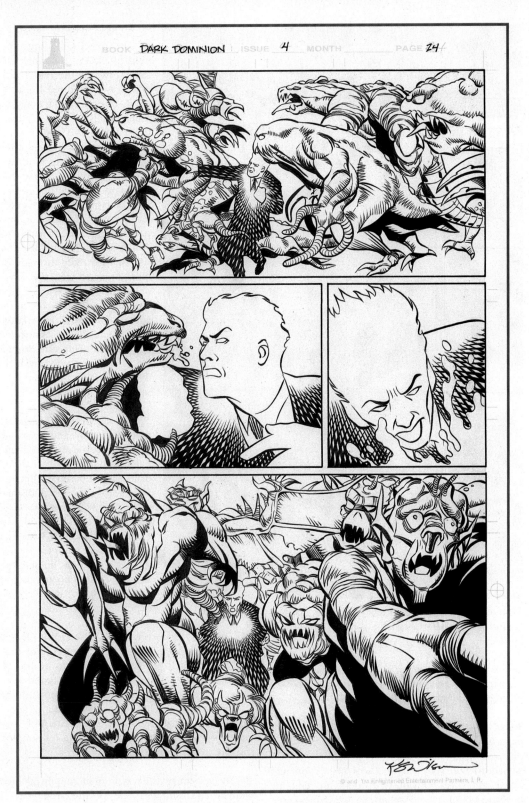

Keith Wilson's original art for *Dark Dominion* #4 Page 24.
Art from Scott Braden's collection.

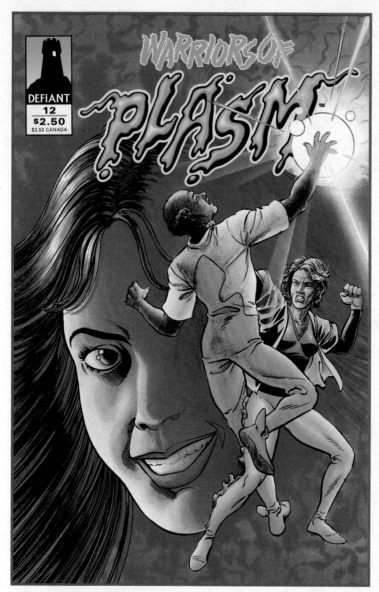

"I worked with a good set of creators, including specifically Dave Lapham," she said. "Towards the end, I only edited two or three books in those lines. I didn't edit that much really – and I picked them up in the end. I knew Dave because I hung around DEFIANT for a long time. And his wife, Maria, of course. And we worked together pretty well. Dave basically worked directly with Jim, for the most part. I think I edited *Plasm* #11, which was where I walked in, was that I worked through the mechanics to get the book out. And for #12, Dave took a break – which was early in my editorship. And, I don't know how we really got connected but I got Tim Eldred to do #12. He is an animation producer now, if I'm not mistaken," she said.

"We worked Marvel style, so there was a plot, and we would illustrate it, and then dialogue it. For some reason, I ended up dialoguing it based on Jim and Janet's story. My first published work was *Warriors of Plasm* #12. I'll be frank: *Warriors of Plasm* dialogue was way fun and it was all completely over the top. But Jim helped me; he was really encouraging of this. It was a really, really good experience," she said.

Soon after, Shooter offered her – a self-proclaimed *Legion of Super-Heroes* geek – a job as an editor at DEFIANT.

"Jim was one of the most influential people in the industry for me. He matched my salary at Ogilvy. I picked up and moved across town," she said.

Weiss landed at DEFIANT following Ed Polgardy's departure.

"I had *Warriors of Plasm*, *Dark Dominion* and *The Good Guys*. Obviously, I could not edit my husband's book [*War Dancer*]. So, Joe [James] edited *War Dancer*, *Dogs of War*. and *Charlemagne*," she said.

"We got this issue out and I was really pleased about it. It looked like what I wanted it to look like. Dave wasn't too happy with it, to be honest, but that is hardly surprising. He was good with the story because I worked it out with Jim, but the artwork was not to his liking. Dave had a different storytelling sensibility, while what Tim did here was closer to his animation. It was a lot simpler," she said.

"JayJay Jackson, by the way, is an incredibly talented woman and she was one of the architects of multiple comic book universes. There is one hell of a brain on that girl."

Weiss said she didn't recall that much of *Warriors of Plasm* #13, Lapham's return, as things were gearing up for *Schism*. The deterioration of the financial situation might also have been a factor.

"It was a great idea to come out with a universe that was figured out. For example, having War Dancer and Michael Alexander [*Dark Dominion*'s Glimmer], introduced in the universe through their appearances in *Warriors of Plasm* was quite brilliant on Jim's part. I think it was more of an issue of what Jim wanted to do, which was to come up with a wholly sprung universe altogether," she said.

"When I was at DEFIANT, I was a newbie. I hadn't done this before. I was more in learning mode while I was there. I was only at DEFIANT for three issues max. I edited two *Good Guys*, three *Plasms*, and some *Dark Dominion*," she said.

"*Dark Dominion* was kind of everybody's baby. Everybody loved that book so much. It was hard to take their stake in it. Len Wein had a stake in it, but J.G. Jones had a very big stake in it. He, as the artist, started to make contributions to the story and some of the dialogue. Janet and Jim loved this character since it was an homage to Steve Ditko. They just loved this book so much. And, it was so critical to the universe overall. Everybody had an investment in *Dark Dominion*," she said.

"J.G. Jones has a tremendous dramatic sensibility. His layouts and sensibility matched the material he was working on. He understood the city and the darkness. I loved J.G.'s work, and it was always on time. I never had a problem with Jeff [J.G.'s given name]," she said.

"I was also in charge of The Bad Guys Contest. The Good Guys, as you know, were selected from a bunch of kids who wanted to be in a comic book for a number of reasons. So, we did another thing with a Bad Guys Contest, but we didn't limit it to kids. I think this was in the works long before I was there. I just kind of took the contest over. I picked a couple of people to be The Bad Guys. One was

David Hillman's colors on War Dancer and Charlemagne. Image courtesy of David Hillman.

a young woman who submitted an entry that was so well-written that I could not say no. The other Bad Guy was a comic book store owner named John Such. He came up with a character that was an imagination stealer and 'I want yours!' It was well thought out, and we were going to mix it with the storylines. It was very cute. It was a lot of fun," Weiss said.

"Of course, it was also a lot of fun to keep in touch with the kids who were The Good Guys. In my office, I had pictures up on my wall, just so I could see their faces. One of The Good Guys was Matthew, who was the son of Jim's cousin, Pete Gyrich. And Pete was one of our business managers. And, why shouldn't we DEFIANT keep in touch? We are portraying these people!" she said.

DAVID HILLMAN • Colorist

Writer-artist David Hillman had one of his first jobs in art at DEFIANT, working in production and then as a colorist, and ended up forging friendships that have lasted through the present.

Overstreet: What had you done prior to DEFIANT?

David Hillman (DH): I was in my early 20s back then. So before DEFIANT, I worked briefly at Milestone Media as a production artist, and before that I was an art student.

Overstreet: How did you get the gig there?

DH: My good friend Joe James, who had just gotten the job as production manager, asked me if I wanted to come work at DEFIANT as one of his production assistants.

Overstreet: What all did you work on?

DH: After spending a few months in production, I moved onto learning how to color the books. The deadlines were really tight, so I ended up touching almost all the books that needed a page quickly colored.

David Hillman today. Photo courtesy of David Hillman.

Overstreet: What was the process like there? Did you know what story was coming or did you just get pages as the inker(s) finished?

DH: At first, I just got pages as they needed to be colored, but later as I was building up to getting a regular book to color, I got to know what new stories were coming.

Overstreet: What was your interaction with the rest of the staff like?

DH: I loved everyone there! I still keep in touch with a few of them, and some are still my closest friends. I miss that place!

Overstreet: What was your reaction when DEFIANT shut down?

DH: Shock! I didn't know it was coming until I walked in one day and everyone was either very quiet or was crying. I looked around and asked, "Who died?"

Overstreet: If you picked one, what would be your favorite project your worked on there?

DH: I got to color a *War Dancer* cover. Usually coloring the covers was JayJay's thing, but she was pretty busy, and the editor asked me if I could color it overnight. It was a rush job, but it came out great!

Overstreet: What memories of that time would you care to share?

DH: As I mentioned, the deadlines were really tight, so a lot of us would spend late nights working together and for a time we all caught the same cold, but the work had to get done, so we just kept on working and it was decided that anyone that was sick and still had work to do would be quarantined in this small meeting room. After a week or so it got pretty ripe in there.

Overstreet: You've branched out a lot since those days. What's your favorite aspect of art these days?

DH: Command Z! Every mistake is fixable. Changing a color back then required using bleach.

Overstreet: What are you working on now?

DH: After many years working in comics and storyboards I recently branched out into writing and illustrating children's books. And I'll be coming out with a new children's book I illustrated sometime in the fall or winter of 2021.

This interview was conducted via email August 4, 2021.

David Hillman colored DEFIANT's serialized comic *Glory* #0 story, which appeared in the pages of *Overstreet's Comic Book Monthly* #15-18. Image courtesy of David Hillman.

J.G. JONES • Artist

Since David Lapham was already a star – if not the superstar he would become later – when DEFIANT started, it seems fair to say that artist J.G. Jones was the biggest "find" that Jim Shooter and company made during the company's brief run.

Following his work at DEFIANT, Jones again teamed with Shooter for Fatale *at Broadway, and then in short succession worked on several* Shi *projects at Crusade,* Painkiller Jane/Darkchylde *at Event, and* Black Widow *and* Marvel Boy *at Marvel before landing graphic novel* Wonder Woman: The Hiketeia *at DC Comics. At DC he blossomed into a mainstay with many high profile projects. He has also taken on other, non-DC work including collaborating with writer Mark Millar on* Wanted *at Top Cow Productions (it was made into the 2008 movie of the same name staring Angelina Jolie), and his own* Strange Fruit *with Mark Waid at BOOM! Studios.*

J.G. Jones at the drawing table.
Photo by Dawn A. Bruno.

A preeminent cover artist, Jones' work is characterized by energy, vitality, power and strong composition. His covers are known for catching – and holding – the eyes of comic buyers, and his originals command serious attention from original art collectors.

Overstreet: DEFIANT was the first place I took note of your work. What had you done leading up to that point?

J.G. Jones (JGJ): That's probably because DEFIANT was my first work in comics. I was living in Brooklyn and trying to make my way in the fine arts gallery scene, which pretty much just means that I was poor and had multiple part time jobs. I had one job as an art assistant (doing all the monkey work for an established painter), another as an

artist and paste-up guy for a weekly newspaper, and then I filled in with illustration jobs, when I could get them. All the while, I was painting giant canvases that no one wanted to buy or show.

I made a friend at the newspaper, Jonathan Larsen, and he was into comics, too. Our Wednesday lunch hour was spent at the comic shop near work, poring over the racks. I could see that my art career was going nowhere, and I needed to make a change, so Jonathan and I created a character called Rant. I drew about six or seven pages, and we shlepped them to a comic con (my first) at the Javits Center in NY. I remember it was winter, and about 2 feet of snow on the ground.

I didn't know who Jim Shooter was, at the time, but he was the first person to review my portfolio. He closed my book and asked if I wanted a job at DEFIANT.

Overstreet: What was your first assignment for them and how did you land it?

JGJ: When I started, they had to convince me to quit my part time newspaper job, which I was reluctant to do. I was as green as it gets, so there was a lot of learning to do before they gave me the keys to a book. I hung around the bullpen, basically learning from Jim, JayJay Jackson, Joe James, and all of the other artists working for DEFIANT at that time. Jim was all about storytelling, not style, so I learned the importance of how to do the basics. I did some color guides and worked on drawing a few little things here and there.

When I was finally ready (not sure that was true), they let me dive in on *Dark Dominion*. That was my first published work.

Unpublished *Dark Dominion* #11 Page 4 by J.G. Jones.
Art from Scott Braden's collection.

Overstreet: What was the experience of working for DEFIANT like for you?

JGJ: I had no concept of what I was doing, and had to have my hand held as I learned to crawl and then walk. Everyone there was so collegial and helpful. People like Alan Weiss, Grey, and Louis Small were kind enough to let me look over their shoulders and learn the ropes. David Lapham didn't work at the office, but when he brought in *Warriors of Plasm* pages, the whole place would stop and crowd around to see what he had just delivered.

Overstreet: Who did you enjoy working with there?

JGJ: I enjoyed working with the entire crew of folks. Everyone was so helpful. I met Charles Yoakum there, and we became good friends. He ended up inking my stuff well into my years at Crusade Comics. Jim, JayJay, and Joe were the heart of the place, though, and we all reformed the band when DEFIANT folded and Broadway comics ramped up.

Overstreet: Did you go into their offices very much or mostly work remotely?

JGJ: The internet then was not what it is now, and most of the comics industry was in or around NY at the time. I primarily worked at home in Brooklyn and brought the pages in to the office, but I would also sometimes work in the office, as well.

The Great Grimmax #0, a giveaway polybagged with *Hero Illustrated*, featured J.G. Jones' first cover work.

Overstreet: You were to play a pretty big role in *Schism*, which would have brought together DEFIANT's storylines into one big epic. Which series were you working for that?

JGJ: I was drawing the main book, *Schism*, and I was pretty far along into this huge, oversized issue when the music stopped and we had to shut it down. It was depressing to put so much effort into something that never got to see the light of day.

Overstreet: You've said before that you were disappointed when the plug was pulled, that your art was improving and you really wanted to display what you had learned. Could you give some specifics?

JGJ: I was still not that good, mind you, but I *was*

learning and beginning to develop a bit of my own style. Telling stories with pictures is hugely different from making a single image or illustration. You have to learn to think like a filmmaker or cinematographer.

Overstreet: As an artist, what did you take away from your time at DEFIANT?

JGJ: I think that I was able to learn the basics from really good people who understood the craft. People now have all these resources online, but back then, you really needed to have access to people who knew the business in order to learn the ropes.

Overstreet: Were there any other creators there whose work you remember liking or were you mainly just focused on handling your assignments?

JGJ: Oh, of course I was looking at everyone's work there. I was a sponge, trying to learn from everyone and anything. I couldn't believe it when they gave some of my first, terrible pencils to the legendary Dave Cockrum to ink. Can you imagine that? My first inker was the X-Men legend, Dave Cockrum!

Alan Weiss had a nice, clean, muscular style that I liked a lot on *War Dancer*. Dave Lapham was an unparalleled storyteller and terrific draftsman.

Overstreet: Did you have any favorite characters there or was it more a case of just being excited that you were able to work professionally as a comic book artist?

JGJ: Pretty much the latter. I was just happy to have work, and a place to learn, and a new little family in the comics business.

Overstreet: Was there a DEFIANT character that you liked but didn't get a chance to draw or did you get to do most of them in the unpublished *Schism* pages?

JGJ: I always thought that War Dancer looked cool, and I did get a chance to draw him a bit in the *Schism* book.

Overstreet: Since those days, in addition to var-

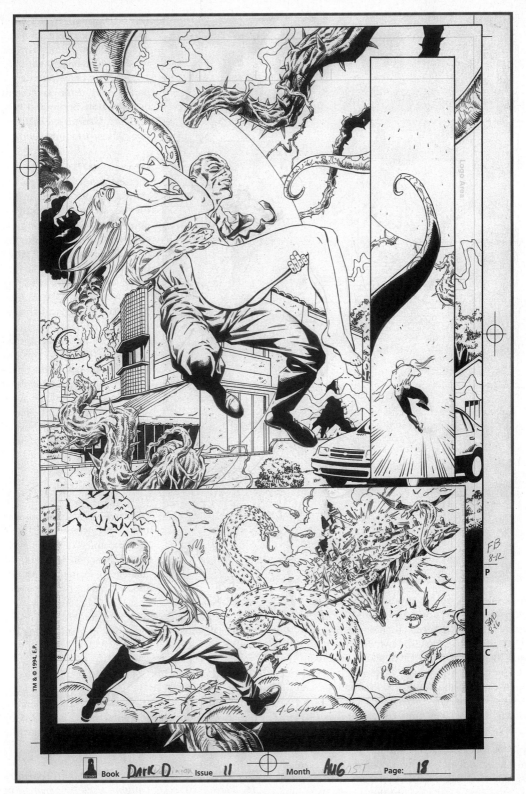

Unpublished *Dark Dominion* #11 Page 18 by J.G. Jones.
Art from Scott Braden's collection.

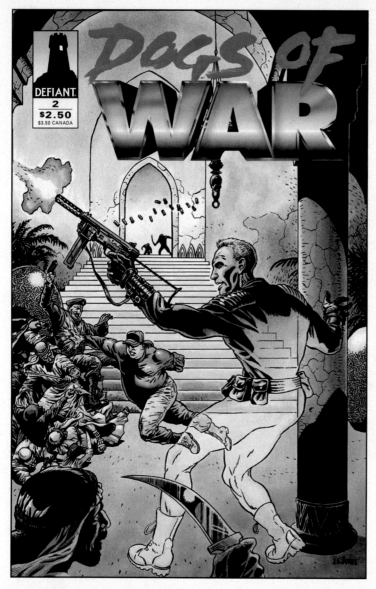

Overstreet: Given its brief life span more than 25 years ago, did you think anyone would still be talking about it?

JGJ: There were so many companies that came and went in the whole boom and bust cycle, I am surprised that anyone remembers those books.

Overstreet: "J.G. Jones was amazing from the get-go. He started at outstanding. It was easy to see he was going to develop into one of the great ones, and he has," Jim Shooter told me a few years back when I was doing an article on your cover for *Great Grimmax* #0. What would you have thought back then if Jim said that to you then?

JGJ: Jim is being more than kind. When I started, I was just awful, but he saw a little spark in there, and was a relentless teacher of the craft. He hammered home lessons that I have relied on throughout my comics career. I have to thank Jim for taking a chance on a nobody who had no clue what he was doing.

Overstreet: After your stint at DEFIANT, you worked with Shooter and company again at Broadway. If you had the chance to team-up with Jim Shooter again on a project, would you do it?

JGJ: I would be delighted to work with Jim, or any of the DEFIANT crew, again. Why? You getting the band back together?

Overstreet: You never know. What are you working on at present?

JGJ: I'm doing a lot of cover work at the moment, but also writing a new graphic novel, and working on a series of illustrations from one of my favorite books.

This interview was conducted via email February 16, 2018. ©2018 *J.C. Vaughn. Used by permission. All rights reserved.*

ious interiors, you've provided the covers for all 52 issues of DC's weekly limited series *52*, and many other DC projects including *Y: The Last Man* #1-17, at Vertigo. You also have done work for Black Bull, BOOM! Studios, CPM Manga, Crusade, Dark Horse Comics, Dynamite, Marvel, Image Comics, Speakeasy, Valiant, Wildstorm Productions, and others, as well as *The Overstreet Comic Book Price Guide*. Where does your experience at DEFIANT rank in your career?

JGJ: It was a definitive time for me because it was my initiation into the world of making comics. I have been doing it for 25 years, now, but there was a certain innocence around those early days, when everything was shiny and new.

Unpublished *Schism* #3 Page 23 by J.G. Jones.
Art from Scott Braden's collection.

ART HOLCOMB • Writer

Best known in DEFIANT circles for his work on the Warriors of Plasm *spin-off mini-series* Dogs of War, *Arthur Loy Holcomb, a.k.a. Art, has published works of poetry, essays and short stories in addition to more than 50 comic book tales. This brought him into contact with such franchises as* Killer Instinct, Magic: The Gathering, *and the* X-Men. He wrote an Eternal Warrior special for the original Valiant and then developed and wrote Eternal Warriors, the revised incarnation of both that title and Archer & Armstrong for Acclaim's VH2 universe. A veteran of stage and screen writing, his work has*

Art Holcomb with Gemstone's J.C. Vaughn, circa 1996.
Photo by Mark L. Haynes.

appeared on UPN (now The CW), Sci-Fi Channel (now SyFy), and Showtime, among other venues.

Overstreet: What was your background as a writer before landing at DEFIANT?

Arthur Loy Holcomb (ALH): I was a screenwriter and playwright. I started my career when I was 13 years old and sold my first stage play to a production company in San Francisco in 1968. Once I saw my words being spoken by actors up on a stage, I was hooked. Since that time, I had written several screenplays and spent time working with the Star Trek franchise at Paramount developing story ideas and scripts.

Overstreet: The tale has been told that you got your gig writing for DEFIANT by having an argument with Jim Shooter at a convention. What's the real story?

ALH: Yeah, that was crazy. I was attending my first Comic-Con in San Diego the years that DEFIANT was launched. It was still a relatively small affair back then and I was walking down one of the halls when a friend of mine, Ron Ontel, grabbed me and asked if I would fill in on a panel on collaboration. Suddenly, I found myself up on the stage with this group of comic book creators I knew nothing about. Being young and contrarian at the time, I took issue with the idea that they were exposing about how art was, by nature, a collaborative affair. We got pretty confrontational.

Afterward, I went up and introduced myself to these people with whom I'd been arguing, and one of them turned out to be Jim Shooter. I, of course, knew who he was, and stumbled through some nonsense about always wanting to write a comic book. He suggested that I send him one of my screenplays and I did so the next week, not really thinking anything more about it. The following week I received a prepaid ticket to NYC to meet with Jim and the DEFIANT crew.

Overstreet: Were you familiar with DEFIANT before you started on *Dogs of War* or did you have to get a crash course on *Warriors of Plasm* first?

ALH: I had been a Marvel fan for years and so I knew who Jim was. I knew I had to bring myself up to speed on the universe, and Jim and JayJay were kind enough to send me an entire run of DEFIANT's books up to that point before I went to New York. The philosophical take on comics and storytelling that Jim had introduced fascinated me and I could

Book DOGS OF WAR Issue 5 Month 5 Page: COVER

Artist Georges Jeanty's pencils for the cover of *Dogs of War* #5.
Image courtesy of Georges Jeanty.

An unpublished *Dogs of War* promotional post card by Georges Jeanty. Image courtesy of Georges Jeanty.

for #1 and an idea of how he wanted the series to wrap up in terms on continuity, but gave me complete *carte blanche* as to the story I told within. It was a chance to really delve into the accidental superhero concept and I loved every minute of it.

Overstreet: What did you perceive as the ups and downs of working on that series?

ALH: The deadlines were something I had to get used to. Writing a complete 22-page book every month was a real challenge in the beginning, but I found myself thriving in this short deadline schedule. There were challenges in working remotely in the days before the internet - when pages and scripts had to be faxed back and forth - but we made it work. The editorial staff at DEFIANT were the best.

Overstreet: You had an issue in the pipeline when the plug was pulled. What was going to happen in *Dogs of War* #6 and any subsequent issues?

ALH: The story was about what happens to someone who is given unimaginable powers and uses those abilities to make a change in the world. But, at its core, these powers ended up being a crucible of sorts, exposing to Shooter - and those he came in contact with - the corruptive nature of power.

immediately see so many story possibilities just in the short runs I had read. Of course, he had great talents like Len Wein and Chris Claremont working there at the time, and so many fantastic artists, that I was immediately won over.

Overstreet: Was it conceived as a limited series or an on-going title?

ALH: It was always planned to be an eight-issue mini-series about the rise and fall of the *WoP* character Shooter.

Overstreet: How much of the story came to you from editorial and how much did you create? What kind of leeway did you have?

ALH: Jim gave me the greatest leeway, and the instructions were quite simple: He gave me the idea

I was looking to tell a different kind of superhero story and it was so sad that it never saw the conclusion in print. In the end Shooter, in despair over his inability to control himself and effect the change that he so badly wanted to see, sacrifices himself in a battle over Manhattan and - while able to defeat his enemy - is killed by being impaled on the spire of the Chrysler Building.

Overstreet: Wow! That would have been an incredible ending to the series. That wouldn't have been the end of your involvement with DEFIANT though. You were supposed to write *The Great Grimmax*, weren't you? How far did you get on that before the plug was pulled?

ALH: Grimmax was a fascinating character. Jim had given me the 8-page establishing story for Grimmax and, as often was the case, I was captivated by Jim's storytelling and the way he could pack an entire, well-rounded tale in just a few pages. I was able to complete a full issue before we ceased production.

Overstreet: His character has been pretty well established in *Warriors of Plasm*. He then went through a pretty significant change, and came to Earth. Jim set him up with the zero issue. Where were you going to go from there?

ALH: Grimmax was the epitome of a stranger in a strange land. He paid little attention to his surroundings, was unaffected by mores and beliefs outside of his own and, by seeming to not fit in at all, he ended up fitting right in to 1990s Manhattan. The best way to proceed with the character, I thought, was to explore the nature of humanity through the eyes of an alien being. Through Grimmax's pure and heroic actions, we were going to cast a light on all that was good – and all that was corrupt – about human society.

Overstreet: Looking back, what do you think you took away from the experience of working with DEFIANT?

ALH: I came from screenwriting and playwriting – both forms of performance-based scripted writing.

A second unpublished *Dogs of War* promotional post card by Georges Jeanty. Image courtesy of Georges Jeanty.

I believe that every time you apply your skills to another form of creating, you get a bit closer to the true nature of storytelling. Working with Jim and the editorial crew exposed me to a larger world and my time with *Dogs* and *Grimmax* absolutely made me a much better writer. I took away from my time with DEFIANT tools and insights I would never have gotten anywhere else. I have always been profoundly grateful for that.

Overstreet: What are you working on these days?
ALH: I continue to write plays and scripts for Hollywood, and have worked as a writing performance coach for several studios for more than decade now. I also run a consultancy teaching aspiring writers how to be successfully producing writers in the 21st Century, and I lecture to students here in Southern California and through the Italian National Film School in Rome, Italy.

This interview was conducted via email August 28-September 4, 2017. ©2017, 2021 J.C. Vaughn. Used by permission. All rights reserved.

In the early days of his career, when he was working at a comic shop and submitting art to various publishers, Georges Jeanty took a shot at impressing Jim Shooter at a local convention. That pitch led to Jeanty's first big break in comics when he was hired to work on DEFIANT's Dogs of War. *Looking back on that time, Jeanty discussed his experiences with the company and on the title, recounted how he got the job, and shared what it was like to work on the title.*

Overstreet: What had you done prior to DEFIANT?

Georges Jeanty (GJ): Well, DEFIANT was more or less my big coming out. My first actual book was with a small company called Capital Comics, it was called *Paradigm*. This was in '94 or so. It was a small, little company. They're still around, technically, but it was just a little, little book. When I got DEFIANT, I thought, "Hey, man, I made it."

Georges Jeanty and friend. Photo courtesy of Georges Jeanty.

Overstreet: How did you get the gig there?

GJ: That was a very interesting story. I was in Florida, I'm from Miami. Jim Shooter was at a convention over there. I had known about it; I was actually managing a comic shop for a couple of years at that point. You know how you stay up to date with things, and of course, if a convention comes to your town, you're the first one there. You see who the guests are. I saw that Jim Shooter was going to be there and I was familiarizing myself with his books and DEFIANT because I knew Jim from Marvel

Comics. Everybody knows his reputation. With DEFIANT, I started to really read, I think at that time, the only thing that had come out or was very popular was something called *Warriors of Plasm*, which was their flagship book. I took it upon myself to create four or five pages of submissions, to draw out a little story with those *Warriors of Plasm* characters. Which, I had been doing with Marvel and DC and getting rejection after rejection.

So, I took it upon myself to do that for DEFIANT and Jim had seen them. He looked at them and was very impressed. If you know Jim Shooter, the guy can have a very stone-face about him. You can't really tell if he likes something or if he doesn't like something. He was just kind of looking at me and he started asking questions about deadlines and how long it would take me to do this. He was correcting me on some of the characters, which I took as a very good sign. He wasn't just looking at submissions, but really critiquing them. He said, "I'm looking for somebody," and "We'll see," and "I'm going to take copies of this, and I'll get back to you." That happens and I'd done it before, and nothing really ever came of it.

A week or so goes by and somebody from the office called and said, "Hey, Jim has seen your stuff and he really liked it. We want to invite you up to DEFIANT." DEFIANT was in New York at the time, they wanted to invite me up

Book DOGS OF WAR Issue 5 Month Page: COVER

Georges Jeanty's inked original art for the cover of *Dogs of War* #5, one of the last issues
released by DEFIANT. Image courtesy of Georges Jeanty.

to talk to me about the book. That's how I got it. What I didn't realize at the time was that Jim was on a mission. Whoever was doing the book *Dogs of War* had backed out rather suddenly. This was information I had no clue about until I had the job. But they had backed out and so he was really in a bind, looking for somebody. He needed to find somebody *that* weekend as I understood it. When I went up to New York I got the job. It was serendipitous and it was talent and right place at the right time. All the stars had aligned in that particular instance.

Overstreet: How did you enjoy working on *Dogs of War*?

GJ: I loved it. It was a very interesting book because all of Jim's titles at that time at DEFIANT were after Valiant. All the stuff that happened at Valiant – he was trying to not have those mistakes happen in DEFIANT. So DEFIANT was – funny enough, this was going on 25 years ago – DEFIANT was more or less how books are published now with subject matter and not necessarily everything needs to be a superhero slant. *Dogs of War* was about a guy who had this power, yes, but it was one of those questions like, "If you did have superpowers, what would you do with them?" The idea was that it doesn't change you necessarily, it just makes you more of what you are. That's pretty much how the book went for the five or six issues that came out.

Overstreet: There was a lot of action in the story, but also a lot of regular people. Did you prefer drawing one or the other or did you like drawing both?

GJ: I was so nervous doing that book because, again, it was my first of what I considered a big break in my career. I was so nervous to get everything right. I didn't even think in terms

of "Oh, this is an interesting book. It has more action. Oh, it has more drama. Or this is more science fiction." Anything like that.

I was very practical because I was working at a comic shop and I had been seeing everything that had been coming out, and funny enough at that time, the Image boom had exploded, and every book seemed to look like an Image book. Even Marvel and DC were getting on that particular bandwagon. I realized my stuff was so not like that. I was just trying to do the best work that I could and just feeling so intimidated. Really feeling intimidated in terms of every single little thing, I was second guessing myself. Somebody's sleeping in a bed, is somebody getting out of bed, is somebody walking down the street - little things like that, I don't even consider these days - I was so bereft by it because I thought, "If I draw one bad panel that's it, this is going to make or break my career."

Overstreet: Did you have any interaction with writer Art Holcomb or did things mostly flow through your editor?

GJ: I forget where he was and I believe at that time the internet, at least for me, was very limited. This was in the early to mid-90s, so not everybody was sending emails. I remember faxing a lot of the artwork or copies to everybody and then getting responses and my editor was my point man. He was my go-between. So, I never actually talked to Art because he wasn't in the studios. I don't think he was even in New York. As I understood it, he wasn't even a comic writer, per se. Jim had really talked him into it and wanted him to do it and really liked his work. He was, I assume, more or less in the same boat that I was. I know that he was an accomplished writer at that point, but in com-

Georges Jeanty's pencil art for *Dogs of War* #4 Page 10.
Image courtesy of Georges Jeanty.

ics with *Dogs of War*, very novice at this stage. So, we were both kind of handholding each other spiritually. Kind of, "Yeah this works," or "This doesn't work," or "Let's defer to Shooter or your editor or something like that." It was a learning curve, but it was one of those where you learned while in the trenches. I had no time to really take it in and be introspective.

Overstreet: We understand you had drawn some of *Dogs of War* that didn't get published when DEFIANT shut down. How far in the series had you gotten?

GJ: You usually work a few months in advance. I think I was either 50 or 80% done with the next issue, which I think was issue 6, I'm not entirely sure where it went to. If I remember correctly, *Dogs of War* was written as a limited series. So, Jim had the whole thing planned out. It was really going to be an eye-opener because at the end of it all, the character inadvertently kills one of the other characters, I believe, from another book called *The Good Guys*, which was a book populated by kids. So, there was going to be this huge, huge drama in all of that. This was a big, big story that was going to go eight to ten issues, I'm not 100% sure. We never did get that far, so a lot of it was written out, to my knowledge, and because they had the idea of where it was going, I had enough time to actually almost finish that issue. And it's so unfortunate.

I still remember to this day how much Marvel just kind of ousted Jim from his company because they didn't like – I don't know if it was a vendetta or something, he could give you more information about that. But, it was so petty and it was really Marvel's attempt to drain Jim of all the money the company had and was making. Theoretically it put him out of business.

So when it happened, it happened very quickly. My editor called me and said, "Hey, whatever pages you've got, invoice them now because stuff is happening." That was the last I heard. I was just, "Oh okay, here are all the pages, the invoices, thank you very much." Honestly, whenever I heard stuff like that, because I had worked for small companies, sometimes you just won't get paid if something like that happens. I kind of wrote off that last issue, thinking

alright well that's work that I did, but I probably won't ever see any money for it. But, sure enough I got my last check for the pieces of pages I did for that book.

Overstreet: What memories of that time would you care to share?

GJ: It was very interesting because this was the first time I was really…I thought I had made it. Consequently, it was also the first time I was making that much money. Which really wasn't that much money, it was maybe a couple thousand dollars. But when you haven't made that kind of money and you're still living at home and you're working at a comic shop, this is a recipe for not a whole lot of money. This was the first time I made that kind of money and checks were coming in and there were two things that happened to me at that time that I'll never forget and that were very significant.

The first was that working for DEFIANT on *Dogs of War* allowed me to buy my first car ever. And when I say that, it was a used car and it was a couple thousand dollars. It allowed me to write a check for the amount of that car that I had never done before. I was struggling over $200 a week and here I was on a monthly basis getting a few thousand, so that really stuck with me. Regardless of how much I make today I always humbly remember those beginnings.

The second thing, which was probably more significant, was my mother – and I'm sure parents of potential comic artists and people who want to go into that business are always saying, "Oh it's really nice" because they don't really understand. Now with the movies being so big, that may not be the case. But back then in the '90s, most parents are like my mother at that time, saying "Yeah this is a nice little thing that you're playing around with, but you should really have something to fall back on. Get a real job or real profession you can actually do *if* the comics don't work out." At that time when I started making money I was living at home and working out of my room, I had gotten my first check and my mom looked at it and thought, "Oh, this is real, this isn't play money anymore." She actually asked me for a loan. [laughs] That was another big thing, I'd come so far that my parents are now asking me for a loan. Those are

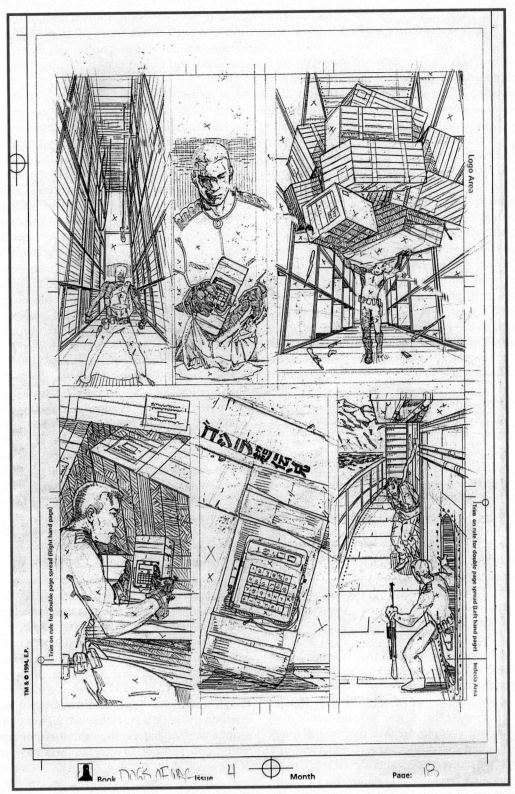

Georges Jeanty's pencil art for *Dogs of War* #4 Page 18.
Image courtesy of Georges Jeanty.

two very significant things that I won't ever forget that DEFIANT did for me back in those days.

Overstreet: What's different between your approach to your art since then and what's the same?

GJ: It hasn't really changed. I think anybody who is going to do this business, do comic books, whether you're writing, drawing, coloring, whatever, you have to learn a level of professionalism. And when I say professionalism, I mean treat what you do like a job. The great advantage or probably disadvantage to what we do is that there's usually nobody over our shoulders. We don't have to go into a job and deal with a boss, per se. Yes, we have editors, but there's nobody over our shoulders looking at us initially. That to me gives way to a very easy sense of just putting things off and not being very professional. I think the first thing I learned drawing was that I need to be professional about this. My work ethic was learned at a very early age, and I have not lost that work ethic since then. It's now going on 20-some years.

The thing that changed is that I'm not so concerned with the minutia anymore as I used to be because you're so critical of yourself. I'm still critical, but I'm no longer, I guess, insecure about that criticism. Now if I'm critical I'm very much, "How does that criticism make me better for the future?" As opposed to that criticism back then making you feel like "oh you're right, I'm no good, I don't know why I'm even trying" that type of thing. Two very significant changes, but in a way, they never leave you because I'm still dealing with those two instances even today. Much more on a professional level, of course, but you still have what you had when you started out.

Overstreet: You've had a tremendous amount of success since those days. What have been your favorite projects?

GJ: Of course, working with Jim Shooter was great. DEFIANT was a really great company and I applaud what they were trying to do. Remember, they were coming out at a time when everyone wanted everything to be Image, and DEFIANT was definitely not Image. *Warriors of Plasm* was nothing like what the Image boys were publishing at all. I didn't real-ize it at the time because I was so in the eye of the storm, but that was a great atmosphere. Everybody loved comics, to my knowledge, in that office and I loved that.

Since then, I've had the great fortune of working at Marvel and DC and Dark Horse and a bunch of other companies. As an artist, you do commercial art here and there, projects pop up. I had the great fortune of working on *Buffy the Vampire Slayer* for many years. Off and on for about ten years. That was such a great, great experience because I realized I like working with good people. In working with *Buffy*, Joss Whedon was such a big comic fan. As much as he is a celebrity or figure head in the business of entertainment, I always felt like he could come down to the level of comics and still be as much who he is with the TV and movies as he is with the comics. I thought that really says a lot for a person to do this particular medium and not look down on it. And not look down on it so much so that he actually would get in touch with everybody who wrote for *Buffy* [the show] back in the day and ask, "Hey would you guys be interested in coming over and writing for *Buffy* the comic book as well." Some of them had never written comic books before and if you do your research, a bunch of those writers went on to become real big figureheads now as writers and showrunners. Working with everyone there was definitely a highlight of my career, for sure.

Overstreet: What are you working on now?

GJ: I'm back at Marvel and I finished something called *U.S.Agent*, which people may have seen just recently with the Disney series, *The Falcon and the Winter Soldier*. But of course, this character has been around since the '90s, I believe. I just did a limited mini-series/trade for Marvel, which was a lot of fun. Currently, I'm doing fill-ins for Marvel at their *Star Wars* property. I'm doing one of their books called *Star Wars: The High Republic*. I'm just a fill-in artist at the moment, and they seem to like what I'm doing, so they keep asking me back to fill-in. I'm currently in the midst of a long time ago in a galaxy far, far away.

This interview was conducted on August 6, 2021.
- Amanda Sheriff

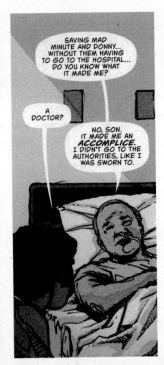

Some of Georges Jeanty's more recent work, *Shadow Doctor* #4 Page 9 (AfterShock, 2021).

TIM PERKINS • Colorist

Writer-artist Tim Perkins, these days best known as the creator of the World's End *graphic novel series, was in the process of establishing himself in the comics industry when a meeting with Jim Shooter and JayJay Jackson at a convention in Scotland quickly resulted in him coloring some of Steve Ditko's work on the* Dark Dominion #0 *trading card set. Soon he would land in New York and start working (some would say living) at the DEFIANT offices…*

Overstreet: Could you tell us a bit about your background prior to working at DEFIANT?

Tim Perkins (TP): I left Art College back in 1980 and worked for about three years for local companies, as a graphic designer. I found some comic book work with Martin Lock's Harrier Comics here in the UK, which lasted for about six months.

Around the same time as I was doing the Harrier stuff, I managed to get a two-page strip entitled *Metempsychosis* into Marvel UK's flagship title of the time, *The Mighty World of Marvel*. I replied to a Marvel UK advert in it, which was asking for any aspiring artists and writers to submit a short comic to be considered for publication in the comic.

I received a complimentary copy of the comic with my work in it and a compliment slip from the guys down at the Marvel UK offices asking if I would like to show my portfolio of work. Whilst at the Marvel UK offices, I met Barry Kitson, who was working on the British version of the Spider-Man comic. Six months later, he asked me if I could help him out on some inking on an issue of *Transformers* that had a tight deadline. My very first mainstream published work *Transformers* #50 of the UK comic. It was here that I met Jim Shooter. I got word back from editorial that he was really happy with my inking. He said I "got it," which has always made me smile.

Tim Perkins coloring a *Dark Dominion* #1 page in the DEFIANT offices. Photo courtesy of Tim Perkins.

Overstreet: How did it come about that you went to work for DEFIANT?

TP: It was in March '93, whilst at GlasCAC, a Scottish convention that I met up with Jim once again. I showed Janet Jackson and him my portfolio of work, and it was my paintings and painted work for 2000AD that they liked. I was really lucky, I suppose, they were looking for painters. I gave Jim my new contact details and he sent me over some of the issue zero *Dark Dominion* card set to paint during May '93.

By August, I had landed in New York for the first time. I was supposed to be out for a week, but whilst out at a meal the night before my flight back home to go on holiday with my young family, Deborah Purcell asked me could I ask my wife, Margaret, if it would be okay to go back for a couple of weeks. This ended up being five months, home for Christmas and back out for another four.

Overstreet: When you started there, who were you working with?

TP: My very first work I did on the first morning in the DEFIANT offices was painting the Steve Ditko-drawn *Dark Dominion* #0 cover. I surprised Janet by informing her over a coffee and cake with Joe James at Grand Central Station's café that I had finished the cover. It was only eleven and she had not expected it to be ready until later that day.

From then on, I was working with Joe, who was a joy to be around. We had a great time both work-wise and out of the office, too. We worked very closely together and planned the issues out. I would ask him to only have such and such inked, leaving me to paint elements thus giving the artwork a lot of depth and making our book different from all of the others.

Tim Perkins' colors over Joe James and Steve Leialoha's art on the *Dark Dominion* #2 Page 1 splash.
Image courtesy of Tim Perkins.

During my time in New York, I was also privileged to work alongside people like, Jim, Janet, Alan Weiss, Dave Cockrum, Len Wein, Oclair Silverio, David Lapham, Louis Small, Jr., Greg Boone, Grey Williamson, J.G. Jones, Charles Yoakum, Bob Downs, and lots of other great creators.

Overstreet: Was this a situation where you were working mainly in the office or from home?

TP: I was working out of the offices and occasionally from my apartment (that Jim had arranged for me to live in) that was two blocks from Central Park. Over time I ended up spending less and less time back at the apartment and would work around the clock, as I was given more and more of the books to work on.

It was great; as well as painting, I was inking, penciling at times, and even plotting. The inside out monster scene with Michael Alexander pulling the creatures tongue so hard it turned itself inside out was my idea. I was only joking really, but Joe liked it so much that he used it.

Overstreet: What was your work environment like?

TP: It was fantastic, I was living the dream: working in New York, working on comics, something I had been dreaming of since I was about eight-years-old. When I heard about Barry Windsor-Smith doing this, I remember thinking, wow, wouldn't that be great, and now, here I was, doing exactly that.

The offices were exactly like you would expect with the logo. They were situated in an office block on 37th street, between Madison and 5th Avenue, and as you looked up there was an old medieval-style crest. It really was incredible.

I have never been treated as well by any comic company at any point in my career as I was there. I had all my expenses paid for, all my materials. It was and still seems too good to have been true. It was quickly arranged for the guys that had been training

under Janet to come in much more often and work under my wings.

Most of the time, we would work on the drawing boards facing Janet's and Jim's offices, but occasionally we would hide away, when under the cosh, to a side office just behind us. The team consisted of Su McTeigue (now Su Laing) and Ben Jung and occasionally Dave Hillman working alongside me. It was brilliant and we had some great times. The offices were always full of artists either working inside them or dropping off artwork or coming in for plotting sessions with Jim and Janet.

Overstreet: What did you think at the time of the people with whom you were working?

TP: I had the greatest respect for them, and I quickly found out that that feeling was very much reciprocated. I was surrounded by an incredible array of talent. Everyone wanted to create the absolute best comics that we could and from what we see nowadays from the DEFIANT comics fans, we did just that. We had a fantastic team of creators in all disciplines, which Jim and Janet had amassed from all around the world. It was also a team made up of veteran and semi-veteran artists alongside new blood and it worked perfectly.

With the Empire State Building serving as a backdrop, Tim Perkins on the DEFIANT office's balcony, 1993. Photo courtesy of Tim Perkins.

Overstreet: Was there such a thing as an "average DEFIANT workday" or was each day different?

TP: Every day (all seven of them) were workdays for me and a lot of the other creators too, but each one was different. I found myself switching between disciplines; one minute I was painting *Dark Dominion*, and the next I was ghosting the style set up by Janet on any of the other books, which needed my attention on them at the time. Then I would be inking to enable the work on *Dark Dominion* to get transferred onto watercolor paper for me to paint, or I could be penciling panels or even a cover or two or spending time plotting with Joe and the others.

Tim Perkins' colors over Joe James and Steve Leialoha's art for *Dark Dominion* #2 Page 5.
Image courtesy of Tim Perkins.

I actually wrote a synopsis for a storyline, which would explain why kids, in the same manner that Michael could see the Quantum creatures, could, out of the corner of their eyes, also do this. It never got a chance to be used, but I ended up using the storyline as the skeleton for the central storyline on a film concept which I worked on at an animation studio I co-set up in the early 2000s.

Overstreet: What were the challenges in coloring *Dark Dominion*?

TP: It wasn't really a challenge, but more of a great opportunity for me to add my mark to a book, which I would be able to create lots of special effects and touches to, which I hadn't seen before in an American comic. A big influence on my work was the three-issue magazine *The Warriors Of The Shadow Realm*, which Marvel put out in 1979 and 1980. This was a big thing for me, during my latter months at Art College. It was the closest thing to *The Trigan Empire* and *TV 21* that I had seen since the 1960s. I had always wanted to work in full color like this and *Dark Dominion* gave me the perfect vehicle to do this.

Overstreet: How was that similar or different than other work you had done?

TP: It was along the lines of the work for some of the Marvel UK covers I had painted for them in the late 1980s, but closer, in fact, to some of the work I did for 2000AD on *Judge Dredd* and *Chopper* for example. It was the work that Jim liked when he viewed my portfolio again at GlasCAC in 1993. It was certainly different than the other DEFIANT books upon which Janet had laid the foundations using watercolor dyes and inks. Using acrylics in this way helped me to give the book an otherworldly look at times and certainly a more painterly look.

Overstreet: Did you have any particular work from your time at DEFIANT that you would point to as your personal favorite(s)?

TP: I think my best stuff are issues 1-3 and 5 of *Dark Dominion* with Joe on pencils, as they were the ones I worked on closest with another creator. Louis Small, Jr.'s pages were similar in allowing for

backgrounds and objects, etc. to be dropped out for the paints and was probably the most paint intensive of the two penciller's runs. Then there are the opening pages of *War Dancer* #2 with Alan Weiss on pencils, which were a hybrid of Janet and my styles. Then of course the opportunity to work over Steve Ditko's pencils was an obvious highpoint for me. Of course, I enjoyed all of the work, alongside all the other great artists and writers, too.

Overstreet: Looking back, what are some of your favorite memories of working at DEFIANT?

TP: The first morning will stay with me forever. The only words to describe the feelings I had were absolute awe.

Then, there was the time that Lancashire met Brazil. Oclair could not speak English and I couldn't speak Portuguese (but then again, no one else could either), yet he and I managed to order him exactly what he wanted to eat, through sign language. Finding out how little he was getting from his agent and obtaining him a massive page rate rise and a consequent breaking away from his agent [is] something I am still proud of.

After a Saturday of John Woo films, I instigated a new game in the office, starting the following Monday, which consisted of any member of the DEFIANT crew suddenly getting up from their positions and firing imaginary guns in the office – a la any John Woo movie - along with the gun fire sound effects I used. This lasted for months. The first week of this saw Jim come out of his office and look around and then say, "I take it [that] it was the crazy Brit that started all of this…?"

Walking in Central Park with Joe James after midnight, where we saw a music video being made. Thanksgiving at Su McTeigue's parents' home. Taking turns to sleep on the DEFIANT couch in shifts. Christmas in New York. Seeing all of the seasons in New York. Watching the Super Bowl with Charles Yoakum…

There are too many others to mention here, but suffice it to say I could fill several books with my tales from that time.

Tim Perkins with Debbie Fix in the DEFIANT office.
Photo courtesy of Tim Perkins.

Tim Perkins' colors over Alan Weiss' artwork for the *War Dancer* #2 Page 1 splash.
Image courtesy of Tim Perkins.

Tim Perkins and Joe James in Central Park.
Photo courtesy of Tim Perkins.

stop doing, the longer I worked in comics. This led to me being headhunted to co-found an animation company where I worked on the writing as well as all the forms of art that were attached to the making of animated features.

The move from comics to theme parks was the right one and I found myself being incredibly prolific once more and imaginative again too. It was the perfect shift of focus for me and enabled me to just slip into film and TV.

Overstreet: What are you doing now?

TP: That lasted until around 2004, when I suddenly realized that what I really wanted to do was create comics again. In truth, I had never stopped loving them or the format. I just hated the politics, constraints and lack of good editorial input. These were the exact opposite poles to what I had seen at DEFIANT, and I suppose I longed for those days once more. So it was in March 2005 that I decided I wanted to return to comics, but not for any of the existing companies. I needed a new vehicle to create my own stories and create them in a visual way too that was true to my sensibilities as a comic creator. I spoke with my wife, who gave me her blessing, and on June 24, 2005 Wizards Keep was born and the graphic novel, science fusion series that I would become synonymous with, *Worlds End*.

Anyone wishing to check out my new work can do so via the websites, www.wizards-keep.com and www.worlds-end.co.uk, and via our social media on Facebook and Twitter. Thanks for taking the time to have me reminisce on my days at DEFIANT. It's always a pleasure to bring back the memories.

We are indebted to Tim Perkins for the permission use of many of the photos in this DEFIANT section of The Overstreet Comic Book Price Guide To Lost Universes. *They greatly added to our ability to tell DEFIANT's story. This interview was conducted by email in June 2019, ©2021 J.C. Vaughn. Used by permission.*

Overstreet: Was it just another gig or did you make lasting friendships working there?

TP: It was never just another gig, and yes, I made many lasting friendships. The majority of the guys there I am still in touch with through Facebook and email. It could never have been like any other gig, as I was living the dream and being treated incredibly well, so much so that upon my return to the UK I had been spoilt. In the nicest of ways of course, and Jim's treatment of me and the respect of everyone else, meant that any gig from then on in had to measure up or I simply couldn't work with that company.

Overstreet: What did you do after DEFIANT closed down?

TP: I worked for another six years in comics working for companies such as Pultiam Press, Tekno (again with Ed Polgardy), Karl Art Publishing, Oyster Books, Arcadia, Newsstand Publications, Caliber Comics, amongst a whole array of others until I found myself totally disenchanted with the industry and decided I needed to get out and find myself again, creatively.

I did this firstly through the world of animatronics and themed attractions creating concept work for theme parks all around the world. The first two weeks I thought every job I did was going to be my last. That was until I finally realized that all the company wanted was for me to use my imagination, something I had increasingly been made to

World's End Volume 2 Page 53, some of Tim Perkins' more recent work.
Image courtesy of Tim Perkins.

Tim Perkins' Scrapbook

THE ENTRANCE TO THE DEFIANT TOWER

DORIAN TENORE-BARTILUCCI

DEBORAH PURCELL

OCLAIR ALBERT

TIM PERKINS, SU McTEIGUE AND BEN YUNG (LEFT TO RIGHT)

HECTOR RAMOS

JIM SHOOTER, BARBARA MORSERF, BEN YUNG, AND TIM PERKINS (LEFT TO RIGHT)

GEORGE ROBERTS, JR.

SHEILA DELACEY

ZACH LYNCH

PETER LUKIC AND PAUL WILLIAMS

DEBBIE FIX

GEORGE ROBERTS, JR.

ROB LAQUINTA

JIM SHOOTER

ED POLGARDY (LEFT) AND JAYJAY JACKSON

JOE JAMES (LEFT) AND ROB LAQUINTA

TIM PERKINS

BEN YUNG

JOE JAMES

HECTOR RAMOS, BRADY DARVIN, PETER LUKIC,
DORIAN TENORE-BARTILUCCI, ZACH LYNCH AND ROB LAQUINTA
(LEFT TO RIGHT)

TIM PERKINS ON THE DEFIANT OFFICE'S BALCONY

Featuring Fawcett's Marvel Family • Marvel 2099 • Ultimate Marvel America's Best Comics • BOOM!'s Stan Lee Universe • Captain Canuck DNAgents • Scout • and MORE!

Timothy Truman's SCOUT

From the pages of *Starslayer*, Grimjack and his graphic novel *Time Beavers* onward through his career, writer-artist Timothy Truman has offered readers hard-boiled action and no small amount of grit. It was at Eclipse that Truman created what is perhaps his signature title, *Scout*. And while Eclipse as a whole was clearly a non-universe, *Scout* and its spin-offs describe a single coherent reality.

"I'd always been interested in Native American culture when I was growing up. My great-grandmother on my father's side was a full-blooded Cherokee, and I'm sure that played a part in it. In college, the interest intensified, and I started reading a lot of scholarly studies and histories about various Native American tribes. Finally, my wife Beth purchased a big, thick book by a historian named Arthur Haley called *Apaches: A Culture and History Portrait* and gave it to me for my birthday. That book really set the scene for coming up with *Scout*. I became intensely interested in Apache culture. It was the Reagan era, so, as an unrepentant leftist, I saw things going on around me that concerned me quite a bit. So, I speculated about what might happen if these things were allowed to progress and eventually pictured this bleak future where America had basically become an impoverished third-world nation. It seemed to me that the only person who might have any sort of hope of existing in such a future would be someone with these old school traditional Apache cultural ideals that I was reading about. So, before I knew it, the whole scenario for the *Scout* series appeared, Truman said.

"The story takes place in the near future in a sort of ravaged, impoverished, dystopian United States. The country has split off into various smaller states or governments, the main one being centered in the American Southwest, called New America. The star of the series is an Apache named Emanuel

Santana who is AWOL from a special Army training program. Scout learns, or at least thinks, that he is the reincarnation of the mythical Apache hero, Child of Water, and that it's his mission to destroy the Four Monsters of Apache legend. The monsters have taken the form of four businessmen and statesmen aligned with acting President, Jerry Grail – himself a former pro-wrestler. The reader never knows whether or not the Monsters are real or just a figment of Santana's imagination," he said.

Scout #1 (September 1985) kicked off the original series, which ran 24 issues and concluded in October 1987. *Swords of Texas* #1 kicked off a four-issue mini-series that same month, and *New America* #1 launched another four-issue mini-series the following month. 1987 also saw the release of the *Scout Handbook*. *Scout: War Shaman* #1 (March 1988) launched a 16-issue run that concluded in December 1989.

"The second series, *Scout: War Shaman*, takes place about a decade or so after the first series, chronologically, during which time Scout married and had two small children, Tahzey and Victorio. After his wife dies, he and the boys set out on a trek across the southwest. Most people were really taken with the second series, the fact that you have this outlaw who has been branded a terrorist by the government, who is on the run and must worry about the welfare and safety of his two small children. In what was a pretty dramatic step for the time, at the end of the series, Scout dies. One boy, Tahzey, is adopted by one of Santana's allies, a militant missionary named Rev. Sanddog Yuma. However, the fate of the youngest boy, Victorio, is uncertain. When we last see him, he's very much alone, hiding in some rocks. Keeping his fate uncertain was a deliberate move on my part, as readers will hopefully discover in Scout: Marauder," Truman said.

FIRST PUBLICATION:
Scout #1
(September 1985)

LAST PUBLICATION:
Scout: War Shaman #16
(December 1989)

REVIVAL(S):
Scout: Marauder
graphic novel (TBD)

Timothy Truman's original art for Scout #8 Page 2 (1986).
Image courtesy of Heritage Auctions.

LOST UNIVERSES

LOST UNIVERSES